Socially Symbolic Acts

Socially Symbolic Acts

The Historicizing Fictions
of Umberto Eco,
Vincenzo Consolo,
and Antonio Tabucchi

Joseph Francese

Madison • Teaneck
Fairleigh Dickinson University Press

© 2006 by Rosemont Publishing & Printing Corp.

All rights reserved. Authorization to photocopy items for internal or personal use, or the internal or personal use of specific clients, is granted by the copyright owner, provided that a base fee of $10.00, plus eight cents per page, per copy is paid directly to the Copyright Clearance Center, 222 Rosewood Drive, Danvers, Massachusetts 01923. [0-8386-4098-2/06 $10.00 + 8¢ pp, pc.]

Associated University Presses
2010 Eastpark Boulevard
Cranbury, NJ 08512

The paper used in this publication meets the requirements of the American National Standard for Permanence of Paper for Printed Library Materials Z39.48-1984.

Library of Congress Cataloging-in-Publication Data

Francese, Joseph.
  Socially symbolic acts : the historicizing fictions of Umberto Eco, Vincenzo Consolo, and Antonio Tabucchi / Joseph Francese.
    p. cm.
  Includes bibliographical references and index.
  ISBN 0-8386-4098-2 (alk. paper)
  1. Eco, Umberto—Criticism and interpretation. 2. Consolo, Vincenzo, 1933– —Criticism and interpretation. 3. Tabucchi, Antonio, 1943– —Criticism and interpretation. 4. Historical fiction, Italian—History and criticism. 5. Italian fiction—20th century—History and criticism. I. Title.
PQ4865.C6Z648 2006
853'.081090914—dc22

2005025469

PRINTED IN THE UNITED STATES OF AMERICA

*For Gina, Anna, and Luciana.
With love.*

"Philosophy cannot be separated from the history of philosophy, just as culture cannot be separated from the history of culture. In the most immediate and literal sense, it is not possible to be a philosopher, that is to say it is not possible to have a critically coherent understanding of the world, without an awareness of the world's historicity, of its historical stage of development and of the fact that this understanding is in conflict with other conceptions or with elements of other conceptions. One's own knowledge of the world responds to specific problems raised by reality, problems that are extremely determinate and 'original' in their topicality. How is it possible then to think the present, a very determinate present, with a way of thinking elaborated for dealing with problems of the past, a past that is often is very far away in time, surpassed by events? If this occurs, then one is 'anachronistic' in one's own time, a fossil and not a modern, living being. Or, at least, a bizarre 'composite.' And, in fact, it happens that social groups who in some ways demonstrate the most highly developed modernity, are in other ways behind the times and therefore are incapable of a total historical autonomy."
—Antonio Gramsci, "Prison Notebooks;" XI, 12

Contents

Acknowledgments	11
1. Introduction	15
2. Umberto Eco	39
The Poetics of "The Model Reader"	39
Life with Father: *Il nome della rosa*	59
Inaction and Reaction in *Il pendolo di Foucault*	90
"Of Me I Sing": *L'isola del giorno prima*	117
Romancing the Family: *Baudolino*	136
3. Interlude: Vincenzo Consolo's Poetics of Memory	156
4. Antonio Tabucchi	174
Back to the Future: On Tabucchi's Poetics of a "Posthumous" Literature	174
Back to the Present: The Self as Other in Tabucchi's "Ekphrastic" and Theatrical Writings	191
Fragments of the Discourses of Lovers and of Other Strangers	207
Who's Zoomin' Who in *Tristano muore*?	220
5. Epilogue: Something's Burning: A Mysterious Flame	243
Notes	253
Reference List	292
Index	309

Acknowledgments

THIS PUBLICATION OF THIS BOOK BRINGS TO MIND MY FRIEND AND mentor, Robert Dombroski. His sudden death deprived me of the opportunity to thank him for all he did for me. In happier times, I discussed the general concept of this book with him, and he read some of the first sections I wrote on Eco before his passing deprived me of one of my preferred interlocutors, sincerest and intuitive critics, and most accurate intellectual compasses. I can only hope the completed work would have met with his approval.

Furthermore, I would like to thank a colleague at Michigan State University, the eminent psychoanalyst Bert Karon, for giving generously of his time and for helping me solve many riddles, particularly while working on the chapters dealing with the fictions of Umberto Eco. I truly enjoy our pleasant, highly informative conversations. Discussions such as these are the reason I went into the profession. That a good deal of what I learned during those talks went into this book is the icing on the cake. I would also like to thank Giselle Galdi and Benjamin Kilborne—for their advice, generosity with their time, and their readings of the *Baudolino* chapter—and Norma Bouchard and Charles Klopp for their kind review of some of the chapters, Eco and Tabucchi respectively, while in production, and for their very helpful comments and suggestions. And I would be remiss if I failed to take advantage of this opportunity to recognize the help given me by Joseph Buttigieg with questions regarding the philosophy of Italian history.

I want also to thank colleagues who invited me to read parts of this work, Lino Pertile at Harvard; Franco Masciandaro and Norma Bouchard at the University of Connecticut. The annual meetings of the American Association for Italian Studies have also provided excellent fora for the exchange of ideas. I must also acknowledge the scholarly journals where chapters, in slightly modified form, have appeared, *Forum Italicum, L'anello che non tiene, Italica,* and *The American Journal of Psychoanalysis.*

Last, but certainly not least, I would like to acknowledge that I would not have been able to carry this project forward and bring it to completion without the unwavering love and support of my raisons d'être, my wife, Gina, and daughters, Anna and Luciana.

Socially Symbolic Acts

1
Introduction

IN THE CHAPTERS THAT FOLLOW I WILL DISCUSS ISSUES OF BROAD cultural consequence through close readings of the prose fictions of three of contemporary Italy's most prominent novelists, Umberto Eco, Vincenzo Consolo, and Antonio Tabucchi. All three are generally recognized among the most important intellectual figures in contemporary Europe. Eco, of course, is extremely well-known in the Anglophonic world. This is due to his remarkable abilities as a raconteur, his skills at marketing his work, and the psychological consistency of his characters, topics we will have occasion to examine in detail in the chapters that follow. Consolo and Tabucchi are equally deserving of such recognition, given the superior aesthetic qualities of their fictions. This is not to say that Consolo and Tabucchi are unknown outside of Italy. Consolo gained international attention with *Il sorriso dell'ignoto marinaio* [*The Smile of the Unknown Mariner*], which has been translated into the major European languages—French, Spanish, German, and English—even though the (pluri)linguistic strategies and experiments that inform his fictions make translating them a challenge. Since then his fictions have attracted an ever-growing bibliography. Consolo's nonfictional essays have been published in major Italian newspapers, in Spain by *El País*, and by the Argentinian *La Nación*, and have been collected in volumes in Italy.

Tabucchi, a scholar of Portuguese literature, is extremely well-known in the Iberian Peninsula and throughout Latin America; his works have been translated into all of the world's major languages. Over the past two decades he has enjoyed consistent and wide popular success in Italy with accessible fictions such as *Sostiene Pereira* [*Pereira Declares*] and *La testa perduta di Damasceno Monteiro* [*The Missing Head of Damaseno Monteiro*]. His most recent works—*Si sta facendo sempre più tardi* [*It*

Is Getting Later and Later], *Autobiografie altrui* [*Other People's Autobiographies*], and *Tristano muore* [*Tristano Dies*]—eschew traditional narrative structures. While a constant throughout all Tabucchi's career as a writer is the exploration through narrative of ways of strengthening interpersonal bonds, these latest works carry forth this investigation in a manner that harkens back to his earlier, more experimental prose of the 1980s. In the more recent works we see more clearly a form of inquiry—present below the surface in *Pereira* and in *Damasceno Monteiro*, but decidedly at the fore of works published in the 1980s such as *Notturno indiano* [*Indian Nocturne*] and *Il filo dell'orizzonte* [*The Edge of the Horizon*]—that perhaps can best be described as the decentering of the locus of consciousness, another topic we will have occasion to examine in depth. In the chapter titled "Back to the Future," I will discuss his poetics as it takes shape after the turn of the millennium in *Autobiografie altrui* (2003). Then, in "Back to the Present," I will take a step backward and examine how his poetics matured and developed in the over the last fifteen years of the twentieth century through the use of ekphrasis and the heteronymic theories of the Portuguese poet Fernando Pessoa. I will then apply, in chapters dedicated to his two most recent works, *Si sta facendo sempre più tardi* (2001) and *Tristano muore* (2004), what I have theorized.

I have chosen to juxtapose the three so as to present a composite—although unavoidably partial—view of Italian letters at the beginning of the new millennium. The texts to be examined historicize our present because they are, to use Jameson's phrasing, "socially symbolic acts" that are to be grasped as imaginary, aesthetic manifestations of real political and social tensions and contradictions (Jameson 1981, 76–82), individual expressions of the society from which they emanate.[1]

The concurrence of the three authors is justified in part by the fact that they are contemporaries. Eco was born in 1932, and Consolo a year later, so they belong to the generation that came of age in the 1950s and 1960s, one that was not forced to choose between allegiance to the Fascist regime and opposition to it, as was the case with writers born a decade earlier such as Calvino, Pasolini, and Pavese. Both Eco and Consolo have worked for Italian State Television and experienced as adults the sociological transformation of the Italians consequent to the economic boom of the late 1950s decried by Pasolini, that is to say the absorption of the peasantry into the lower-middle class and the advent of mass culture.

Eco, of course, gained international recognition as a semiotician at a relatively young age, but became known as a novelist only in the 1980s with *Il nome della rosa* [*The Name of the Rose*]. Consolo gained wide acknowledgement as a writer with the 1976 publication of the classic *Il sorriso dell'ignoto marinaio*, after his debut novel, *La ferita dell'aprile* [*April's Wound*] (1963) went largely unnoticed. Tabucchi, born in 1943, is a decade younger than Eco and Consolo. However, like Consolo Tabucchi gained prominence as a writer with the Italian public in the mid-1970s. His works from the 1980s also reflect the turbulence of the previous decade, years marked by the ongoing contestations of the Student Movement and organized labor on the one hand, and on the other by the "strategy of tension" (the terrorism of the extreme right and left, which many believe share a common antidemocratic matrix), events that influenced the fictions of Eco and Consolo also. Like Eco and Consolo, Tabucchi's debut as a writer was conditioned by the neorealist tendency of the post war period and the neo–avant-garde movement of the 1960s. Moreover, and again like Eco and Consolo, Tabucchi has reached a stage of maturity from which he can appraise the civic and literary legacy left us by the twentieth century, as is clearly evinced by *Tristano muore*, and propose an agenda for the years to come.

Our three authors also share the view that Italy is a country where it is more and more difficult to declare one's democratic propensities because of the monopolization of the proprietorship of the mass media by Prime Minister Silvio Berlusconi. However, while all three writers most definitely fall within the broad umbrella of progressive opposition to the conservative reflux that has dominated Italian politics since the early 1990s, in speaking of Eco's opposition and social commitment we must accentuate much more heavily the cultural than the political. Indeed, his frequent interventions in Italy's major periodicals can be seen in part as manifestation of his commitment to use the media to 'unmask' today's reincarnations of Italy's Fascist past.

A specialist in media studies, Eco has found fault with many of the conservative policies enacted by the governing coalition. He is very concerned by the antidemocratic domination of the media by a prime minister who owns controlling interest in many of the country's largest print outlets, its three nationwide private television networks, and is able to dominate the administration of the nation's three public television networks: a state of affairs that allows for a strong pro-government bias in the way the news concerning public policy is reported.[2] For Eco this muting of opposition voices has led to a situation where a leader can claim to be the interpreter of the common will, inferring that this repeats, mutatis mutandis, the concentration of power in one man's hands that occurred in Italy in the early 1920s.[3] Furthermore, concentration of ownership suffocates the industry's capacity for self-criticism, causing what should be society's unending search for freedom and liberation to atrophy and dissipate.

However, the "lay religiosity" (Martini and Eco 1996, 70) and weak teleology that inform Eco's views are quite distinct from "morally earnest" laicism of Tabucchi (Klopp 2001, 98) and of Consolo. Eco's "lay" or "natural ethics," comprehends remorse due to the contravention of a set of "objective" norms governing human behavior, binding on all people alike, even in the absence of a superhuman legislator who punishes or forgives transgressions (Martini and Eco 1996, 77). Eco's weak teleology looks to absolve the "critical function of disinterest toward the future" while constantly reexamining the errors of the past (Martini and Eco 1996, 11–12). Thus, it is a quest for a constantly evolving, hence absent—that is to say nonobjective—structure of knowledge whose locus is in language, which in turn is defined as a Beginning in which it is possible to seek out relative "criteria for truth" (Eco 1980, 496).[4]

At the same time, while intellectual investigation can indeed contemplate "possible worlds," it must be careful to interrogate that which can be known. For this reason it can make no pretense to incisiveness in the present. Consequently, Eco defines social commitment as understanding the past, and living in the present in a way that sets examples for posterity. In other words, the intellectual can do no more than leave "messages in a bottle" for future recipients (Martini and Eco 1996, 76). Hence, Eco's narratives take inward, self-reflexive paths, investigating the genesis, the causes and the effects of intellectual and literary traditions and controversies. His narratives follow a linear, cause-and-effect progression. They are all told in flashback form: they let us know how we got where we are.

Tabucchi is interested in exploring what is not known, in examining trails that diverge from what the course of past events would lead us to anticipate. Therefore, he traces a path that leads first through the subject of narration and then outward, toward the other. For Tabucchi the act of narration has an ethical connotation; it is form of agency and a means of knowledge of the world. It is both understanding of the ways and means by which individuals participate in society and of how they modify the world. Similarly, his characters all share an "abiding preoccupation" to confront fundamental questions of right and wrong (Klopp 2001, 99).

For his part, Tabucchi uses Italy's major dailies as tribunes—in a manner reminiscent of the poet Pier Paolo Pasolini, author of well-known *corsaro* [pirate] editorials in the 1970s—to call to task the president of the Italian Republic, Carlo Azeglio Ciampi, for not safeguarding the integrity of the Italian Constitution; to criticize the failure of politicians to lead the "moral renewal of Italy" after the scandals of the early 1990s; and to decry the return to Italy of the fear of the Other, evidenced by *revanchistes* nationalisms and xenophobias (Parazzoli 1998, 77–80).[5]

Consistent with the views mentioned above, Eco defines the "intellectual function" as that of "critically recognizing that which is considered a satisfactory approximation of one's one concept of truth," and of coherently "bringing ambiguities to light." He claims that this "intellectual function" is always practiced in anticipation of events or after the fact, and only rarely effects what is in progress: "This is why Cosimo Piovasco di Rondò [the protagonist of Calvino's *Il barone rampante* [*The Baron in the Trees*]] lived in the trees: not to exempt himself from the intellectual duty to understand one's own times and participate in them, but to better understand them and direct them from above the fray" (Eco 1997b; 11, 23, 24).[6] Indeed, Eco has maintained that intellectuals should not intervene in discussion of pressing social issues that fall outside their area of expertise.[7] In taking a stance similar to that assumed by Lyotard, Eco affirmed that the intellectual, by definition, embodies disinterested knowledge above social conflict (Lyotard 1983, 4).

This pronouncement by Eco sparked a rebuttal from Tabucchi, who called Eco to task for assuming this reassuring posture, one that defers questions with ethical bearings to technicians whose are not compelled to consider the moral implications of their policy decisions. Tabucchi—a writer for whom "the literary vocation is in itself, intermittently, a commitment to explore political and ethical ends" (Smith 2000, 102)—affirmed that the role of the intellectual in society is "to put in crisis," to disseminate disquietude by questioning what is known, that is to say by undermining inherited certainties. Indeed, literature is defined by its "cognitive function," its capacity to interrogate and to oblige us to speak of that which we do not know. For this reason he argued that literature does not follow events, as Eco had claimed, but precedes them. To use Tabucchi's own phrasing, literature is not the effect of a cause: because literature deals in uncertainty and in speculation, it is the "posterior cause of an anterior effect." In other words, literature demands "a rethinking" of the present when it assumes a "posthumous" stance, one that is "not immediately tied to reality" but instead requires the reader to use literature as a tool for looking at our present from the perspective of the future (Tabucchi 1996a, 122).

In other words, Tabucchi's commitment is defined by his opinion that literature must ask precisely those questions that society is not yet prepared to answer. Literature does not exist for the present but as *witness to* the present. Therefore, it is a constant reminder that our actions will be submitted to posterity for judgment. In his own words, "Literary commitment consists . . . of reminding others, in providing a testimony that is perhaps futile, but whose futility may perhaps have a different value for posterity" (Tabucchi 1996a, 123).

Tabucchi contends that because literature provides testimony it also furnishes the reader with a means for interacting with the past. In this way literature is able to remind us that things do not have to be the way they are. And this cognizance, that history may have followed alternate paths, is the key to our freedom. Hence, his nostalgia for the future, his longing for "something other" than what is.[8] This restoration of the temporal moorings lost to the eternal present of postmodernity is for Tabucchi—and for Consolo, as we shall see—a way of historicizing the present. Indeed, the difference in views on the function of literary communication separating Eco from Consolo and Tabucchi allow us to understand the reasons behind the divergence in how the three historicize in their narratives how we live our present.

For his part, Consolo claims, with a touch of hyperbole, that the average Italian is no longer a citizen of a democratic Republic but must now be considered a subject of a culture founded on advertising campaigns that have succeeded in substituting memory with a reality consumed by information overload (Parazzoli 1998, 26–28).[9] Consolo's linguistic experimentation responds to what he sees as an interruption in the relationship between literary text and social-historical context and the resulting inability of prose fiction to communicate. He does so by adopting a poetic mode of expression that allegorically restores what is in danger of being lost, the local dialects, Sicily's urban- and landscapes, all of which embody "the history, the ancient splendor, and the recent decadence" of the Island. Together these historical relics exemplify a culture at risk that in turn serves as metaphor "for the [imminent] end of [Western] civilization" (Consolo 2002, 9). Similarly, Consolo's *Requiem* for victims of the Mafia (written shortly after the assassinations in the 1990s of the prosecuting judges Giovanni Falcone and Paolo Borsellino shocked Italian public opinion catalyzed an immediate and general outcry) belies Eco's stance regarding the duties of the intellectual we cited above—that whenever intellectuals intervene in topical activities they are not performing as specialists, but are participating in subsidiary activity—by expressing in his art the desire to understand what happened and demand irrevocable change. As is the case with all his fictions, Consolo's *Requiem per le vittime della Mafia* [*Requiem for the Victims of the Mafia*] was written with the antagonistic intention of re-inserting art into its social context, triggering debate, and catalyzing a process of transformation.

Thus, our analysis of Consolo provides a transition between the two larger sections of this book—the first dedicated to Eco, the second to Tabucchi, who gives relatively greater weight to the political in proportion to the cultural—because just as Consolo's linguistic experimentation serves to reintroduce prose narrative into Italy's national debate, his ekphrastic retrieval of the past invites the reader to participate in the fate shared by all whose destiny is to live this dawn of a new millennium.

The comparison of our three authors' similar, but diverging perspectives on topical events and on the role of literature, and the analysis of novels whose humus is a cultural environment comparable but very distinct from our own, may hopefully give us fresh ideas on how literary studies and culture in general might resist an authoritarian involution of planetary dimensions and contribute to the sketching out of new relations between globality and locality, diversity and solidarity at a time when "a triumphalist right has been boldly reimagining the shape of the earth, [and] the cultural left has retreated into a dispirited pragmatism" (Eagleton 2003, 52). Indeed, that which unites Eco, Consolo, and Tabucchi, and that which separates them, especially as concerns the role of literature and the intellectual in society, cut to the heart of what it means to practice literary scholarship at the outset of the twenty-first century.

Over the past fifteen to twenty years the tendency toward involution has converged with the amorphous term globalization, whose meaning has evolved from denoting the electronic linkage of the remotest corners of the globe to now connote also a *pax americana* that is synonymous with the increasing marginalization of the United Nations and the World Court as arbiters of international affairs and the Pentagon's equation of the national interest of the United States with the best interest of all humanity. After the collapse of the Soviet bloc, the world was left without an alternative to free-market capitalism at a time when the United States found itself at the head of the information technology revolution. As a result, the U.S. became exponentially more powerful, economically, technologically, and militarily. The "peace dividend" promised the American public in the early 1990s was quickly gobbled up by the Pentagon while Bush senior and Clinton paved the way for Bush junior to anoint himself sheriff of the planet and unilateral enforcer of a "new world order," Bush pere's euphemism for the end of the period in diplomacy crafted after the end of World War II based on the balance between superpowers. At the same time, the cultural hegemony of the United States, buttressed by that nation's military might, created a situation where U.S. ideas on the economy and the organization of society became 'common sense' all over the world.

In point of fact, a recent analysis of political phenomena such as Thatcherism and Reaganism describe how these two national, conservative political discourses articulated a new hegemonic common sense, that is to say a new political wisdom and a consensus that have taken on global form through local applications by producing the discourses through which even neoliberals and social democrats now operate (Cvetkovich and Kellner 1997, 17).

Furthermore, as Vattimo indicates, these new hegemonic discourses have succeeded in filling precisely that void left by the 'postmodern' dissolution of foundational thought and by the 'end of ideologies,' a state of affairs that became particularly pronounced after the collapse of the Soviet bloc. In practical terms, this meant the discrediting of deductive planning in favor of a trial-and-error form of liberalism made of baby steps and pragmatic concreteness (Vattimo 2003, 87).

Harvey contends that in the 1970s "The term [globalization] spread like wildfire in the financial and business press, mainly as tool for legitimating the deregulation of financial markets. It helped make the diminution in state powers to regulate capital flows seem inevitable and became an extraordinarily powerful political tool in the disempowerment of national and local working-class movements and trade union power" (Harvey 2000, 13).[10] In the humanities, globalization supplanted an equally amorphous term, postmodernity, which heralded, by negation, the end of modernity. We did not know what or where we were, but we 'knew' we were no longer modern: grand, metaphysical narratives were no longer valid, but new points of orientation had yet to be determined.

Thus, the term "postmodern" came to connote a period of general uncertainty, anxiety, disorientation, and frustrated attempts at regrouping such as the nomination of John Kerry for president in the name of electibility: we compromised because we knew we could not have what we wanted, but we knew we did not want Bush. "Postmodern" indecision was a reaction not only to extraordinarily negative events throughout the world (such as the proliferation of war and the ongoing destruction of the environment), but also to advances in medicine—that challenged the very definition of what it means to be human—to the insecurities provoked by a highly volatile global economy, to the evolution of society, and to the loss of 'common sense' temporal anchors wrought by advances in technology.

Parenthetically, Best and Kellner, while coinciding with Harvey's assessment—that globalization under technology strengthens "the dominance of a world capitalist economic system, supplanting the primacy of the nation-state with transnational corporations and organizations, and generating a new global culture that is eroding all local cultures and traditions"—also underscore the phenomenon's positive aspects: "the new global economy, society, and culture are increasingly digitized and interactive, with rapidly expanding wireless networks supplementing the wired society and producing new forms of connectivity." They remind us that "these technologies engender ubiquitous communication and interaction, and innovative forms of culture and everyday life" (Best and Kellner 2001, 207). The hybridization of cultures fashioned by globalization expands possibilities for self-definition. However, they also note that globalization forces new conflicts and choices onto individuals (for whom the weight of the past in significant decision making has been undermined by the instability within postmodernity) in search of identity and values: "For some theorists, this allegedly postmodern heterogeneity is positive, but for others it makes it easier to manipulate fragmented selves into consumer identities, synthetic models produced by the culture industries" (Cvetkovich and Kellner 1997, 11).[11]

In sum, globalization is a multivalenced phenomenon. It recontextualizes and places under broader scrutiny violations of human rights and other injustices and is capable of promoting greater acceptance of diversity and heterogeneity where homogeneity and sameness had been the rule. However, globalization has also contributed to the resurrection of ethno-nationalisms, religious fundamentalisms, and other forms of resistance to the homogenization and Westernization associated with some forms of globalization (Cvetkovich and Kellner 1997, 18).

If this appraisal is accurate, then our task becomes one of articulation, of understanding how various societal components are organized; of using literary studies to analyze the emotional and subjective dimensions of private life. Since "the intrinsic object of literary studies is knowledge of the human being" (Tabucchi 1997b, 122), the critic must underscore the "necessary reciprocity," to use Gramsci's term, linking literature and the broad public context, so as to provide for a charting of lived experience, as well as the social and historical forces that condition and determine individual existence, and to suggest linkages of cognitive and affective mapping that attempt to represent modes of experience and history.

Parenthetically, it is precisely at this juncture that we come upon the social relevance of the prose fictions of our authors. For example, the psychological depth of Eco's protagonists, the unresolved battles with oedipus that plague them through senescence, cast into high relief the articulations of patriarchal power relations, especially the ways and means power is held, administered and perpetuated through successive generations, and provide us with unsettling portrayals of where we are and how we got here. Analysis of the interactions within Eco's societies of men allows us to contextualize these relations within a specific matrix, so that we might better understand their function and effects in other microcosms. By shedding light on a specific manifestation of a more general condition we may perhaps induce how different locations are related to one another.

Consolo and Tabucchi indicate potential ways out of this state of affairs. Consolo examines the effects of detritus of a past that are still with us, while Tabucchi invites us to contemplate possible directions for the future. Both do so with prose fictions that suggest means for reestablishing the "instinctual and sensuous roots of that solidarity which makes the fate of the other part of one's own fate" (Marcuse 2001, 137) severed by media culture, the high-tech culture of the image.[12] In Tabucchi's fictions especially there is a reciprocity that allows individuals to receive themselves "back as a subject from the Other;" that is to say, the reciprocity of self and other permits the subjects of his narrations to realize their intrinsic "nature in a way which allows the other to do so too" (Eagleton 2003, 169–70).

To close the parenthesis and backtrack a bit, Marramao proposes that modernity was characterized by a process of secularization—defined by a rise in electivity (the individual's right to choose), the legitimation of change, and the growing specialization of the workplace—and by the increasing importance of the experience of time (IX). With the invention of the mechanical clock time became less a quality,[13] and more a measurable, quantifiable commodity. The validation of electivity and change lessened the importance of the past in significant decision making and legitimated the concept of prospective time in which the future predominates over past and tradition and also over the present (33). This change in perspective was accompanied by an idea of progress as an "irreversible-cumulative temporality" of unique, unrepeatable events (XXXII). In other words, time as change and as constant transformation defined Modernity and provided the paradigm for all scientific and political thought (LI).[14]

However, a sea change in temporal perspective began with the bombing of Hiroshima and Nagasaki. Fear of the negative capabilities of science set in; we began to lose faith in science as panacea as the motor for the "omni-pervasive," unstoppable, forward march of progress. The radically shortened time perspectives of modernity underwent a shift. The loss of confidence in prospective time caused a temporal entropy. Indeed, it might seem that in postmodernity the present is all there is. Furthermore, with the end the logic of linear time and the unitary sense of history—that is to say in the absence of an *arché* or Beginning and an eschatological telos or end to history—we were left to ask how we were to restore a sense to history and define a postmetaphysical social ethics.

Lost (this is especially the case with the younger generations) within a present characterized by severely weakened temporal moorings, we also found ourselves dealing with a media culture that generates sanitized collective memories and nurtures uncritical aesthetic sensibilities while producing "images that mobilize audience desire into certain modes of thought, behavior, and role models that serve the interest of maintaining and reproducing" the values of its corporate proprietors. The merchandise peddled by media culture demonstrates—at times subliminally, at times explicitly—who has power and who is allowed to exercise force and violence. Its audience voluntarily submits to a form of cultural pedagogy that "contribute[s] to educating us how to behave and what to think, feel, believe, fear, and desire" (Kellner 1995, 1–2; 78). As a result, whatever future possibilities left to the spectator, us, are absorbed into a nonconflictual arena that "instantiate[s] rather than critique[s] the idea that 'there is no alternative,' save those given by the conjoining of technological fantasies, commodity culture, and endless capital accumulation" (Harvey 2000, 168).

Public reaction to the criminal destruction of the World Trade Center in Lower Manhattan and of the lives of more than a thousand innocent civilian workers within the Twin Towers, the commandeered airplanes and the Pentagon the morning of September 11, 2001, made evident the extent to which inner freedom has been whittled down by technological 'reality.' Calmer heads were not allowed to prevail because they were denied airtime by a corporate news establishment hungry for the elevated ratings the reporting of hostilities supplies. The evening news fanned flames and pumped patriotic pride to the extent that among many Americans there was, to use Marcuse's phrasing, a "*mimesis:* an immediate identification of the individual with his society, and, through his part of society, with society as a whole" (53). As a result, civil rights were restricted; room for dissent was limited; diplomatic solutions were jettisoned; and something unheard of, at least in recent memory—a "*preventive* war" of conquest that knows no limits in space or time—was set in motion.

This unmediated, 'voluntary' identification of the American people with their president served to erase the distinction between the individual's defining humus, his or her community, and society at large. For once, almost all of us, including Italy's Prime Minister Berlusconi, were flag-waving Americans, outraged by the offense to our national honor, supportive of the war effort, and willing to suspend the Bill of Rights. The rest of us were afraid to speak up. Common sense dictated as much: opposition to the war was said to place our troops—young men and women who had volunteered to put themselves in harm's way—in jeopardy, an act considered treasonous by Attorney General John Ashcroft and therefore punishable by firing squad. Freedom of thought and speech were seen as obstacles to the "war against terror," as was the right to privacy, while the Justice Department began to make the case in favor of suspending the right of habeus corpus.

At a deeper level, beneath all the rational justifications, there circulated a libidinal affinity that bound American subjects to their rulers. This was especially the case within the white majority, which had access to no point of view other than that of a warmongering Administration. Public opinion passed through the filter of Condaleeza Rice's National Security Council prior to distribution through the mass media. And once this narrow universe came to coincide for most Americans with the identity of their nation (then with their race, and then with their equals [and superiors] in status), any human universal that fell outside those increasingly restricted boundaries and might, however feebly, invoke the "solidarity which makes the fate of the other part of one's own fate" became an abstraction, something intellectual, "at best a moral or religious command which one can violate without much consequence" (Marcuse 2001, 137), as demonstrated by the treatment reserved for Iraqi and Afghanistan prisoners of war and those detained at Guantánamo Bay, Cuba. Real issues receded before the instinctual affirmation of the televised image, and the majority of Americans 'found themselves,' at least for a while, in George W. Bush.

Critique was decisively outmatched by the established facts the Pentagon channeled through the media. Dissent was stifled while the individual's capacity for independent thought atrophied. This situation—the logical outgrowth of the relationship just described between rulers and ruled, administrators and administered—was installed by a media culture that sets the agenda for masses who do not determine policies, but instead voice their preferences on choices that are predetermined for them (Marcuse 2001, 83)[15] by a concordance of government agencies, the large multinational corporations who locally sponsor elections and media campaigns, and mass media outlets that have traditionally defined 'mainstream' opinions (Wolf 1992, 188).[16] As a matter of fact, in the United States this tendency has recently been extended to the circumvention and supplanting of 'real' journalism—the traditional news reporting that respects the bias of its corporate patrons—by a new category in the cultural marketplace, "infoganda" or "faux journalism"— fake news shows starring pseudo-journalists emanating directly from the Bush administration (Rich 2004; Rich 2005). And when these 'velvet glove' tactics did not do the job, reactionary forces highly placed in the media took out and applied the iron fist. Indeed, the Disney Corporation's attempts at muzzling director Michael Moore are a monument to corporate America's ability to censor speech and indoctrinate the public (Rutenberg). After all, those who appear on television do not hold power; power belongs to those who can hire and fire those who appear on television.

The filtering of what is sent over the airwaves has reached grotesquely large proportions in Italy with the affirmation of the power of Berlusconi, "Sua Emittenza," the undisputed and uncontrolled landlord of Italian television. The ability of corporate monopolies to shape public opinion and funnel debate is nothing new. But in Italy the muzzle placed on the media, and the prime minister's attempts to make the magistracy ineffective and usurp the authority of the president of the Republic, have reached frighteningly antidemocratic proportions. As Ben-Ghiat points out, Berlusconi's "patrimonial ambitions do not stop at the creation of a vast financial empire, but extend to a proprietary vision of the state in which public and private interests are indistinguishable." Moreover, the extent to which the younger generations in and outside of Italy have fallen prey to technological determinism and 'common sense' views of society and culture as the result of "the creation of a mental structure which responds to, and reflects the requirements of the system" (Marcuse 2001, 170)[17] makes painfully evident the need for a "deep" liberation, that is to say a liberation of the unconscious from the false cathexes of media culture.

In such a context literature can be an effective tool for dealing with the mediations or instruments for the building of hegemonic consensus identified by Gramsci. It can also submit to critique the depth dimension of satisfactory submission to the power structure. In sum, our close readings of the prose fictions of Eco, Consolo, and Tabucchi are prompted and informed by the need to catalyze a "permanent revolution" (Harvey 2000, 243), a social project that understands the need for continual negations. To paraphrase Browning, "Ah but a society's reach should exceed its grasp, or what's a heaven for?"

In order to keep the background—against which our three authors write, while looking closely at their fictions—clearly in view, I will use an approach whose point of departure and arrival is the text but whose cornerstone is the poetics of the author, as evinced in extraliterary and nonfictional writings. This will allow us to read the prose fictions of Eco, Consolo, and Tabucchi in the light of the dynamic intellectual and artistic personality of each, while considering their experiences within their literary, cultural, moral, and historical context so that we may see how a poetic-esthetic agenda is transformed into art. For this reason, my approach to the three individual writers is descriptive, not prescriptive, in that I attempt to react to what reverberates most clearly in their work.

My reading of Umberto Eco's fictions comes in response to the resonance, especially of his first novel, among an international mass audience. All five of his works of fiction merit close attention because they reveal different facets of the same type of behavior. Eco's protagonists avoid oedipal conflict and resolution and, later on, offer up brief and weak challenges to paternal authority before submitting to it in the hope of receiving it in inheritance. The unresolved oedipal issues that run through Eco's fictions and the role these conflicts play as a result in perpetuating structures of patriarchy have clear and broad implications outside the covers of the novels. When Eco's protagonists avoid confrontation with the Father and oedipal resolution, socially constructed gender roles under patriarchy are reaffirmed, and the reader is comforted by tales that reproduce what is already known, that which was digested in childhood as factual and natural, despite its contrived foundations (Sobieraj).

Thus, the implied intent of each of the chapters dedicated to Eco's prose fictions is to document how patriarchy is constructed socially, then reproduced and transmitted individually among a mass readership. Eco's audience is composed of kindred spirits, both men and women, who see his characters replicate their own conscious and unconscious responses to social expectations of gender. In Eco's societies of men socially constructed gender roles are reaffirmed—men dominate while women are either sublime, virginal mother figures or degraded as whores—along with socially desirable behavior for their respective gender identities. It may very well be the case that Eco's female readers reenact the dialectical process by which typified gender identities are internalized, a hypothesis that might explain his mass readership among both men and women: "Model Readers" of both genders are assuaged when they underwrite that which they already know, socially constructed reality perspectives on a shared reality. Indeed, all Eco's protagonists console their readers by tautologically verifying and legitimating the world as we know it: things are exactly as they must be.

Indeed, as we read through Eco's fictions, it becomes increasingly clear that the popularity of his narratives is due to a great extent to his ability to actively tap into the communal myths and dreams, the needs and goals of his target audience, a specific segment of Western society.[18] Hopefully, an analysis of Eco's fictional texts will draw attention to the fact that Eco's novels succeed in revealing concealed aspects of our humanity when they bring to the fore shared, deep-seated complexes, the result of repressed, unresolved battles with oedipus, but reaffirm the status quo and thereby fail to activate literature's capability to transform the present. As we shall see, Eco's fictions seek to escape culture's historical dimension and exorcise transgression of the status quo by circumscribing debate within the rules of a well-defined game.[19]

Consolo provides an "interlude" between the lengthier sections on Eco and Tabucchi, because a reading of his fictional and nonfictional writings that focuses on the novel *Retablo* [*Altarpiece*] succinctly raises key issues to our topic: the role of literature in society, the nature of the literary artifice, and the decentering of the locus of narration. *Retablo*, whose main character is a Milanese painter who travels to Sicily in search of antiquities, is an exemplary work within Consolo's ouevre because a recurring motif in his fictions is the weaving in of figurative art.[20]

Set in the Age of Enlightenment, *Retablo* provides the historical antecedent for other fictions by Consolo that, when placed together, summarize the collective history of Italians since national Unification in 1860.[21] The fictionalized history of the Risorgimento recounted in *Il sorriso dell'ignoto marinaio* is continued by *Nottetempo casa per casa* [*Night-time, House by House*], which tells of the birth of Fascism. The story of a young man's coming-of-age related in *La ferita dell'aprile* takes place against the backdrop of the end of World War II and the birth of the Republic, events that echo in the account of the "years of lead" and terrorism related by *Lo spasimo di Palermo* [*The Spasm of Palermo*], his last novel to date. *Retablo* also makes evident many of the themes and ideas that inform Consolo's poetics while enabling the reader to see how literature is capable of restoring a sense or direction to history that is lost in postmodernity. Furthermore, the chapter on Consolo introduces the topic of ekphrasis prior to consideration of its use by Tabucchi, whose investigation in this area has proven to be a crucial element in the latter's development as a writer.

Ekphrasis, for Consolo, is a means for the recovery of those aspects of Sicilian civilization—the language, the traditions, the landscape and monuments—in risk of extinction.[22] It is also a means for catalyzing what we may call a collective anamnesis intended to restore a "resilient past" to our future. Ekphrasis, to borrow Dainotto's phrasing, allows us to "supplement our historical loss with 'topographical knowledge'" (18).[23] The integration of the lexicon of Sicilian dialects into standard Italian not only locates Consolo's prose in time and space, but is also an integral part of a linguistic experimentation whose purpose, like that of his ekphrastic works, is to dignify and restore what has been marginalized, that which is at risk of being written out of history: the language and culture of Southern Italy's subaltern populations.

Consolo responds to the perception that the relationship between literary text and the historical and social context have been interrupted—resulting in the dissipation of the audience for literary works, and literature's loss of social relevance—by developing a unique mode of expression. This is the state of affairs depicted in the clash between a philosopher and his son-in-law poet in "Catarsi" [Catharsis], the first of the two one-act dramas recently collected in the volume *Oratorio* [*Oratory*]. In "Catarsi" the corruption emanating from a perverse concordance of government and intellectual superstructure results in a "stasis": guilt by association results in the physical paralysis and aphasia of innocent family members. Catharsis, symbolized in Consolo's writings—both nonfictional and fictional—by the image of the *nóstos* [*homecoming*], Odysseus' return home to Ithaca, occurs when individuals return to their defining communities. But in Consolo's fictions communication ceases when atonement is precluded: reascent from the abyss is impossible because the home and the community have been degraded and because the polis, the context in which individuals realize themselves, has been defiled. The second *pièce* in *Oratorio* and Consolo's most recent example of creative writing, "L'ape iblea. Elegia per Noto" [The Bee of the Iblei Mountains. Ælegy for Noto] (which served as libretto for the composer Francesco Pennisi's *Oratorio*, whence the title of the volume) constitutes an attempt to "restore," lyrically, the "history, the ancient splendor and recent decadence of a city destroyed by earthquake in the hope of forestalling, musically, the disappearance of a civilization.

Indeed, Consolo's narratives are deeply rooted in the historical reality of Sicily; and, following Sciascia, Consolo utilizes the Island as metaphor for a broader condition, for all that is wrong with contemporary Italy. Sicily as metaphor is an ideological tool of analysis; it is a move *toward* history and away from atemporal, essentialist, allegedly natural explanations of a 'Sicilian way of being.'[24]

For this reason we may say that Consolo gives a direction to history when he retrieves the past allegorically, in the Benjaminian sense. For Benjamin allegory interrupts homogenized, continuous, linear, sequential, causal history, replacing the imaginary continuum of past and present with disjunctive memory

(Eagleton 1981 and Benjamin 1998). Repressed, historically recyclable material is remembered and reinterpreted through allegory, reproducing moments that are antithetical to the present. When these fragments or recollections are reinterpreted in the light of their new context, meaning is created. In this way a nonantagonistic "literature of replenishment" (Barth) is replaced with an antithetical literature of fragmentation and negation composed of the displacements of nonchronological and nonsubjective memory, of "living images" that interrupt the habitual and open the present up to review and to interpretation while exposing subjective perspectives to the objectifying perspective of debate.[25]

At the same time, the nonsubjective perspective created by the use, in *Retablo*, of three distinct narrating voices underscores the lack of a centralized locus of narrative consciousness. Thus, the author undermines the attempts of the main character, the bourgeois painter, to absorb the stories of all others within his own. In fact, following Dombroski, we may say that the tripartite structure evoked by the title of this work reflects a more general condition of disorder and fragmentation, and also responds to that situation by searching for a way to represent this "complexity of practices and material conditions without submitting them to some overarching concept of totality" (Dombroski 1998, 262).[26]

Like Consolo, Tabucchi participates in collaborative ekphrastic works. But while Consolo does so with the intent of retrieving what has been lost to history, Tabucchi takes from this exercise an important lesson in alternative perspectives.[27] In this way he acquires a tool for decentering the subjects of his narrations, which "replicate the effect of Lacan's topological models of mental functioning, where the inside is continuous with the outside, and the whole cannot be grasped in a single moment" (Smith 2000, 88). A distinguishing feature of Tabucchi's narratives is the examination of diversities and "the interrogation of reality through another's eyes" (Tabucchi 1996a, 121). The exploration of interiorities is never an end unto itself, but follows a path whose depth is matched by its extension to the other. Following Eagleton, who equates such decentering, or the doubling of the ego, with a "disinterestedness" rather unlike Calvino's, we may say that Tabucchi's characters do not view "the world from some Olympian height, but [participate in] a kind of compassion or fellow-feeling." They try to sense their "way imaginatively into the experience of another, sharing their delight and sorrow without thinking of [themselves]" (Eagleton 2003, 133).

This strategy can be contrasted to Eco's installation of a seemingly plural narrative viewpoint, one that is a contamination of multiple subjectivities (those of the empirical author, the narrating voice, and the protagonist) and the underwriting of the Barthesian concept of the 'death of the author' as a way of passing authority over the text to yet another subjectivity, that of the reader. In Eco the center of narrative gravity is strengthened, not undermined, because the apparent multiplicity of perspectives created by the strategy of the Model Author allows Eco to present as objective his own indirect subjectivity. Readers willing participate in this deception because narrative resolution, or closure is always achieved (all Eco's novels are told as lengthy flashbacks)—and closure of any sort, as Harvey maintains, "contains its own authority because to materialize any one design, no matter how playfully construed, is to foreclose, in some cases temporarily but in other instances relatively permanently, on the possibility of materializing others (Harvey 2000, 196)—and because the pseudo-objectivity of the tales transforms fabulation into a viable means of editing, or rewriting the past in a way that explains and justifies the way things are in the present.

However, the retrieval of the past by Consolo, as we have seen, and by Tabucchi is future oriented. Tabucchi's characters make use of the mnemic time-image to present the reader with a direct, qualitative image of thought. His narrations cognitively organize time through what Rodowick, following Deleuze, calls the juxtaposition, or irrational geometry, of the interval. To explain, representation of the flow of time is not subordinate to movement through space (as is the case in Eco's fictions). The "interval" is a source of discontinuity; it divides and regroups diegesis (Rodowick 1997, 15): seeing and hearing (memory) replace the linking of images through motor actions. The organization of narrative sequence in time-images assures that the flow of time and thought are disjoined: there is no quantifiable, linear sequence. Instead, time is continuously splitting off toward an undetermined future, and disappearing into a past that is preserved as an accumulation of nonchronological strata while remaining present as a potentiality, as the locus in which all the past is stored.

When utilized in narrative, the Deleuzian "interval" makes possible the recovery of what was not initially perceived—the out-of-field, to use a cinematic term; or to phrase it differently, the outside, or the detritus that was written out of the past—and its insertion within the diegetic flow. Thus, the time-image produces an image of thought as a nontotalizable process: when the chronological series is no longer a succession of instants in space, but a time-image that fragments the present, the regrouping of temporal relations realistically portrays a concrete image of nonchronological memory and thought. Closure is not possible because the actual opens up to the virtual. The reader is not presented an image of what can be objectively known, but instead is confronted with an unending quest for a fragmented, subjective truth. The time-image gives history a sense, albeit one of unpredictable change: duration is neither linear nor chronological, but introduces a future in continuous transformation (Rodowick 1997, 24–25). For this reason we can affirm that it too is a realistic way—perhaps more realistic than traditional linear narratives—of representing and historicizing the present.

Since the time-image denotes subjectivity as an ever-changing construct—a "becoming multiple" (Rodowick 1997, 140)—and thought as the nomadic comprehension of all temporal dimensions, the reader receives the work in a way that is neither subjective nor objective, but may be described as nonsubjective, or objectifying. Because no one character authenticates or verifies the historical truth of the text, the reader cannot adjudicate the veracity of any one character's narration with respect to another. There is no Truth to uncover. Instead, "there is a set of transformations where narrations continually confront one another in series that may just as easily contradict as corroborate one another" (Rodowick 1997, 100).

Thus, it becomes incumbent on readers to extract and elaborate their own meanings and conclusions from the "essential elements" of the story (Tabucchi 1988e). Furthermore, the 'boundaries' of Tabucchi's texts (prefaces, covers, etc.), as we shall see in the chapter dedicated to his poetics, serve not to clarify and guide the reader, but almost always complicate things further. Indeed, Tabucchi uses the paratext (Genette) not to shed light on hidden aspects of the creative process but to disquiet, to raise questions that remain unanswered so as to underscore the fact that all literary descriptions of reality are mendacious: such translations are always distortions that blur distinctions between reality, memory, and fabrication.

At the same time, Tabucchi believes that ludic, combinatory games of exhaustion and replenishment are merely a "melancholy artifice" intended to assuage the reader, a "set of Legos that can be assembled and re-assembled in an infinite number of ways."[28] Art, he asserts, is a "dream," an interiority made manifest, imagination that has become reality. He compares the writer to the actor who "transubstantiates" or projects outward and becomes one with the character portrayed. He explains that in the theatrical fiction, actors cannot simply make believe they are someone else; they must "suffer the anger, the sadness, the bile, the desperation and triumph as did Shakespeare for Hamlet." In other words, they must "feign the pain they truly feel." Similarly, writers transform life experiences into their fictions.

Tabucchi takes this notion of the "depersonalization" or doubling of the writer in the character, from Fernando Pessoa's *poeta fingidor*,[29] who carries forward a process radical introspection through the creation of autonomous alter egos: his heteronyms, five poet-characters invented in minute detail—biography, somatic features, aesthetic taste, cultural preparation, tics, and so forth (Tabucchi 1971, 35–37).[30] The projection of the writer into the character is, admittedly, another "lie" [*una menzogna*], but it is also the *primum mobile* of narrative (De Caro), because, as we have seen, for Tabucchi narration denotes the sharing of experience. The literary 'falsehood' of empathizing with the fate and the suffering of another because they are one's own pain and suffering provides us with the means for self-understanding and for reaffirming and strengthening interpersonal bonds. In fact, Tabucchi's self-analysis aims outward, toward enhanced intersubjective understanding and communication. Intersubjective understanding is possible because the introspection carried forward by Tabucchi's characters necessitates looking at the self from the outside, from the vantage of the other. They do so because part and parcel of their author's poetic involves striving to obtain a diverse form of awareness of his own subjectivity, to see himself as others see him. For example, in *I volatili del Beato Angelico* [*The Winged Creatures of Fra'Angelico*] a character named Antonio Tabucchi asks his interlocutor/alter ego to believe him when he says that he is a novelist, and therefore he is a liar (Tabucchi 1987, 47). However, the Möbius strip, inward and outward trail thus followed is not an intellectual game, nor is it an end unto itself. Instead, it traces a path ever deeper within and ever further outside the self.

Thus, the divergent definitions of the literary artifice put forward by Eco and Tabucchi afford us two differing ways of using literature to come to grips with the challenges and possibilities of the new millennium. For both Tabucchi and Eco literature is a falsehood. Both use this term to indicate that it is something other than a materiality; it is a creative, mental exercise. Eco, however, emphasizes literature's ludic qualities and capabilities because they allow us a glance at a beginning, a primordial trait of humanity revealed through language. He is particularly interested in signifying phrases from which multiple meanings can be extracted—enigmas, paradoxes, and lies—because, like poetic expression, they raise issues germane to the essence of language (Eco 1989, 86), thereby revealing the nodes of a "combinatory logic whose purpose is to produce possible instruments for the explanation of reality."[31]

Eco, in addition to his many other talents, is also a master at composing and solving of puzzles and riddles. Like the enigma, deceptions and falsehoods must obey the logical structure of language if they are to be credible. Eco cites the intent of the agent as his main criterion for distinguishing between imitations on the one hand, and, on the other, forgeries and counterfeits (Eco 1990, 165). An authentic, original work of art is something irreproducible and unique, while "the notion of counterfeit generally implies a malicious act" (168).[32] Lies undermine the compact on which social interaction is grounded because they are part of "a game that suspends the underlying rule of our relationships with other speakers" (Eco 1976a). In contrast, narration is a game that allows writers to absolve themselves from the ramifications of the stories they tell. For Baudolino, prevarication, like narration, is done without the conscious intention to deceive, and since Baudolino sincerely believes what he says, he is absolved of responsibility for his (mis)representations.[33] Therefore, both prevarication and narration are creative acts, and both are synonymous with fabrications.[34]

In any case, Eco's theorization of probability or of linguistic play—simulation, paradoxes, and falsehoods—is an intellectual exercise in metaphysics that contemplates both an indeterminate origin, or fullness of presence, and the eschatological End that are lost to postmodernity. His is a search for certainties within relativity and chaos; it is an attempt to understand why things are as they are. On the other hand, Consolo efforts aim at restoring lost aspects of the past so as to restore a sense, or direction, to history. Tabucchi mines the past so as to enable us to contemplate how things might be. His narratives compel us to contemplate alternatives—negations of the present—that are rooted in present possibilities, whose aim is a utopia that will always exceed our grasp.

2
Umberto Eco

The Poetics of "The Model Reader"

The concept of "Model Reader" as developed by Umberto Eco in his essays informs his novels and is therefore fundamental to a critique of his fictions. According to Eco, Model Readers do not submit to the writer's authority, but create what he calls a Model Author, and, ultimately, write their own text. In other words, in response to the so-called postmodern crisis of representation in literature that challenges what writers know and can legitimately depict, Model Readers actively move to nullify the determining effect of the author's influence on how texts are read, what Foucault has called the "author-function." Model Readers do not allow the empirical author's biography and poetic vision to condition their reading, but interact only with the work. Writers, overwhelmed by the impossibility of fully knowing a chaotic and rapidly changing reality, necessarily forfeit the right to impose meaning. They distance themselves from what they have written through the creation of a narrating voice in whom Model Readers vest the authority to narrate, the Model Author.

Eco's Model Reader willfully participates in the illusion of an author who 'dies,' as Eco phrases it, or relinquishes control to the reader after completing the act of writing. The reader, who is "no longer manipulated by an authorial point of view," becomes "the one who extracts, invents, creates a meaning and an order for the people in the fiction" (Federman, 8). However, Eco's apparent distancing from his novels through the use of superimposed layers of narrative subjectivity is the cornerstone of a consistent attempt to camouflage a persistently strong authorial voice.

When Model Readers underwrite the illusion of the author's invisibility, they cease to read critically and absorb the ideology encoded in the text. Once liberated from the authority of the empirical author, Eco's Model Readers fashion their own texts by constructing a theoretical Model Author, who is a projection of the wishes and desires of the empirical reader. By purposely ignoring the imprint of the empirical author, Model Readers free themselves to accept what the empirical author determines is the "literal sense" of the text. When the readings of author and reader coincide and corroborate each other, their consensus as to the "literal sense" of the text makes their readings normative.[1]

This is accomplished through what Carla Benedetti, in discussing Calvino's work, has called the Apocryphal Effect, the invention by the writer of a fictitious persona to whom the writer assigns authorship. In an essay titled "I livelli della realtà in letteratura" [Levels of Reality in Literature] Calvino claims that within the work, between the writer and the narrating voice, there exists an additional level of subjectivity, what he calls "the author." In his definition the author is "a voice, a style, a self-projection, a psychological position, a rapport with the world" that does not necessarily coincide with the writer's personality. Calvino believed the imposition of this author between empirical writer and text, nullified the Foucauldian "author-function" because it prevented the reader from using information about the writer to justify a strong interpretation of a work of literature. This compounding of narrative strata within the work increases in turn the chasm between writer and the text and further justifies the author's abdication of responsibility.

Eco takes Calvino's concept one step further. While Calvino's author is a projection of the writer, Eco's Model Author is a projection of the wishes and desires of the Model Reader. Therefore, Eco's Model Reader is both a hermeneutic and a poetic. It is also an ingenious marketing strategy. His 'open' works strongly suggest reading strategies,[2] even though they claim to invite the spontaneous collaboration of his target demographic of impressionable middle-brow Model Readers who are flattered by the offer of writerly collaboration. Eco explains that "the *possibilities* the work's openness make available exist within a given *field of relations* pre-determined by the author; there is "an organizing rule which governs these relations." Therefore, "the *work in movement* is the possibility of numerous different personal interventions, but it is not an amorphous invitation to indiscriminate intervention" (Eco 1984c, 62; his emphasis). When "the author offers the interpreter, the performer, the addressee a work to be completed [h]e does not know the exact fashion in which his work will be concluded, but he is aware that once completed the work in question *will still be his own*" (Eco1984c, 62; my emphasis).[3]

I must stress from the outset that my own realization as critical, not Model, reader is that there is at all levels of narration (Eco, narrating voice, etc.) a willingness to absolve those who would release the narrator from responsibility various 'culpable acts,' for example, fabrication. This makes me question what the narrator is trying to conceal from himself and from others. This, in turn, causes me to ask myself why, how, and to what extent I empathize with the plight of a narrating voice who struggles with oedipal guilt, gender issues, and the constraints placed on individual development and behavior by a patriarchal power structure. This allows me to imagine myself being observed—by the author, the characters in his novel, and other readers—as I read. This "dialectics of looking" (Kilborne) allows me to consume the text in a way that might be described as nonsubjective because of the tension it installs between interior and exterior realities: as this self-interrogation proceeds, critical self-awareness and comprehension of the text enhance each other reciprocally. Reading, however, does not follow the path of the hermeneutic circle as decribed by Eco (see Eco 1990 and Eco 1998), because the text ceases to be an inert presence onto which I transfer my own personal history. It assumes its fully transitive, antagonistic, historical force when it engages me in a dialogue that enables me to bring forth and elaborate what I have concealed from myself. Thus, it permits me to avoid the tendency to identify with the narrating voice and the tendency to absolve all, myself included, from responsibility for 'culpable' behaviors. Dialogue with the text then opens the door to a critical reading that catalyzes the transformative, future-oriented power of the literary work.

In any event, Eco's Model Reader strategy was tested with great success in *Il nome della rosa*. His first novel presents itself as a *conte philosophique* designed to illuminate the theological disputes of the late Middle Ages while evoking a multitude of canonical and lesser-known texts. Real and fictitious historical figures mix in what presents itself as a personal memoir dealing with events that transpired in a monastery in November 1347. In addition, *Il nome della rosa* utilizes a defining postmodern stylistic device, parody of a popular genre—the detective story—when it seems to frustrate reader desire for closure. "Seems" because while it is true that the conclusion of *Il nome della rosa* overturns conventional detective story structures with the victorious self-destruction of the assassin who is never brought to justice, and the self-criticism of the investigator who fails to solve the case in a timely manner, it is also true that when Jorge tells all, including how he lured the Abbot into his deathly trap, closure is achieved. All mysteries are solved, chaos is dominated, and order is reinstalled (Ferretti 1983, 36).

All Eco's novels are lengthy flashbacks whose conclusions return the reader to the point of departure. The ultimate fate of Casaubon, in *Il pendolo di Foucault* [*Foucault's Pendulum*], is of limited consequence. When he succeeds in understanding Belbo's behavior, including the motivation for his friend's passive acceptance of death, all the important loose ends are fastened down. What happens to Baudolino after his final departure from Constantinople is of little interest and of less consequence, as we shall see in the chapter dedicated to that novel. The same can be said of Roberto de la Griva after he leaves the *Daphne*. In other words, Eco's Model Readers are neither challenged nor transformed, but comforted and gratified when expectations are satisfied. Linearity of plot above life's perplexities and vicissitudes facilitates reader acceptance of the author's imposition of a limited number of 'common sense' interpretations of the work. Model Readers embrace the opportunity to write their own text and are grateful that their options are simplified and limited. Thus, Eco, who minimizes in theoretical settings his importance as empirical author, enables himself to surreptitiously induce his Model Reader to submit to his authority.

Although Eco's poetics of the Model Reader would nullify the influence of the empirical author, all his novels are works *à thèse* that purposively intervene in contemporary political and intellectual controversies.[4] Therefore, any reading of his novels must be accompanied by a consideration of the literary, cultural, moral, and historical contexts of his fictions in relation to his dynamic personality as an artist, intellectual, and scholar. This in turn necessitates examining the manner in which his ideas on literature inform his novels. The contextualization of his fictions not only transforms readings from mere exegesis to critique, but also helps the reader avoid the idiosyncrasies of the reader-response hermeneutic that Eco himself advocates as an integral part of his poetics of the Model Reader.

In the late-1950s and early 1960s, Eco first came to prominence in Italian letters as a theoretician of *Il gruppo '63* [*Group 63*], a neo-avant-garde movement that claimed to respond to radical social transformations brought on by rapid industrial development and the growth of the culture industry. One aspect of the debate within *Il gruppo '63* regarded devising new forms of narration capable of reinvigorating Italian fiction after the demise of neorealism as a dominant trend. In a theoretical work produced at that time, *Opera aperta* [*Open Work*], Eco spoke of the positive aspects of the culture industry and of the utility of "literary engineering." He also anticipated the notion of the "death of the author" that was developed more fully a few years later by Roland Barthes.

In *Opera aperta* Eco proposes that readers supplant the writer, who willingly abdicates authority over the text, and actualizes the "open" literary work with personal interpretative interventions. However, despite repeated statements to the contrary, "Eco has never embraced the Barthesian notions of 'the death of the author' or of the modern author that has become a mere *scriptor*" (Capozzi 219). Unlike Barthes, Eco argues that the open text predetermines the extent to which reader collaboration must be controlled, encouraged, directed, and transformed. Although writers appear to relinquish control when they declare themselves superfluous to the appreciation of their texts, they cannot in fact completely abdicate control of the narrative process through which the disorder of the universe is reordered for the reader.

Eco's historical metafictions actively strive to move beyond the postcognitive perplexity McHale contends is endemic to our postmodern condition.[5] Eco argues that contemporary art must deal with and resolve for its public the turmoil caused by the breakdown of the traditional Order set out a millennium ago by the great Medieval summae. Because the world codified by such writers as Thomas Aquinas has collapsed, modern art cannot reflect a conception of the cosmos as a hierarchy of clear and preestablished orders of existence. So Eco investigates how contemporary artists give form to a world dominated by "chance, indeterminacy, probability, and ambiguity" (Eco 1962; 5, 16–17, 50), and he determines that the writer dominates chaos by setting the parameters for the reader by establishing the literal sense of the work, which predetermines 'common sense' readings.

As Eco makes clear in the Postille al *Nome della rosa* [Afterword to *The Name of the Rose*], as author he identifies with his text. While writing his first novel, he "wanted, with all [his] strength to sketch the outline of a reader who, after having been initiated, became [his] prey, that is, the text's prey" (Eco 1983b, 523). Eco indeed accomplished this—as his sales figures attest—through literary engineering, a deft marketing strategy that determines the novel's packaging (or, in more traditional terms, narrative structure). For example, *Il pendolo di Foucault* is parceled out in brief chapters, in deference, perhaps, to the short attention span of the inveterate TV viewers who figure heavily in Eco's mass readership. Exposition of "The Plan" is broken down over chapters 85–95, a tactic that allows for frequent breaks from reading. The only significantly lengthy chapter is 113, the one that coincides with the culmination of the plot, a point where the reader would find a commercial break more annoying than relaxing.

The term "literary engineering" denotes a process of writing by which erudite works of 'high' literary value are prepackaged to first create and then meet the needs of a mass reading public. Such planning and construction of the literary product necessarily takes into account reader tastes and desires from the very outset of the creative process (Ferretti 1983, 27–30). Accordingly, the writer's preferred interlocutors are readers capable of identifying erudite citations and other undeciphered linguistic codes and who enjoy their status as the select public of a writer with Eco's distinguished academic credentials.[6]

Thus, the extraordinary success of Eco's fictions is not at all serendipitous. Prior to trying his hand at writing novels, Eco, a recognized expert in media theory, discussed this very practice. The object of analysis in *Apocalittici e integrati* [*Apocalyptic and Integrated Intellectuals*] is a "craft whose goals are consumption, escapism, and the popularizing of acquisitions." In other words, Eco seeks to legitimize theoretically the "mediation" and "vulgarization" of an elite cultural experience for a mass audience. And so, in *Apocalittici e integrati* he juxtaposes pulp novels to works capable of transferring "avant-garde" experiences to a higher level of consumption in an intelligent and productive way.

In "Ricerca e Lettore Modello" [Research and Model Reader]—an essay published in a collection titled, interestingly enough, *Letteratura tra consumo e ricerca* [Literature between consumption and research]—Eco equates nonconsolatory art with "esthetic elitism," asserting that amenable readings—such as his fictions—need not necessarily be considered unartistic (Eco 1984b,103). In his opinion, a text can be both pleasurable and artistic if its "complexity and organicity are such as to permit us to reconstruct within ourselves the text's designated reader" (105). He then distinguishes his fictions from avant-garde efforts by defining his own work as experimental. While avant-garde provocations are ends unto themselves, experimental literature "offends, but with a pedagogical intent, and in order to reach a consensus." Experimentalist writing deludes expectation, but "wants to be accepted by a wide reading public," and, over time, to "become the norm" (98). Eco goes on to say that consumption, market success and reading pleasure are not compatible with avant-garde texts, but they are the necessary complement of the experimental work. Although experimentalists test the horizon of expectation of their readers, they do so not to make themselves inaccessible, but to forge new Model Readers capable of "understanding him, appreciating him, and loving him." For this reason, he excludes from his intended public "first-level readers," those who read only for plot, and aims for second-level "Model" readers who appreciate the craft of writing and can identify intertextual citations (98–99,101).

Eco does, however, reject third-level high brow readings that would reconstruct the artistic and historical personality of empirical authors within the cultural and political context of their times, claiming he is not interested in the writer's dialogue with contemporaries and the literary tradition. Since his target audience is the reader who is primarily interested in legibility, that is to say the plot and the craft of storytelling, Eco rejects as interlocutors those professional critics (105) who are resistant to his narrative authority. Yet a glance at Eco's curriculum vitae[7] shows that he is very mindful of erudite treatments of his work. Moreover, Eco has gone to great lengths to influence scholarly interpretation through interviews and self-commentary.

Eco's Model Reader *"wonders what sort of reader the story would like him or her to become* and . . . wants to discover precisely how the model author goes about serving as a guide for the reader." He explains that, "Only when empirical readers have discovered the model author, *and have understood . . . what is wanted from them*, will they become full-fledged model readers" (Eco 1994b, 27; my emphasis). In other words, Eco's Model Reader first seeks to appreciate the writer's craft, then attempts to follow "the strategy [the author] designed to enable a reader to explore . . . endlessly" (46) the world created by the narrator. In the final analysis, the act of reading is a process of adaptation to the intentions of a Model Author (75). Model Readers must strive to "be faithful to the suggestions of a voice that is not saying explicitly what it is suggesting" (112). Eco's "Model Reader" looks at "the textual strategy as a system of instructions aimed at producing a possible reader whose profile is designed by and within the text and who can be extrapolated from it and described independently of and even before any empirical reading" (Eco 1998, 34).

Eco's Model Readers adapt their horizon of expectation to the text, and conform their reading to the anticipated requirements of a Model Author. As we have seen, Eco's Model Author is both a narrative strategy and a set of instructions that must be accepted if we are to behave and perform as Model Readers (Eco 1984, 15). Eco argues in fact that "the Model Author and the Model Reader are entities that become clear to each other only in the process of reading, so that each one creates the other" (Eco 1984, 24). Therefore, the Model Author is gleaned from the text by its reader. And since the empirical author purports to have died, that is to say ceased to exert authority over the text, the entire process takes place *within the mind of the reader.* That Model Reader refrains from looking outside the work for an objectifying, historical context and stays strictly within the confines of "the still valid hermeneutic circle" (Eco 1998, 39–40). The Model Reader purposely ignores what Marcuse calls the antagonistic force of the work within its here and now. Put differently, the Model Reader underwrites the self-concealment of the empirical author. The Model Reader engages only the Model Author, who is a well nigh metaphysical entity, or, in Eco's own words, "a voice without body or sex or history" (Eco 1994b, 25), an invisible ventriloquist of ideology.

Eco contends that this strategy is "socially incisive" because it "transforms" the reader, who is modified through the act of reading-interpreting (Eco 1979, 45). Since the "Model Reader" is "not to think of anything at all except what the text offer[s] him" (Eco 1983b, 523), this "transformation" is catalyzed by the reader's self-authenticating interpretations of the text, which are the result of the interplay between an understanding of the work's component parts and an evolving comprehension of the whole. However, this raises a question that Eco leaves unanswered: how can a Model Author or a text be considered somehow above temporality, and transform the reader without the transitive presence of a historical, empirical interlocutor? In other words, if the transformation of the reader is to be achieved through the "complicity of text and reader" (Costanzo), the point of departure must be an awareness of the text's historical alterity, which is precisely what Eco admonishes his Model Reader to ignore.

Since the Model Author Eco envisions is no more than "a textual strategy . . . that asks to be imitated" by the reader (Eco 1994b, 25), it is a projection of both the image of what the reader *thinks* the author wants the reader to become, and of the image of what the reader wants the author to be: a benevolent validator of the Model Reader's reading, an author re-created in the reader's own image. In sum, the reader validates the author's abdication of responsibility, while allowing the writer to maintain authority over the text. Eco's Model Readers do not create a Model Author as much as they re-create themselves by convincing themselves that there is an exclusive Reader-Text relationship outside history and in the absence of dialogic exchange.

When Model Authors reorder the chaos of the universe their readers are comforted by what Eco calls the "manageable totalities" of narrative worlds where there is neither doubt nor metaphysical uncertainty. For example, because *Il nome della rosa* is a whodunit, Model Readers may assume it emphasizes human agency; however, all action is in fact circumscribed by an invisible, but very firmly established divine order.

In any event, in closing his Norton lectures, Eco told his audience that for him writing is the gateway to participation in an experience tantamount to returning to the womb. Reflux through narration allows him to approach the unreachable object of desire and experience a feeling of oneness with the universe and its creator. Regression allows him to approach a feeling of plenitude, an impression that allows him to believe he is "for a moment, the model reader of the Book of Books" (Eco 1984, 140). On other occasions Eco has compared the pleasure of writing to the Oneness of "living in a narrative uterus" (Stauder 1996, 3), while praising the sense of false security that can be gained through the act of reading. To use his own words, "I think that we read novels because they give us the comfortable sensation of living in worlds where the notion of truth is indisputable, while the actual world seems to be a more treacherous place" (Eco 1984, 91). For this reason, Eco aims to create in his novels escapist "ontological worlds" that allow his Model Reader to believe what the empirical reader knows cannot be true (Eco 1984, 107), that the world is not chaotic, but ordered.

Thus, we see the extent to which Eco's poetics of the Model Reader is an adroit marketing strategy that plays on the insecurities of his target demographic of middle-level readers. The Model Reader wants the author's acceptance and approval, and, more importantly, is happy to retreat to Eco's ordered narrative universes above the indeterminate flow of postmodernity. Eco maintains that all his prose fictions ask "the only problem that philosophy always poses to itself, if the universe is ordered." Therefore, in all his novels there is a search for *el punto fijo* [*the fixed point*], at the center of the universe. Because Eco believes "there is a minimum of order in the universe" the finitude of his novels reflect those laws that circumscribe and govern the narrative worlds he creates.[8]

Beginning with the tale of Adso da Melk, all of Eco's novels give the past "a somehow coherent identity" (Pike, 327) by utilizing (auto)biography as an element of the narrative strategy. An elderly Baudolino tells of his life to his faithful amanuensis, Niceta. Casaubon, in rewriting Belbo's life, narrates his own. The life of Roberto de la Griva is recounted through his letters, memoirs and a shipboard diary. Eco's (auto)biographers look back on their lives and, through the screening process of memory, level the past within the present. In so doing, they can rewrite the past, justifying in terms of the present the actions they say and believe really took place. Eco's faithfulness to this strategy endows his novels with a remarkable psychological consistency: all his narrator-protagonists are engaged in grand struggles with oedipus and with patriarchal power. And all of his autobiographical subjects, even the 'Medieval' Adso and Baudolino, are endowed with a very modern self-awareness and sense of personal identity, evidenced by their pursuit of self-interest and their use of autobiography as a narrative device.

Following Burton Pike, I suggest that true pre-Renaissance protagonists would have been much less concerned with their own individuality than Adso and Baudolino. However, all Eco's narrators, including Adso and Baudolino, need to assert their identity as autobiographical entities before death overtakes them. Autobiography is their means of affirming their identity through an act of consciousness because they view their personal death as a much more emphatic event than would have someone who lived in pre-Renaissance, God-oriented times (see Pike, 328). Eco's autobiographical subjects write about themselves so that they can "vault over the walls of space and time and . . . become God, or God-like" (Pike, 329). They reinvent the past, giving it a new coherence, and flatten it into a present that is timeless because discrete, rational moments such as seasons, birthdays, and years are screened by and superceded in memory. By writing their lives the subjects of Eco's fictions condense and compress a very modern, that is to say fragmented and relativized, sense of time into the eternal present of their text. In this way they resolve the conflict between linear, historical time and the undifferentiated time of memory (Pike, 332).

As Pike indicates, the nineteenth-century autobiographer saw History as a "progressive cosmic force." The ego determined linear, chronological time, which provided the autobiographer with "ideal external support" for individual problems with identity (Pike 330). However, by the end of the nineteenth century in Western culture, personal identity was no longer seen as fixed, but as relative to evolving functional relationships (340). But even though the past was no longer considered an objective entity, a "sense of the past" gave a complex reality the unity that underpinned the multiple perspectivism and relativism of modernity (Harvey 1989). This modernist internalization of the past "enables the ordering mind to escape temporarily" from the determining influence of the ego and to incorporate the "timelessness of the unconscious" into narrative. As a result, the immersion of the autobiographical subject into the narrative-as-it-is-being-written creates the illusion of permanence outside the flow of time: "the present is the compounded result of an individual total past" (Pike 339).[9]

In postmodernity the weight of the past is drastically reduced and future horizons are radically shortened in meaningful decision making. Jameson uses Lacan's account of schizophrenia as an aesthetic model to argue that postmodern art is conditioned by the accelerated reshaping of structures of temporal experience wrought by the revolution in information technology. Indeed, personal identity is to a great extent the effect of the temporal linkage of past and future with one's present, but in postmodernity the present is all there is.

Eco, however, does not seek to guide and transform postmodernity beyond the loss and absence of metaphysical foundations and eschatological ends.[10] Instead, he retools a modernist model: the use of autobiography and the strategy of the Model Reader both serve to detach the narrative from historical contingency. The poetics of the Model Reader seeks to conceal the time, place, and conditions of production of the text. Eco's autobiographies console the Model Reader when they restore coherence and manageability to the temporal experience. They do so through an act of consciousness that does not by restore lost depth to the past, but condenses it into an autobiographical present outside the flow of time. "Autobiography appeals to readers," Pike contends, "because the psychological structures inherent in the way a writer attempts to re-create his life activate a latent response in the reader. The reader responds to conscious and unconscious patterns in autobiography because they correspond to conscious and unconscious patterns" in the reader (333). The Model Reader, whose adult habits and repressions preclude an editorializing access to the personal past, identify with Eco's autobiographical subjects because, by giving voice to ideas and feelings that the reader's active consciousness tends to reject, they allow the reader to participate vicariously in their struggles with oedipus and with patriarchy.

In point of fact, the struggle with oedipus is a leit motif in all of Eco's novels. To quickly explain, Adso—the narrator-protagonist of Eco's best seller *Il nome della rosa*, never confronts his paternal figures. Oedipus is left unresolved. Adso is sent away from home before reaching puberty, and as a teenager he does not defy the paternal surrogate Abbone, but confronts him vicariously through his nurturing mentor, Guglielmo. He takes vengeance on his elders only after they have all long since passed away, and he can do so without fear of reprisal. When Adso—the only witness to and interpreter of what happened—finally sets his memoirs to paper, he absolves himself of all blame for his role in the destruction of the monastery and makes public the shortcomings of everyone else. In *Il pendolo di Foucault* Casaubon challenges the paternal surrogate Agliè, but regrets having flirted with The Plan, and ultimately submits to the Father's judgement. Roberto de la Griva avoids confrontation with paternal figures by learning to "acquiesce, or at least give the appearance of acquiescing" to the authority he intends to inherit (253). Baudolino is an elderly man when he tells of himself and of the physical and verbal abuse suffered at the hands of his biological father and of his mentor Otto, of unreleased aggression against his idealized adoptive father, and of his sublimated love for his surrogate mother. Oedipus, once again, remains unresolved. Unable to elaborate or de-cathect having been sold by to the Emperor Federico by the biological father whom he was incapable of pleasing, Baudolino spends his adult life hoping to satisfy vicariously, through his adoptive father, his need to please his biological father by finding Prester John.

In battling oedipus, patriarchy, and rejecting parents, Eco's fictions touch deep chords in the Model Reader, who are also consoled by the works' closure in the face of life's open-endedness, and feel an affinity when the autobiographies prove that the past can be rewritten and fixed for posterity in terms favorable to the narrating subject. All this is accomplished in an amenable way when Eco deflects attention away from the turmoil within his narrating voices by challenging his Model Reader to identify citations from canonical and lesser-known texts.

Eco uses another typically postmodern device, pastiche, to reconstruct a world that we already know, and condenses the literary and historical past into the reader's present. He does not cite texts we have already read to parody or undermine tradition; rather, Eco uses a stylistic technique that reflects the acquiescent behavior of subjects who want to appropriate, not challenge, what is already in place. Despite claims that his "experimental" fictions offend in order to modify the reader's horizon of expectations, Eco's use of pastiche is ludic, without significant dialectical thrust. And because Eco's "citationism" (Vassalli) does not aim beyond the dejà lu, it nullifies the transformative power of literature. Since his novels are designed for readers who already exist, reader expectations remain unchanged. The Model Author skillfully blends the old and the new within the plot and the Model Reader uncovers the probable and the foreseeable. Together, the two arrive at preordained truths that reaffirm traditional Order (Ferretti 1983, 32–37). Therefore, the act of reading Eco's fictions is not future-oriented, but eminently reassuring: Model Readers learn that things are the way they must be.

Eco's autobiographies re-create the past, but they do not restore its historical depth. Following Rodowick's exegesis of Deleuze's writings on the cinematic image, we may say that in Eco's narratives time is subordinated to movement in space; time is represented indirectly, the result of spatial succession. In classic realist cinema, when physical actions link linearly to create continuity, time is measured in quantitative intervals. Similarly, all Eco's prose fictions follow a rational progression of events that projects a model of stable Truth. His plots reflect determined and predictable relations that are predicated on a definition of time as becoming in space (33). Parenthetically, we will see further on how Tabucchi portrays the direct, qualitative image of time; time is independent of movement. For example, *Si sta facendo sempre più tardi,* diegetic progression is catalyzed not by action, but by memory. Irrational progression divides and regroups diegesis, destabilizing and overturning the subordination of time to movement while upsetting the concept of a stable Truth reaffirmed in Eco's fictions.

For his part, Eco assuages the insecurities of those who must live with the electronic volatility of postmodern work- and market-places and contend with the effects of the revolution in information technology on real living conditions. Furthermore, while he claims that scholarly readings of his fictions do not influence his creativity, his Model Reader is enticed and encouraged to consume by the professional validation of scholars who also read Eco. As is the case with Eco's middle-brow audience, many literary critics and scholars are not immune to Eco's use of "allegorical fun, polyvalence, and analogies." They, too, are attracted into his marketing web by his ability to create a "neo-Baroque *divertissement,* characterized by "wonderfully varied and tangled possible avenues of connections," and are more than willing to dedicate exegetical energy identifying them (Hutcheon 1997, 320–25). Often, high-brow readers prove to be just as susceptible to Eco's marketing strategy as their middle-brow counterparts. Moreover, these same literary scholars are often predisposed to render positive evaluations of Eco's fictions by their agreement with positions set forth in his theoretical works.

As Bondanella notes, intellectual affinity for Eco's nonfiction "paved the way for a positive reception" of Eco's first novels among academics (290). In citing nonfictional writings by Eco in order to identify "the key to the plot" (288), and "the key to Lia's function" in *Il pendolo*, which is itself "a key which requires a specialist's knowledge" of *The Divine Comedy* (296), Bondanella reinforces the boundaries set forth by Eco for interpreting *Il pendolo*. In other words, Bondanella encourages consumption of the book first by underwriting its literary value and then by providing the middle-level Model Reader with instructions for reading it. Bondanella then points out: "Eco's conclusion is an extraordinary ending for a novel written by one of the world's authorities on semiotics. It paradoxically praises a moment in which things represent, signify, symbolize, stand for, or allude to nothing but themselves—in short, a state of grace in which there is absolutely no need for semiotics!" (299). Indeed, precisely this "state of grace"—above the paradox—buffers the reader against the doubts and insecurities characteristic of our shared postmodern condition.

Moreover, as Eco himself indicates, his fictions allow the Model Reader relatively easy access to contemporary intellectual debate, which too often isolates itself from a wide audience by excessive reliance on academic jargon. Since, as Federman, author of seminal essays in North American postmodern literary theory, has pointed out, "there is too much to know and comprehend" (8) recourse among specialists—"lay clergies," in Eco's parlance—to the "ritual languages" of New Critics, Deconstructionists, and Lacanian critics raises "market issues" that Eco, a publishing consultant, argues can and should be exploited by novelists. He explains that writers can increase their market share by reproducing in their fictions the "mysterious," "sacred" languages of intellectual coteries and make them accessible to a wide audience (Costa and López, 119).

Although recourse to the terminology of specialists serves to obscure the "literal sense" of messages and inhibit reception, Eco also attributes a positive value to self-imposed limitations on intellectual debate because its use among specialists reflects their shared 'common sense' and "communitary knowledge." Precisely because of their high institutional positions, specialists serve as arbiters of common sense and therefore are charged with "filtering and organizing all available contents" in order to avoid the "parcellization of knowledge" on intellectual frontiers such as the Internet (Arpaia). In Eco's opinion this state of affairs justifies the preemptive "evaluation" by specialists of what goes online. Eco is willing to admit that such "mediation" restricts intellectual freedom, but avers that de facto censorship of the marketplace of ideas is a price we must be willing to pay in order to "guarantee a certain community (in which we can place our faith) has filtered the essential" and validated what we read. "Without filters," he continues, "we risk the anarchy of knowledge. No one of us can reconstruct alone and *ex novo* a totality of knowledge" (Latrive and Rivoire); knowledge must be received through an institutional filter that in his opinion coincides with the ideological and political center. The ideological filter Eco proposes is endowed with the duty and the right to define normality and ban all forms of deviance and dissent by placing them out of bounds. Such 'common sense' normativity is given concrete demonstration in his admonishment—one would assume in the guise of Model Reader of himself—of Theresa Coletti's negative assessment of his female characters.

Eco has stated that he has "repeatedly tried . . . not to speak about [his] novels" (Eco 1992, 819) because he does not like giving opinions on his fictions. However, he also jocularly admitted that "if you twist [his] arm, [he] will" (Rosso and Eco, 247).[11] However, not only does Eco give suggestions on how to read his fictions, but, when an empirical reader such as Coletti resists transformation into Model Reader, Eco rebuts quickly and surely. Coletti—in Eco's own laudatory words, "the kind of reader that any author would dream of"—wrote "one of the first sympathetic and perceptive reviews of *Foucault's Pendulum.*" But she is also the author of an article that makes remarks critical of Eco's attitude toward gender, a charge Eco cannot accept. He recognizes that Coletti's reading "is legitimated" by his text "as read according to a given system of expectations." Unfortunately, those expectations do not coincide with his. So, he "prudently propose[s] an equally possible alternative reading" to Coletti's offering. In effect, he chastises Coletti for a reading he claims falls outside the boundaries set by the literal sense of his novel. Paradoxically, the poetics of the Model Reader would dictate that Eco clarify why Coletti should not be free to propose her own Model Author or at least explain how she has misunderstood the literal sense of *Il pendolo*. In point of fact, Coletti's reading follows that of Jacques Le Goff, who underscored the "decisively medieval quality in [Eco]'s figurations of gender," specifically, the subalternity of the women of *Il pendolo* whose destiny is, in Le Goff's words "to be at the side of men."

In other words, LeGoff provides both 'common sense' and scholarly corroboration of Coletti's reading. What remains unclear is whether Eco responds to Coletti as a strong, living empirical author or as a Model Reader who creates and projects a Model Author in his own self-image. Eco affirms that "Narrators, as well as poets, should never be able to provide interpretations of their own" work (Eco 1992, 820). He then adds: "In this dialectic between the intention of the reader and the intention of the text, the intention of the empirical author becomes rather irrelevant, even when authors cannot refrain from commenting upon the pages of their critics" (822). However, aware of the contradiction into which he has fallen, he remarks, "I think that it is also possible for authors to act as reasonable but not particularly privileged readers of their own texts, and to argue about cases in which they think a text does not legitimate a given interpretation—or might also legitimate a complementary one" (822).

Reasonable, as we shall see presently, is a fundamental term in Eco's attempts to limit interpretation. Reasonable, hence commonsensical, normal, therefore normative, because the effect is that of a strong, living author ostracizing one 'abnormal' reading of his work while implicitly validating others. In fact, when Eco asserts that "the work institutes, *authoritatively*, as *free and unpredictable*, for whatever the oxymoron is worth" the "fundamental relationship between work of art and interpreter" (Eco 1990, 20), he fails to mention that free and unpredictable readings come into effect only after the conditions of reading are limited by the literal sense which he neglects to mention is imposed on the work by what Foucault has called the "author-function."

Parenthetically, when we consider the audience in front of whom Eco voiced his objections to Coletti's reading—a group of undergraduates at a small, competitive liberal arts college in upstate New York—the carrot-and-stick method inherent in the marketing strategy/poetics of the Model Reader becomes quickly evident. Coletti may or may not be taken in by Eco's initial recourse to flattery. However, of much greater consequence is a

Hamilton College audience that is much more representative of his target demographic. Therefore, Eco tells his more impressionable public that he "was fascinated by the different ways they found to enter [his] novel and walk around in it." Every reading they offered during his colloquium with them was "a 'good' one." He found their response especially gratifying because, he confided, he "wrote his novel thinking of and looking for the sort of Model Reader they all proved to be," readers who, unlike Coletti, *accept him on his terms*. After all, his "text is a machine conceived for eliciting many interpretations (provided they are 'good')" (Eco 1992, 824). So, while high-brow readers may or may not be immune to Eco's siren song, given the "star system" in academia (whereby literary-academic audiences often identify with celebrities in their field)[12] how can Eco's young Hamiltonians be expected to resist?

In *I limiti dell'interpretazione* [*Limits of Interpretation*] Eco claims that once a text has been "emitted" its detachment from the concrete circumstances of its utterance causes it to float in "the void of the potentially infinite space of possible interpretations. Therefore, no text can be interpreted according to a definitive, original, final, authorized sense" (Eco 1990, 6–7). But the historicist approach that Eco implicitly engages in polemic in this essay does not propose utopias of definitive meanings. In fact, its recognition of the inaccessibility of the object of linguistic desire necessarily acknowledges the "absent cause" (Jameson 1992) behind all texts, the real world that predetermines all critical constructs. Linguistic traces of the empirical author, a nexus of ideological and psychological concerns, subsist in the text (this is certainly the case with the empirical author of all Eco's novels). Therefore, even though a narrative may seem to recount nothing more than itself, thereby concealing the author, the subjectivity in language forces the reader to consider the subject of language: the empirical author. Consequently, collaborative readings cannot ignore the process by which the moral, intellectual, and cultural force of the author informs the text.

Eco claims that individual linguistic "encyclopedias" link to each other rhizomatically, thus forming a "labyrinthine" totality composed of an infinite number of "encyclopedias." Since an individual's "subjective-connotative encyclopedia" signifies through consensus as to meaning and the context furnished by the circumstances of enunciation, it constitutes a weak system.[13] However, precisely because weak interpretations are necessarily historical they cannot avoid consideration of the *intentio auctoris*, as Eco maintains. In arguing against the relevance of a dialogue in absentia with the empirical author, Eco writes, "That which renders the encyclopedia fruitfully weak is the fact that it never gives a definitive and closed representation; it is never global but always local. It comes in response to specific contexts and circumstances; it constitutes a limited perspective of semiotic activity" (Eco 1983a, 75). Indeed, the historicity or materiality of the text necessitates the contextualization from which we derive meaning. The materiality of the text links it to both its time and to the reader's time and necessitates the identification and reestablishment of "an organic connection with the temporality and the sociality of the human experience" (Luperini 1999, 25). The radical historicity of the text, in turn, makes eminently necessary the recuperation to our present and the valorization of what Benjamin has called "the detritus of history," the untextualized traces of past reality that survive in conscious and unconscious memory and in orally transmitted knowledge. The "detritus of history" have been deemed unreasonable and consequently deleted by histories written in function of the present in the name of a 'common sense' that too often has proven to be erroneous.

As already stated, Eco makes a fundamental distinction between what is reasonable and what is rational, arguing that intersubjective controls determine what is reasonable. In contrast, what is 'rational' includes the radically idiosyncratic, and limiting cases such as Nazism and Stalinism (Lyotard). Therefore, Eco concludes "our behavior should be reasonable, not rational" (Rosso and Eco, 244). And since radical rationality can coincide with its opposite extreme, irrationality, Eco—implicitly setting aside what Kuhn has written regarding the 'deviance' of the catalysts of scientific revolutions—maintains that what is reasonable should define the 'norm.'[14]

In an essay of contemporaneous gestation as *Il pendolo*, "L'irrazionale ieri e oggi" [The Irrational Yesterday and Today] (Eco 1987), Eco equates "opposite [political] extremisms" blurring all distinctions between political engagement within the democratic process on the one hand, and, on the other, support and complicity with terrorism. In this essay he uses the same rhetorical strategy utilized in an essay for Vittorini's *menabò* in the early 1960s, one that Calvino described as "dumping one argument on top of another to confute both" (Calvino 1995, 705).[15] He then contrasts various fanaticisms and what is "reasonable," and moderate. The irrational, in his definition is what exceeds a norm, and falls outside "just limits and measures." It cannot be stressed strongly enough that in "L'irrazionale ieri e oggi" what is reasonable for Eco lies squarely within the confines of European civilization and shares its foundations. In fact, he proposes we use as the basis of our considerations the Greco-Latin model of rationality, so that "we can prudently define as irrational everything that appears to deviate from the limits imposed by the norms that are at the origins of our culture" and then ostracize as not 'normal' what falls or has fallen outside the mainstream. Eco then very deftly strings together various manifestations of 'aberrant' contemporary thought, declaring each guilty by association with the others. Claiming that they all share a common, irrational matrix, he cites as examples romantic idealism, Marxism in its Lukacsian and Leninist incarnations, Heideggerian existentialism, the Nietzschean superman, and Derridean deconstructionism. He then proceeds to trace, in juxtaposition to such irrationalities, a contrasting grand history of ideas that links and identifies Christianity with Western rationalism.

Neither Eco's conclusions nor the logic he utilizes to reach them are of great import here. What needs to be underscored is how the irrational is equated with rebellion from the norm in Eco's fictions, allowing for a temporary deterritorialization (Deleuze and Guattari) or "unchaining" of desire from socially restricting forces. However, after a relatively brief period of rebellion, all Eco's autobiographical subjects obey the call to return to the patriarchal Order they are in line to inherit. Much like the author of the unsigned introduction to *Il nome della rosa*, Eco's Model Readers do not write—which, *pace* Barthes, remains an active, transitive verb—but passively "transcribe, with no concern for the present," what the author provides, after surrendering their right to read critically. Model Readers identify with their author, who allows them to participate vicariously in "the great dignity of the Man of Letters" *au dessus de la melée*. They "take comfort and consolation" in stories that are "incommensurably distant in time," and "gloriously bereft of any relationship with our world and lives, our hopes and securities." They read books that do not discuss human consortium, but other books. They read Eco to escape from their "dreariness of their daily lives" into a parallel world created by an author whose "pure love of writing for writing's sake" and his "simple love of storytelling" have led him to seek "repose everywhere and in everything, but has found it no where except in a corner with a book (15).

Life with Father: *Il nome della rosa*

Our reading of *Il nome della rosa** is grounded in the concept of Model Author as analyzed in the preceding chapter. This allows us to examine how the voice of Adso da Melk is given shape by the author as it passes through the filter of the novel's narrating voice. The concept of the Model Author also enables us to question our relationship with Adso, be it one of critical distance and/or empathy and unwitting identification. The self-interrogation catalyzed by a critical reading raises questions regarding the affinity felt by both critical and empathetic readers for the protagonist as he struggles with a patriarchal power structure. This causes the critical reader to ponder why Adso writes, which raises questions concerning the manner in which Adso comes to be (re)presented through the various levels of frame tales. In addition, and this matters more, it leads us to ask how the various narrators of this tale distance themselves from the text and why this causes Model readers to assume responsibility for it and to accept Adso's refusal of culpability for actions intended, at a deep level, to injure his parents and parental surrogates.

To explain, while Adso's tale ostensibly is of his own coming of age, he remains for the most part a passive observer/recorder of the actions of others.[16] Furthermore, Adso claims that writing is a means of expiation, yet he sees no real need to be ashamed of his actions. Not only does he tell of everyone but himself, but in this "confession" Adso tells *on* everyone but himself. Following Freud, we can note that Adso's "complaints are really 'plaints' in the legal sense of the word"; since everything derogatory Adso says of himself "at bottom relates to someone else" (Sigmund

---

*Unless otherwise specified, citations refer to Eco, *Il nome della rosa*. All translations from the Italian are mine.

Freud, "Mourning and Melancholia," 169). In the words of the empirical author, Adso prepares for death by convincing himself that everyone else is a fool (Padovani).

At the same time, Adso's text achieves great popular success because it taps into the "kindred wishes"—that is to say the needs and goals—of Model Readers who see themselves reflected in Adso. Adso never defies the Father, but does participate in the challenge to patriarchal authority carried forth by Guglielmo da Baskerville. However, when the efforts of the two end in defeat, Adso submits to the father imago, Father, and assumes his power. Then Adso takes vengeance on all parental figures by creating a narrative that leaves them humiliated and destroyed.

For their part, Eco's Model Readers accept what is recounted as fact, take Adso at his word that the text is a "faithful chronicle" of what transpired, and gloss over the fact that anyone who could refute Adso's testimony is long dead before Adso sets plume to parchment.

By framing his story as the decades-old recollection of a "senescent" man, the elderly Adso-narrator abdicates responsibility for his role in the destruction of one of the monuments of the civilization he claims to hold very dear, just as the Model Author utilizes the strategy of the found manuscript to abdicate authority over his text. Nonetheless, Eco's Model Readers immerse themselves in the character: there is no pretense of Brechtian distancing. The dichotomy young Adso/Adso-narrator is lost; and subjective perceptions that have filtered through decades of memory tautologically take on a truth value of their own.

As we have seen, Model Readers by definition underwrite the strategy of the Model Author,[17] which Eco sets out as a condition for reading *Il nome della rosa* in his introduction to the novel. The reader is given a text that is purportedly an Italian redaction of a French translation of memoirs of an elderly man, Adso, who wrote many years after the actions occurred and almost entirely without the benefit of written records. Eco's recourse to the strategy of the found manuscript would allow the Model Author to absolve himself also from any responsibility for authorship of the text. In fact, the reader is told in the introduction that an Italian redactor worked without benefit of the French translation, with only lost notes as his guide (12) and wrote "as if enraptured by a vision" (12–13). The introduction is not signed, and one would assume that this is done to allow the empirical author, Umberto

Eco to distance himself from the Model Author. After all, who, if not Eco, anticipates reader needs and facilitates consumption of the text by inserting in the paratext a map of the Abbey and a chronology of a medieval day? Adso's reader would most certainly not have needed the chronology.

The introduction to the novel tells us that certain passages were left in Latin while the bulk of the text was translated from French into Italian to "preserve the spirit of the times" (14). However, the use of Latin to indicate a distinctive stylistic register does not reflect the intellectual climate of Adso's lifetime because Adso produced a text written almost entirely in Latin, the lingua franca of literate men of his time. Adso slips out of Latin and into his German vulgate only once, in order to keep the agnosticism of his "theological conclusion" beyond the comprehension of many of his intellectual brethren. Adso's seventeenth-century French editor leaves licentious[18] and elitist passages in Latin, which becomes a language of sexual repression and snobbery. When Eco's Model Author underwrites this critical stylistic decision through duplication, Latin becomes a language of occlusion and of titillation of the target demographic.

Adso claims he writes to expiate his sins before death overtakes him. Yet, his closing declaration of agnosticism (503) would lead us to believe he is less concerned with an afterlife as one might expect. He also claims that he writes to preserve for himself the memory of what happened at the convent. However, his advanced age gives credence to the suspicion that he writes for the collective memory of posterity. Oddly, he suppresses the names of two very important elements of his reconstruction: those of the monastery and the Abbot. It would seem that his failure to definitively identify them shields the institution from blame and the man from guilt for what transpired. Yet they are easily discernible because Adso has absolutely no qualms about naming the monks who reside and work in the convent, nor the convent's visitors. He places the events in a recognizable geographic setting and within very precise historical parameters. Thus, he places responsibility for all that happened squarely on the shoulders of his elders in the Benedictine order, the Abbot and Jorge da Burgos, who prevented him from gaining access to the knowledge preserved in the Library and would have forbidden him from disseminating what he learned.

Adso's agnosticism gives voice to the "natural" or "secular

ethics" Eco has proposed in an extraliterary context (Martini and Eco, 76–77). Adso is a nonbeliever, and doubts that there is anyone on high who can forgive him. For this reason, he participates in "the cleansing rite of public confession, asking the forgiveness of others" so that he may be forgiven. Thus, it would appear that Adso's public confession is both an act of forgiveness and of contrition. But this is not the case. Adso deludes himself into believing that by not naming the Abbot, a paternal figure, he gives reparation for the oral violence he commits against his elder through testimony. Similarly, by signing his text, Adso submits to his reader's judgment the actions of the biological father who sent him away from home.

Since it is safe to assume that Adso is not primarily concerned with the well-being of his soul, we may advance the hypothesis that he is more preoccupied at a deep level with finding a path to psychological freedom as he awaits death to overtake him (253). Indeed, writing allows Adso to elaborate the remorse that haunted him since his week at the Abbey. He writes after his nostalgic obsession with the past finally reaches a stage where he is able to digest this culmination of his youth and come to some sort of resolution. This can occur only after he returns to the scene of the fateful events and collects detritus—pages from books ruined by the fire that destroyed the Abbey decades earlier—in an unsuccessful attempt to piece together a book that would somehow encapsulate his experience there.[19]

Adso does, in fact, confess sundry, minor peccadilloes. At various points in his story he admits to feigning prayer to gain access to Ubertino (224); to disobeying the Abbot and eavesdropping on a conversation between the latter and Guglielmo (146); to having felt pride at his prowess as a lover (247). He also confesses to 'borrowing' a lantern in order to explore the library with Guglielmo and to having had sex with the unnamed young woman. These last two sins were absolved at the time by his indulgent confessor, Guglielmo, hence not in strict need of a second, very public divulgence.

This raises the fundamental question of why Adso eases his conscience publicly, outside the hermetic seal of the sacrament of penance, as one would expect of a devout cleric. By converting the private therapy of the sacrament into a public spectacle Adso normalizes his own behavior during the week in question and also the desires that remained sources of shame and self-reproach into his old age.[20] Writing allows him to avoid the exploration and possible uncovering of deeper realities concerning himself and his actions. It allows him to forestall interrogation of the modalities of his own participation while allowing him to avenge himself of the parents who rejected him and the authoritarian parental figures into whose care he was entrusted.

Adso justifies his decision to commit his story to paper by telling of a reverie that "had accompanied his childhood as a novice"—in other words the period immediately after being sent from home—that ordered him to "write what he saw in a book" (52). This statement would suggest an unconscious desire for vengeance against his father, the man who sent his unwilling son out into an inhospitable world. Of course, Adso would deny this. He explicitly claims that the decision to enter a convent was his own, and not, as one might think, imposed on him against his will by his father. However, Adso does acknowledge in passing that monastic life is for many "an excessively heavy burden" (143). After all, his life in the convent is without maternal nurturing, emotional warmth or object-relatedness—his descriptions of the camaraderie among novices reveal no joy whatsoever in participation—and he is beset by sodomite monks. Moreover, when he questions the sagacity of what was in fact his father's decision, Adso slips and contradicts himself: "While getting into bed I concluded that my father should not have sent me out into the world, which was more complicated that I thought. I was learning too much" (160).

Adso explicitly accepts what his father imposed on him when he was still a child, and never speaks of any inner unrest or outer rebellion in conjunction with puberty. In other words, oedipal resolution and maturation are postponed indefinitely by the decision to send him away from home. Instead, Adso defends himself psychologically by regressing. That is to say, rather than giving in to an outflow of libido, the teenaged Adso identifies with a leader, the Abbot, and alters his own personality consequentially. At the same time, his repressed resentment for the rejecting father is transferred to the authoritarian Abbot. And so Adso writes to exact vengeance through his text on his parents and on parental figures. Therefore, following Sterba (1940), I would propose that since Adso "cannot discharge his libidinal energy through satisfaction in real objects," he "gains, or tries to gain gratification through fantasy," through the written editing of his past that informs Adso's "faithful chronicle."

By confessing publicly Adso also avoids recognizing and assuming responsibility for any of the tragic events that occurred during his week at the Abbey. That is to say, he deflects away from himself any blame for the long-range consequences of his actions, which include the destruction of the monastery, particularly, but also the deaths of the young woman, the Abbot, and Jorge. And since he admits to no serious transgression, the Roman Catholic rite of penance is of no use to him: he cannot request forgiveness and absolution, nor can he promise to 'sin' no more. The confession is made near the end of his life, and therefore cannot raise future expectations of behavior. Furthermore, Adso's public confession is a form of disobedience; it not only shatters the seal of silence the Abbot would have imposed on the young monk (a condition Adso willingly accepted as a term of membership in the Benedictine order), but allows him to tell the world of the shortcomings and failures of his father figure, the Abbot. Writing allows Adso to relive the pleasure of seeing the Abbot stripped of his property, authority, and life, and of seeing another parental figure, his mentor Guglielmo, fail in the missions assigned to him, that of mediating the conflict between Emperor and Pope, and that of solving of the convent's murder mystery. In other words, writing allows Adso to deny the enjoyment he secretly experienced when his parental surrogates were humbled.

A public confession is, of course, an act of self-humiliation. And we must remember that the desire to avoid and to inflict the humiliation gives structure to this society of men and is also a key element to comprehending Adso's behavior. He humbles himself before the Abbot; he subjugates himself and asks forgiveness when necessary, kneeling before his superior and kissing his ring (451). By accepting the discipline of the Benedictines and his place at the bottom of their hierarchy, Adso knows he will receive in exchange admittance into the order's power structure and the right to participate in its grandeur.

Humiliation is a social form of shame, and is distinct from ego-based, individual, intra-psychic shame. It reflects learned masculinity among males, especially the need for acceptance by peers. It "pervades the same-sex relations of boyhood groups, male rites of passage, and even adult inter-male relations" and is a powerful mechanism for shaping normative behavior and attitudes. Within this same dynamic, the mentor relationship meets "a vital need for male nurturing." The mentor has a special power, in that he can accept "the boy as a person, with his own unique qualities and foibles, despite the rigid parameters of traditional masculinity." On the other side of this same coin, "Authority is the civilized form of male pecking order" (Jennings and Murphy, 24; 27). Adso defines all male-male relationships in terms of a pecking order established through humiliations.[21] Thus, Adso's concern with humiliation and pride provides us with a paradigm for understanding the interpersonal dynamics among the monks who interact with him. It is of particular importance for understanding the relationships he establishes with his superiors: with the active yet benign influence of the nurturing, combined parental figure[22] Guglielmo on the one hand, and, on the other, the authoritarian Abbot.

Adso submits to Guglielmo's humiliations, which Adso consciously attributes to Guglielmo's excessive pride (31, 162, 448, 469, 470, 474). This understanding of Guglielmo's foibles and limitations endears the mentor to his pupil; tempers the younger man's resentment for harsh treatment; and also allows Adso opportunities for revenge. Guglielmo actively defends his intellectual superiority from periodic challenges from his student, and is not averse to embarrassing Adso in front of others (171, 366, 367, 369, 370). Neither is Guglielmo disinclined from attacking Adso's masculinity. For example, the elder man, after observing one instance of Adso's clumsiness, mocks his charge's fantasy of being a "warrior" of evangelic truth and a "soldier of Christ" (168, 176). Nonetheless, Adso accepts Guglielmo's treatment, identifying with his mentor in triumph, and feeling pride in an association that raises Adso socially above his peers (33). At the same time, ambivalent feelings toward the master causes Adso to feel satisfaction when Guglielmo fails in his missions as a detective (394, 396) and diplomat (385, 500).

Any pride taken by Adso in his own knowledge and acumen is soon quashed by Guglielmo. However, when Adso feels "oppressed by remorse" for having sinned against the flesh, he confesses to a surprisingly indulgent Guglielmo. Guglielmo is condescending (calling him "my dear little wolf" [256]), but is also careful to flatter Adso's masculinity. And so Adso must "confess" to the reader to having felt "the sweetest sort of pride" (256) in his own beauty [*venustà*] and prowess as a lover (247). Thus, by humiliating himself through this double confession, Adso exalts himself, thereby satisfying a deep-seated desire to supersede Guglielmo as a man of faith. In fact, Adso monopolizes the moral highroad when he affirms that he spent the rest of his life praying that God would forgive Guglielmo "the many acts of pride that his intellectual haughtiness [*fierezza*] led him to commit" (501).

Adso's place in the male pecking order is contingent on his relationship with Guglielmo—below the Franciscan but firmly attached to his coattails—and so Adso's perspective on their relationship is implicitly reflected in the way Adso addresses and refers to his mentor. In acknowledging Guglielmo's superior intelligence, Adso refers to him as "my master" (127, 200, 300, 442, 444, 445). However, on those rare occasions when Guglielmo is seen as an authority figure, the Italian redactor has Adso use the formal *voi* (for example, 409). Adso refers to Guglielmo by name when the older man's authority is grounded in the Law, for example, when Guglielmo's participation in the Inquisition is evoked (118) or when Guglielmo stifles Adso's attempts to assert himself (127). Only once is Guglielmo perceived as a member of the ministry, when Adso seeks absolution from his sin of the flesh, and is referred to as "Frate Guglielmo" (254). Adso's mentor is transformed from "Guglielmo" to "my master" when the Franciscan proves himself Jorge's intellectual peer in debate (137). In fact, the term "my master" is used to express Adso's admiration. Adso also uses it when he can participate in Guglielmo's superiority—and rise, as a consequence, in the male hierarchy (33, 79, 82, 112, 116)—and when Guglielmo's errors lower him closer to his student's level (174).

Guglielmo's strong, proto-Renaissance sense of individuality is at the root of all his mistakes. It leads him into the triple checkmate of failure as a diplomat, as a sleuth, and as savior of Aristotle's lost text. In contrast, Adso staves off any threat of succumbing to "abduction [*rapimento*] into the depths of identity" (248) through self-humiliation. Furthermore, Adso's self-effacement allows him to supersede his master on a nonspiritual plane by providing him with gradual access into the monastic power structure he ultimately inherits.

At the same time, because Guglielmo is of lower social rank—he is a mendicant friar—he can make less strict superego demands than Adso's Benedictine elders, and can condone Adso's acting out id impulses (178).[23] In granting Adso absolution for fornication, Guglielmo enjoins the young man to forget the incident ever happened (255). Guglielmo then abruptly changes the subject, setting a pattern for complicitous silence that will be repeated when their plot to subtract control over the Library from the Abbot and Jorge ends in tragedy. Their "painful parting of ways" will cast into full relief the guilt they share. Their shame, "as if by tacit agreement," causes the two of them to never discuss the role they played the destruction of the Abbey (500).

Adso, who typically demonstrates an insatiable curiosity for the adult world, fails to ask why Guglielmo was "visibly moved" [*commosso*] by his confession. However, he does question the "rather energetic slap [*manata*] on the head" given him by Guglielmo at the conclusion of this conversation. The "guilt" felt at the precise time of the transgression causes Adso to think that Guglielmo's reaction was occasioned by a sort of sort of "good-natured jealously, typical of the man, who craved new and lively experiences." However, after years of reflection a less innocent Adso interprets Guglielmo's act "as proof of his paternal and virile affection, or perhaps as indulgent penance" (257). "Indulgent penance" in the form of corporal punishment would certainly help assuage Adso's obsessive guilt for his newly acquired carnal knowledge. But what is of greater import here is his raising through negation questions about the true nature of their relationship (see Sigmund Freud, "Negation," 214). Adso takes pain to point out that their relationship was chaste and pure, free of even the "shadow of lust" (23). He also insists on assigning "paternal and virile" attributes to an idealized figure, whose treatment of his charge may equally be described as maternal.

Adso does not question the nature of their relationship nor ask why Guglielmo inexplicably went looking for him in the middle of the night after the young man was assigned his own, separate, sleeping quarters (254).[24] In depicting their final separation Adso finds masculine strength and resolution in Guglielmo's maternal tenderness: "I had to distance myself from him, with many tears, from my kind mentor.... then [Guglielmo] hugged me tightly, with the tenderness of a father, and discharged me [*mi congedò*]" (500–1). Despite the use of a verb more typically associated with the military, "*congedare*," Guglielmo showed maternal tenderness in dressing the nearly naked Adso in the aftermath of the fire after saving Adso's possessions from flames and looters (490). And Adso, can 'tell all' in his text only because Guglielmo, the more constant of Adso's parental figures, interceded when the Abbot would have forced the young man to swear that he would never repeat what he had seen (451–52).

Adso, who is proud of his acquired abilities as semiotician, inexplicably fails to ponder the modalities and dynamics of the relationship between the parental figures, Abbone and Guglielmo. When they first meet, the Abbot asks Guglielmo to conduct a murder investigation that the former knows—through various prelates' confessions—may reveal illicit homosexual practices among his monks (33). When Guglielmo presses for information the Abbot is not at liberty to provide, Abbone responds: "Vi prego frate Guglielmo, fratello Guglielmo [I beseech you Brother William, brother William]," accentuating both frate and fratello, both of which translate as "brother." Guglielmo quickly grasps the subtle request for complicity implicit in the distinction, blushes bright red and responds "Eris sacerdos in aeternum" [you will be a priest forever] (42), using a term, "sacerdote," that makes reference to earthly power.[25]

While reading we must also keep in mind that Adso-narrator is not the teenaged ingenue represented in his memoir; when he writes he is an elderly man who knows what was implicit in the Abbot's request and in Guglielmo's response. Nonetheless, he fails to explore why the Abbot repeats the distinction between *frate* (brother-priest) and *fratello* (brother-confederate) a second time, in discharging the Franciscan near the end of the tale. Had he done so, Adso would have acknowledged that Guglielmo is *frate*, a brother monk, when the Abbot asserts his superior rank in the Church hierarchy (448, 457), and *"fratello tra i fratelli,"* a brother among brothers (452), when the Benedictine wishes to convey a sense of betrayal and his disappointment that Guglielmo's loyalties in conducting the investigation were, at least to the Abbot's mind, with others than he.

The outward appearance of Guglielmo, whom Adso remembers as remarkably youthful and energetic for his age, are vividly recalled and depicted. Adso is enthralled by his mentor's quick wit, encyclopedic knowledge, strikingly attractive appearance, which he describes in detail (23). However, soon after describing Guglielmo "once and for all," Adso cannot resist furnishing his reader with a second, more detailed study of the master's physical characteristics (38). Later on Adso cannot resist furnishing another, even closer look at his master's face (82). Only in the course of recounting an excursion into the Library does Adso remember that he was much "smaller and lighter" (178) than the British monk, whose uncommonly tall stature allows the two to gain access to the most inner recesses of the Library (462).

In contrast, Adso is parsimonious in his description of the Abbot, even though the latter is a key figure in Adso's narration. Within the context of their first meeting, Adso stresses only those aspects that reflect the Abbot's authority and lack of affection, his "severe glance" and "pale cheeks" (22). This is not surprising, because at this time Adso says he will not indulge in descriptions (22). Nonetheless, just as Adso expends great effort in describing Guglielmo, he also depicts in minute detail the wealth of the convent ruled by the Abbot (147, 149, 159) and describes almost all the others he encounters. Salvatore fascinates Adso, as does the sodomite Malachia, and so both are presented in great detail (53–54, 80). The same can be said of Jorge (86). The critical reader, of course, cannot help but note the extent to which what Adso describes and what he leaves to imagination serve to indicate the modalities of his participation in his world.

Indeed, not only does Adso avoid describing the Abbot, but Adso never mentions his name, even though the affectionate augmentative, "Abbone," might lead the reader to assume that the Abbot's physical stature is commensurate to his temporal and moral authority. The Abbot's apparent position 'above the fray' within the monastery allows Adso to gloss over the fact that Abbone is Italian (131), hence subject to all of the moral flaws and limitations the Northern European Adso prejudicially associates with the residents of the Peninsula.[26] Furthermore, the Abbot succeeds in asserting himself physically over the uncommonly tall Guglielmo, twice pulling the British monk close, embracing him, and kissing him on the mouth (33, 159). Thus, the reader is very surprised to learn at the tale's culmination that the Abbot was quite short and unimposing, the state that allows Jorge to trap and kill him.

Adso's silence regarding the Abbot, a paternal surrogate, is due to ambivalent feelings that make him feel anxious; he avoids dealing with this anxiety by saying nothing. Nor does Adso describe his parents at any time in this lengthy narration. The silence that surrounds the Abbot also encircles the biological father who sent his son out into the world with no concern, it would seem, for his son's feelings. It is no small coincidence that while Adso attributes great importance to his family's social status, he never refers to his family by name. He signs his text "da Melk," which of course is not a surname but a place of origin. Adso's father is never named nor described. The reader is simply told that he was "not the least important of the Emperor Ludwig's barons" (21). In other words, the father is not identified, but sufficient information is provided to inculpate him for the vicissitudes that subsequently overtook his son. As for Adso's mother, she is totally absent from the narration and so there is no way of ascertaining the exact nature of her contribution to Adso's psychic development. In any event, the parents' physical appearance is evoked only once when Adso walks through the ossuary and he "swear[s] that the killing sneer [*ghigno mortifero*] of those naked heads reminded [him] of the smiles of [his] loved ones" (181).

Similarly, Adso fails to describe himself. While this may be attributed to his struggle against a sense of individuality, his recurring use of the term "child" [*fanciullo*] to depict himself during the week in question causes the critical reader to raise an eyebrow. It serves to deflect all responsibility and create a childlike image of innocent bystander, even though he was past puberty when the Library was destroyed.[27] As we have already mentioned, Adso's proud status as Guglielmo's "scribe and disciple" (22, 109, 303) places the young man above the other novices in the male pecking order and makes available to him special food and lodging privileges. In addition, his association with Guglielmo gives him access to knowledge of the adult world hidden from the other novices (457). Adso is well aware of the precarious nature of his privileged status, and this awareness accentuates the shame Adso feels at the public exposure of his indecently "unfledged" [*implume*] chest, after he took off his tunic to fight the Library fire. He would have preferred this occurred under the shadow of night, the felicitous setting for his one sexual encounter: the young woman was prevented by darkness from seeing his hairless chest. Nonetheless, he is uncomfortable in knowing that the young woman could not help noticing his lack of facial hair (247), which Adso equates with a lack of manliness.[28] The equation of body hair and virility is reinforced in his description of one of the cadavers. He is embarrassed by the female qualities of one of the cadavers because they remind him of his own perceived physical inadequacies: "His body, white and soft, without hair, looked like that of a woman, except for the obscene spectacle of his flaccid pudenda. I turned red, and then shivered" (259).

Adso struggles to become a man by acquiring the knowledge prohibited by the Father, patriarchal authority. Indeed, his text is the story of his belated, that is to say postpubescent, attempt to supersede Father by wresting away authority over the Library while sublimating instinctual desires. Adso instinctively craves knowledge and comes to understand that it has two venues, intellectual and carnal. Carnal knowledge is precluded to novices, and the Abbot strictly limits access to the Library. Therefore, Adso circumvents both paternal interdictions by studying contemporary heretical movements. He admits he is "obsessed by the idea of Fra' Dolcino" even though he does not know why (197). The heretics that interest Adso sought to wrest control of the Law away from the Father: they undermined patriarchal authority by proposing a diverse way of knowing God, and by transgressing property rights and sexual taboos, such as incest (see 156). In this, they reflect Adso's idealized personality: adult, independent, and equal to Father.

According to the Abbot, heretics "threaten the order of the civilized world" (155). They do so through their transgressions of property rights and sexual taboos. Ubertino and Guglielmo explain to Adso that while the Franciscans are not orthodox in their dedication to a feminine ideal of "madonna povertà" (155), living on charity and refusing ownership, the brothers, unlike the heretics, respect the property of others. Moreover, while Franciscans contest the Pope's authority, Francis recognized the power of the Church, and was rewarded by seeing his order consecrated by the Pope (226–29). In contrast, "heresy is wedded to the revolt against the wealthy" (229). Franciscans do not engage in illicit sexual practices whereas heretics threaten established order with their "filthy thoughts" [*pensieri immondi*] (155), that is to say their incestuous practices.

This distinction between "*mondo*" [world][29] and what might appear to be its opposite, "*immondo*" [which does not translate as "not-world," but as "filth"], is fundamental to understanding Adso's views. In other words, the "*immondo*" is the grotesque deformation, not the diametrical opposite, of *"il mondo,"* established order. Like Adso's mirror image in the Library, the *immondo* parodies and undermines the Law of the Father. To explain: the firmament, or *"universo cosmo"* (34) surrounds the Earth. The Earth is divided into the *"universo mondo"* (282) and the *"immondo."*[30] The *immondo* (the not-clean, the impure, that which transgresses tradition and order) does not negate, but parodies the *mondo*. The floorplan of the Library honors God by reproducing the geography of the *"universo mondo"* (316). Following this logic, the Devil may be called euphemistically *"la bestia immonda"* (45, 451); since Lucifer is an angel gone awry, he is not the opposite but a transmogrification of Good. Similarly, *"animali immondi"* are potential sources of food whose consumption is prohibited (190). This same etymological perspective justifies Guglielmo's distinction between Inquisitors who have "clean hands" [*le mani monde*] and the torturers whose hands were sullied, made *immonde* with the blood of their victims, doing what they believed was God's work (378).

The reader watches along with Adso as Guglielmo and Jorge clash over the power to determine what knowledge is *mondo* and what knowledge is *immondo* and is to be banned outside the metaphorical walls of the *universo mondo* as defined by the Library. Jorge, who controls the Library, would continue to expel laughter and carnivalesque frivolity because they are "dirty [*immonde*] parodies of order" (477), as are the teachings of Aristotle, who to Jorge's mind is an *"immonda auctoritas"* (479). In contrast, Guglielmo would Christianize the teachings of Aristotle, canonize the Greek philosopher's treatise on comedy, and give him a place of honor within confines of the Library.

The distinction between *mondo* and *immondo* also informs Guglielmo's view of women, whom he considers *"immonde"* (255): "unclean." They exist as a function of the male's potential for both good and evil. When seen from Guglielmo's proto-Renaissance perspective, woman is a key to the dignity of man: when desire for her is sublimated, she can provide access to God; when known carnally, she provides man with a distorted, perverse, *immondo*, way of knowing. In both cases, she is property of the Divine Father and his earthly vicars, hence to be avoided, lest one be guilty of incest. Therefore, while carnal knowledge is a *"bruttura"* (279), filth to be repressed and denied, and woman's physicality *immonda*, woman can be virtuous nonetheless if she sublimates her sexuality while the male who sublimates desire for her as part of a quest for spiritual knowledge is uplifted.

Adso applies Guglielmo's abstract dichotomy just outlined to a real woman, Adso's love interest, and splits her into something *monda* and *immonda,* determining that she is both a virgin and a whore (442). While in the middle of having sex with her, and even though he knows she is fresh from a liaison with Salvatore, Adso convinces himself of her chastity (248). Then, after Guglielmo has proven to Adso that the young woman is not a prostitute, Adso mentally reduces her to savage. This allows him to place her outside all moral categories and justify his own behavior: "I realized, in a confused way and almost denying to myself the truth of what I felt, that that poor, filthy [*lercia*], impudent creature that sold herself (who knows with how much arrogant constancy) to other sinners, that daughter of Eve who, so weak, just like all her sisters, had made commerce so many times of her flesh, was nonetheless a thing of splendor and worthy of great admiration [*mirifico*].... How beautiful was the spectacle of nature not yet touched by the often perverse knowledge of Man" (281).

Adso's virgin fantasy and belief in her innocent savagery restores and safeguards the spiritual purity of his union with her. At the same time, her status as savage assigns her the role of sexual predator. This allows him to blame her (and absolve himself) for his sin of the flesh and for what he considers, at a deep level, an incestuous relationship with his spiritual sister.[31]

Thus, the young woman, an unvoiced presence and a source of the complicitous silence shared by Adso and his confessor, metonymically embodies desire for Eco's society of men. This unspeakable, hence unnamed, totemic desire for the Father's authority and dominion over women is sublimated in a power struggle for knowledge, symbolized by Aristotle's lost treatise on comedy, the *liber acephalus de stupris virginum et meretricum amoribus,* the untitled codex about raping virgins and making love to prostitutes (287, 475). The woman embodies the ancient, primitive desire—the rose—that gives Eco's comedy and Adso's texts their title. As Adso writes, "stat rosa pristina nomine, nomine nuda tenemus" [The ancient rose exists in name, we hold the bare names] (503).

For Adso, the young woman is a source of knowledge—both intellectual and carnal—and therefore a crucial element in a belated, postpubescent attempt to possess the mother imago, Mother. Adso's unrequited longing for his mother become painfully obvious when he describes his pollution while contemplating the statue of the Virgin (165). As we have seen, the early departure of Adso from his childhood home prevented him from partaking in the open defiance typical of puberty and adolescence. He accepted the life his father chose for him and bypassed the traumas usually associated with oedipal resolution. The lack of a stable mother figure provoked a preadolescent search for a mother image. Puberty, which was supposed to be a time of oedipal triumph for Adso, instead brought to the fore the trauma associated with maternal deprivation and the need for an accepting mother. He willingly submitted to a new mother, the Church, in exchange for the security of communal life (see Gilberg 382). Submission allowed him to retreat from many oedipal problems associated with competing with the father. Since he bypassed the traumas of puberty and oedipal resolution, his feelings toward the mother were never repressed, and regression, rather than rebellion, allowed Adso an object choice other than the mother: Guglielmo, the surrogate whose approval Adso comes to crave. When Adso gains Guglielmo's acceptance, he satisfies vicariously through Guglielmo, his need to please his biological mother. Once this occurs, he can detach libido from Mother and transfer it to new objects. However, Adso does not transfer libido to a sexual partner, but identifies with a leader, the Abbot, who represents certain ideals. This transferal affords Adso a new sense of independence from the parents who are treated with indifference bordering on callousness (see Anna Freud 1958, 266). To spite the father whom Adso resents for having sent him away from home, he commits acts the Abbot would find objectionable: he violates Mother (the Library) and has sex with his putative sister (at the height of ejaculative "rapture," Adso calls his lover his "sister" [249; *sorella mia*]).

When all is said and done, Adso's "initiatory journey" (Capozzi) retraces an adolescent phase of vacillation in which he engages in the forbidden before denying all instinctual gratification. After he leaves the Abbey, a life of asceticism provides Adso with a masochistic remedy (penance) for the guilt associated with having helped precipitate the events that concluded his week there. Pain, as Guglielmo teaches him, is more exciting than pleasure, and, if not taken to excess, is a virtue (67). So Adso spends the rest of his life renouncing physiological needs for bodily comfort, and repudiating the genital aspects of his personality.

Adso immerses himself in the sublimated femininity of the "santa madre chiesa" [holy mother church] (64), who is open to all men (492).[32] Once Adso has been inducted into the Church as a novice he contests dominance of the labyrinthine Library. In this way he competes with father figures for the affection of idealized, asexual mother figures, the Library and the Church (both are indicated by feminine substantives in the Italian), desexualizing or sublimating a forbidden aim.[33] He is frightened by the Library (492), in his words "a lair of powers a human mind cannot subdue" (289), due to its uncanny resemblance to the womb (see 143: "*le meraviglie celate nell'ampio ventre della biblioteca*" [the wonders hidden in the ample womb of the library]). Yet he cannot resist returning to it, in an attempt to wrest possession of it from the Abbot. He remembers that Alinardo compared the Library to the world, so that departure from it was tantamount to death: "Intranti largus, redeunti sed nimis artus" (For one who is within [it], it is big; for one who is leaving [it], it is too small [164]). However, given Adso's psychological state, Alinardo's remark can also be read as a metaphor for what Adso would like to forget, the separation trauma of birth. When Adso ventures into the Library on his own, he almost gets lost. Overtaken by fear, he almost vomits (180). When he finally finds his way outside the labyrinth back into the world, he inadvertently reveals that his fright was occasioned in fact by claustrophobia: "How beautiful the world is and how ugly labyrinths are!" (182).

Frustrated in his efforts to conquer the Library, Adso almost sets it on fire, several times, always 'accidentally' (168, 176, 462). When the moment of truth arrives, that is to say when he and Guglielmo are about to take control of the object of their quest, Aristotle's lost treatise on comedy, the youthful Adso, his hands trembling (485), 'inadvertently' lets an infirm, elderly, blind man regain possession of the contested volume and set the Library on fire (486). Adso considers the Library, a "sublime" entity that did not deserve to be destroyed by a "vulgar accident, like a peasant's hut" (489). Yet, in fighting the fire he is, in spite of himself, a model of comic, unmanly, mute impotence: "the agitation made [him] clumsy and disabled [*inabile*]," (488). He falls to the ground, exhausted, unable to speak. He tries gesticulation, but he was "almost naked, having thrown [his] tunic on the flames, and the sight of the boy that [he] was, bleeding, face blackened by the soot, an indecently unfledged body, dull-witted [*istupidito*] now by the cold, certainly did not inspire confidence" (489).

Investment in desexualized female images—*la Chiesa* and *la Biblioteca* [The Church and the Library]—defends Adso against incestuous wishes for the mother (see Linda Joan Kaplan 172–73). Furthermore, he isolates himself from the id by underwriting Ubertino's enraptured, transgendered visions of himself as Mary Magdalene, the reformed prostitute. But when Ubertino goes so far as to tell Adso that ecstatic love is asexual, Guglielmo counters that such a radical quest for knowledge of God can easily lead outside the boundaries of the *mondo* to the sensuality of the *immondo*, and to sins of the flesh (64, 65). The reader is not informed of Adso's reaction, but does know that this lesson is not lost on Adso-narrator who acknowledges that he used the same terminology to describe both the heretic Fra' Michele's matyrdom and his own "most foul" [*turpissisma*] sexual ecstasy (251) with his spiritual sister (249).

Distortion 'absolves' Adso-narrator of the unconscious sin of incest, and distances him from a crime commonly attributed to heretics such as Paolo Zoppo, who seduced women by calling them "sister" (193). Adso-narrator remembers that his own "sister" was "young, almost adolescent, perhaps she was sixteen, eighteen, or twenty years old" (247). Thus, despite the fact that she was an adult, Adso depicts their copulation as the embrace of two innocent children, a *fanciullo* [young boy] and a *fanciulla* [young girl](251), and he will repeatedly describe her as a "fanciulla" while telling of her trial. In any event, he gets to have his cake and eat it, too. He has sex with his sister but is relieved of all guilt because this spiritual sister is not his mother's child, as Freud pointed while discussing the concept of the family romance.[34]

Following Freud, we will use the term "family romance" to refer to Adso's self-image as a child born of distinguished parents. For Adso it is a means for regulating feelings of self-esteem and a response to feelings of rejection by parents who sent him away from home and to his hostile feelings toward his father. Since the new parents of the family romance are usually "equipped with attributes that are derived entirely from real recollections of the actual and humble ones" we can glean much of Adso's relationship with his real family from his views of parental figures. Guglielmo, as we have seen, is a man who combines the nurturing qualities typically associated with the mother. In the Abbot is reflected Adso's perspective of his father. The elders Jorge and Ubertino will assume in Adso's mind characteristics that—if I may continue with the metaphor—make of them putative grandparents, paternal (Benedictine) and maternal (Franciscan) respectively.[35]

The Abbot is "of noble extraction" (102, 187). He is very interested in maintaining and increasing his wealth, symbolized by his gems (147, 149, 215), and his temporal power through painstaking cultivation of the relationship with the emperor (150, 350). He is the master of *l'Edificio* [Edifice], a masculine substantive in the original Italian. This "City of God" (29–30) symbolizes a temporal power that Guglielmo and Adso do not contest: the identification of biological father and the Abbot is all too clear. Adso craves the Abbot's approval and acceptance and appreciates being addressed "paternally" (101) by the man who presents himself as "common father" of all those who fall under his sway (159). The Abbot considers himself wise only because he is severe, a disciplinarian (46) who can impose the Benedictine code of silence on the young man. The ring he allows Adso to kneel and kiss is not only symbol of his power, but also, and this matters more, grants him the authority to assign meaning to signs and to symbols, such as his gems (451). Furthermore, he can impose silence on fellow Benedictines. In addition, should someone not subject to his direct influence attempt to discredit him or his convent, the Abbot has the power to see to it that his words will be interpreted as the idiosyncratic ramblings of a madman. For example, in discharging Guglielmo, the Abbot tells the disgruntled Franciscan: "Tell all [of what you have seen], if you wish; no one will believe you. And even if some small part of your fantastic reconstruction of events were true. . . . Even then, everything is now back under my control and my responsibility. I will control everything; I have the means; I have the authority," (452). In other words, the Abbot embodies the Word and the Law. He is the arbiter of all semiotics, hence, of all knowledge. For this reason, when Jorge proves the Abbot wrong—by demonstrating that the Abbot's power had not yet passed from Jorge's to the Abbot's generation—Adso rebels against the delay in the transfer of authority by 'inadvertently' starting the fire that destroys the

Abbot's corpse and all symbols of his wealth (492-93). Although Jorge demonstrates his continuing control over the Library and the knowledge it stores by killing the Abbot, Adso believes the file rendered the Abbot's authority "res nullius" [null and void] (427).

Adso takes great pride in belonging to the Benedictines, whom he believes enjoy a privileged rapport with God, the Almighty Father (414). Adso happily accepts the obligations and sacrifices that come with acceptance of privileges associated with the Benedictine novitiate (109, 186, 310). By underwriting an idealized image of the Father, Adso acquires needed self-esteem, while entrance into the Benedictine order allows him to reject the family who rejected him. For this reason he is "confused and humiliated" (454) when Guglielmo takes umbrage with the Abbot's extolling "the reserve, the secrets, the mysteries . . . and the sense of honor, and the vow of silence" on which the Benedictine's greatness was founded (452).

Adso's disappointment with his real parents causes him to retain their preferable aspects and reject the disillusioning aspects (see Linda Joan Kaplan, 170). He never mentions the death of his mother and father who, we may assume, passed away while Adso was in Guglielmo's care: Adso's ambivalent attitude toward his parents is cast into full relief when he tells his reader that he was made to abandon Guglielmo when called home, not by his mother and father, but by his relatives (500). Although Adso is present for the murder of the Abbot and witnesses Jorge's suicide, he does not look back until many years later, making manifest his unspeakably high level of loathing for paternal figures. Adso pauses to elaborate the deaths of the Abbot and Jorge only after years of contemplation, finally fulfilling a promise made many times to himself to revisit events that haunted him for decades: "Once again I promised myself (old copyist of a text never written before now but that has spoken in my mind for many decades) to be its faithful chronicler, and not only for the love of truth, nor for the most worthy desire to teach my future readers. But also to free my memory which is withered and tired of the visions that have exhausted it my entire life. And therefore I must tell all, with decorum but without shame. And I must say now, clearly, that which I thought then and almost attempted to hide from myself" (280-81). Shortly thereafter, he tells the reader he "hides nothing, since [he] decided to write always and only the truth" (291). In other words, he had debated many times with himself whether or not to set his thoughts to paper, and had even contemplated rendering an unfaithful chronicle of the events, raising the questions of how, why and to whose detriment would he have consciously skewed his tale.

When Adso is finally capable of mourning the objects of his affection—men and institutions reduced to "ashes of ashes," whose demise made his world poorer and emptier—he is at no time given to shame and self-reproach for the role he played in their destruction. He finds no aspect of his conduct morally unsatisfactory. Instead, takes pleasure in the public exposure of his story. His only self-criticism concerns the ugliness of his hairless, youthful body. He can tell his tale only after becoming "canuto" [having very white hair][36] like Jorge, venerable in years experience (187), hence in knowledge and authority. He is "*senesco*" [senescent, growing old, aging], but not "*imbecille nel corpo*" [a physical imbecile] (164), as was Alinardo. And so, as his individual death and the collective Final Judgment approaches, Adso identifies with *il mondo incanutito* [the grey-haired world] (503 and also 19, 23), that is to say, he believes he has taken the place of Jorge and the Abbot and has come to incarnate the divinely established, age-old boundary between order and the *immondo*.

Adso proudly identifies with Abbone. Both are Benedictine monks, hence dedicated to the contemplative life (33). Adso's self-image as a member of a select caste of intellectuals is of a piece with his family romance particularly his self-image as a child born to distinguished, wealthy parents. Prior to gaining Guglielmo's confidence, Adso associated manual labor with illicit sexual intercourse. To use his own words, "the mechanic is an adulterer" (25). In Adso's opinion, the study of the natural world (Guglielmo's excuse for getting his hands dirty), should be subordinated to a life of pure intellectual contemplation in "most chaste nuptials." Adso's elitism causes him to show minimal regard for the convent's workers, in his opinion so many "oafs and louts" (499). Like the young woman whose name Adso never learns (409), the cooks and other convent workers are nameless and faceless (188, 199) as are the novices and their director, to whom Adso feels superior because of his association with Guglielmo (456). Adso's class prejudice allows him to delude himself that he can easily repress his desire for the young woman: the "priestly state and the duties" he "imposed" on himself out of respect for his "family's rank" "save" him from temptation (328).

His haughtiness is grounded in his familiarity with Latin, the lingua franca of the learned men of convent (54), and in his ability to communicate in writing. It places him above the "oafs" who need the icons carved above the Church portal to understand the word of God ("pictura est laicorum literatura" [49]). Since induction into the Word equals power, Adso's illiterate, therefore silent love is predestined for tragedy (334). Despite his infatuation, his professions of love and his feeble attempts to save her from the Inquisition, Adso—who spoke some Provençal and knew a smattering of Northern Italian dialects (191)—addresses the young woman in German during sex, "scaring her greatly" (247). Similarly, he derides Salvatore's "most comical" attempts to enter into the jargon of entitlement, Latin (223). Adso walks "indignantly" away from a conversation with Salvatore about common carnal experiences because "engaging that scoundrel in combat" would violate his station of both "noble and novice" (312).

Nonetheless, since Salvatore lived among heretics, Adso spends a great deal of time with him, enough to reconstruct, piecemeal, a sufficiently complete biography. Guglielmo is the only person whom Adso comes to know more intimately. Adso is struck by this odd state of affairs, but prefers not to pursue why he is fascinated by Salvatore; instead, Adso quickly rationalizes and moves on (272). Furthermore, he hides information regarding Salvatore's association with Fra' Dolcino from Guglielmo— protecting Salvatore and hindering his mentor's investigation (223)—while furthering his own inquiry into this specific form of heresy. Because of this, and because of their common association with the young, unnamed woman, Adso believes himself bound against his will to Salvatore by "a common secret." This allows him to displace his own guilt onto Salvatore, "his accomplice and companion in sin" (272), transforming the older man into his own grotesquely deformed mirror image. Salvatore, in Adso's words "a gluttonous and lusty beast" (72), incarnates the man Adso is afraid he truly is: insufficiently educated, and a slave to the sins of the flesh. Readers who identify with Adso may or may not share this sense of inadequacy; however, we can say with a great amount of certainty that Salvatore is a composite of all the vices that besiege Adso throughout his adult life: "in his tale I recognized many of those whom I had already known or met in my travels, and many others that I met later and recognize now. This is true to the extent that I wonder if I am not attributing to him, after these many years, adventures and crimes that were perpetrated by others, before I met him and after I met him, who now blend together in my tired mind to form a single image, forced together by an imagination that unites the memory of gold with that of a mountain to compose the idea of a mountain of gold" (191).

While encroaching on the Abbot's Library Adso is surprised and terrified by a deformed mirror image of himself. He later confesses: "I was in constant fear of finding myself in front of another mirror, because the magic of mirrors is such that even when you know they are mirrors they do not cease to disquiet you" (243). Adso's experience in front of a mirror forces on him an awareness of his own subjectivity. He resists developing a sense of himself as an individual and moving, to use Lacan's term, into the symbolic order. The Library mirror presents him with a means of self-identification that brings to the fore precisely that which he wants to deny: the direct, dialectical confrontation of his inner and outer realities. He recoils in horror at this sight of himself, and purposely forgets what he has seen. He keeps his lantern burning, wasting oil unnecessarily, to ward off further surprises and revelations (245).

Adso's avoidance of inner realities is placed clearly in evidence by his expeditious dispatching of his desire to meet a mythical unicorn. While engaged with Guglielmo in a seemingly innocent discussion of diverse ways of knowing (whose only consequence seems to be the deciphering of the organization of the Library), Adso mentions in passing that he would like to meet a unicorn in the woods and participate in a virgin capture. He then reminds Guglielmo that the unicorn—a symbol of Christ and of chastity—can only be captured by placing a virgin in a wood. Attracted by the maid's "most chaste smell,"[37] the unicorn places his head on the maiden's lap, offering himself as prey to the hunter's snares (318). However, Adso omits the tale's dénouement, the unicorn's execution by his captors. When confronted with Guglielmo's skepticism as to the orthodoxy of the tale, he replies: "What a disappointment. I would have liked to meet a unicorn with crossing a wood. Otherwise, what pleasure is there in crossing a wood?"

What pleasure, indeed. According to Mohacsy, in the Middle Ages unicorn tales enjoyed widespread credence and currency even among the learned (see Mohacsy 1984, 390). If this is truly the case, then Guglielmo's skepticism is more modern than medieval, indicative of the postmodern handprint of the doubting empirical author. As for Adso, his investment in the tale reveals unconscious processes crucial to understanding his character.

Adso's unicorn is, of course, a phallic figure, while the virgin capture condenses symbols of both incestuous and parricidal desire. The duality of the female in this tale—she is pure but also the traitorous seductress who lures the unicorn to capture and death—gives evidence of residual oedipal guilt. The dual nature of the maiden, her simultaneous innocence and perfidy, is symbolic of the child's double image of the mother. On the one hand, the oedipal child longs to restore the early mother-child fusion. On the other, the child perceives the danger of his longing: retaliation from Father who sets the hunter's deadly trap.

Like the unicorn, the heretics who serve as models for Adso's challenge of paternal authority are tricked by women and burnt at the stake. So, in repressing the death of the unicorn, Adso implicitly recognizes the he, like the unicorn, "is not active, but passive. He is not shrewd and enterprising, but artless and defenseless" (Mohacsy 1984, 409). Any oedipal fear he may have of challenging Father is reinforced by the spectacle of real persecutions and executions, all occasioned by the heretical femmes fatales that fascinate him so, the women responsible for the deaths of Fra' Dolcino and Fra' Michele: "this monk, called Michele, was in truth a very pious man, who had preached repentance and poverty, repeating the words of Saint Francis. He had been dragged in front of the Inquisition because of the maliciousness of certain women, who, feigning to want to be confessed by him, accused him of making heretical propositions to them" (236). Sublimation of the carnal desire that entraps the unicorn allows Adso to avoid dealing with the pain, vulnerability, and dependency love can cause. Participation in an erotic of denial, that is to say refusal of sexual fulfillment, allows him to avoid both the snares of women and the threat of an avenging Father.

Adso gives a lengthy description of Fra' Michele's trial and execution, which took place shortly before the young man joined up with Guglielmo. The procedure made such a profound impression on Adso that he not only copied the death proclamation, but he preserved and kept the parchment with him throughout his entire adult life (238). Michele blends in reverie with Dolcino (242) who, according to Ubertino, was guilty of preaching against the property of others, a trait that distinguished Dolcino as a heretic. Michele and Dolcino were heretics because they challenged authority. Heretics not only advocated the expropriation of the ecclesiastical and private property but, and this matters more, trampled on all sexual taboos, including incest. Franciscans such as Guglielmo and Ubertino refused their own inheritances and challenged the Pope's temporal claims, but respected patriarchal order. In other words, the Franciscans respected the divine investiture of the Pope and the Emperor, whence they derived their own authority as learned men, or "*sacerdoti*" (225).

Adso-narrator underwrites this reasoning, perhaps because it provides him with a point of entrance into the power structure: he remembers thinking, "I am a novice, but I will be a monk and later a priest [*sacerdote*]" (224), that is to say a man invested with the power to make holy, hence authority over the foundations of knowledge. This represents a recantation of his youthful, energetic participation in Guglielmo's challenge to the Abbot's control of the Library. Indeed, while writing his text, the elderly Adso remembers distrusting Guglielmo's intellectual curiosity because it constituted a challenge to the authority Adso aimed to inherit. Adso-narrator tells his reader that over the course of time "I always learned to distrust such inquisitiveness, even though I know very well that to my master this attitude was not displeasing" (142).

In other words, the heretics reflected the youthful Adso's idealized grown-up personality. However, their tribulations taught him that independence from and parity with Father are not worth the potential punishment: it is best to submit, wait one's turn, and painlessly inherit. Guglielmo's description of the fate of Remigio and Adso's love interest confirms what the young man already knew firsthand from watching other heretics burn at the stake. Thus, any patricidal ambitions he may have had are associated with the funereal bonfires of Michele and Dolcino. Adso looks patriarchy in the face, sees how it fights to preserve itself with "diabolical determination" (486), and is frightened by the heat of the pyre. He draws toward to the flame of heresy, but only to retreat.

Although Adso is attracted to Guglielmo's inquisitiveness, he does not care to acquire self-knowledge. In fact, Adso is more than willing to repress desire and sublimate prohibited carnal knowledge. When his attempt to supersede Father ends in the tragedy of the Library fire, Adso shuns the doubt and relativism that inform Guglielmo's teachings. As we have just seen, after a youthful 'walk on the wild side,' Adso comes to agree that access to knowledge should indeed be limited; and that authority should neither be discussed nor challenged (188): "I felt confused and was afraid of my thoughts. Perhaps they were not proper [*non si addicevano*] for a novice who was only to follow scrupulously and humbly orders [*la regola*], for all the years to come—which is what I did, never asking further questions" (189). Adso submits to authority (325), and admonishes his reader against "covetousness of new things, and the lust for knowledge" (187).

Adso's ultimate distancing from Guglielmo's utilization of doubt as a means of knowing is foretold throughout the book. With hindsight he recalls his frustration with Guglielmo's refusal to provide him with foundational truths and "universal knowledge" [*conoscenze universali*] (158, 219). When he tells his story he remembers rooting against his mentor and the other Franciscans, and for the affirmation of Papal authority. He claims he wanted truth to prevail over doubt when the Franciscans prepared to engage the Pope's representatives in debate (308-9).[38]

The young Adso is depicted as caught between conflicting desires. He wishes to challenge authority and understand, on the one hand, and, on the other, to arrive at a foundation of knowledge. His inability to resolve this dilemma leads him beyond Guglielmo to the elder Franciscan, Ubertino,[39] who vaunts a direct, mystic relationship with God. Ubertino impresses on Adso that all women are to be avoided. Almost all are inferior beings—most are "the demon's vessel" (226); the passage through which the devil gains access to men's hearts (228); almost all, to use his word, are "manure" (334). The remaining, select few are idealized and sanctified.

Ubertino's exchanges with Adso are very physical. The young man enjoys the caresses and embraces,[40] whose purpose, Adso believes, is to convey the elder man's "knowledge or ardor" (225). Ubertino's stroking comes in stark contrast to the aloofness of Adso's father figures, and gives credence to Ubertino's androgynous vision of himself as Mary Magdalene (60-61), the harlot restored by Christ to a life of chastity. Ubertino's mystic persona dovetails perfectly with Adso's unicorn fantasy. In the Christological interpretation of the unicorn tale, the mythological beast purifies poisoned waters by dipping his horn into them. For Adso, such water-conning make metaphorically possible both sex without pollution and the restitution of the mother's virginity through sex with the son.[41] It also 'purifies' after the fact his liaison with the young woman.[42]

However, Adso resists Ubertino's mystical charm. Adso is not ready to give up his ego boundaries, and so Ubertino's charisma cannot be effective. In other words, at no time does Adso express a desire to efface himself and unite with "the ultimate source of religious sentiment, the Cosmos" (see Sterba 1968). Adso's ambitions are much smaller: he is not interested in uniting with something larger than himself. Adso turns inward, away from the Infinite offered to him by Ubertino, seeking refuge in the intimate oneness of the family bosom whose surrogate is the Church.

Adso is silent about the time spent with his biological family. He has almost nothing to say about his life with his parents and siblings prior to his being sent off by his father. The reader does not know if Adso resented those siblings who were allowed to stay at home. Adso never mentions them, and so we have no way of knowing if there were brothers or sisters who inherited his parent's wealth. The reader is told only that Adso was given to the cloister by parents who recognized his superior intellectual gifts. The one sibling he mentions, the spiritual sister with whom he has sex, is bastardized by her extraction her from a lower social class, legitimizing Adso by implication.[43]

Adso's admittedly "obsessive" curiosity for the women heretics is a response to the resentment he harbors for having been sent from home. It allows him to picture himself in potentially erotic situations with mother and sister figures, thus obtaining revenge and retaliation against both his parents. Adso's family romance holds together in the face of such feelings because he believes that the equal love for all children of the Father,[44] God, and of the "Holy Mother Church" has real application. One would have expected the liaison with the young woman to liberate Adso from adult authority, since the carnal knowledge acquired is incompatible with the revelation of the parents' sexual activities (Sigmund Freud "A Special Type of Choice of Object Made by Men," 170). Instead, Adso's resents the powerless independence thrust on him at a young age that left him prey to sodomitic monks. Indeed, he continues to crave the dependence and the nurturing denied him as a child when his father separated him from his mother by sending him away. And so Adso resolves his family romance in a pathological way—by fantasizing a return to an idealized mother and renewing his dependence on Father—by overinvesting in it.

Once taken into the bosom of the Church, Adso happily assumes the role this new family assigns to him. He identifies with Jorge, the "omnipresent" (136) yet invisible 'grandfather,' the Benedictine paterfamilias who divides the world into strict black-and-white, Manichean categories of good and evil (138). While still an unempowered youth, Adso fought to wrest control of the Word and of power from Jorge (486), while struggling with sexual drives and his superego.

Jorge believes that his fight to restrict knowledge is supported by a divine will. Guglielmo, who seeks to make knowledge more accessible, also believes that God is on his side (475, 482). Guglielmo's challenges to the established order open the door, in Jorge's opinion, to the legitimization of the *immondo*, a world turned on its head (441, 482). For this reason Jorge considers Guglielmo the Antichrist. Guglielmo's irony and doubt (150, 481) and especially his quest to give the Word, the right to speak, to the poor, would legitimate the carnivalesque parody of an institutionalized social hierarchy. Thus, when Adso sees Guglielmo repeatedly humbled by a higher authority (459, 487, 495) he cannot help but agree with Jorge's argument, that "the simple must not speak" (482), a view validated in and by the fire.

Once the deaths of Abbone and Jorge clear Adso's way to becoming a man of authority, Adso-narrator justifies and perpetuates Jorge's obscurantism, a choice justified by the "divine chastisement" of the pyre, a punishment that conferred perpetual validation on Jorge's struggle to limit access to knowledge. Consequently, Adso becomes an obfuscator; moreover, as the reader will remember, the confession conveyed by his original text is in Latin, the language of a restricted intellectual elite.

While watching the fire destroy what Guglielmo had held most precious, Adso gains vengeance on his mentor, who had humiliated him repeatedly throughout their week together at the convent. Finally, when he sees his master rendered helpless, Adso can feel filial piety for Guglielmo: "I saw just then Guglielmo himself who emerged [*sbucava*] from the refectory door, his habit smoking, holding in his hand a large cooking pot and I felt pity for him, this poor allegory of impotence" (490). After witnessing Guglielmo's humiliation at God's hand (495) and seeing how Guglielmo's effrontery brought on a "divine malediction" (493) and a "divine chastisement" (496), Adso "dares, for the first and last time in [his] life, a theological conclusion" (496). In other words, Guglielmo's mortification clears the way for Adso to assert himself as the rightful interpreter of the transcendental signifier, God (503). Subsequently, Adso will live his family romance, his wish of belonging to a different family, the Benedictines. He will regulate self-esteem through his relationship with that order when he inherits the power held by his predecessors. Only many years later, when he is secure in this role of authority, will he elaborate what happened and confess to his extended family, his audience of readers (see Linda Joan Kaplan; 193, 195; and Harvey Kaplan).

Adso can narrate his story only after he has distanced himself from Guglielmo's inquisitiveness—that is to say, when Adso's youthful search for a foundation of knowledge (129), for order and certainty has come full circle—and he comes to agree with Jorge that ignorance of others can indeed be blissful. Thus, Adso's "faithful chronicle" is grounded on a foundational truth, the "Word of God." Adso's status as God's vicar is a manifestation of this "incontrovertible truth," one that he repeats daily with "psalmodizing humility" (19), after inheriting the power of Jorge and Abbone.

In other words, after attempting to resolve oedipus through a belated rebellion against paternal authority Adso submits to the Law, participates in and, finally, expropriates and perpetuates Father's authority. So, when telling his tale—one of a lifelong struggle to repress intellectual curiosity—Adso presents his ability to sublimate as a universal model. He admonishes his readers to all be good little monks, repress their intellectual pride, and "copy without understanding" (287). In other words, seminarians and readers should follow the example of Adso who did not seek to supersede Father, but submitted to Him, and got everything he wanted in the end.

Indeed, since Adso is the only living testimony to what 'really happened,' he can proffer a narrative destined to outlive all throughout eternity; a story that cannot be contradicted in which he alone can assign blame—perpetrating oral violence against his parents—and absolve himself of all guilt.

Having exchanged libidinal drives for a good relationship with an object, the Mother Church, through whom he communicates with an ideal subject, God, Adso fulfills a libidinal aim while avoiding shame and guilt (see Fairbairn). Power—*il potere*—over heaven and earth, symbolized by Peter's keys, is a masculine attribute made possible by participation in the feminine *santa madre chiesa* through whom one must past to arrive at God's mercy and to salvation. Adso identifies with the transcendental signifier, God, who in Adso's definition, "is a big nothing; he is touched by no now and no here" (503).[45] That is to say, God is absent, yet spatially and temporally pervasive. Eco's narrator, who has identified with the transcendental signifier, assumes Jorge's role as arbiter of knowledge, and in so doing dons the mantle formerly worn by the elder Benedictine, that of collective superego.

This brings us full circle, back to the question of the role and the posture to be assumed by the reader, the person called to submit to that collective superego. Eco's Model Reader walks away from this text knowing that knowledge, symbolized by the Library, is a proper source of contention. However, dominion over the law, symbolized by the *Edificio*, is never challenged. When the Abbot, a paternal figure, seeks to wrest control of the library from Jorge, the Benedictine paterfamilias kills him. When Guglielmo engages Jorge, the intensity of the confrontation reinforces the lesson Adso took from the trial of the young woman and Remigio: when the higher-ups fight, it is best to not get involved: "the humble [*i semplici*] always pay for everybody, even for those who speak on their behalf." This concept is driven home by his mentor, who tells him "one day the big dogs . . . will make peace by passing over the bodies of the smaller dogs who brawled in their service" (409), and Adso, who has already learned to submit to authority and the benefits of the contemplative life, learns to disengage. Adso's reader would do well to follow his example.

Guglielmo's *avant la lettre* postmodern metaphysical doubt keeps him far from the extremisms of the Ubertino, the heretics and the Inquisitor Bernardo Gui (73). Following his master, Adso tells his readers to stay squarely in the middle of the political road, and resign themselves to their fate: "we must not transform the order of world even if we must fervently hope in its transformation" (230). Politics is a game played high above the average person's head, one the masses would to well to avoid (157–58, 195); hope should be placed in an enlightened few, an elite class of men like Guglielmo, who have learned to remain close to the experience and virtues of "*i semplici*" [the humble, literally the simple] in order to paternalistically reform their world (208). Like Saint Francis, Guglielmo would "integrate the marginalized, those who are ripe for rebellion" (205). Even Guglielmo, who advocates a more democratic administration of knowledge, places limits on access and diffusion; he tells Nicola that *i semplici* should not concern themselves with questions of orthodoxy and heresy, and stay clear of the power struggle between the Emperor and the Pope.

Adso identifies ideological extremism with the radical quest for knowledge and such "cognitive lust" with the carnality he has learned to sublimate (398–99). Just as Adso disengages, so does the Model Author who "transcribe[s] without worrying about the present." In the introduction Eco's voice explains that

> The years in which I discovered the text of the Abbot Vallet, the persuasion that one should write only engaging the present and with the intent of changing the world held a certain currency. Now, ten years or so later, the man of letters (who has regained his very high dignity) is consoled by the fact that it is possible to write for the pure love of writing. And so now I feel free to narrate, for the pure love of narrating the story of Adso da Melk and I take comfort and consolation in finding it so incommensurably removed in time (now that the vigil of reason has chased away all the monsters that his sleep generated) so gloriously bereft of any relationship with our times, so estranged in time from our hopes and securities. (15)

In other words, just as the narrating voice represses the unresolved psychological traumas that haunt the narration, the Model Reader is invited to escape from the real world to Eco's world of books that speak of other books (15), and only coincidentally of life. If Eco's Model Readership is defined by its passive reception of what is encoded in this text, then they do not utilize the text as a tool for investigating through participation in a "dialectics of looking" (Kilborne) wherein they watch themselves being watched by others to then question their affinity with Adso and their identification with his oedipal struggles. How the critical reader chooses to behave is another matter.

Inaction and Reaction in *Il pendolo di Foucault*

Eco's novels all deal in the acquisition, administration and transmittal of patriarchal power. *Il pendolo di Foucault* [Foucault's Pendulum] is no exception. None of his protagonists oppose its structure; all of them accept their subservience in the hope of inheriting what 'belongs' to those in authority. Paternal humiliations seem to constitute a rite of admittance into a male pecking order structured by authority and shame; these degradations are always accepted by Eco's protagonists, but with a tolerance laden with the frustration and resentment associated with the inability to supersede Father. Moreover, Eco's novels all underscore how the power structure is perpetuated when the heir identifies with the aggressor, the authoritative paternal figure, and mistreats those who would follow in his footsteps. Indeed, there are overriding similarities that link Eco's protagonists; their psychological consistency justifies using them as a point of entrance into a discussion of how patriarchy self-perpetuates.

As we have seen, *Il nome della rosa* deals in the modalities of inheriting institutional authority over knowledge from the Father and the administration of that inheritance. Adso, the character with whom the reader is invited to identify, is a fledging intellectual. The central character of Eco's second novel, known to the reader only as Casaubon, is a bit older, a university student when the book opens. Like Adso, Casaubon also equates knowledge with the power he would like to wrest from a paternal surrogate. Here, too, as we shall see, the strategy of the Model Author allows everyone—the empirical author, the narrating voice, and those kindred spirits who constitute the target demographic—to avoid responsibility for acts they believe are culpable.

However, the influence of ideas and theories that inform *Il pendolo di Foucault* at the level of empirical author are so pervasive in this *conte philosophique* that little space is left to the humanity, maturation, and development of the characters. As Zamora has argued, a serious shortcoming of *Il pendolo* is that "too much is told, too little dramatized" (334). Indeed, it is almost impossible to discern any emotional development in any of the characters. At best, we can record a certain form of intellectual development in the narrator, Casaubon, when he passes from a youthful incredulity to the skepticism of his adult years.

The details provided by the text of Casaubon's sentimental life are skeletal, as are those of his involvement in the world outside his studies. We are afforded a minimal glimpse into his childhood, and his relationship with his wife Lia resembles an intellectual sodality more than a marriage (he considers her his intellectual Beatrice [407], his *donna angelicata*). As a young man Casaubon is completely removed emotionally from the political tumult of 1968–69. He is approximately twenty years old when labor unrest gives rise to Italy's Hot Autumn, which he lives as a spectator, dressed "in jacket and tie" (120). Casaubon considers student and worker rebellions as no more than a "simulated revolution" (58, 117), a sort of made-for-TV movie, and dreams of a painless, effortless social palingenesis, "a Golden Age . . . in which you became aware that the Revolution not only would take place, but that it would be sponsored by the Chamber of Commerce" (90).

Casaubon bypasses all the important historical events of his lifetime with extreme indifference. While a student at the *liceo*, he succeeds in ignoring the tumult of 1968. In 1972, only two years after matriculation, he is already at work on his thesis (61). He was too young, he tells himself in retrospect, to participate in the incandescent, revolutionary atmosphere of 1968–69 (646), and his long stay in Brazil removes him physically and emotionally from the Student Movement of 1977 and the *affaire Moro*—the kidnapping in March 1978 and assassination, almost two months later, of Italian statesman Aldo Moro by the Red Brigades. He is in Paris in search of Belbo when Communist secretary Enrico Berlinguer dies, and is in hiding when the Italian Communist Party briefly becomes Italy's first party in elections for the European Parliament. He lives his entire life as a precociously old man. At the tale's conclusion he is "ashamed" to admit he is a forty-year-old, self-styled "elderly bourgeois" (646). Therefore, it comes as no surprise that the Parisian protests for and against the Savary Law (337)[46]—events he witnesses as a disinterested foreigner—are mere fodder for a taxicab driver's facile, indiscriminate invective against all political unrest (642), a harangue Casaubon gives the appearance of endorsing with his silence.

The moral of Casaubon's story seems to be have no ideals, do not place your trust in any movement, religious or political, larger than yourself. In fact, the novel is united by a subtle subtext that would discredit any form of political activism. He subscribes to the self-serving understanding that participation in society's grand events is spurred not by principles, but by economic self-interest or subservience to fashion. Such pessimism is reinforced by the cameo appearances of secondary characters such as the bookshop owner "who once sold the Cultural Revolution" but now find books on mysticism more profitable (390).

Other secondary characters, who also completed the swing from radical Left to radical Right, afford Belbo the opportunity to expound on his typology of "imbeciles, fools, and madmen" who submit manuscripts to his publishing house (72–73). The only 'sane' option the reader might glean from the work, it seems, is to avoid engagement. The elaboration of The Plan, a conspiracy theory, drives this point home when it places Casaubon, who "had always distrusted analogies," at the center of an ideological maelstrom, "caught up in a feast of analogies, a Coney Island, a May Day in Moscow, a Holy Year of analogies" (381). Hindsight will tell him that the best plan of action would have been inaction, the skeptical abstention from participation in the strange confluence of Left and Right exemplified by the association of the elitist psychoanalyst Dr. Wagner and two radical Leftist groups (245; see also 97).

Wagner's involvement with political extremists allows Eco to equate left and right extremists by underscoring the irrational matrix they shared. As he told one interviewer: "many political formations of our history, rightist and leftist, should be reinterpreted in the light of their religious foundations" (Adornato 104), even though the Eco, in an extra-literary setting, strongly denied making any allusion in his novel to right-wing subversion (Stauder 1989, 7, 8). Indeed, it would seem that the focus of the novel's critique is directed toward the left: in Eco's own words, *Il pendolo* "is a way of telling about what happened in Italy. In other words, what happened in Italy with the Red Brigades happened in Brazil with Amparo. There is this grand psychedelic debauchery in the irrational" (Stauder 1989, 6–7).

"What happened in Italy" was an increase in the threat of both left- and right-wing coups in proportion to the growing popularity of the Italian Communist Party among the working and middle classes through the 1960s, 1970s, and into the 1980s. Indeed, subsequent to the student uprisings of 1968 and organized labor's Hot Autumn in 1969, a strategy of tension, consisting of acts of terrorism of indiscriminate political coloring, increased in intensity, revealing the extent to which the authority of the state was in doubt (Ginsborg 1990, 423). In 1981 the existence of a subversive Masonic lodge, the P2, was discovered. Its members included prominent figures in the secret services, armed forces, in business and in the world of politics (La strage, 323).[47] Although the precise objectives of the lodge have remained obscure, there is little doubt that its venerable master, Licio Gelli, was seeking to construct an anti-Communist network within the highest echelons of the Italian State. The close bonds linking Gelli and right-wing terrorism (whose purpose was that of preparing a military coup d'état) would indicate that in 1980 Gelli was for all intents and purposes the occult leader of Italy's secret services (De Lutiis, 353). In fact, his "secret Masonic Lodge constituted a 'State within the State,' a hidden power structure that had succeeded in infiltrating the highest strata of the secret services and the military, and the most sensitive apparatuses of the Government, even the Council of Ministers." This invisible concordance of wealth and government "placed at risk the very democratic order of the Nation" (Flamigni, 403–404).[48] At the same time, acts of right-wing terrorism were utilized in order to denounce in the court of public opinion a "theory of opposite political extremisms" that lumped together leftists and neofascist subversion, in order to suggest that the political center was the only safeguard for the preservation of liberal democracy and that a market economy was the only possible choice for social organization.

By the late 1980s (*Il pendolo* first appeared in print in 1988) middle-level Italian readers (Eco's target demographic) had grown justifiably tired of almost twenty years of urban violence. They would typically fail to distinguish between the destabilizing acts of neofascist terrorism (that, unbeknown to the average Italian, benefited from complicity at the highest levels of government) and the pseudorevolutionary strategies of the Red Brigades (whose motto was "Strike at the heart of the state"). In fact, the two extremisms were easily equated by their similar rhetorical styles, which masked a common goal, the installation of a dictatorship, even though their methods differed (the Red Brigades were more closely associated with targeted political assassinations, while the neofascists typically opted for indiscriminate bombings of public spaces). Although the Parliamentary Left had vowed to uphold a Constitution it had helped write and ratify, in the final analysis this "strategy of tension" served the electoral ends of Italy's secular and religious centrist governing parties. Since the average, apolitical citizen did not discern between the Red Brigades, who bandied about the classic texts of the Marxist tradition, and the Italian Communist Party, the latter was considered guilty by association and held accountable at the polls, while the political center (the coalitions that coagulated around the Christian Democrats) was seen the only 'reasonable' alternative to social chaos. In *Il Pendolo di Foucault* this logic of *reductio ad unum* of a complex and evolving social and political history is extended to include the organized labor movement (59, 72–73, 97, 99–100, 105), in other words, it would seem that anything other than Casaubon's "skeptical" *qualunquismo* [noncommitment] is a 'paranoia' to be avoided.

Belbo's political *centrismo* becomes apparent when he relives his adolescence. In his recollections of the Resistance the main colors of Italy's political spectrum—red, white, and black—blend together. Mortal enemies are seen forming a "spiritual cavalry," *au dessus de la melée* (310, 314). Belbo's *rêveries* of his youth and of a time when his Uncle Carlo—who had compromised himself with the Fascist and Salò regimes—was able to find and occupy a common, human ground with his longtime adversary—the sharecropper Uncle Carlo exploited—and with the local Partisan commander (since Belbo's narrative is told from the perspective of the landholding class, the peasant Canepa's motives are ignored [346]). His recollections of what "probably" happened (313) blur all distinctions between Fascist loyalists and Resistance fighters in a revisionist negation of the historical reality of Fascist dictatorship (130) and tacitly justifies the continuation and consolidation of the traditional state structure and administration inherited from fascism by nascent republic (Ginsborg 1990, 91). Belbo's recherche uncovers an "unequivocal" revisionist world of apolitical martyrs where "a dead man was a dead man was a dead man" (345). He remembers the survivors of the war extending the Resistance concept of democratic unity to include Fascist loyalists: "it didn't matter who had been a Fascist and who hadn't been, it was a matter of honoring our war heroes" (666). In fact, the battle name of one of the partisan commanders is "Ras," earned through heroism in the Fascist colonial campaign against Ethiopia (663–65, 668). The most positive model of this nonpartisan civility during a world war is the local priest, who embodies values that transcend quotidian concerns. Don Tico not only neglects his own well-being when safety of the flock is threatened, but he willingly puts life on the line to safeguard the purity of his art: "Priest, yes, and anti-Fascist, but above all art for art's sake" (666).[49]

However, Belbo's reminiscences are not all positive: he cannot forget the opportunism of the politically divisive: "Cantalamessa said he was Communist, Bo claimed to be a Fascist; both were willing to sell themselves to the other side for a slingshot" (351). The crowning glory of the obfuscation of boundaries is the politically ambiguous Remo. Although the reader cannot be sure if Remo was a Black Shirt or a partisan who infiltrated Fascist ranks (521–22), Belbo remembers "with certainty" that Remo was a partisan who died a heroic death. Whether this was the case is of no consequence. What matters is what Belbo recollects through the screen of memory, and he remembers an idealized politics, an *embrassons-nous* where combatants at some critical juncture stop shooting at each other and remember they are, after and above all, Italians.

Like Belbo, the adolescent Eco experienced firsthand the combat between Resistance fighters and the Nazi-Fascist occupiers (Mitgang 204). Moreover, Belbo, Diotallevi, and Casaubon "have important autobiographical links to the author's experience as a young man during the war and as an associate of major publishing firms in Turin and Milan in the early years of Eco's career" (Bondanella 290). Both Eco and Belbo were born in 1932 (69, 121; Diotallevi, in his late forties at the tale's conclusion [597], is their contemporary). Too young to participate in the combat, the generation into which Eco was born was able to avoid the fundamental life choice between declaring fidelity to Fascism and filling the ranks of the partisan movement.

While I have no intention of using the author's biography as a key for reading *Il pendolo di Foucault*, the parallels between

Eco's life and those of his characters drawn by some critics cannot be ignored. They underscore the ideological imprint left by the empirical author on this text: the novel's characters repeat verbatim comments and observations made by Eco in extraliterary writings. In other words, Eco's nonfictions facilitate exegesis because they help us place the novel in historical and critical relation to the dynamic personality of its artist, justify our identifying the heavy hand of the empirical author, and, our theory that this is a novel *a thése*.

As already mentioned, Zamora has found *Il pendolo* lacking in plausible character development. While I agree with Zamora that Casaubon and the others are unsympathetic characters, I would argue that they are extremely plausible from a psychological standpoint. Eco's characters realistically project from the two-dimensional page into our four-dimensional world. There are, in fact, those who empathize with the characters, flow into the Model Reader demographic, and absorb the text's ideology; others, those who find the characters less than congenial, are more able to gain the distance necessary to decipher what the author has encoded in the work.

Eco's characters are off-putting because they live only for ideas, not for sentiment. Casaubon, Belbo, and Diotallevi live cloistered from society, in their own little ivory-tower world filled entirely with books. Yet there remains a distance between them: when the story draws to a close, even after extended period of close collaboration spent practically isolated from the outside, the three continue to address each other formally, using the *Lei*, and by their last names. Furthermore, they have no familial support system: neither Belbo nor Diotallevi seem to have any living family; Casaubon's parents are recollected only very fleetingly, as we shall see. However, the two references to Casaubon's youth do allow us to speculate that at the root of his failure to develop emotionally is an unresolved oedipal conflict. Prior to doing so, I submit that Casaubon, because of his stunted psychic growth, projects his internal reality onto Belbo and Diotallevi to such an extent that the three must be treated as alter egos, and not as distinct individuals.[50] In fact, the text leaves open the possibility that the latter two characters are figments of Casaubon's imagination.

The events of *Il pendolo* appear to be recounted by two distinct narrative voices, those of Casaubon and Belbo, author of the

Abulafia (Belbo's nickname for his computer) files that are read and inserted verbatim into the narration by Casaubon. The use of this particular narrative device gives the semblance of a decentered, polyvocal response to postmodernity. That is to say, it would seem that in *Il pendolo* the relativistic, nonfoundational truths and *petits récits* that characterize the polycentric reality of postmodernity are charted by the plural, hence mutually objectifying, perspectives of the novel's first-person narrators. McHale argues that the retrieval of the computer files by Casaubon allows access to Belbo's "alternative view of the same events." However, I would argue that access to Belbo's computerized memoirs allows Casaubon to appropriate events of which he would otherwise have little or no knowledge.

When Casaubon frames or retells the significant events of Belbo's life, Casaubon's theories concerning Belbo's behavior verify themselves tautologically. When Casaubon believes he can speculate-project-reconstruct 'what really happened' to Belbo, Casaubon can live out his fantasy: he becomes the all-knowing detective, a self-styled "Sam Spade/Philip Marlowe" (36, 38, 238, 242, 422/239, 324), or secret agent (240). This is consistent with his professional posture. He does not consider himself a literary critic because he does not engage in the subjective interpretation of texts (662). Rather, he is a researcher, a dispassionate, faithful, and positivistic recorder-annotator of the facts he empirically observes.

By the same token, the use of flashback to interpolate files into Casaubon's present does not change the temporal perspective of the narration, as McHale contends (183). The entire narrative takes place in an abbreviated timespan, Casaubon's temporally dissociated—or to use Jameson's terms, "schizophrenic," "postmodern"—continuous present. As is the case with the frame-tale strategy, the use of flashback also serves the purpose of endowing Casaubon's tale with the semblance of omniscience. His story is not lived within a process of becoming, but relived without any doubt as to how the story will unfold. In fact, once the stage has been set (in the first two sections of the book, "Keter" and "Hokmah"), Casaubon mentally returns to his here and now (see 53) and using hindsight constructs a narrative that strictly adheres to the chronology of events. He takes leave of temporal order only to evoke Belbo's memoirs, which fill in the lacunae of what he previously did not know, as they become necessary for the advancement of the plot. When Casaubon writes history backward, that is to say, as a function of his present, he reifies Belbo's nonfactual testimony. Once Belbo's narrative becomes part of Casaubon's reality, which is to say, his own remembered experience, the illusion of reality supersedes any and all debate as to whether or not the events narrated really happened. It does not matter if the narrative is fiction or nonfiction. Casaubon assigns a truth value to his tale because it is real for him. Belbo's written word is fact, a verifiable and verified foundation for knowledge. Thus, the decentering is more apparent than real: a unitary personality constitutes a very strong center of narrative gravity. Model Readers adapt to a textual strategy that ignores the distortion to which memory is always subject and underwrite the false objectivity of the text.

Casaubon identifies completely with Belbo. In fact, he succeeds in cracking the password that gives access to the Abulafia files after he "becomes" Belbo (47). This can take place because Casaubon's curiosity for the minutiae of Belbo's intimate life (354) allows him to think like and incarnate Belbo (610). Indeed, what Casaubon believes might be the last hours of life are not spent contemplating life with his wife and child, but reading the Abulafia files so that he might reconstruct Belbo's biography.

Casaubon's attention to the details of Belbo's life (343, 348) startles the object of his gaze (344, 522), especially when Casaubon remembers not only what Belbo has forgotten, but what Belbo has forgotten having told him. Casaubon, undeterred, perhaps spurred on by this recognition of thoroughness of his care, becomes as one with Belbo: "The others did not understand, I intuited—and now I know" (345).

At the novel's conclusion, Casaubon believes he knows all there is to know about his alter ego (660). And when Casaubon's quest culminates—in the uncovering of the "Key Text" (662) that resolves all enigmas surrounding Belbo and his past—the identification of Casaubon and Belbo is sealed. Casaubon can perceive himself as more than a mere reader of Belbo; he "relives" Belbo's past through his texts (663). This is true to the extent that Casaubon does not reproduce Belbo's final "confession" (602), he paraphrases it. In other words, he expropriates Belbo's text, and makes Belbo's life his own. Indeed, even though *Il pendolo* is told as an interior monologue, Casaubon respects Belbo's suppression of the name of the town of the latter's country retreat (in Belbo's texts it is called ***, even though there are clear indications as to its location).

Once he believes he is the incarnation of Belbo's text, Casaubon achieves a fullness of presence that legitimates his use of conjecture to fill the narrative lacunae left in the computer files. In other words, the gaps in what Casaubon knows are either deemed of no consequence (244), or filled in by speculation (577 ["probably"], 344 ["it must be"], 582 ["it must have been"]). When Casaubon becomes one with the text, he can tell of Belbo's life as if it were his own autobiography, an autobiography that, as we have seen, maintains the illusion of objectivity. More importantly, the relationship between Casaubon and Belbo reflects the one advanced by Eco for Model Authors and Readers.

In other words, Casaubon enters a fictional universe where he takes on a dual role of reader-author. He creates a text that is more real than life itself. It is hyperreal, reality to the second power: experience validates itself through sheer redundancy when he conflates perceived and apperceived reality. As we have also seen, the symbiosis of Casaubon and Belbo is completed when the former reads the latter's computer texts subsequent to Belbo's execution at the hands of the "Diabolicals." Thus, Belbo heeds Eco's admonition to the Model Author, to "die after having written. So as not to disturb the progress [*cammino*] of the text" (Eco 1983b, 509). Casaubon—the privileged, Model Reader of Abulafia—serves as perfect *pendant* to this Model Author, who "dies so that the reader might accede to his truth" (671). Belbo's death allows Casaubon to project his own inner world onto Belbo's autobiography.[51]

The linking and overlapping of the two personalities give credence to the hypothesis that they are alter egos, a manifestation of the deep defense mechanism developed by Casaubon in response to his disappointment in his father prior to puberty and the lad's failure to rebel. Casaubon does not split his investment of positive affect between interpersonal communion and work—as the reader might hope (see Tomkins 203)—because he is totally absorbed in his job. Even though Casaubon occasionally alludes to his personal life, it is of minimal importance when compared to his obsessive involvement in The Plan. Casaubon does not revisit his past, except for one important instance in which he tells of his loss of childish innocence, a corollary to a life lesson gleaned from his father's incredulity.

To explain, the ten-year-old Casaubon wants to subscribe to a weekly magazine that publishes illustrated versions of literary classics. He justifies his request by explaining that the declared purpose of the publication is to make education pleasant. But Casaubon senior makes known to the boy the ulterior motives of the books' publisher: to sell copies and make a profit. In so doing, the father reveals his own parsimony: Casaubon senior's declared "suspicion of comic books" does not succeed in masking his purpose (57). In this unpleasant way Casaubon fils learns to read between the lines, to always seek ulterior motives, and to distrust the world.[52]

Since the text does not provide details, we can only speculate on the extent of Casaubon's disappointment in learning these harsh realities, and in being denied his comic book. Nor can we determine with certainty the magnitude of the trauma associated with an assertion of paternal authority: Casaubon's testimony resists analysis. However, it would appear that this specific (ab)use of paternal authority strengthens a will to defy in the child. Incredulity (rebellion against paternal hypocrisy and authority) becomes a patterned, repetitive response and gradually develops into a vaunted skepticism (19, 41). In fact, awareness of the hypocrisy of both the magazine publisher and Casaubon's father sets in place behavioral patterns that preclude meaningful social interaction. Casaubon learns to trust no one, including his alters. He will declare, "I had made of incredulity a scientific duty, but now I had to distrust even the masters who had taught me to be incredulous" (380).

While recollecting this event, Casaubon—who apparently has no siblings—speaks not of his own father, but of "our father" (57), raising the event to a macroscopic level, that of a universal human trait. Similarly, he ascribes Belbo's memories to the supraindividual level of the "collective imaginary" (522). Significantly, this episode from Casaubon's past is mirrored in Belbo's life when the latter tells of the parsimony behind his own father's refusal to buy him a trumpet (69). 'Total' understanding of this particularly embarrassing episode (see 69–70) is achieved at the novel's conclusion, when Casaubon comes upon the "Key Text," the file in which Belbo's successful sublimation of his sexual frustrations is recounted.[53] As for Casaubon, when he decides he wants to father a child, he determines that he will raise his offspring not in his own image, but in that of his alter, Belbo, by insisting the child "quickly learn the trumpet" (353).

The precocious nature of the Casaubon's discovery of his father's duplicity effectively forestalls the more open defiance typical of puberty and adolescence. When Casaubon identifies with Belbo, who is slightly less than a generation older Belbo assumes for Casaubon the guise of an older brother who, in imparting the importance of skepticism teaches Casaubon how to supersede his father. A more exact discussion of Casaubon's relationship to his father is not possible because the text is silent in this regard. Nonetheless, his mute challenge to the father, through skepticism, is not without consequence.

At a key stage of his life, immediately after his return from Brazil, Casaubon measures himself against his father. The young man takes stock of his situation, and realizes to his chagrin that he is almost thirty years old, an age when his "father was a father, knew who he was and where he lived" (234). It takes Casaubon two years of work to establish himself, and to reach a place where he can be "satisfied with [him]self" (240). We do not know if ultimately he felt guilt or filial piety as a result of the comparison with his father. Neither does the text shed light on the ambivalent nature of his relationship with his father, which leads Casaubon to desire sexual possession of mother surrogates. However, it is clear that Casaubon lives this fantasy, as we shall see, in his relations with Amparo and Lia, and vicariously, through his alter ego Belbo, who will approach the primal instinct of copulation with the mother through his relationship with Lorenza Pellegrini, whom he calls a "prostitute" (320) but in her own mind is both "prostitute and saint" (48, 322, 621).[54]

Because Casaubon, to the best of the reader's knowledge, never openly challenges his father, his identification with Belbo allows both men to reexperience the shame associated with their youthful observations of their fathers' hypocritical frugality. At a very early stage in their relationship, Casaubon and Belbo impulsively conceal what they know of Colonel Ardenti from police inspector De Angelis, an authority figure, but do not know why they do so. Upon reflection, Belbo comes to believe that he has repeated the cowardice characteristic of his youth. Casaubon convinces himself he acted on principle (unnamed schoolmates taught him "that you lie to police"). Although the two do not consciously consider their actions a rebellion against a paternal figure, feelings of guilt for having defied the Inspector prevent their communicating with each other for a lengthy period of time: "But that's the way it is," Casaubon pronounces, "a guilty conscience poisons friendship. After that day, I didn't see him anymore. I was his remorse, and he was mine" (170). However, the shame they feel ultimately serves as a means of self-identification and of segregation from the world (see Tomkins 216).

The multiple personality Casaubon-Belbo contains both the subject (the active voyeurism of Casaubon who subjects his alter to intense scrutiny) and the object of affect (the passive exhibitionism of Belbo who wants to be seen and therefore reveals to his young associate that which he had concealed: his youthful poetry ["There you go, after I am dead, remember, there is all my early literary production" {342}] and, later, his memoirs). The active alter loves, or observes, while the passive, narcissistic alter (whose need to be loved autoerotically inverts onto itself) sublimates sexual desire. In fact, the active alter, Casaubon, sees himself as the true creator of The Plan and Belbo his follower (558). He also believes Belbo is "humiliated" by the fact that his inability to create artistically forced him to turn to editorial work (32, 561). While Casaubon's observations of Belbo are geared toward uncovering what Casaubon himself is, Casaubon is the man Belbo wishes he had become. Belbo "scolds" Casaubon for being part of a generation that is beyond good and evil, having 'sold out' to the first bidder (253). However, this reprimand (a *"paternale"* in the original Italian 263) is quickly followed by a confession, of Belbo's jealousy of the material success typically enjoyed by those of Casaubon's generation and of Belbo's regret for having allowed professional scruples to deprive him of material comforts (253).

Belbo writes because he is incapable of living. He is well aware he does not have "the makings of a protagonist" (40) and so he keeps a diary that is protected by a secret password. His means of self-expression, hiding in a computer a text not intended for publication, is the quintessence of communication without affect. Because his only interlocutor is himself, storing his texts becomes a means of distancing himself emotionally from what he writes. A secret password not only restricts access to his intimate diary, but for Belbo is a means of self-denial. Casaubon gains access to the computer files when he stumbles onto the password, answering "No" to Abulafia's "obtuse" prompt ("Do you know the password?") "out of hatred" for the computer (50). Casaubon considers this success a "violation" (50), a euphemism for carnal aggression, thus equating his "penetration" into the secrets of Abulafia with possession of Belbo's love interest, Lorenza Pellegrini, something denied Belbo (49).

Belbo does not interact with the world around him (see 63, 71), but lives a life of remorse and self-denial for his failure to act at critical junctures in the past. Not by chance Belbo desires a woman who does not reciprocate his affection. Belbo's entire adult existence is one of regret for having failed to choose, even incorrectly, and act (121). Not having lived, he feels he is not worthy to write about life. Therefore, his response to his own ineptitude is that of the classic antihero of modernist literature whose inability to live causes him to write about living. Belbo limits his activity to editing the works of others. However, guilt leads him to introspection, which in turn leads him to writing.[55]

Belbo knows that "a guilty conscience is not enough for redemption" (128), and so he writes "by mechanical reflex" in Abulafia, the secret "pseudo-diary" of a "simple spectator of the world" (64–65). Belbo attempts to attain reasonable self-knowledge without the guide of a professional analyst who would direct him through such an examination. He coyly scatters evidence of his past, but eschews dialogue, and consequently the means and methods of the psychoanalytic method. This predetermines the propensity of the two alters toward their individualistic method of self-discovery, introspection. However, such confession, without a deeper understanding of the psychic process and the consideration of the possibility that unconscious truths may exist beyond the reach of the interior monologue squirreled away in his computer, is not sufficient for gaining self-understanding (see Horney 296–97). This rugged individual's *recherche* fails in its attempt to achieve a fuller self-awareness, thus forestalling his learning how to negotiate a place for himself in society, literally conducting him to the gallows.[56]

Belbo's retreat from the world is taken one step further by Casaubon, who lives vicariously through his alter ego. For this reason we can aver that Casaubon resembles the antihero of ludic postmodern narratives who neither live nor write about life, but instead write about writing. Casaubon effects an "overturning of the paradigm" (90) when he moves beyond Belbo's modernistic monadism toward an even more radical isolation, into a world of books and erudite footnotes written for a very limited public of specialists. He does not communicate through a text of his own; he documents the texts of others as a vocation, while his obsessive avocation becomes the documentation of Belbo's life of remorse. However, unlike Belbo, Casaubon is not concerned by his failure to interact with society; he feels no need to communicate with anyone through a text. Instead, Casaubon lives vicariously through his research into Belbo's non-life. He sympathizes and identifies with Belbo, and simply observes life with the "spirit of he who confronts discourses on Truth in order to prepare himself to correct the page proofs" (59).

Casaubon skepticism and emotional removal from society leave him without a moral compass. Diotallevi hopes that "one day a Manuzio edition would reveal a new combination of the Torah to him" (268) and the cynical Belbo sees the success of the Manuzio scam as an example of the lengths of "human foolishness" (253). However, for Casaubon duping the "Self-Financing Authors" is a source of "entertainment, a practical joke" (268). Because he rarely makes a commitment and almost never acts, Casaubon has very few occasions to feel remorse. He neither lives life nor writes about it; he merely observes it. Since Casaubon is not one of life's active participants, he can do no wrong. For him, since his only errors are mental, not material, they without consequence. He strays only twice from the straight and narrow. He errs intellectually—when excogitating The Plan—and sexually—when pining for Lorenza (in chapter 58, dedicated to "the chaste prostitute" [Table of Contents]), Belbo's mother fantasy, whose relationship with the father figure Agliè, is a source of great jealousy for Belbo. However, in neither case does Casaubon act: his illicit sexual desires for her are never made explicit.

Casaubon's discovery of his father's duplicity allows him to bypass the traumas associated with puberty and oedipal resolution, and so his feelings toward his mother are never completely repressed. His observation of Belbo's relationship with Lorenza—whom Belbo admits "adoring" as one would an "ancient and universal aunt" (415)—allows Casaubon to delude himself as to the nature of his relationship with Lia: Belbo, not he, is the one trying to have sex with his mother.

In any event, Casaubon slips, "protected and guaranteed," into the "aristocratic" world of an "official Culture" that ignores the humanity whose history it pretends to comprehend and whose civilization it believes it advances (60). While enrolled at the university, his enlightened self-interest leads him to fancy himself student rebel in the morning and to curry favor with his professors in the afternoon (60). His estrangement from the world magnifies that of Belbo, whose computer files reveal the process of introspection utilized to revisit the determining events of his youth. The existential noncommitment of the two men, that is to say their refusal to see themselves as part of a societal grouping larger than themselves, causes them to avoid dialogue and distrust psychoanalysis (see 598)—which is reflected in Casaubon's depiction of Dr. Wagner, sinister link between the radical Left and the fascistic "Diabolicals"—and by extension any exploration of the irrational unconscious.

Just as Belbo seeks self-recognition through introspection, Casaubon's unwritten testimony, *Il pendolo di Foucault,* is an interior monologue. Casaubon's tale has no addressee; all his remarks are directed only to himself. He does not write, but thinks his text. Casaubon is his only interlocutor (679). Therefore, the preference of Belbo and Casaubon for introspection is the cornerstone of an attempt to achieve self-understanding and freedom from inner bondage that, tragically, is not linked to a desire to change, grow, and develop their best potentialities. The introspection of Casaubon, especially, has no aim; at no point does he recall his past in order to rectify mistakes.

Belbo's skepticism precludes faith in the supernatural (251). Since he is a nonbeliever—if we follow arguments advanced by Eco in a nonfictional venue—Belbo enjoys no guarantee of divine forgiveness. Therefore, one would not expect him to feel remorse. For this reason Belbo underwrites the "natural ethics" Eco proposes for the non-believer in a different context. Belbo's "secular ethics," along with the awareness of his failings and misdeeds, combine in his *recherche* to cause feelings of anxiety and helplessness that, in turn, lead Belbo to seek out a death that will perhaps serve as an example for posterity (Martini and Eco, 76).[57] His overriding sense of guilt causes, first, his "unlimited solitude," and then his "desperate death." For this reason Belbo seeks out "the cleansing" of introspective confession as a way of atoning for the remorse he feels (Martini and Eco, 77).[58] To a very limited degree, the same can be said of Casaubon, even though Casaubon's confession (the unwritten text of *Il pendolo*), is completely internalized, as one would expect of such an isolated personality.

Guilt leads both Casaubon and Belbo to allow Agliè to decide whether they live or die. Belbo permits himself to be drawn into Agliè's trap where he remains "calm," even though he has a noose around his neck, knowing, in Casaubon's words, that "he had no other choice" (602). Prior to finding himself in checkmate, Belbo shuns all possibilities for self-preservation because they are unreasonable. He never considers changing his identity and fleeing: this would constitute a break from the alter. He does not surrender himself to the police: this would result in punishment meted out by someone other than Agliè. And so Belbo spends four days typing his "testament" into Abulafia (601). Casaubon finds this statement along with a lengthy file, file "Il ritorno di San Germano" (524–35), in which Belbo predicts the manner of his own death.[59]

Before heading for Paris, Belbo leaves ample clues that would enable Casaubon to find him and rescue him, should Casaubon so desire. Belbo phones Casaubon from Paris to apprise him of what has transpired with the "Diabolicals." He says that everything Casaubon needs to know of his plight is in Abulafia, in numerically ordered files. He tells Casaubon to read them, and then says, "you decide" what to do (30, 36). In other words, Belbo actively pursues a passive aim, the fantasy of being rescued in suicide (see Jensen and Petty). Casaubon, in fact, will be put in the position of choosing between rescuing Belbo and showing his aversion by abandoning his friend to his death. Since we are dealing with an alter ego, the fact that Casaubon dispassionately watches Belbo die serves to underscore the depths of self-loathing felt by the protagonist of *Il pendolo*.[60]

At a deep level Casaubon believes himself culpable of having experienced the primal fantasy of intercourse with the mother (Amparo/Lia), of having desired the mother (Lorenza), and of having competed for the affections of the surrogate mothers Amparo and Lorenza with Agliè (see 189).[61] He also believes he is guilty of having tried to supersede the paternal surrogate by besting Agliè in the field of occultism. Once Belbo has met his fate, Casaubon can do no more than quietly await his own judgment (whether it takes the form of punishment or pardon is of no consequence) at the hands of the avenging father figure, Agliè.[62]

As we have seen, Casaubon's response to the discovery of his father's imperfection is not open aggression and so there is no suppressed guilt. He continues to compete with a father figure for the affection of women, mother figures who remain idealized, asexual personae, desexualizing or sublimating a forbidden aim (see Sterba, "A Contribution"). His repressed oedipal situation creates a tension in his life that is overcome by the identification with his secondary personalities. By displacing repressed patterns to these personifications Casaubon absolves himself from responsibility for his actions and saves himself from the blame of the super-ego and society (see Alexander). In addition, unresolved oedipus causes ambivalent feelings toward the father surrogate (Casaubon and his alters identify with Agliè and seek his approval for their advanced knowledge of occultism [see 460, for example]). At the same time they try to satisfy their aggression toward him by using him as a dupe in their vanity press scheme and trick him by inventing a secret society the three uncannily name "Tres." Initially, they think The Plan is a clever parody of Agliè's competence in the field of religious history (452–61, 537). They feel a certain filial piety when he cannot keep pace with their schemes; in fact, The Plan gains real impetus when Casaubon determines that he knows more about the topic than Agliè (474). Later, they will perceive Diotallevi's illness as the punishment for their impertinence (546; 598, 599 [for his part, Diotallevi will be "ashamed" that others knew of his illness (577)]).

At the novel's conclusion, neither Belbo nor Casaubon considers telling Agliè what the latter wants to know—that The Plan they concocted was all a hoax—because they must continue to defy him with their superior cynicism. Thus, when Casaubon waits for Agliè to either castigate him or rescue him from death, a prototype of the parent-child relationship is acted out. Casaubon projects a share of his own aggression onto the person he holds responsible for his fate. Like Belbo, Casaubon is willing to go forward with his threat to literally make Agliè a murderer should the rescue fantasy not be fulfilled (Jensen and Petty 138).

All three alters are of one mind intellectually. Belbo's search for an "absolute truth" is motivated by the "unbeliever's nostalgia for certainty" (Cannon 1992, 898), is shared by Casaubon, and is reflected in the positivistic, commonsensical empiricism Casaubon appropriates from Lia. Since the only thing of which the three alters can be certain is their regret for mistakes they have made, they underwrite a weak teleology that is not future oriented. Instead it limits itself, to use Eco's own phrasing, to absolving the "critical function of disinterest toward the future and constant re-examination of the errors of the past" (Martini and Eco, 11–12).

Shame leads Belbo and Casaubon to resign themselves to their fate, as calmly as Diotallevi submits to his cancer. Curiously, Diotallevi dies in synchrony with Belbo during the night of June 23–24, 1984 (649) after repenting for having "sinned against the Word, that which created and maintains the world" (598). For his part, Belbo must also deal with his lost faith. But he comes to understand that his open-ended search for the object of his desire is not a lost *arché*, but the telos. As he tells Abulafia, "The thing whose address I have lost is the End, not the Beginning. Not the object to be possessed, but the subject who possesses me" (560). He then admits to having participated in The Plan because of this "flaw of faith."[63] When Casaubon reads in Abulafia the "Key Text"[64] for understanding Belbo's sublimation of sexual tension, Casaubon projects an inner peace onto his friend. This allows Casaubon to believe that Belbo's ultimate defiance of the Father constituted the tardy resolution of oedipus necessary for Belbo to die in peace.

As for Casaubon, he can resign himself to awaiting Agliè's judgment once he gains a fuller understanding of how Belbo sublimated his frustrated sexuality: in one lengthy but almost imperceptible trumpet note ("it was clear [that] in that instance he was possessing Cecilia" [670]). Casaubon's 'sins,' as we have seen, are intellectual. He gives in to a "passion of the mind," and challenges the Father, when he strives to be a "genius" (72) and concocts The Plan. However, Casaubon bites off more than he can chew and throws reason to the wind. As a result, this self-styled "Mr. Incredulity" (19) commits the mortal sin of credulity (57), closing the circle, so to speak. He joins radical rationality (genius) with its opposite extreme: madman.[65]

Casaubon's youthful "political choice" was a retreat from the polis into "philology" (59). Since his motivation for participating in political marches was merely "to follow a girl who disturbed [his] imagination," he assumed that the political engagement of his cohorts was tantamount to a sexual experience. But what his fellow students lived with "passion," sex and politics, Casaubon wanted to experience as nothing more than an intellectual curiosity. For this reason, any sexual desire that may have "disturbed" him was purposely redirected toward his research, specifically his thesis on the Knights Templar (58–59).

During one of his first meetings with Belbo and Diotallevi, Casaubon told the two of having "lived with" the Templars for two years while writing his thesis and of his having "fallen in love" with them (100). He described the Templars to them as a fraternal sodality (much like the Garamond *équipe* [team]) whose vow of chastity led to their often being described as a company of sodomites. In his own words, "their regulations stated that women were most dangerous and that they might only kiss their mom, sister and aunt" (93). After bringing this enraptured description of the Templars to a close, Casaubon notices to his chagrin that he "had dreamt, with true feeling (how embarassing!), and aloud . . . with passion and compassion" (105).

Important aspects of the Casaubon's personality come to the fore through his observation of Belbo's frustrating relationship with Lorenza, a self-styled "prostitute and saint" (48). In fact, it is interesting to consider Casaubon's relationship with Lia in light of his suppressed desire for Lorenza because in so doing we underscore the extent to which his wife is mother figure for him. To explain, while on a working vacation in the country with the Garamond *équipe* Casaubon is disturbed by an unfamiliar sensation, a strong physical desire for Lorenza, who has accompanied the three men on their excursion (353). To subdue his feelings Casaubon literally hides his head under his pillow and forces himself to think about his wife. But his longing for Lorenza is not easily restrained (368). He returns to Milan "with much remorse." Although sight of Lia allows him to contain his yearning (380), Lorenza's effect on Casaubon is lasting (48). Even as he watches her execution she appears to him "as pure and languid as a Pre-Raphaelite adulteress," "too diaphanous to not stimulate [his] desire one more time" (620). Although he does not mourn the death of either of his alters—Belbo's murder is liquidated intellectually and with great haste (635–36)—thoughts of Lorenza's death move him to tears (636, 638). Subsequently, the trauma of her execution causes images of Lorenza and Lia to conflate in memory: remembrance of Lorenza's sexuality is superimposed on a daydream of Lia maternally cradling his head between her breast and her armpit and whispering to him to "be a good boy" [*stare buono*] (642).

We know much more about Lorenza than about Casaubon's wife, Lia. Certainly the conjugal relationship does not come close to matching the intensity of the bond between Casaubon and Belbo. Casaubon's marital life remains largely unexamined, except for two fleeting mentions of the physical union (242, 385). Their relationship begins with her telling him he is too thin and needs to eat more (241), the same admonition behind which she will hide the announcement of her pregnancy, a state that will transform her in his eyes into "a Flemish Madonna" (403). After marrying, Lia respects the traditional gender roles of wife and mother (462), retreats from the workplace, and transfers to her husband her suppressed professional ambitions, even though Casaubon willingly admits she is a better researcher than he. She warns Casaubon of the dangers of his research prior to his diving into The Plan (he interrupts this scolding with a refrain of "Yes, mommy," to which Lia replies, "Of course, my baby" ["*Certo che sì, bambino mio*" {383}]). He delays telling her about The Plan because he "is ashamed" (563). Ultimately, she convinces Casaubon that The Plan—his means of challenging the paternal Agliè—is foolishness, "humiliating" her mate (573).

Lia's 'commonsense' approach to life helps Casaubon to further occlude what he has already repressed. When she feels he has been working too hard, her maternal instincts kick in, and she forces him to take a vacation. While on holiday, he tells her of The Plan, but reticently, and with great shame, in anticipation of reprobation. Lia does in fact proceed to quickly cast asunder what the three men had painstakingly put together. She does so by obliquely reducing The Plan from documented historical fact to unsubstantiated, subjective narrative. To prove her point, she uses the parable of another subjective narrative that has been reified: Freud's theories on the unconscious.

She explains to Casaubon that the popularity of Freudianism has become so widespread that it is now an ideology, coloring and informing our view of the world. For many it has become a self-fulfilling prophecy: we see oedipal conflicts where there are none, and it has even become a form of faith healing for the laity (563–64). In other words, in debunking The Plan, she proposes a positivistic approach to self-understanding that mirrors the research method she and her husband utilize in compiling their erudite footnotes, on the one hand. On the other, her exclusive reliance on what can be empirically observed, individualistic introspection, reinforces the refusal of dialogic clinical transference and countertransference as a means of self-recognition. Monologic introspection, as we have seen, is also the method utilized by Belbo for reaching self-understanding, while positivistic empiricism is utilized by Casaubon to comprehend the personality of his alter, Belbo.[66]

Lia embodies traditional values of motherhood and family, and, more importantly, catalyzes the culmination of the plot by echoing statements made by the empirical author in extraliterary contexts, identifying and denouncing the "psychosis" of a "Conspiracy Syndrome" which raises suspicion to a metaphysical level (337). Casaubon keeps the details of his machinations hidden from her out of shame (491, 495), but when things get complicated he must confess. In response she uses 'common sense' to provide "the only true answer" (337) to that which confuses him. She makes clear to Casaubon that acts of terrorism, such as the placing of bombs on trains (foreseeing the ruse used by the "Diabolicals" to trap Belbo) by both Leftist and Rightist "fanatics" [*esaltati*] (567), is a perverse search for God, for a totality, in other words, for both a metaphysical *archè* and an eschatological end, or telos (337).

Before meeting and marrying Lia, Casaubon has a romantic relationship with another mother surrogate, the Brazilian Amparo. As is the case with all the female characters, Amparo is a secondary character. She is a foil whose only narrative functions are to underscore aspects of Casaubon's personality—such as justifying Casaubon's decision to stay far away from political engagement—and to provide concrete demonstrations of ideas discussed by Eco in essays and interviews. Amparo embodies Eco's extraliterary descriptions of leftist reflux away from the social commitment, beyond identity politics to mysticism. She is also the limiting case who incarnates and makes narratively plausible even the wildest conspiracy theories, while validating the confluence of opposite political extremisms.

When Casaubon first meets Amparo in Milan, she appears to be of a rigorous political and moral coherence (128–29). However, observation of Amparo in her native surroundings permits Casaubon to condescendingly note that she is full of "splendid contradictions" (176). Although a "convinced Marxist," after returning to her native Brazil she embraces the mysticism of her ancestors, creating her own hybrid of Marxism and *santería*, and places her hopes for social renewal in the local bishop (an ex-Nazi sympathizer), and in Wall Street's "barracuda." Thus, she makes clear to Casaubon the similarities between diverse religious traditions—Judaism, Christianity, the religions indigenous to Brazil, and fideistic Marxism (186, 190)—and attributes the resemblance to their atavistic commonality of source. While she claims she does not believe in popular religions—she calls them the "opiate of the people" (176)—she knows they are "real" (178).

Therefore, back in Brazil she is susceptible to the influence of Agliè and to occultist theories she comprehends "not with her mind, but with her uterus" (190). Agliè reminds her that her training in Continental philosophy was not an emancipation but in truth a repetition of submission to European hegemony over its Third World dominions. Such training (in Agliè's parlance a euphemism for ideological indoctrination) is standard practice among those who liberate slaves. The colonized and enslaved are given nominal freedom, but are forced to surrender their true identity: their language and beliefs. In other words, the Marxism she embraced while in Europe repeats the perverse liberation of Africans first set in motion by the slave trade that brought them to the Western Hemisphere. Thus, Agliè helps her arrive at the conclusion that Europe is to blame for the ideological confusion and political instability of the Third World. However, she does not fault European imperialism. In fact, she tacitly underwrites Casaubon's affirmation that she should be thankful that slave traders captured and sold her African ancestors, saving her from a life under apartheid (206). The Europe to be blamed for turmoil in developing nations is progressive Continental theory, "the smattering of historical materialism that made her forget" her past while abroad (194).

Amparo and Casaubon soon part company. Nonetheless, at the novel's conclusion he evokes her in memory. While awaiting Agliè's vengeance or forgiveness, he ponders the need to face one's fears monologically, or introspectively. Within this context he recollects the example of Amparo who, while returning to the home she purposely chose in one of the worst neighborhoods of

Manhattan, would challenge would-be sex offenders by offering her body to them before they had the chance to rape her. Even though Casaubon considers Amparo's behavior courageous, it is difficult not to be taken aback by this passage, set in relief from the rest of the text as its own laisse, and its reassertion of ancient male concepts of the woman as property. Amparo's willful consent to sexual violence raises the specter of a compulsion to repeat, on her part, of submission to acts of intimidation and physical conquest, invasions that fall somewhere between robbery and assault (see Brownmiller).

This rape fantasy is, of course, cut from the same voyeuristic cloth as Casaubon's morbose observations of Belbo and Lorenza: in the rape fantasy he mentally watches Amparo have sex with someone else. Moreover, this particular rêverie allows him to believe that while he was with Amparo, she somehow maintained her sexual purity (each time he saw her, it was like their first time [207]). Only after they part ways, does he remember that Amparo was the partner who habitually provoked illicit sensuality.[67] Therefore, he can blame her (and absolve himself) for what he believes, at a deep level, is an incestuous relationship, thus safeguarding the asexual purity of his union with Lia (see Benedict). In retrospect, he can perceive Lia as unadulterated, the virginal *pendant* to Amparo's vamp, in yet another mother-prostitute binomial. That is to say, he can imagine Amparo as seductress, available to all men, and Lia as a woman interested in sex only insofar as it is a means for giving a child to her husband.

Like the women, the "Diabolicals" are also undeveloped, superficial characters, willing dupes for the Garamond vanity press scam. They, too, serve to bring forward otherwise hidden aspects of Casaubon's personality. However, the most diabolical of them all, Agliè, does not fit their mould. He is lucid, cogent, not given to excess. In contrast to the "Diabolicals," he is not susceptible to "overtly paranoid textual interpretations" (Bondanella, 291). Agliè considers himself a true occultist, and sees himself as very distinct from his exhibitionistic, "puerile" (299, 622), "exoteric" cronies (459), whom he is quite capable of coldly observing with irony and skepticism (297, 374–75). He cynically exploits their credulity by aiding and abetting Garamond's swindle (338, 453). He always lucid, even when his life is threatened (622, 628–31), and succeeds in defrauding the deceitful publisher, Garamond.

Ultimately, Casaubon will undermine his own narrative, as we shall see presently. This gives the narrative the appearance of postmodern indeterminacy, but at no time does Casaubon approach a postmodern understanding of himself and his alters as perceiving subjects and objects in terms of time, history, change, and becoming (Best and Kellner 1997, 203). Rather, he embodies the quintessence of postmodern schizophrenia, or temporal dissociation, masterfully described by Jameson. Because the three alters are static characters (see Zamora), Casaubon "re-territorializes" (Deleuze and Guattari) with predictable facility: he docilely returns to the patriarchal mainstream, never remotely approaching the catharsis (Gramsci) or class consciousness to which the "de-territorialized" subject may accede. In other words, Casaubon never fashions an ethics out of indeterminacy.

To explain further, at the outset of the novel Belbo, Casaubon, and Diotallevi, constitute a single territorialized body, to use a term coined by Deleuze and Guattari. That is to say, the productive energies of all three are tamed and confined, desire is repressed. However, their involvement with The Plan catalyzes a process of deterritorialization whereby both material production and desire are "unchained from socially restricting forces." Their involvement with the series of occultist texts opens a door to escape from the role forced on them by their employer as economically exploited accomplices in the vanity press scheme. The creative rebellion inherent in creating The Plan raises the possibility that desire might "move outside of repressive social codes and restrictive psychic and spatial boundaries" (Best and Kellner 1991, 88). In the context of this novel, their "schizophrenia is not an illness or biological state, but a potentially emancipating psychic condition produced within capitalist social conditions, a product of absolute decoding" (Best and Kellner 1991, 90). However, after this brief rebellion, the three repent for their disobedience and willingly return to the normative fold.

At the novel's conclusion, Casaubon is not emotionally liberated, much less transformed. Rather, he has set aside all desires, and has allowed himself to be reterritorialized within normalizing capitalist institutions, casting to the wind any chance for emancipation from and/or subversion of the forms of subjectivity they authorize. In other words, Casaubon's identification with (an)other is not followed by a move beyond monadistic atomization toward socialization; instead, he regresses. The same holds true for his alters. Diotallevi abjures his her(m)etical belief in unlimited semiosis on his deathbed. He peacefully accepts his immanent death just as Belbo's submission to the Father prepares the stage for Casaubon's final surrender to Agliè. At the end of this novel, as was the case with *Il nome della rosa,* and despite Casaubon's attempts to undermine his own narrative, chaos is dominated and closure is attained.

By this I mean to say that *Il pendolo* is a very "readerly" work, to use Barthes's term. Although Casaubon lives an idiosyncratic, monologic reality[68]—he undermines the truth value of his tale by raising the possibility that his recollections are no more than those of a madman—his story does not "force the (willing) reader to construct his or her own paranoid mapping of . . . byzantine plots, . . . characters, and intricate historical events and forces" (Best 74–75), but instead moves in the opposite direction toward univocal meaning. By the end of the narration all loose ends have been tied down. Moreover, the reader is provided the illusion of a happy, life-affirming ending when Casaubon evokes his son while waiting for Agliè to arrive and pass judgment. The lad is Casaubon's vehicle for the felicitous self-perpetuation through the renewal of his genetic text; the heir who will vicariously set things aright for his father, who mentally associates the boy and Belbo's achievement of oedipal resolution through defiance of Agliè (659). More importantly, through the nascent son Casaubon can contemplate a vicarious return to the Oneness within the womb of the wife-mother, the site of the fullness of presence and of the fortunate state Eco wishes for both Model Reader and Model Author while strolling through his *Narrative Woods.*

Belbo, Casaubon believes, achieves such Oneness in defiance and in death (633). This understanding answers many enigmas. Prior to this partial resolution, Casaubon had gone to Paris for reasons he himself did not understand (602). Before departing he ruled out contacting Garamond and Inspector De Angelis, but never considered notifying the police. Nor did he consider renting a car and returning to consult with Lia: her deconstruction of The Plan had prompted his abandonment of her. After returning from Paris where he witnessed the ritual killings, Casaubon prefers solitude in Belbo's villa to Lia's company. At any rate, Casaubon's initial reaction to Belbo's phone call apprising him of the situation, consistent with Casaubon's personality, is to not get involved. Yet, he cannot help but wonder and fantasize about Belbo's predicament, casting it in the form of a suicide fantasy (602).

This flight of the imagination entices him to travel to the place where Belbo is held prisoner, the Conservatoire. Once there, instead of keeping vigil, Casaubon falls asleep. The mortal ceremony awakes him, and he overhears the "Diabolicals" say that he, Casaubon, also represents a threat to them (622). His spontaneous reaction is to leave his hiding place and mix in with the "Diabolicals," risking capture, which he later justifies by stating that he needed to better observe his friend (625). After the executions, he returns to his hotel and takes an overdose of sleeping pills (645). After he awakes, he repeatedly tells himself that he has "no guarantee whatsoever that what [he] remembered was true" (647). He avoids dealing with the issue of why he is not at peace with himself (679, 680), and, as the novel ends, he is the prey of the nightmarish "Diabolicals," metaphor of all his repressed demons, that is to say, of his own "flaw of faith," of his own unresolved oedipus and of the latent sexuality that informs The Plan.

As for The Plan, as Guglielmo confesses at the end of *Il nome della Rosa,* "there was no plot . . . And I discovered it by mistake" (494). In other words, while The Plan may be a mere fantasy for Lia, it is reality for Casaubon. This enigma is placed by Eco, a master of riddles and puzzles, inside a second, at the level of literary device or narrative strategy. As we have noted, at no point does Casaubon set his story to paper. What we read all transpires in his mind; the culmination of *Il pendolo* is presented as the sum of Casaubon's reading of a computer text written by Belbo and Casaubon's interior musings. In other words, Casaubon frames a text already objectified or framed by Belbo, who had stored The Plan in Abulafia as the apocryphal memoirs of someone else (577).

In turn, Casaubon's interior monologue is reported/framed by an empirical author who feigns death and hides behind a Model Author, who as we have seen is a projection of the empirical reader. In fact, as theorized by John Barth, the frame-tale strategy is a means at the disposal of authors who wish to distance themselves from their texts. That is to say, the act of producing a text necessitates the creation of a narrating persona, which according to Barth is an extension of the author's personality. Once the author's life has been so "fictionalized," the author uses the persona to distance herself from, or "frame," the narrative. Readers then "frame" both text and author by "reading/re-narrating" the work. As a result, both the author and the work are extensions of the reader's personality. Readers are then framed/fictionalized by acquaintances who read/recount their lives. Hence, for Barth, the inherent fictionality of the author's—and by extension everyone else's—life: life is fiction, and fiction is life (209).

This posture dovetails with the "postmodern attitude" to which Eco subscribes. For Eco, in postmodernity life is supplanted by literature through the subordination of the real events referred by the narrative to the act of narration (Eco 1983b, 529). This purposive act of concealment, when accepted by a Model Reader as a condition for reading, creates the illusion of the writer who communicates without affective involvement. Any emotion catalyzed by the text is entirely the reader's: whatever the author may have felt while writing is negated and denied. Eco claims that he attains "the essence of the postmodern" when he embeds Belbo's tale within Casaubon's story (Stauder 1989, 4). While this distancing might appear to give an objective quality to Belbo's story, we must remember that the *emboîtement* within the frame-tale does not go beyond the retrieval of computer files that bring to the fore, verbatim, Belbo's highly subjective first-person narrative. Thus, the retelling of Belbo's tale serves to create a false omniscience that aims to comfort the reader while surreptitiously reasserting the empirical narrator's authority over the text. This narrative strategy dovetails perfectly with a marketing strategy calculated to sell a literary product. To seduce, Eco flatters and amuses his reader, a stance he has defended in his theoretical writings.[69] Once caught in the web, the Model Reader creates and then identifies with the Model Author, and duplicates Casaubon's submission of the invisible yet determining paternalism of the Author of the Text.

"OF ME I SING": *L'ISOLA DEL GIORNO PRIMA*

Eco's third novel, *L'isola del giorno prima* [*The Island of the Day Before*] (Eco 1994a), contains numerous ludic, metafictional self-references to the craft of writing. As was the case with *Il nome della rosa*, the strategy of a found manuscript is utilized, and again the identity of the redactor remains unknown. A mystery also surrounds the protagonist, Roberto de la Griva, who, like Adso da Melk, may be a historically verifiable character, or pure fiction. This infuses Roberto's story with doubt, since, as Bouchard has pointed out, it "is dispersed in several manuscripts, and is often incoherent and full of gaps, the narrator is well aware that 'all must be based on conjecture'" (358). More importantly, the narrating voice creates a story even though he is not capable of telling "precisely how the manuscripts of Roberto were transmitted nor where the events in question occur" (358).

Roberto's texts reflect the same oedipal tension characteristic of Eco's other fictions. In addition, the narrative device is again a fictionalized (auto)biography; and again there is a frame-tale: Roberto's biography is purportedly told reported by a third party, the narrating voice who pieces together a narrative from Roberto's letters, love poems, and unfinished novel. This distancing of the narrating voice from the main character, with respect to Eco's earlier novels, endows the narrating voice with God-like power over his creation, the narration.

Paradoxically, while the narrating voice acknowledges his role in constructing Roberto's story, he is disinclined from taking responsibility for the text. He attempts to avoid accountability by informing the reader at the outset that his work was compiled from a composite of papers miraculously recovered from an abandoned boat that caught fire centuries ago in the middle of the South Pacific. He then seeks recourse in postmodern uncertainty and play, repeatedly and explicitly underscoring his own lack of omniscience, which necessitates his filling the blanks in Roberto's story with conjecture.[70] In other words, the narrating voice intentionally places himself in the contradictory position of undermining the truth value of his tale in order to absolve himself of responsibility for it while at the same time asserting his right to narrate through reiterated references to his own expertise as a storyteller, and implicitly reaffirming his authority over the text by vaunting the plausibility of his conjectures.

The narrator reinforces this paradox by repeatedly undermining all distinctions between art and reality with metafictional musings that equate the craft of writing and divine Creation. Indeed, his representation of God reflects perfectly his self-image as narrator. "God . . . evidently knows how to manage different times and different stories, like a Narrator who writes different novels, all with the same characters, but having different events befall them in each different story" (248). Like the narrator, Roberto has "taken from the novelists of his century the practice of telling so many stories contemporaneously at the same time that it is difficult to keep them all in order" (392). However, Roberto cannot aspire to God-like status: he spends the entire novel overwhelmed by life's vicissitudes. Unable to redact his own tale, Roberto remains forever mired in his story, the first-person narrator of unpublished manuscripts destined for oblivion until 'saved' for posterity and objectified by the narrator.

By placing in evidence Roberto's ineptitude, the narrating voice creates a bond of complicity between himself and his Model Readers, who must acknowledge the skillful and entertaining way in which an incompetent Roberto's story has been packaged. Moreover, when the narrator casts in relief his superiority over his subject—through ironic, metafictional commentary (on Roberto's lot, and on the condition of narrator)—Model Readers accept the credibility of the narrator's assumptions as a premise for reading.

When the Model Reader identifies with the perspectives of the narrating voice Roberto's idiosyncratic, first-person subjectivity is transcended. Once this has taken place, Model Readers can see Roberto's tale of lost Order from the same objectified—not omniscient—vantage of the narrator. In this way the narrating voice structures chaos, showing himself to be more God-like than God, who is responsible for Roberto's untoward fate, and, by extension, for the vicissitudes of the life of the Model Reader. When Roberto passively accepts the fate meted out to him by the Transcendental Father, he provides the reader, who identifies with the object of narration, with a template for the sort of submission to a higher authority exacted by the narrating voice over his literary creations. Indeed, Roberto is grateful that Fate forced him to withdraw from the world so that he might better contemplate life's Great Mysteries: "This is why he had been thrown on the *Daphne*, Roberto told himself. Because only in that restful hermitage would he have had the ease to reflect on the only question that frees us from all apprehension regarding non-being, giving himself up to the wonder of being" (433).

Fortunately, the Model Reader's lay God, that is to say the narrator, sets aright what the metaphysical God has cast asunder. As the narrator tells the reader: "in real life things happen because they happen; only in the Land of Novels do things seem to happen for a reason or providence" (470). Thus, the narrator-*cum*-Model Author restores the reader's world to manageable, human dimensions and provides overwhelmed Model Readers the structure and closure they ardently desire. Moreover, once the narrator has assumed these metaphysical proportions, he can assuage his readers greatest fear, that of our mortality. The narrator does so by first reminding his readers that he has perpetuated himself in time through his text (he writes: "when authors finally decide to die, Novels often write themselves, and go where they want" [446]). Then, he removes from consciousness the question of what follows biological death by setting aside consideration of the state of having been—the eternity of no-longer-being—in favor of a meditation on nothingness, that is to say his "apprehension regarding [the epochs] of non-being" that precede birth: "That which assails the philosopher is not the naturalness of the end; it is the mystery of the beginning. We cannot be interested in the eternity that will follow us, but we cannot subtract ourselves from the terrible question of what eternity preceded us: the eternity of matter or the eternity of God" (433).

This statement provides rare opportunity for observing what the narrating voice would conceal: that which he has introjected prior to projecting, in transmogrified form, onto his protagonist: an insecurity that prevents contemplation of the future and makes incumbent a search through the past for a Foundation for thought.

The narrating voice of *L'isola del giorno prima*, in telling Roberto's story, tells of himself.[71] And, the narrator's lack of omniscience absolves him from delving into aspects of Roberto's character that the narrator would prefer leave unexamined: writing is a retreat into an internal world of literary fantasy that shelters all authorial *rêveries* from reality testing. This fantasy world can flourish externally because kindred spirits, or Model Readers, identify with the voice's dramatizations.

At this point, I must open a brief parenthesis and make clear that I have no intention of asserting that works of literature can or should be read as manifestations of the return of the repressed of the empirical author. Readers may not apply the psychoanalytic method to writers about whom there is always much we cannot know with certainty, and who are refractory to the crucial element of the psychoanalytic process, transference. Nonetheless, following Richard Sterba's reading of Sigmund Freud we may say that artists recycle *rêveries,* impersonalizing them enough so as to be acceptable to others, while linking to the representations of unconscious fantasies a quantity of pleasure sufficient to outweigh the repressions of their audience. Indeed, the practice of art is always to some extent "an activity whose aim is to assuage unappeased wishes" for both the artist and the person who enjoys it, and a means of reconciling conflicting forces of desire and prohibition (Sterba, "The Problem of Art in Freud's Writings" 257, 258). Therefore, we may legitimately ask how the artist overcomes the conscious refusal of kindred spirits to participate in his individual fantasies. Eco accomplishes this by distancing himself from the narration through various levels of *emboîtement,* by creating narrating voices who allow the reader to return to a very early phase of psychic development, that of "the omnipotence of thought" (265), in which "the individual still looks upon himself as omnipotent because wishes are experienced at this period as if their fulfillment in reality were achieved by the mere act of wishing" (265).

In any event, and to close the parenthesis, Model Readers identify with narrating voices who, we may say following Anna Freud, surrender their instinctual impulses to their protagonists. For example, the voice of *L'isola* makes manifest through the protagonist the introjected identity of the paternal authorities to whom he was exposed: Roberto identifies with the Father, internalizes paternal criticisms of his behavior, and incorporates them into his superego (Anna Freud 1966, 116). After projecting prohibited impulses onto Roberto, the narrating voice can watch with interest and pleasure a game in which he has no stake himself, while his desires are satisfied vicariously by his protagonist. In other words, the narrating voice avoids unpleasant self-criticism by assigning to Roberto what the narrating voice recognizes about himself as blameworthy: acknowledgment of someone else's wrongdoing substitutes for guilt and self-reprobation. Furthermore, the voice's indulgence toward Roberto is intended primarily to reflect back onto himself (Anna Freud 1966, 119). At a higher level of *emboîtement,* the same can be said of those readers who identify with the narrating voice.[72]

Model Readers of *L'isola* identify with a pseudo-reality where life's travails are explained and given meaning. Then, they feel profound satisfaction when thought (the narration of that pseudo-reality) structures chaos and suppresses doubt. When the voice alludes to, but effectively excludes from the narration the re-creation of Roberto's childhood, he forestalls examination and understanding of the psychic forces at work in himself, and of how instinctual forces have broken free from repression and discharged themselves in his text.[73] Then, the narrative distancing effected through the device of the found manuscript conceals and precludes consideration of endopsychic processes at work within the text with which the Model Reader identifies.

For this reason, the narrator's justification for writing, that is to say for reconstructing Roberto's life, is of fundamental importance. However, the narrator never answers his own question: he asks, but fails to explain why Roberto's story is relevant to himself and his modern-day reader, or why he believes it should be shared (470). Instead, the question the narrator repeatedly asks is always "where to begin?" (9). The question he never asks is why begin?

This notwithstanding, the narrating voice takes pains to underscore the historical plausibility of his tale (see 227). He is also careful in the final chapter to convince the reader that Roberto's story may have a basis in historical fact and to explain how a manuscript may have been recovered from the remains of the *Daphne*. However, it would seem that he does so to deflect his and the reader's attention away from his own deep reasons for writing and toward metafictional issues. Model Readers agree with the voice that *L'isola del giorno prima* is about Roberto and his recovered papers (466), and that the narrator is extraneous to the events he reports.

Thus, the narrator and the Model Reader accept Roberto's evasion from topics related to his childhood that would cause him anxiety, particularly his parents' relationship with Roberto's Carmelite tutor. Furthermore, the compact between narrating voice and Model Reader is contingent on their silent accord that the blanks in the proxy-protagonist's story may be filled in with the narrator's wish-fulfillment and conjecture: "Roberto allows us to understand very little about the sixteen years lived before the summer of 1630. He mentions episodes from his past only when he believes they shed light on some connection with his present situation on the *Daphne,* and so the chronicler of his chronicle must spy between the lines of what he wrote" (22). This apparent redundancy—chronicler of his chronicle—is noteworthy because neither Roberto's letters nor the text of *L'isola* is a chronicle. They are narratives that reorder, give hierarchy to, and offer interpretations of events. Had Roberto simply kept a chronicle, his laconic treatment of his youth might have been expected. However, his written record of time spent shipwrecked is very much a *recherche* into his past. Therefore, his indisposition to discussing childhood, puberty, and adolescence would indicate ambivalence toward those with whom he was closest, his parents especially. This condition allows kindred spirits, the anonymous narrating voice and the Model Reader, to identify with Roberto.

My own critical—not Model—reading of the narrator's "chronicle" reveals that Roberto's father was a strict disciplinarian. Roberto saw disobedient subordinates beaten (30). Even though paternal indulgence excluded real thrashings, Roberto was subjected to a rigorous military training (48), and so he took his father's threats of corporal punishment very seriously (31). Furthermore, the text makes no mention of any real bonding between father and son, and the distance between them is increased by the father's failure to consistently address his son in a single language of affect. That is to say, the father was multilingual and adapted his speech to contingency. He "spoke French to his wife, in dialect to the peasants, and in Italian with foreigners. With Roberto he expressed himself in different ways depending on whether he was teaching his son to fence, or going on horseback through the fields cursing the birds that were ruining the harvest" (22). Roberto's story, including the young man's letters to his French beloved, is reported in the language of the anonymous narrator, present-day Italian (11), as are the father's conversations with French interlocutors (71). Parenthetically, it is interesting to note—we will return to this topic further on—that no conversations between Roberto and his Francophone mother are directly recorded. In any event, while the narrator presents as fact his own wish that Roberto's father had felt warmth for his son, this hypothesis is not corroborated by the tale. Indeed, the reader is told that father communicated with his son very little, using with Roberto "the taciturn coarseness characteristic of the men of those lands" (24).

When Roberto is sixteen he witnesses his father's heroic death in battle. The "elder Pozzo" had put himself in harm's way to defend his son, who was stunned by the ferocity of combat (48).

Roberto's paralysis under fire is a form of passive aggression against a father who had imposed a rigorous code of chivalric honor to Roberto as an eight-year-old boy (26).[74] Roberto will avenge himself, but is guilty about the result: the loss of his father disorients Roberto, who "finds himself suspended between sky and sea" (50). In recompense, he would like to prove himself his father's worthy heir by emulating the courage demonstrated by his elder under fire (71), but Roberto is of insufficient mettle: "When everyone complimented [Roberto] on his father's heroism, he would have liked to have mourned with pride. Instead he sobbed." Roberto is then overtaken by the thought of his father's disapproval of such shows of weakness. He remembers at this point "that his father had taught him that a gentleman must learn to support with dry eye adverse fortune." But he is quickly liberated by the awareness he was now an orphan, and therefore his father "could no longer demand an explanation." Over time he learns to permit himself an additional weakness, that of self-commiseration: "it is useless to habituate oneself to the loss of a father, because it cannot happen a second time. You so might as well leave the wound open" (72).

Roberto suffers his father's death egoistically, and then feels remorse for not having properly observed the socially prescribed period of mourning (82). Just as Adso prays for a haughty Guglielmo in *Il nome della rosa* (501), Roberto prays for the soul of a father who may have died outside the state of grace. This allows the narrating voice to project onto Roberto a "filial piety" for the martyred father who is thus superseded in the most anodyne of ways by his son (50, 82).

After the death of his father, Roberto becomes "the legitimate lord of La Griva, heir to the family name and fortune" and—thanks to his orphan status—exempt from further military duty (73). Nonetheless, he follows social convention and begs his superior officer to be allowed to take part in the combat, knowing in advance that "this would not be granted to him" (136). Unable to follow in his father's footsteps, he surpasses his parent through cowardice which he camouflages as intelligence. Roberto quickly learns to live a life of compromise: while he avers that he would love to emulate his father, he does not want to die. He learns to avoid not only the sort of heroic, yet futile combat that cost his father his life (87), but all confrontations, particularly with his surrogate paternal figure, the Jesuit Father Caspar, with whom Roberto is shipwrecked, as we shall see.

After the death of Roberto's father, the philosopher Saint Savin, half a generation older than Roberto (74), takes the young man under his wing. In a manner reminiscent of Belbo's mentorship of Casaubon in *Il pendolo di Foucault*, this 'older brother' teaches Roberto to respect the status quo (76), to shun valor and embrace prudence (103, 125). Then, Saint Savin's death at the hands of a priest offended by the former's atheism underscores the hypocrisy that masks and justifies all grand causes (133). Indeed, rather than learn to assert himself as master of his own destiny, Roberto understands the importance of passively following his fate.[75]

Similarly, all Eco's protagonists avoid conflict at decisive junctures in their lives. Jacopo Belbo is able to sidestep the fundamental life choice forced by World War II on those only a few years older than he. Then he spends his life longing for the order lost when a single-party dictatorship was replaced by the ambiguity and chaos of a multiparty Resistance and Republic. His younger charge, Casaubon, also resents political upheaval, refutes all forms of activism, and escapes participation in the student revolts of his Italian contemporaries. Both Adso da Melk and Baudolino, in the eponymous novel by Eco, are sent away from home just as they enter adolescence, never to confront paternal authority. Rather than challenge power, they learn to acquiesce. Both believe that if they obey, they will inherit what Father owns. Baudolino dedicates his adult life to legitimizing his place in the feudal hierarchy, while Adso comes to consider his place at the bottom of the Benedictine pecking order a privilege, because it initiated him into the power structure he later inherits. Roberto, too, as stated by the narrator in the epigraph, is "proud of his humiliations" (5, 8–9) because they confirm his place in the social order.

Eco's protagonists do not challenge patriarchy because they cannot tolerate uncertainty and disorder. Therefore, they structure their lives in such a way as to meet their need to be in a world where people comply with authority. They convince themselves they are "men of peace," a euphemism for succumbing to the power they hope to inherit. Roberto desires the riches and authority associated with possession of what belongs to his father: the mother imago, the family name, and patrimony (376). Once the death of his father permits him to take possession of this inheritance, guilt for his passive killing of his father causes him to turn his back on his legacy, abandoning mother and the family estate. He does so because, to borrow Sigmund Freud's phrase, he is made "criminal from a sense of guilt" (Sigmund Freud, "Some Character Types"). In other words, he cannot accept his successful killing of his father, which gave him everything he desired: the family name and fortune, and Mother.

Roberto's relationship with Father Caspar replicates the pattern of passive killing of Roberto's father. While marooned together on the *Daphne*, the Jesuit becomes for Roberto a paternal figure and the incarnation of power (253). Roberto allows the older man to expound theories Roberto knows are outdated because "Roberto had learned well enough the ways of the world to know that one must give the appearance of assenting" (253). At the same time, he amuses himself by tormenting Caspar, provoking his elder into explaining concepts and ideas that Roberto easily rebuts by utilizing "the entire repertory of arguments he had heard in the feasts of men the Jesuit considered, if not emissaries of Satan, at the least boozers and gluttons who had transformed the tavern into their own Lyceum" (277).

Nonetheless, Roberto is forced to admit to himself that some of Caspar's physical theories were sound, because the Jesuit was successfully teaching Roberto to swim, a skill that would enable Roberto to save his own life, and that of his counselor. However, Roberto refrains from taking any initiative, limiting his actions to passively carrying out Caspar's instructions (300–2; 306). In fact, all efforts are destined to fail, despite Caspar's acumen, because Roberto's "modesty" prevents him from undressing before another man, and the weight of his clothes precludes his staying afloat (332). Moreover, because Roberto follows Caspar's instructions to the letter, all failures are attributed to the master. So the older man, overcome by frustration, goes into the water himself, and dies trying to accomplish what he believes Roberto cannot learn to do. Thus, Roberto, whose ineptitude in combat was the cause of his father's death, also causes Caspar's demise.

Once Caspar has disappeared under the sea, Roberto doffs his clothes, goes in the water, and swims. The narrator depicts Roberto's moment of his success in the following manner: "With a yell of exultation he had arrived at the bowsprit, he had grabbed onto the prow, and had arrived at the Jacob's ladder—and may Jacob and all the Holy Patriarchs of the Holy Scriptures be blessed by the Lord, God of the Armies" (362).

This passage is of particular interest because the use of free indirect discourse makes the exclamation attributable not to Roberto, but to the narrating voice. Whether or not Roberto thanks God for his success is not ascertainable; rather, the wish that the God of the Heavenly Armies bless Roberto and the Holy Patriarchs is filtered through the voice of the narrator who expresses the belief that Roberto deserves this blessing because he obeyed the instructions bequeathed him by his deceased father figure, and succeeded in swimming. The narrator insists on using Father Caspar's term, "Jacob's ladder," to refer to the anchor chain (6), thus perpetuating the commemoration of the father of the twelve Patriarchs of *Genesis*. In so doing, the narrating voice follows Roberto in extolling the God who punishes those who rebel against patriarchal authority.[76] In this way the narrator—whose story accepts without question Roberto's concealment of the passive methods the young man used to rid himself of both his fathers—reveals his belief that the young man is to be praised for refraining from open rebellion, and for twice waiting for a Father to die—a process Roberto was adroit at hurrying along—before striking out on his own.[77]

In this way Roberto's ambivalence toward both paternal figures and his unresolved oedipal issues come clearly to the fore. In fact, Roberto demonstrates affection for the Jesuit only after the latter has vanished under the sea, never to return: "In the few days since he had fled, [*sfuggito*] Father Caspar had become for him friend, brother, family and fatherland. Now [Roberto] realized that he was once again unpaired [*scompagnato*] and lonely [*romito*]." (315–16). The narrator also reports that Roberto is less concerned with the demise of his friend than with his own "refound solitude." It must be noted that again Roberto's state of mind is filtered through the narrator, whose use of free indirect discourse indicates a mimesis of vision between the narrator and that of his protagonist. In this way the narrator appropriates Roberto's sentiment that Caspar's attempt to reach the island and death are tantamount to an abandoning, even though this is clearly not the case. The use of free indirect discourse also allows the narrator to make his own—while distancing himself from—

the seeming redundancy of "scompagnato" and "romito." It also allows the narrator to project ambivalence toward paternal figures onto Roberto, who resents his fathers and is annoyed by their domineering ways, but enjoys living in idyllic isolation with them.

While Caspar is alive Roberto has cause to take exception to the only person who had ever read—and without Roberto's consent—the secret confessions hidden in the love letters a timid Roberto had not intended to share with anyone, not even their addressees (234). As a lad Roberto felt similarly violated by his father's destruction of all illusions surrounding the mother's sexual purity. To explain, as an adult Roberto remembers seeing a pained expression on his mother's face—"as if [his father] had awakened in her an already placated anxiety"—whenever the elder Pozzo would pick up the five-year-old Roberto, his only child, and call him his firstborn (24). It does not occur to Robert that the apparent pleonasm might be a wish for additional offspring; instead, it causes him to suspect the existence of an illegitimate, older brother: "Roberto was at first too little, then too modest, to ask himself if he and this brother shared a father or a mother (and in both cases the shadow of an ancient and unforgivable offence would have fallen on one of his parents)" (24). Roberto allows both parents to share the blame for this "unforgivable sin," even though this "expression of paternal joy" indicates that if an older sibling had been born out of wedlock, it was undoubtedly the mother's progeny. At the same time, Roberto represses awareness that his mother harbored a sensual nature she kept hidden from him, along with the suspicion that she might have even engaged in illicit sex. So when the thought that an illegitimate older brother sired by someone other than the elder La Griva might exist becomes a conviction, Roberto is tormented by not knowing which of her children his mother loves more. Although he is comforted by the bastardization of the brother, Roberto nonetheless needs to assign to Ferrante guilt for all the pranks Roberto commits (25).

As a lad, feelings of loneliness and exclusion had made Roberto susceptible to the overriding influence of his own thoughts (51); he "passed his time without friends" and frequently lost in fantasy. The privilege of being the young lord of the manor further isolated Roberto from other children. He had gone off with his father to war, hoping to: "give life to his chivalrous dreams, which had been fostered by poems he had read as a child: to be of noble blood and to finally have a sword at his side meant becoming a knight in shining armor who risked his life for his king or to save a damsel" (51). So when Roberto takes pride in his humiliations, renouncing sexual fulfillment and accepting his isolation on the *Daphne*, he gains, as recompense, tremendous narcissistic gratification in doing penance not only for his own sins of lust and parricide, but also for those of his father, who may have died outside the state of grace. At the same time, he makes no mention of atoning for the "unforgivable"—because unspeakable—"sin" against the family name just mentioned, his mother's possible extra- or premarital affair.

The removal from thought of the possibility of un-avenged family honor is of a piece with Roberto's family romance, a means for regulating self-esteem and for defending against reality. It allows Roberto to unconsciously split the parents with whom he identifies, that is to say, he retains their preferable aspects and rejects their disillusioning ones. He imagines them perfect and redirects his disenchantment with them onto an imaginary, illegitimate half-brother, Ferrante.[78] In other words, he represses the suspicion that Ferrante is the fruit of the mother's secret love affair with the Carmelite mentor.[79]

Then, the death of the biological father lifts all inhibitions of Roberto's love strivings. Roberto has no amorous interest prior to the death of the "elder Pozzo," which occurs when Roberto is sixteen years old (80). Shortly thereafter he exhibits a behavior more characteristic of those enthralled in the first great infatuation of their pubescent years. Roberto falls in love with a peasant, his social inferior, whom he is ashamed to identify to Saint Savin. Like the nameless love interest of *Il nome della rosa* she is both virgin and vamp: "that virginal figure, that quintessence of fertile beauty and of martial fury, together with the suspicion of immodesty . . . had made her precious to him, and had sparked his senses" (Eco 1994a, 109)." When Roberto's shyness makes the woman who may or may not be the "whore of the French army" unapproachable, he idealizes her. He dares not advance toward her, but loves Anna Maria or Francesca (her name is of no great importance to Roberto [126]) passionately, but from afar, writing letters he will never send, and taking pleasure in an erotic of denial. In the words of the narrator, "His first imprecise love convinced [Roberto] for ever that the object of love resides in distance, and I believe that this experience marked his entire destiny as a lover" (118). This monologic, fantasy relationship soon ends with a suggestion of impotence. When Roberto, after rising from his sickbed, chances to see the object of his love ravished by the plague, the narrator declares "Love becomes intellectual only when the body desires and the desire is violated. If the body is feeble and unable to desire, love's intellectual aspect vanishes. Roberto discovered that he was weak and unable to love" (Eco 1994, 126).[80]

Indeed, "this experience marked [Roberto's] entire destiny as a lover." Roberto will love only once more, and will repeat the same pattern of impotence masked as courtly love, defined by separation, suffering, and refusal of fulfillment. Roberto's infirmity precludes his demanding reciprocity in love; he learns to derive sensual pleasure from his asceticism. When Roberto finally falls in love, he suppresses his instincts and creates a subliminal image of the woman. His love is pure, without need of reciprocation, because he does not love in her what he loves in himself. Rather, he defines "true love," as did Guglielmo da Baskerville, as "wishing the loved one well" (Eco 1980, 399). Later, Roberto will find consolation in his solitude, where he cannot be forced to confront his own sensuality and that of his idealized love: "it is better to isolate oneself at sea, where he could possess his loved one in the only way allowed him" (183). Again, as was the case with Eco's first novel, the narration underwrites the superiority of unrequited, ascetic love over gratification of instinct: "perfect love is not in being loved, but in being a Lover" (Eco 1980, 183).

Roberto's silent hostility toward his mother is made evident by his failure to write to her to inform her of the death of his father. He assumes that those compatriots who had already returned home would have told her: "He asked himself if he should not be close to her at that time, but no longer understood what his responsibilities were" (136). The mother-son relationship is further obscured by the fact that she was not conversant in the local languages young Roberto spoke daily. Roberto eventually returns home after the death of his father, but his papers "allow us to perceive [*intravedere*] very little about the years that passed between his return to La Griva and his entrance in Parisian society. One can cull from a few scattered allusions that he stayed on until he was almost twenty years old to assist his mother, discussing half-heartedly with the stewards of plantings and harvests. The minute his mother followed her husband into the tomb, Roberto realized he was estranged from that world. He must have entrusted the estate to a relative, assuring himself of a healthy income, and traveled around the world" (144).

After the mother's death, he spends two years in Southern France before moving to Paris, and—after living there for several years—meets and falls in love with "La Signora" (144, 148). The reader never learns with certainty the identity of the object of Roberto's affections (149–50); but one thing is certain: his love remains unrequited. Roberto's love letters to La Signora—as is the case with all his other writings—are not attempts at establishing dialogue with a reader. Some letters are not signed, while the others remain unsent (150). In fact, Lilia, or "La Signora," is much more the product of Roberto's imagination, of his outward projection of an internal reality,[81] than anything that may or may not have existed in the flesh.[82]

Roberto's papers say almost nothing about the mother who may have given birth outside the bonds of matrimony; to avoid anxiety he remains silent. Fear of the mother is deflected to the domineering father, who, as we have seen, is never challenged by his son, and superseded only through trepidation disguised as cunning. Yet, there is cause to suspect that Roberto's lesser apprehension of the father displaces that for the mother, who is much more essential to the continuance of his life.[83] In *Il nome della rosa* and in *Il pendolo di Foucault* ambivalent feelings for the mother cause Eco's protagonists to be silent in her regard. In *L'isola del giorno prima* Mother figures, but ever so slightly, in the narrator's evocations of infancy and childhood; Baudolino, as we shall see, will restore her partially to consciousness.[84] In any case, anxiety associated with Mother pushes Roberto to radically internalize the love experience and precludes his communicating with adult love objects.

In other words, Roberto compacts within the mother imago visions of both goodness and of evil; she is a pure woman who offers love to other men, but not to him. Similarly, his love interests are women he must degrade before he can idealize them by denying their sexual nature. As an adult Roberto loves women he does not desire, because he cannot love the woman he desires, Mother. He represses incestuous wishes by psychically debasing the love object, either by loving a woman of an inferior social class,[85] or by overevaluating one who is his social equal. By splitting the mother imago into virgin and vamp, he can repress desire for the original object and substitute objects that are not able to bring the sexual instinct to full satisfaction. When he refuses fulfillment and sublimates he can take pride in his acceptance of the insurmountable difficulties placed in the way of libidinal temptation.

Roberto's erotic of denial allows him to reunify his cosmos. Like Mother, all women can be chaste and belong to more than one man. So, mom and dad are good; and evil, which exists only in the ghost of the half-brother Ferrante, can be exorcised for Roberto by the narrator who fits everything into a grand scheme that justifies and gives resolution to Roberto's sufferings and deprivations. And when this happens, all the fears of the Model Reader—who participates vicariously in Roberto's conflicts—are laid to rest.

For all this to happen, Roberto must remove from consciousness any interrogation of his parents' triangular relationship with his Carmelite tutor "who, it was said, had traveled in the East, where—the mother mumbled while making the Sign of the Cross—people insinuated he had become a Moslem" (23). The narrator avers that "only one thing is known about the Carmelite" (23): during one of the monk's stays at La Griva, he exposed Roberto to the *unguentum armarium*, or powder of sympathy, the substance that played an important role in Roberto's adult peregrinations. However, this assertion is belied in the final chapter, when the narrator reports that while considering the possibility of an Intruder on the *Daphne*, Roberto looked skyward and "remembered how at La Griva, when the decrepit family chapel had collapsed, that his Carmelite preceptor who had lived in the Orient advised reconstructing that small oratory in the Byzantine style, round with a central cupola, a style that had absolutely no precedent in the Monferrato region. *But* the elder Pozzo did not want to stick his nose into affairs of art and of religion, and had listened to the advice of that holy man" (470; my emphasis).

This passage raises several unanswered questions regarding the Carmelite's presence and influence within Roberto's family. The most apparent regards what seems to be a solecism: the narrator's use of the conjunction "but"—which indicates contrast—when 'and' would appear to be more appropriate. In other words, 'and' would have suggested the father's decision was the direct consequence of the Carmelite's proposal. On the other hand, "but" implies an ellipsis in the narration because it counterposes one thought against another that is not formally stated. This raises the question of who objected to the Carmelite's suggestion and was overruled by the father. A legitimate assumption is that this unnamed presence is the same person who was able to maintain in her employ a religious tutor suspected of heresy (even though the narration leaves her motive for doing so equally vague), precisely because of the father's lack of expertise and interest in religious matters.

In any case, the narrator does not question the dynamics of the relationship between these three adults and the effects of their interaction on young Roberto, even though the metaphysical contemplations that define Roberto's adult life were determined by the Carmelite's influence. Indeed, the narrator's silence in the monk's regard is deafening.[86]

When, at novel's conclusion, Roberto once again contemplates the way in which "the world articulated itself in "uneasy architectures" [*stranite archittetture*] (51) and remembers the monk, it occurs to him that "the sky of the Antipodes" resembles the starry firmament painted on the La Griva oratory, a metaphor for Roberto's family. He also recollects that as a child he imagined that the *universo mondo*—the known world and heavens—was as fixed and unchanging as the vault on which it was depicted. But then it occurs to him that "At Casale, in the middle of a plain, he had understood that the sky was vaster than he thought, but Father Emanuel convinced him to think of the stars as concepts, rather than look at what was observable" (471). Once again, the critical reader is struck by the eccentric use of the conjunction "but," where 'and' might have been expected, which raises the question of what has been removed from the narration. One may surmise that the elision makes implicit reference to a conflict—between the speculations of Emanuel and the empiricisms of the father, who taught Roberto to farm and hunt based on a close acquaintance with the observable natural world—that has been repressed from the thought process.

In any event, whatever is suppressed within the ellipsis is at the root of Roberto's mental turmoil, whose initial manifestation coincides with the series of traumata associated with the shock of combat: "In a brief period of time Roberto had lost his father, his beloved, his [sexual] health, his friend [Saint Savin], and perhaps the war (133). However, Saint Savin had already deprived Roberto of the certainty that the war in which his father so deeply believed was endowed with any real meaning or political consequence, and in so doing convinced Roberto that what is empirically observable never coincides with real substance. Moreover, repressed from this list of Roberto's losses is that of the transcendental father (see 58), the ultimate source of all certainty. In the words of the narrator: "From the way he speaks of it on the *Daphne,* I contend that at Casale, while he was losing his father and himself in a war loaded with and bereft of meaning, Roberto learned how to see the world [*l'universo mondo*] as an unstable web of enigmas, behind which there was no Author. Or, if there were, it seemed lost in the multiplication of the perspectives from which it could be seen" (137). Resistance to this realization catalyzes Roberto's search for a *"punto fijo,"* a fixed point that is geophysical but also metaphysical. Geographically, his quest takes him to the Antipodes; mentally it pulls him into a state in which he is unable to distinguish between past, present, and future,[87] and between fact and fantasy.[88]

The use of irony in depicting Roberto's plight allows the narrator to lead his Model Readers—who observe Roberto exclusively through the narrator's eyes—into identifying with the narrating voice's detached and objective, but admittedly not omniscient, point of view. Once this has been put into effect, the empirical author, through the interposed narrating voice, can make his case to the reader in favor of pragmatic semiotic practice at the expense of idiosyncratic hermeticism, the result of Roberto's extreme solitude (see 337 and also 15). According to Bouchard, the narrator "obtrusively comments on the various practitioners of semiosic drifts, while appearing to engage in something of a Pragmatic model of interpretation" (358).[89]

While this is indeed the case, it is also important to stress that when we look beyond the narrator's explicit intentions we see that he utilizes a screening device, one that encourages psychological readings of Roberto as a means of diverting attention from himself. Indeed, the "shames and fears" (78) that motivate the creation of Ferrante are explained in oedipal terms by Saint Savin, who he tells the young man: "Perhaps you did not love your father as much as you believe; you were afraid of the severity with which he pushed you to be virtuous, and you attributed a guilt [una colpa], to then punish him not with your guilts, but with someone else's guilts" (79). In other words, by anticipating questions and responses concerning the mental state of the object of narration—Roberto—the narrator discourages the Model Reader from asking why the subject of narration—the narrating voice—projects these issues onto the protagonist.

As is the case with all Eco's protagonists, Roberto is not capable of living with ambiguity; he needs to obey someone. But when his search for a lost transcendental foundation leads him to relive in his mind the clash of world views that engaged his father and Father Emanuel—and he finds that he must side against his father—Roberto retreats into an hermetic isolation that is first physical, and then linguistic. However, it must be noted that for Roberto language is never a means of affirmation or self-expression—whence his refusal of epistolary exchange with his beloveds. Instead, it is the vehicle for his passive adaptation to and reconciliation with the conflicting polyglossia of his elders. Then, his psychosis is foreshadowed when the narrator points out the linguistic disorientation of a subject no longer capable of "conjugat[ing] verbs as the God of the Italians commands" (244), that is to say, of obeying an established order. Thus, if the origin of Roberto's infirmity is found in the conflict for the mother between his biological father and Father Emanuel, it culminates when the empirical science of the surrogate father Caspar fails to lead him to back to the certainty of his biological father by means of the discovery of the coveted *punto fijo* but rather plunges him into even deeper metaphysical uncertainty: "If the Creator agreed to change his mind, would the order he originally imposed on the world still exist? Perhaps he had imposed many orders from the beginning of time; perhaps he was inclined to change them daily; perhaps there was a secret order that reigned over that changing of orders and perspectives, but we were not destined to ever discover it. Perhaps we were destined to follow the play of changing appearances of order that reorganized themselves after each new experience" (472).

The narrator then allows the reader to avoid the anxiety associated with Roberto's metaphysical and oedipal doubts by inviting participation in the delusion of metafictional certainty "where we make believe we are telling about things that really happened, never admitting that we are faking" (473). As the narrator indicates, Roberto "wrote for himself, it was not literature" (9). If this is the case, then the same can be said of the narrator's text.

In fact, the narrator knows that which Roberto has great difficulty admitting: "that Order does not exist. It is only one among many possible states of repose that disorder occasionally reaches" (Eco 1971, 150–51). And so the narrator portrays Roberto with an ironic detachment designed to conceal that his protagonist's pledge to univocal order and frustrated desires for completeness and finality are themselves projections of the narrating voice's desire for metafictional Oneness, a state the narrator achieves when he provides his reader with an overarching plan above all possible orders and disorders.

He does so by means of the perfect mother, literature, *la letteratura*, a feminine substantive in Italian whose model mate is the narrating voice, the deified father-author of the metafictional "Book of Books" (Eco 1994b, 140).

Romancing the Family: *Baudolino*

In *Baudolino* [*Baudolinus*] Umberto Eco returns to the Middle Ages, the setting for his highly successful first novel, *Il nome della rosa*. In this work Eco uses a modern-day narrator, as he does in another historical fiction, *L'isola del giorno prima*. But, as he did in *Il pendolo di Foucault*, he sets aside the device of a found manuscript, the strategy used in *Il nome della rosa* and *L'isola*. Nonetheless, a constant throughout all the novels—accentuated in *Baudolino*, above the variations in narrative strategy—is Eco's ironic abdication of narrative authority. In all his fictions Eco utilizes what Benedetti has called "the apocryphal effect" (Benedetti 2002, 141), whereby the writer declares I am not the person writing, thereby refusing responsibility for the role played by the text in catalyzing contemporary debate. Indeed, in *Baudolino* Eco uses the apocryphal effect to set in motion a process by which authority over and responsibility for the text is assigned to everyone (Baudolino, Niketas, the narrating voice, the reader) and therefore to no one.

To accomplish this, the empirical author creates a fictionalized extension of his own personality, a narrating voice who deflects responsibility for the culpable acts made manifest in the text—the attempts to control through narration anxiety for the way the various narrators believe they appear to others—away from himself. He does so, by first inducing the reader to endorse the truth value of the tale and then paradoxically undermining that truth value. This is accomplished when historically verifiable persons—for example, Niketas Choniates, the protagonist's principal interlocutor—and occurrences are fictionalized by their incorporation into an inventive plot that includes imaginary characters and events.

The plot is driven by the 'reproduction' of conversations in which Baudolino, as recompense for having saved Niketas's life, asks that his life story be textualized by Niketas. Niketas is the "logothete of secrets," Chancellor of the Basileus of Byzantium (18).[90] In other words, Niketas is the high-ranking official charged with the administration and safeguarding of the empire's narratives, the historian who edits the past, rendering for posterity the official version of what 'really happened.' So he is eminently qualified to serve as Baudolino's biographer. However, the text is replete with reminders of the unreliability of the raw material at Niketas's disposition, the information that filters through Baudolino's vaunted mendacity. In other words, Baudolino's disclaimers implicitly authenticate the veracity of fictive events: even if everything Baudolino tells Niketas is not perfectly true, his conversations with the logothete may have really happened. Once the author has created this smokescreen of authenticity, he uses it to draw attention away from the inherent subjectivity of Niketas's professional activity—that of rendering a narration of narrations—and his own, when he tells of Niketas' tale.

This is why readers are surprised by the enigma presented them at novel's end that tells them what they knew all along: that Baudolino's story was not written by the logothete, but by an even "greater liar" (525–26) than the protagonist, the imminent narrator. Readers respond to this conundrum by falling back on the one thing they can know with certainty: the thoughts triggered within their mind by the act of reading. Since the author cannot be known with complete certainty, noncritical readers tend to ignore that writing is the author's means for engaging the reader in dialogue. Noncritical, model readers tend to isolate themselves with the text, and ignore the writer's role in producing the work and the work's potentially transformative force within the historical contingency.

Reading becomes their means of escape from the world, the flow of time, and the historical context. They read, following the idiosyncratic, monologic path of the hermeneutic circle, which seeks validation only in their successive readings. When they eschew using the work as locus for a dialogue in absentia with the author, the text ceases to be an antagonistic presence in the here and now of the reader. It is transformed into an inert presence, a blank page onto which noncritical readers can transfer their own personal history and install themselves as putative authors of the text. But because it is Baudolino's tale, not theirs, they can observe his story as kindred spirits while he performs culpable acts they believe do not regard them.

Baudolino wants to expose himself: he wants to see his life story immortalized on paper. But he is reluctant to do so because he is afraid of the reception that may await his efforts.[91] So he expresses himself, but through the filter provided by the writer, who is thus given the authority to interpret Baudolino's words when preserving them for posterity. Furthermore, Baudolino, the son of a peasant, wants to be written by Niketas because the latter is a member of the Byzantine nobility, a man who enjoys many of the positive qualities Baudolino would like to possess.

The conversations between the two have an almost therapeutic quality about them: Baudolino "seemed anxious to speak with someone, as if to free himself of things that he had held inside for who knows how long" (33). He makes known all his negative qualities and actions, particularly his propensity to prevaricate, while Niketas listens indulgently. Thus, Niketas takes on the guise, for Baudolino, of an ego ideal, someone who recognizes and verifies Baudolino as Baudolino fantasizes himself to be (Ragland-Sullivan 1987, 129).

At the same time, Niketas is not a passive object of transference for Baudolino. Their relationship is marked by the reciprocity of the countertransference from Niketas onto Baudolino. Moreover, concealed behind the dialogue between the two is the projection of the narrating voice's inner realities onto both Baudolino and Niketas, who assume responsibility for what are more accurately described as the narrating voice's fictions. In sum, Baudolino and Niketas allow the narrator to watch from the sidelines interactions that readers are led to believe do not regard him because his characters have assumed all responsibility for the telling of his fictions.

For both Baudolino and Niketas the act of narration has a negative valence. They associate narration with prevarication, a culpable act. At the root of their guilt is the equation of storytelling and the ability to edit the past. For both, but especially Baudolino, narration is a cause of shame: his radical propensity to rewrite the past is a dissociative response to external pressures, specifically, parental neglect and abuse, something he would prefer to keep hidden. So, by having himself written into presence by another, rather than by himself, Baudolino can conceal things he prefers to keep hidden.

Throughout the text Baudolino uses imagination to escape the present. His childhood lies are prompted by the harsh environment of his parents' household. They protect him from paternal wrath and help him cope with maternal indifference. In sum, they shield him from suffering for which he believes himself blameless. At the same time, parental abuse and neglect cause Baudolino to believe that if his true nature were known, no one would like him. And so he comes to use falsehoods to conceal his self-loathing.[92] He will habitually obfuscate his true nature, even to himself, with successive layers of untruths: as he tells Niketas, "I always confused that which I saw and that which I wanted to see" (35), an observation seconded by his interlocutor, who responds, "you've lied so much you don't even know who you are any more" (45).

It seems that Baudolino does not want his stories to be taken seriously. He knows they are false; so, very often, they are deliberately transparent. At other times it appears he wants to be caught in his lies; this would force his interlocutor to give him the attention he did not receive as a child. Indeed, his narcissistic tendency to expose himself, which makes manifest an inadvertent yet ineluctable dependence on others, functions as a defense against his fears of being ignored, as he was by his parents. He needs to be noticed, and so he will often undermine his lies with declarations of their mendacity. By proclaiming himself a liar, he exposes himself in a way that allows him to control how others see him, preventing others from seeing him in a way he does not want to appear (Kilborne 125, 52).

As a member of Frederick's court, Baudolino uses his imagination to defend himself from awareness of the unjust disadvantage imposed by nature upon a child with his prodigious intellect in denying him a noble birth (see Freud, 1957b). His fabrications also help further his career, and allow him to believe he will be allowed to ascend socially, perhaps be named Frederick's heir: just reparation for the early wounds to his self-love. Later on, the trauma associated with the negative effects on his ambitions envisioned because of the loss of his protector Frederick will cause Baudolino to lose control over his imagination: in other words, he will lose contact with reality. Indeed, Baudolino is aware that as the son of a peasant, he can aspire to no more than the rank of ministerial, the intellectual's equivalent to the warrior-knight and to certain nobility (60). Nonetheless, the narrator predestines his protagonist to crave a position in the Emperor's entourage when he assigns to Baudolino's family the name Aulari (160), which translates into English as "courtier."[93]

Later on, Baudolino's very real fear for his life after the death of Frederick opens the floodgates to uncontrolled dissociation. Baudolino becomes absorbed in a distorted internal world. Regression into fantasy serves a defensive, compensatory function, affording Baudolino an increased sense of authority over his own destiny that will culminate in his 'encounters' with Ipazia and Deacon John. Upon learning the he was Frederick's killer, Baudolino will inflict pain on himself. Escape into fantasy allows him to give consistency, stability and integrity to his conflicting self-narratives (see Lynn, Pintar, and Rhue 1997, 296–97).

However, the reader cannot know the extent to which childhood traumata—paternal ill-treatment, the Imperial Army's occupation of his hometown, the anxiety associated with separation from his parents and the feelings of rejection consequent to being sold to the very man who had placed his homeland under siege leaving the child to face alone an overwhelming threat to his survival—effected Baudolino's experience of identity. More significant is the fact that the narrating voice avoids discussion of this topic. This absence or vacancy gives structure to the work when it allows readers to project their own individual internal realities onto it. When this occurs, the reader is indeed transformed into the 'author' of Eco's 'open' work.

Model Readers inadvertently empathize with Baudolino's chafing under parental criticisms, and the struggles with incestuous desires for the mother imago. They relate to the manner in which Baudolino introjects the paternal identity and internalizes paternal disapproval into the superego. Model Readers take pleasure in indulgently watching—through the prism of the narrating voice—while forbidden impulses—such as Baudolino's repressed parricidal wishes and unresolved oedipal desires to possess Mother—are dramatized in a way that liberates them from guilt and self-reprobation.

In this way, Model Readers, both male and female, underwrite Eco's literary reproduction of their responses to social expectations of gender. In Baudolino's society of men, socially constructed gender roles under patriarchy are reaffirmed—men dominate while women are either sublimated into virginal, maternal figures or degraded as whores. While this may seem paradoxical, in effect readers are comforted by pages that do not challenge, but reproduce what is already known: socially constructed perspectives on a shared reality that was digested in childhood as factual and natural, despite its contrived foundations (Sobieraj).

This leaves unanswered the question of why Eco's Model Readers would pay any heed at all to the self-confessed "liar" who narrates *Baudolino*. Eco himself has written that the social use of language presumes truthfulness and that those who admit to fabricating transgress something more than of a rule of logic; they violate "a conversational rule" that forestalls communication (Eco 1976b). The answer may be that readers enjoy observing from their hidden vantage a game where both Baudolino and Niketas seek intellectual dominance rather than attempting to engage (an)other in dialogue.

Another reason may be readers' desires to enter with the narration into "possible worlds" not necessarily grounded in present reality but posited by speech acts of simulation. In an extraliterary context Eco draws a favorable parallel between this sort of speculation and the disinterested "ivory tower" research of many academics, which goes forward, as he phases it, "without immediate concern for applicability," and "divorced as much as possible from political contingency." That is to say, Eco equates linguistic simulation to pure, disinterested science whose objectivity, he argues, can be attained, but only by a necessarily "dissociated personality," one that separates theory and praxis; thought, or intellectual work, from engagement in the *polis* (Eco 1976b).

For Eco, the act of creating a possible world, one not necessarily connected to reality, inheres in the process of literary narration also. He has elsewhere extolled the ability of the novel to "give us the comfortable sensation of living in worlds where the notion of truth is indisputable, while the actual world seems to be a more treacherous place" (Eco 1994, 91). His views on this topic are of special interest here, because they allow the reader to glimpse into Eco's literary workshop and, more importantly, because they bring into play what in his opinion is the role of the reader-interlocutor within the process of narration-simulation: "The reader has to know that what is being narrated is an imaginary story, but he must not therefore believe that the writer is telling lies. According to John Searle, the author simply *pretends* to be telling the truth. We accept the fictional agreement and we *pretend* that what is narrated has really taken place" (Eco 1994, 75; his emphasis).

The establishment of a novelistic pact or fictional agreement between writer and reader based on the suspension of disbelief reflects the mode of communication between characters in *Baudolino* (where the agreement to use something other than reality as the basis for communication conditions the intersubjective relations between Baudolino and Niketas). Since communication is dependent on agreement on something in the world, then purposive deception severs that which binds the story (literature) to its context. However, when linguistic agreement ceases to be goal-oriented—that is to say, when narrator and addressee do not communicate with the intent of modifying something in the world—narration ceases to be a cooperative, collaborative locus of dialogue and interpretation.

Nonetheless, Eco argues that suspension of disbelief allows both the storyteller and his audience to escape into another world, one ordered by the narrator above the chaos of reality. And as long as the characters and events recounted in the fiction parallel those of the real world, the audience may believe the story is true (Eco 1994b, 107). He contends that readers want to believe that the ordered, fictitious story is true, because if it is, then our chaotic world makes sense. So readers willingly suspend disbelief because they "live in the great labyrinth of the actual world, which is bigger and more complex" than the world described in any novel: "It is a world whose paths we have not yet entirely mapped out and whose total structure we are unable to describe. In the hope that rules of the game exist, humanity throughout the centuries has speculated about whether this labyrinth has an author or more than one. And it has thought of God, or the gods, as if they were empirical authors, narrators, or model authors" (Eco 1994b, 115). And when we believe that the story is true, we enter a "possible world" where all wrongs are set aright, inequities are overcome, and power is painlessly transferred from one generation to the next.[94]

Baudolino lies or fabricates narratives to evade reality, and justifies his prevarications by citing a utopian vision of "possible worlds;" he tells himself that if we "imagine other worlds we end up changing the one we live in" (104). He believes he always lies "for a good reason" [*a fin di bene*] (182). In fact, the deep motivations behind Baudolino's prevarications—to conceal his self-loathing, to control how others perceive him, and to escape punishment and advance his career—imbricate. This is particularly evident with his youthful sightings of Saint Baudolino: this super-enabled vision of himself is used first to escape punishment for not doing his chores and then to advance in stature within the Emperor's household (8–9, 36).

Yet Baudolino's tendency to invent narratives is the result of his feelings of shame and increases his sense of guilt. Indeed, when Federico first appears, in full battle armor, Baudolino thinks the real San Baudolino has come to carry him off to hell (9–10). Subsequently Baudolino will repeatedly punish himself and perceive himself being punished for his transgressions throughout the course of his 'adventures.' After perfecting his apocryphal Prester John letter—which he admits is a manifestation of the idiosyncratic, "personal dream" he would prefer "not share with anyone else" (178)—Baudolino carelessly gets drunk and loses it to his rival, Zosimo (218); later on he will lose the counterfeit Grail (321). Moreover, Baudolino considers the death of Beatrice his punishment for having loved Colandrina (248), whose death is seen by the protagonist as punishment for his recidivist inconstancy both in his love for Beatrice and in his loyalty to Frederick. Another, even more fitting punishment to his mind for his propensity to falsehood is his only heir: Colandrina's monstrous, stillborn child, whom Baudolino describes as "a lie of nature" [*una menzogna della natura*] (239). The loss of Ipazia is for Baudolino yet another castigation, one that causes the protagonist to lose contact with reality for six and a half years (462–63).

Baudolino learns as a child to perceive negative events as just punishment for his errant behavior. Unlike his parents, who "broke their back working all day," Baudolino would play in the woods where he met a monk who taught him to read (11–13). However, the monk tries to molest him, a turn of events Baudolino ascribes to his not having listened to his mother, who always disparaged the literate (173). Nonetheless, Baudolino is pleased that his ability to read and write grants him superiority over his father, Gagliaudo (16). Thus, literacy is assigned a contradictory valence: it allows escape from the present, but the access it affords to new worlds removed from contingency and necessity is always tinged with guilt and with feelings of shame associated with his humble social provenance.

Shortly after his removal to the Imperial court, literacy will cause Baudolino to 'sin' and feel remorse again. Following Frederick's example, Baudolino begins drafting a rudimentary autobiography (17) on parchment stolen from Otto (5), inadvertently destroying a completed draft of the Emperor's life story. Otto cannot explain the loss, but blames and punishes the Canon Rahewin for it (50): "Two years later [Otto] decided to rewrite; I was his scribe; and I never dared confess to him that I had scraped away the first version of his *Chronicle.* As you see, [divine] justice exists, because I too have lost my own chronicle, only I never found the courage to rewrite" (44).

Otto, the European *pendant* to the Eastern historian Niketas, kept a double set of books for his master. While Otto's *Chronicle* of Frederick's life was the more realistic of the two, in the *Gesta* he gave vent to a more utopian vision of "possible worlds." In this alternate biography, written in a lower stylistic register, Otto fantasized a "world [that] could not but always go better" (45). Baudolino, who spent his life hoping to emulate his adoptive father, yearned to have his life story recorded also, and began keeping a diary on the parchment stolen from Otto, as we have just seen. However, his feelings of inadequacy precludes his keeping notes for a *Chronicle*—his notes were to serve for his own *Gesta Baudolini*—but once again he is 'punished' for his less-than-ethical behavior. As he tells Niketas: "Through all my journeys I brought this story of my life with me. But while escaping [from the Kingdom of Prester John] I lost those papers. It was like losing life itself" (17).

Baudolino's life story was not to adhere strictly to what really happened. Rather, he intended to write a tale of possible worlds. A self-proclaimed "man of peace," he prefers to look away when, in the real world, emperors such as Frederick humiliate sons and cities (51, 62). Baudolino knows he cannot aspire to having his life recorded in a *Chronicle*, and not only because he is the son of a peasant, a fact belied by his hands.[95] It is also due to the fact that he is not fit to succeed Frederick because men of peace such as he are not suited to lead a warrior caste. Therefore, during moments of stress and discomfort he unwittingly uses his hands to stroke a much more obvious source of the shame, the scar on his face acquired not in battle, but fleeing from a jealous husband (71). The scar is a constant reminder of his cowardice, and a highly visible contradiction of his conscious self-image.

Baudolino will compensate for his humble origin and regulate feelings of self-esteem with a family romance—that is to say the fantasy of being the offspring of distinguished parents—a response to his feelings of rejection by parents who sent him away from home. The creation of new parents who are "equipped with attributes that are derived entirely from real recollections of the actual and humble ones" allows Baudolino to compensate for his hostile feeling toward his father and his ambivalence toward his indifferent mother. The family romance also responds to feelings of shame and inadequacy inflicted by parents who were extremely covetous in their approval.

Baudolino's prodigious ability to learn foreign languages does not impress his father, Gagliaudo, who mocks, scolds, and hits his son, before selling him to a stranger (7–8, 9, 10, 14, 41). Gagliaudo and his wife are skeptical of the young Baudolino's visions (9) and believe they are merely a subterfuge to avoid work. When Baudolino returns home as a successful adult, his father misses no opportunity to disparage his son and to minimize his accomplishments, reinforcing a deep conviction that the parents who sold him never wanted him. Therefore, in order to please his father, Baudolino spends his adult life trying to find Prester John, Baudolino's paternal ideal, in the vain hope of satisfying vicariously, through his adoptive father, his need to please his biological father. Finding Prester John—both *rex et sacerdos* (128), an earthly God and source of all legitimacy above both emperor and pope—would legitimate both Frederick's reign and Baudolino's succession, despite his genealogical shortcomings.

Baudolino attempts to win his mother's love by overachieving. He believes he has reached his goal when he returns home in triumph as the Emperor's envoy. His mother, however, is not terribly impressed, and says to those standing by, "He is harnessed like the dog of a lord." A much more positive spin is put on this event by the narrating voice who reports, Baudolino's "parents ate him up with their eyes; his mother . . . was dazed" [*abbacinata*] by the splendor" (244). The narrating voice immerses himself in characters' language in order to provide a contamination of his own perspective and Baudolino's subjective sentiments. In this way, the narration presents as objective the indirect subjectivity of the author. This objectivity draws readers in, inducing them to further identify with the narrator. As Deleuze, following Pasolini, has pointed out, this mimesis between the character's subjective vision and that of the writing subject creates an effect wherein the text "does not simply give a vision of the character and his world; it imposes another vision in which the first vision is transformed and reflected" (Deleuze 1997, 72–76). In the final analysis, the perception that "the true object of [Baudolino's] desire was the unreachable kingdom of Prester John," and not "the woman of his dreams," Beatrice (97) must be attributed to the narrating voice, not to Baudolino.

Baudolino blames his father for sending him away, and defends his "blessèd mother" (9) by depicting her as powerless to prevent Gagliaudo's abuse of her son. Baudolino claims he cried when sent from home because he perceived his mother weeping "as if he were going off to his death" (14). However, upon returning home after a fifteen-year absence, he embraces his father but neglects to even ask of his mother, or of her whereabouts (184, 186). Then, when he chances upon her, he "hears angels sing." In her turn, she equates him with her livestock and with a demon: "O Lord, O Lord, two beasts in one night; one is born and one who returns up from Hell" (174).

In point of fact, the text does not corroborate Baudolino's proclamations of maternal affection for him. He cannot comprehend her indifference—he would like to believe that if she does not love him, it cannot be that she does not want to love him—and so he deals with the prospect of malevolent mothering and reduces his feelings of resentment by splitting the mother imago. Beatrice is both idealized—she is attentive and loving—and debased, that is to say sexually available (until Baudolino avoids the possibility of reprisal from Frederick—and reinforces his self-image of the good son—by denying libido).[96]

Throughout life Baudolino attempts to win Mother's approval by feigning perfect intelligence or God-like status. He hopes to accomplish this by perfecting his narrative abilities. As Niketas indicates, when Baudolino lies, he subordinates all others to his fabrications: since only Baudolino knows the truth, everyone else is dependent on him. (88–89, 45, 297). Indeed, as a boy Baudolino may have not have been worth keeping, but if he were omnipotent, Mother would have to love him. And so Baudolino deludes himself that she believes his concoctions, even though her words belie him: "she yelled at me: 'You lazy, good-for-nothing bum, you are the worst of them all; what have I done to God to have a son who sees saints?'" (9).

Although Baudolino depicts his relationship with his mother in the most positive terms, the text indicates that he has screened his negative memories of her: when she dies, Baudolino meditates "on the way he thought of the woman who had generated him, and to whom he had never shown tenderness" (278–79). His indifference slips forth again when he calls the blows with which he tortured the traitorous Zosimo "mother's kiss" (276). He would have liked his mother to represent a locus of security, but when he sought refuge with her from his father's beatings, she was too preoccupied tending her flocks of animals to afford him the consolation he desired (36). As a result, Baudolino would escape to the local woods, because there he could feel as if he were back in his "mother's womb" (34).

For Baudolino Frederick is a leader who embodies many of the ideals in which Baudolino believes, and the diametrical social opposite of his parents.[97] Furthermore, Frederick benefits greatly from Baudolino's prevarications. Indeed, their relationship is grounded on silent complicity and shared guilt, beginning with Baudolino's invention of a vision of San Baudolino that the Emperor exploits for political and military ends (13, 36). Later on, their collusion will be confirmed by their underwriting of the less-than-honorable face-saving expedients excogitated by Baudolino to allow Frederick to withdraw 'honorably' from his siege of Alessandria (203). Although Frederick's inclemency makes punishment by Gagliaudo pale in comparison (15), Baudolino accepts mistreatment from his stepfather. Indeed, the protagonist comes to think of Frederick as his real father (while Gagliaudo's physical appearance is never depicted for the reader, Frederick is described in great detail by Baudolino [36]), presumably because the Emperor, unlike Gagliaudo, never rejects him.

News that the Emperor will marry causes Baudolino to feel

jealous; he fears he will be forced to share Frederick's affection (53). However, Baudolino falls in love with Beatrice the moment he sees her (54). He is sixteen years old and this is his first time he has felt this way (61). For her part, Beatrice is an adult woman, at least five years older than Baudolino. Nonetheless, he imagines the love object as closer to his own age, and describes her as an adolescent. To use his words, she is a "twenty-year-old girl" [*fanciulla ventenne*] (61). Baudolino ignores the social and economic chasm between them (Beatrice, even if she had not been Empress, comes from an extremely wealthy family), and he succeeds in holding his emotions in check—at least initially—by telling himself that a relationship with a stepmother would be incestuous. He reminds himself of the need to respect Father's totemic rights over Mother (54), and takes pleasure in an erotic of denial (Scaglione), writing love letters he will never send (83, 84).

At first Baudolino feels culpable for what he imagines are forbidden desires. However, according to the narrating voice, when news of the Emperor's savage vengeance on Baudolino's countrymen reaches the protagonist, "in a very dark way, without Baudolino even noticing it, [Frederick's behavior] persuaded [Baudolino] that he was not guilty for having loved the Empress" (93). Baudolino then returns to the Imperial Court, and, according to the title given by the author to the relative chapter, "reprimands the Emperor and seduces the Empress." However, Baudolino neither "reprimands" (in fact, he "cries" while rebuking Frederick, who sternly counters Baudolino's charges [109]) nor "seduces." So Baudolino retreats, and surreptitiously punishes his stepfather by revealing his emotions to the object of his affections.

Beatrice's response is less than encouraging: she calls him a "boy," but then softens the blow by maternally caressing the nape of his neck, and then his scar. Encouraged by this, Baudolino kisses her, but Beatrice turns pale, pulls back, looks him straight in the eye, and says firmly, "In the name of all the saints in Heaven, never do that again" (111). He will not. Instead, Baudolino will anguish over the many infractions committed in his celebration of this "blasphemous Mass." Of course, one of his most serious violations in this instance was that of almost tarnishing his idealized image of his stepmother (111–12). Baudolino vows to respect her honor, and for her part she 'helps' him avoid having sex with her by never showing anything more than maternal concern for him, and helping him comport himself with dignity in her presence (175-76).[98]

Since Baudolino's adventures are all told as a long flashback, critical aspects of his tale come forward indirectly from the narrating voice who presents as objective the subjective sentiments he projects onto Baudolino. For example, the encounter between Beatrice and Baudolino, who returns after a lengthy absence to the imperial court, is depicted in the following way: "Baudolino kneeled to kiss her hand, without looking up at her face. Beatrice hesitated an instant. *Perhaps* it occurred to her that if she did not acknowledge affection and confidence she would have belied her embarrassment. And so she placed his other hand on his head and maternally ruffled his hair—forgetting that a woman barely in her thirties could no longer treat him—now that he was a grown man—that way, a man not much younger than she" (154; my emphasis).

Saving Frederick from a very close encounter with death gratifies Baudolino; he has restored the gift of life to his surrogate father, who, as we have seen, has supplanted the biological parent in Baudolino's mind as his true father (whose life had already been spared by his son's negotiation of a peaceful settlement for the siege of Alessandria). After rescuing Frederick Baudolino can identify with the father of his family romance, and elaborate his desire for Beatrice, whom he has possessed vicariously through Frederick: "In that precise instant . . . I understood that, by saving the life of my Lord, I had paid my debt in full. But for exactly that reason I was no longer free to love Beatrice. And so I realized that I no longer loved her. The wound had healed" (211).

The desexualization of Beatrice allows Baudolino to continue to split the mother imago. He will idealize the objects of his affection and reject all disillusioning aspects, as he does with his mother, whom Baudolino fantasizes loved him unconditionally. Indeed, all Baudolino's amorous relationships will repeat this pattern of behavior. After Beatrice, Baudolino will look backward to Mother through his wife, the "blessèd" Colandrina (whom Baudolino considers a daughter [236-37]), and through his final love interest (this one young enough to be his granddaughter [462]), Ipazia, that "purest of virgins" (516) who reveals her sensuality to no man but Baudolino. When Beatrice dies, his recollections of the Empress blend with and fade into reminiscences of Baudolino's parents. These memories then merge with thoughts of his late wife Colandrina (355), forming a conglomerate figure in his mind.

When Colandrina announces her pregnancy to Baudolino, he begins "to look at her as if she were the Virgin Mother" (237). When she goes into labor she takes on the semblance of "a waxen Madonnina" (238). She dies giving birth and is transformed, in Baudolino's mind, into a "heavenly angel" charged with sending her "blessings" earthward toward him (246). After her passing it takes "Baudolino a year to come out of the melancholic folly that had overtaken him, a year of which he remembered nothing, except that he took grand cavalcades through wood and field, and would then stop and drink until he collapsed into long and agitated sleep" (241). When Frederick dies, she assumes corporeal form, reappearing as her brother Colandrino, "an earthly angel, like his poor sister" (401), and one of Baudolino 'companions' on the 'expedition' to the Kingdom of Prester John.

The journey to the Kingdom of Prester John is prompted by the death of Frederick (316). This is an extremely traumatic event; first, because it puts an end to the dynastic ambitions of Baudolino—considered at court the Emperor's "bastardello" (318). More importantly, the succession of Frederick's son, Henry, who was jealous of Baudolino's favored status at court, represents a very real threat to Baudolino's life. Thus, the Emperor's death precipitates an emotional crisis that had been brewing at least since Baudolino's student days in Paris, when he invented his alters (see 497). The quandary sets Baudolino off on a journey that physically may possibly have taken him from Turkey to Asia Minor, but is primarily through the hidden recesses of his psyche.

Indeed, Baudolino actively forgets the "cursèd name" of the river in which Frederick drowns (297). The four years immediately following this event are also lost to memory (330), but are spent in places of which no one has ever heard, where they speak languages unfamiliar to Baudolino's polyglot cohort (328), and are inhabited by creatures that exist only in books. What matters more, although Baudolino's speech immediately before and after gaining awareness of the death is reported directly, his behavior at the most critical of junctures—while coming to that awareness—is conveyed by the narrator through free indirect discourse (316–17).

Baudolino's 'guide' throughout his 'expedition' is Gavagai, a prepubescent boy approximately the same age as Baudolino when he was sent from home tenderly described by the narrating voice as "a *baby* of ten or twelve years" (370; my emphasis). Gavagai explains to Baudolino that the Son—Jesus—is of similar but not identical substance as the Father; the Son is an adoptive creation, yet one and the same as the Transcendental Father (375, 404–5). As stated in the Nicaean Creed, Jesus was begotten, not made, and is one in Being with the Father. Jesus' relationship with God elucidates to Baudolino's mind, by implicit analogy, the relationship between the Prester and his deacon, causing Baudolino to assume that it should have also applied to himself when the time came to succeed Frederick.

According to the Gavagai fantasy, deacons—and by extension sons—are chosen not because of lineage, but on the basis of prodigious abilities demonstrated in early childhood (for example, Baudolino was "joyously surrendered by the family" and moved to court where they prepared him to "succeed [the] adoptive father, fear him, honor him, and love him" [398]). However, like Baudolino Deacon John never receives his inheritance. The Deacon is overtaken by an advancing case of leprosy—a projection of the self-loathing learned by Baudolino in early childhood[99]—and predeceases his spiritual father, just as Baudolino was denied the chance to succeed the Emperor. So Baudolino compensates by granting transcendent qualities to his alter, the deacon.

During his travels Baudolino meets and deals with numerous monsters, or repressed fears and anxieties. He is accompanied by Gavagai and a contingent of alter egos. One of the most significant yet least visible of the companions, as we have seen, is Colandrina-Colandrino who gives manifest shape to an undefined but "painful memory" (235): fear of the combined parent figure, to use Melanie Klein's term (103—4), the image of both parents united against the child, the abusive father Gagliaudo and the neglectful, phallic mother.[100]

Baudolino's journey culminates with Ipazia, with whom he converses in Greek (424), a language that reflects a split, because it is both the scholarly language of his ideal, Niketas, and the sublime *eloquio* of Prester John (371) on the one hand, and, on the other, the debased tongue of carnal knowledge imparted to him as a young student by a Parisian prostitute. When Baudolino first sees Ipazia, she is with a unicorn (422), reminiscent of the armored horse on which Baudolino first saw Frederick (9). Even though Baudolino tells Niketas that he had not been with a woman for a very lengthy period of time, Ipazia's "angelic countenance" inspires in him "a feeling of pure adoration" (422), and he is transformed into "pure gaze," a state Niketas admits he envies (423).

When she returns for a second encounter—without the phallic symbol, the unicorn (425–26)—he "re-became [*ridiventato*] a baby who seeks his mother's breast, and cries when the mother absents herself because he is afraid she will not come back" (428). Like Beatrice and Colandrina, Ipazia is virginal but sexually available. She does not belong to another man—she has taken a vow of chastity (429)—but is predestined to give a sort of virgin birth by copulation with an anonymous fecundator.[101] As for Baudolino, his choice of an uncommon verb, "re-becoming," and eccentric use of the conjunction "and" to indicate ellipsis give credibility to the hypothesis of an unsatiated infant's repressed disillusionment with an unloving mother.

As a child Baudolino wanted to believe in a familial utopia grounded in his triangular relationship with his parents. However, the offense to his narcissism by a mother he had to share with his father destroyed that illusion and brought to the fore oedipal worries associated with the fear of the combined parent (Klein), that is to say trepidation of both parents united against him. Ipazia forces Baudolino to confront the split by asking him how could a loving God link the possibility of eternal life along with that of eternal damnation? (432).

When Baudolino proves unable to answer, Ipazia explains to him that a perfect God did not create, but was saddled with evil. More importantly, she defines God as the Oneness of Incarnation; precisely what Baudolino believe he has found in his union with Ipazia.[102] Indeed, the Ipazia fantasy allows Baudolino to regress while neutralizing the bad maternal imago in a marriage symbolized by his own incarnation within a womb that is purified by his presence. It allows him to believe that the world created by the Father is good, and "what seems to us as evil is simply God's will poorly misunderstood" (see Mohacsy 1988, 89).

Resolution of the split paternal imago—"God is the place, or the non-place, where opposites mingle," Ipazia tells him (435)—enables Baudolino to confront those insecurities associated with the dual vision of the mother as loving, idealized provider and a betrayer, belonging to another. Bliss becomes possible when the phallic unicorn, Father, is sent away. Baudolino would like to believe that women like his mother do not have sex, and that Ipazia is like his mother. That is to say, Ipazia belongs to a group of women who are only supposed to have sex once, to procreate, and then renounce it forever. When he undresses her, he discovers her animal-like sexuality—her goat legs—and intuits that his biological mother also had sex—but only once—in order to conceive her child. Therefore, when Baudolino and Ipazia copulate, he gets what he has always wanted: sex with Mother. He feels rejuvenated, eternal, as if he had "overcome death" (448). In fact, in the absence of the unicorn, Baudolino can monopolize the mother imago's attention, penetrate her, and re-occupy her womb, which he purifies through the "perfect love" (443) of his self-incarnation. Having thus mentally transformed himself into a Christological figure, Baudolino relives his deflowering of his neighbor's daughter, which he had justified at that time with a fabrication in which he testified to hearing "a voice from the Heavens" telling him that he "was the unicorn who took away the sin of the world" (9). According to the narrating voice, the proxy Niketas listens to this tale in silence, "dominating with great difficulty his envy" (444).

Like Baudolino, Niketas is an intellectual and a narrator; not a man of arms. Nonetheless, Niketas not only participates in the activities of the court of the eastern empire, but writes (hi)stories that define the reality of that court (28). In other words, he too is a God-like narrator, who can "weave a providential design" (18) into the textualized identity he promises to create for Baudolino.

As the dialogue between Baudolino and Niketas progresses, the protagonist ignores that he gave the gift of life to Niketas by saving the logothete from European crusaders. This event, explicitly acknowledged by both Niketas (17) and the narrating voice (18), is a repetition of what Baudolino did for both his fathers. Thus, Baudolino can extend to Niketas the protection Baudolino wishes he had received from biological father who abused and sold him when he was a helpless child. Niketas, who for the most part avoids commenting on what Baudolino tells him, takes umbrage upon hearing that Baudolino allowed another to receive credit for his literary creations. Niketas calls the deliberate creation of apocryphal works an "atrocity" comparable to a "father giving away the fruit of his own loins" (88–89).

Baudolino does not respond, but cannot help but remember the many instances of his own acceptance of paternal abuse, including forced alienation from the home, which he explains in the following way, mingling images of his true and adoptive fathers: "it was one thing to defend yourself when the Emperor put you under siege, and another to attack of your own initiative. In other words, if your father strikes you with his belt, you have the right to try to grab it and pull it out of his hands—it's self defense—but it you raise your hand against your father, well then, that's parricide" (193).[103]

Although Baudolino willingly submits to his fathers, he describes to Niketas a dream in which Moloch-like cannibals devour their own children (341). As we have seen, Baudolino takes pleasure in superseding his fathers, and when Pafnuzio tells Baudolino that he was materially responsible for Frederick's death, Baudolino's self-analysis is immediate and epiphanic: he admits that his repressed hatred for Frederick was the reason he had never ceased desiring his adoptive mother. While he had believed he had desexualized Beatrice, he acknowledges that he remained "infected with this [incestuous] leprosy" (the leprosy projected onto Deacon John), a state that led to his fouling Ipazia.

After Baudolino vanishes, the voice (who up to this point has encouraged the reader to invest emotionally in the fate of the protagonist[104]) must shift the center of narrative gravity from Baudolino to Niketas. But before beginning to compose a biography of Baudolino, as promised, Niketas consults with Pafnuzio—falsifier par excellence (511).[105] Pafnuzio reminds Niketas that the latter's history of Constantinople need not be objective or exhaustive: Niketas has the authority to exclude Baudolino from historical reality. Pafnuzio then admonishes Niketas to leave to someone else, "a bigger liar than Baudolino," the task of writing Baudolino's story.

That "liar," the narrating voice, creates an image of omniscience for himself by reporting on Niketas' thought processes (see, for example 66; 125), which is undermined when Baudolino's thought processes are left opaque. Furthermore, while the tale seems to be verisimilar—because it is open-ended (it is impossible to know what happened to Baudolino after he leaves Constantinople)—closure is achieved, and the reader gratified, when a plausible theory explaining how Frederick died is produced. When all is said and done, what really happened becomes irrelevant.

Eco's Model Reader identifies with the narrating voice who splits into Niketas and Baudolino. In stark contrast to the firebrand Baudolino, Niketas remains blissfully detached—continuing to enjoy the privileges and luxuries of his life as a writer—while a war of planetary dimensions destroys the world around him. He can do so because he believes that his tale has nothing to do with that world: he is simply narrating the narrations of others, constructing his fabrication on top of other fabrications. It is a simulation, real only to the extent that author and reader agree to imagine it real.

Readers enjoying imagining that the story may have happened, but need not have happened. Indeed, it is within this conundrum that Eco's Model Readers—the select few who can locate and appreciate the enigmas Eco has encrypted in the text—find validation. They can also observe with amusement, but more importantly with consolation, as Baudolino creates, ex nihil, foundational myths that tautologically legitimate superstructure of the world as we know it (see, for example, 63–66, 170–72, 409), which, therefore, must be exactly as it is. Reality is the renarration of the déja lu. Baudolino's monsters exist because he has read of them and can tell Niketas about them. He visits kingdoms that are real only because they exist in his mind. Prester John exists only because Baudolino spent two thirds of his life searching for him.

Model Readers enjoy watching Baudolino submit to the Father, rather than confronting him, in the hope of painlessly inheriting what is his, and then passively killing him (as did Adso da Melk and Roberto della Griva). They also enjoy observing Baudolino splitting and possessing the mother imago, and perpetuating the structures of patriarchy. Similarly, they enjoy watching the author pile fabrication upon fabrication, so as to distance himself from his tale, because, since there is no apparent act of agency on anyone's part, no one can be held responsible for the state of affairs subtending the text, which is written by no one and by all, but describes a "possible world" they can believe has no relationship to the real world, but is in many way a very accurate reflection of it, and is one they may passively inherit.

3

Interlude:
Vincenzo Consolo's Poetics of Memory

THE NARRATIVES OF VINCENZO CONSOLO ARE CHARACTERIZED BY a poetics of memory and by an anti-Orientalist inflection.[1] That is to say, his writings contrast an essentialist and racist characterization of the heterogeneous peoples who inhabit Southern Italy and Sicily, a categorization that reified subsequent to Unification in 1860. Consolo's native Sicily is a metaphor (one of many metaphors necessary to understand for an appreciation of his work, as we shall see) for the all the Souths in a world where the term North corresponds to an ever smaller and "evermore warlike and oppressive" portion of the world's population. The world's Souths, in Consolo's parlance, are those places where the myth of a utopian North is constructed. For this reason southerners need to willfully counter their inherited complexes of inferiority and subalternity (Consolo 1995, 81–82). Consolo moves toward this end by elaborating and refining a poetics of memory defined by three main elements. The first is a linguistic investigation motivated by the desire to restore a lost dignity to the popular dialects of his native Sicily by using their vocabulary in such a way as to enable them to gain national acceptance. A second thread woven into this pattern is the will to oppose the loss of social consequence inflicted on the novel by a hegemonic media culture centered in Hollywood; to this end Consolo adopts a mode of expression, the metaphor, charged with re-invigorating the language of prose fiction. The third is to be found in his contributions to collaborative ekphrastic investigations of the civic and natural vestiges of the Island's past, projects whose multiplicity of witness reflect a defining characteristic of his prose fictions, the decentering of the subject of the narrating voice.

For Consolo the function of literature is that of restoring to our present the detritus of the past (Consolo 1993a, 28) in anticipation of what Benjamin calls the Messianic moment, instances when allegorical vision recalls dialectical images, reconfiguring them so as to catalyze their liberating potential. Consolo restores these ruins or living images of the past to "the time of the now" (Benjamin), opening them up to review, interpretation, and discussion. In this way subjective perspective is absorbed into the objectifying perspective of debate. This process of reinserting lost remnants of the past into the present is for Consolo a form of political activism (Rossi, 21), a way of restoring the central place of a sustained narrative critique in Italy's national argument.

According to Benjamin, narrative intelligence derives its "authority" from its spatial and temporal otherness; stories "come from afar." Because storytellers are defined by their ability to give counsel for their audience, their stories are future oriented: their purpose is to impart knowledge that will be useful to the audience in the future. Narrative does not transmit disconnected bits of information, but conveys experience embedded in the storyteller who passes it to those listening. Indeed, Consolo agrees that since narration is synonymous with the sharing of experience, it is an intrinsically democratic action in which inheres "a practical idea of justice and a profound need for morality." It is a political act because it rises from the same social and historical context that it addresses, interpellating its here and now with its own allusive, literary language, one that utilizes metaphor to evoke our shared human condition (Consolo 1999b, 144, 229).

All Consolo's fictions are faithful to his youthful desire to narrate the reality of Sicilian populace through "sociological writings of extreme communication" where the unusual term "extreme communication" is not intended to connote a mimetic "realistic-testimonial" narrative, but a prose that is "memorial and metaphoric; not logical and referential, but highly transgressive and expressive" (Consolo 1993a, 13–14). For Consolo, the use of metaphoric expression is justified by the conviction that traditional prose narrative forms cannot communicate with a society dominated by visual media and that literary expression must be in tune with this historical reality. Texts must connote, not denote, lest they be overwhelmed and integrated into the information highway. Therefore, the writer who wishes to communicate must paradoxically refuse communicativity and narrate poetically through metaphoric images, as theorized by Pasolini in the oft-quoted essay on "The Cinema of Poetry." Consolo, to substantiate his argument, notes that verse in the regional languages of the Peninsula has prospered because, following Pasolini's example, many poets now refuse more accessible and marketable forms of expression. Following this line of reasoning, Consolo concludes that "the return to documentation and to historiography must have poetic expression as its starting point. Only then can we begin to narrate again, and to write novels (Consolo 1995, 87).

Indeed, Consolo describes himself a *"contastorie,"* a storyteller or popularizer (Rossi, 21). He finds that the "fundamental problem of writing novels," already identified by Gramsci, is that of always finding oneself behind the times. To explain, novels are the end result of lengthy process of contemplation, and, therefore, narrators tend to write with their eyes directed toward what they know, the past. Often, sudden and unexpected events overtake the process of writing, so that literary texts are often outdated before they are published. Because of this, Consolo concludes that only the narrative recuperation of memory through metaphor can make the novel once again current—what the novel loses in topicality, it gains in social relevance when it depicts the latent traces of the past that determine and condition our behavior in the present—and make prose fiction a harbinger of the future (Consolo 1999b, 28).

Although Consolo's fictions are deeply rooted in his native region, he does not adopt an essentialist posture. Instead, he allegorically recuperates the perspective of the vanquished. Following Dainotto, we may say that Consolo uses graphic texts to remind us "of what historical memory has lost and yet continues to exist as symptom." The ekphrastic text, "a supplement to memory" serves as "a place of argumentation from which . . . the anamnesis of a traumatic loss can begin" (19). By contrasting the radical, postmodern lessening of the weight of the past and tradition in meaningful decision making and the length of future expectations a lost sense or direction may be restored to history.

Consolo grounds his prose in the real living conditions of contemporary Sicily, which is not spoken of directly but, following Sciascia, is elevated to universal symbol of evil, of all that is wrong with Italy (Sanna, 26). And, it must be stressed, evil is always spelled with a small *e* so as to depict a circumstance that is neither atemporal, existential, or metaphysical, but deeply rooted in history (Consolo 1993b).[2] In reacting against a current of Sicilian literary art that goes back to the nineteenth-century naturalist Giovanni Verga, which sees history as an illusion and looks instead to nature and myth for explanations of a Sicilian essence (Consolo 1999b, 178), Consolo proposes that all Sicilian writers shoulder the burden of retrieving lost aspects of the Island's history. Unlike Northern writers, to use his parlance, such as Hemingway and Graham Greene, cosmopolitans who enjoy the luxury of traveling widely so as to tell of the truths of others, Sicilian writers—and all Southern writers for that matter, southern Italians, South Americans, and so on—are called on to ground their writings in the history of their native reality: "The greater the social unhappiness of a land, the more that country's writers must . . . respond to the need to explain and understand that land's pain and suffering" (Barina, 123).

Consolo schematizes the divergent approaches of various Sicilian writers in geographical terms, claiming that Eastern Sicily has always been, for geological and topographical reasons, more susceptible to the whims of nature, earthquakes, for example, and the eruptions of Etna. As a result, "existential and psychological problems are grist for the mill" of the writers of that region. In contrast, those from western Sicily—where the mining of sulfur in the nineteenth century created a historically new category of industrial workers, a phenomenon that gave rise to violent conflicts of capital and labor—tend to structure their narratives in more logical terms of reason and history (Sanna, 18–19).[3] Consolo has averred that his work oscillates between these opposing poles of history/reason and poetry/myth, a practice he explains in almost astrological terms: his home town, Sant'Agata di Militello, falls just to the east of the 'border' separating eastern and western Sicily.

However, he specifies, over time his youthful tendency to express an existential condition or otherwise transcend the quotidian gave way to metaphoric representations of historical and social analysis (Sanna, 17, 19).[4] Indeed, writing for Consolo is a form of ideal, moral, and historical engagement, a means for interacting with the world (Consolo 1993a 5; Sanna, 40). However, his literary commitment must be described by negation, that is to say by its opposition "to all power structures, injustices, forms of oppression, abuses of power, and violence: the evils and the horrors of our time" (Consolo 1993a, 70).[5] Therefore, following Marcuse, we may say that Consolo strives to create a situation where the sensibility of the individual is not only the medium for the *principium individuationis*, but also for its opposite, universalization: and from within the resulting dialectic of the universal and the particular *humanitatis*, solidarity among individuals, may emerge (132).

In his nonfictional writings Consolo refers metaphorically to the ills that define our contemporary condition in terms of Homer's *Odyssey*. To use Consolo's own phrasing, "*The Odyssey* is a story of guilt and expiation of remorse (Consolo and Nicolao, 21). Odysseus' 'return to Ithaca'—verbal shorthand for a process of catharsis, absolution,' and 'salvation' that occurs within the individual but is possible only "within a civil consortium, and culture"—or *nóstos*, evokes a return home, to childhood, memories, traditions, and affects. The *nóstos* is the revisiting of our "olive trees"—the tangible signs of our individual and collective contributions to civilization and society—the journey away from the unregulated 'progress' that disregards our shared humanity and from the "fanatic desire for wealth and possessions" (Consolo 1994a; 17, 51, 58, 77). But the degradation of cityscapes and countryside perverts its meaning. Here, the return home is both descent into the depths and ascension. So that the *nóstos* is more than the return to this sentimental Motherland; it also connotes our duty to leave home a second time to arrive at the Fatherland, or history, metaphor for an understanding of one's place and role in the polis (Consolo and Nicolao, 18).

As mentioned, Consolo's use of metaphor instantiates his lack of faith in the ability of traditional narrative forms to reflect contemporary reality. The novel, "the most political and subversive of literary genres," has been "disarmed and reduced to a pitiable object of consumption" (Consolo 1993c). It "is in crisis because it is no longer able to assuage our collective fears of massive annihilation caused by Auschwitz, Hiroshima, Stalin's Gulags, Vietnam and Sarajevo." Moreover, it is no longer capable of helping us 'return to Ithaca' because "directly or indirectly, wittingly or unwittingly," the contemporary novel, for the most part, supports or praises the powers that be (Consolo 1993c).[6] Therefore, the novelist has lost social consequence and "risks being accused of complicity and collaboration with a structure of domination that perpetrates injustices and crimes" (Consolo 1994b, 49).

Both Consolo's life and literary itinerary resemble the Homeric *nóstos*. He and his protagonists return from Milan, where Consolo has spent most of his adult life, to their 'Ithaca' and 'Penelope,' Sicily, but do not find her as they left her. Unlike Ulysses, Consolo cannot return to a recomposed world—to the olive trees of his youth—and to the internal and external harmony of times past, because they no longer exist. Instead, he returns to a degraded Sicily of *olivastri* [uncultivated olive trees], a land of unplanned and unregulated development, and of unbridled damage to the landscape and to the environment.[7] And so this modern-day Homer expresses his rage by placing plainly in view, ekphrastically, the remains of what was and now appears to be destined for extinction. Through the collaboration of word and image, and the plurality of witness it affords, Consolo involves readers in the destiny of those olive trees, a fate they are implicitly asked to share.

At the same time, Consolo restores dignity to the language that gave birth to literary Italian, the Sicilian dialect, but was written out of the language after the Piedmontese colonization of the rest of the Peninsula (see Scafoglio and Cianflone 1977; and Piromalli and Scafoglio 1977). Farrell avers that Consolo extends "his feeling for the underdog, his identification with Sicily into the sphere of writing" (64). Whether or not this is a completely accurate portrait, it is true that Consolo's project is consistent with a "linguistic 'ideology'" that consists of retrieving "words that cannot be found in any Italian dictionary, but have their own history and philological dignity, whose etymologies link back to Greek, Arab, French, Spanish" (Consolo 1993a, 55). Following Pasolini, who in the well-known essay "Nuove questioni linguistiche" [New Linguistic Issues] acknowledged the sociologic and linguistic homologation of the Italians (that is to say the absorption of the workers into the lower middle class and consequent end of class conflict on the one hand, and, on the other, the assertion of the pragmatic, technological, bureaucratic interregional *koiné* of the lower middle class as the national language [Consolo 1997]), Consolo "exhumes a specific lexical patrimony, names objects, evokes characters emblematic of a vanished world" (Consolo 1993a, 28). The preservation of memory imparts an understanding of the present that enables us to imagine the future. "*Omeros,*" as Consolo points out, "in classic Greek means 'hostage.'" By extension the poet can be said to be "the hostage of literary tradition, of memory, and, above all, literary memory" (Consolo 1999b, 266). However, this does not mean that he limits his efforts to the ludic quoting of canonical texts, that which the writer Sebastiano Vassalli calls "*citazionismo.*" Rather, there is a transgressive force at work in Consolo. In refuting the linguistic homologation wrought by the state bureaucracy and the mass media, Consolo's formal investigation affirms and defends a cultural identity in danger of extinction (Sanna, 10–13). In so doing, his linguistic undertaking reaffirms a weakened intellectual freedom because it helps restore the capacity for "individual thought after its absorption by mass communication and indoctrination" (Marcuse, 51).

In this way Consolo intervenes in the centuries-old *questione della lingua.* First, he distances himself from both neorealist and neo-avant-garde experimentation. Neorealism, the tendency that predominated in Italian letters during the decade after the Second World War, emphasized content over form, a reaction to "the dominion of the word over the world" that characterized Italian literature under fascism. Neorealist linguistic investigation was for the most part limited to the mimesis of a spoken Italian replete with calques from the dialects in the name of a heightened realism and the reduction to the absolute minimum the literary mediation of language (Manacorda, 466–67).

Consolo's critique of neorealist inquiry tends to be neither direct nor explicit. Nonetheless, it is easily deduced from his objections to the positivistic mimesis of Verga, the model for neorealist inquiry. Verga justified the use of dialect cadences and expressions as a means of dispassionately recording reality and consequently made stylistic choices for Consolo are tantamount to a surrendering of the writer's authority over the text to the characters.[8] Consolo not only attempts to avoid the populist limitations of neo-*verista* inquiry, amply documented by the Gruppo '63 and others such as Asor Rosa, but also takes issue with the proposals of certain exponents of the neo-avant-garde and their "a-historical," "artificial" "re-inventions of the Italian language" (Sanna, 13; Consolo 1993a, 15). Consolo contends that the *koiné* decried by Pasolini imbricates with and supports the linguistic experiments of the Gruppo '63 and its heirs (Consolo 1993a, 15). Consolo believes there the prevalence of this "technological, business Italian" (Pasolini) in the media and among Italy's youth has put an end to the confluence and continual reciprocal enrichment of literary language and the popular languages, the dialects. As a result contemporary Italian—in both its colloquial and literary forms—has become "rigid and fragile because it has been invaded by the language of an alien, economic super-power." Contemporary writers have reacted to this state of affairs either by adopting a highly stylized language, or by reproducing directly on paper what they hear on the street. Therefore, Consolo also distances himself from the *avant-gardisme* of many contemporaries, whose "neo-naturalist" imitations of the younger generation's slang and cadences, and the inflexions and syntax of the mass media have compressed the historical depth of the language.

Consolo argues that today's novelists are not able to communicate because society ignores them. He responds to the resulting "aphasia," a term than in his parlance indicates the sundering of the necessary reciprocity of literary text and social context (Consolo 2001b, 11), by utilizing a stylistic mode characteristic of poetry, the metaphor (Consolo 1999b, 282). Following Marcuse, we may say that the aphasic silence Consolo decries characterizes a society wherein media saturation leaves no area of life, including the instincts, free from social management and administration.[9] In this "total society," the intellectual's task is to help people learn to see and think independently again, and to break the power of imposed information and indoctrination (Marcuse, 93). This is precisely the goal Consolo's ekphrastic project sets for itself. As Consolo asks himself, in the "weak light" of this "zone of uncertainty" and forgetfulness that is media culture, are "temporal progression, order, and narrative" still possible? (Consolo 1989, 10).

He believes it is, but to achieve his goals he must utilize a language that is more musical than prosaic, and takes recourse in the visual image.[10] In the writer's own words: "As the years passed I came to understand that visuality, painting, was for me a way of balancing my stylistic research, in the sense that I follow a sort of musicality of the phrase in my prose. I try to give a meter, a tempo, a rhythm to the phrase, so that my writing approaches poetic composition. I balance this sonority with a visual element, to create a sort of balance between sound and vision" (Consolo 2001b, 17).[11] Indeed, the "narrative poem"

L'olivo e l'olivastro (Consolo 1994a) comes in direct response to the aphasia just mentioned. Here Consolo adopts the stylistic models of poetry to reduce the gap between writer and reader and restore to prose narrative its ability to communicate logically and engage the reader in dialogue (Consolo 1999b, 282). Following Benjamin, Consolo proposes that poetic narration—when it reenters latent traces of the past into legibility so that a new value, relative to the present, may be assigned to them (Consolo and Nicolao, 38)—is capable of restoring dialogue between writer and world.[12]

Consolo claims that his linguistic inquiry is in the mould of Gadda and Pasolini, who aimed for language that was expressive, not communicative or denotative, and steeped in the history of the language (Sanna, 13). But unlike Umberto Eco—who, in *The Island of the Day Before*, took care to exclude words that came into the Italian after the seventeenth century, the period in which his novel is set—Consolo emphasizes stylistic concerns, especially the function of each word in the broader context, that is to say the manner in which lexical choices bring to the fore those ideologies and social relations the author intends to demonstrate. In his own words, "it is not an antiquarian operation, but a process that responds to a more vital motivation" (Bibolas, 15).[13]

However, like Eco, who directs readings of his prose fictions through extra-textual self-commentary, Consolo also gives philology a head start in *Lunaria* (Consolo 1985a)—a work that is set, as is Consolo's *Retablo* (Consolo 1987b), in the 1700s—by affixing to his novel a lengthy appendix that elucidates questions related to the historical context and to style: that is to say, he casts in relief the temporal depth of his lexicon, which draws on both the erudite languages of the Viceroy's court—Spanish and standard Italian—and the local dialects. However, and in contrast to Eco who feigns his 'death' in order to simulate the passage of authority over the text to the reader, Consolo "shows his hand" (Consolo 1985a, 116) and indicates his sources. He does so to valorize the linguistic detritus he has recovered, while making available points of access to the historical depth of a document whose linguistic strata intertwines with the transformations over time of the civic monuments also discussed in the book's appendix.

INTERLUDE: VINCENZO CONSOLO'S POETICS OF MEMORY   165

The inclusion within the text of dialogue in Spanish, Tuscan, and Latin reflects the linguistic disenfranchisement of *Lunaria*'s lower socioeconomic classes, synechoche not only for all the subjects of the Kingdom of the Two Sicilies before the Unification, but, more importantly in this context, for their descendents: the millions upon millions of emigrants from Italy's *Mezzogiorno* to places of linguistic and social hostility spread out all over the planet: Northern Italy, Europe, Australia, and the Americas, where—like Porfirio, the Viceroy's "eternal servant"—they were made to assume the role of "Negroes of the New Indies" (Consolo 1985a, 19). Unable to speak or read the dominant, colonial language, they were deaf, dumb and blind before antagonistic social, political, and economic structures of dominance.[14]

Like the appendix to *Lunaria*, *Museo Mandralisca* [*Mandralisca Museum*] (another collective, ekphrastic volume [Consolo 1991c]) provides its reader with a key for reading a work by Consolo, in this case *Il sorriso dell'ignoto marinaio* (Consolo 1976).[15] Here Consolo illuminates aspects of his historiographic research conducted in preparation for the writing of the novel, and his own admiration for Baron Mandralisca, a character whose professions of faith roughly coincide with the convictions of the author (Segre, 86), thereby providing Consolo with a vehicle suitable for commenting metaphorically on Italy in the 1970s, the period in which the novel was written. Similarly, Consolo contributed to the anastatic reprinting of the periodical *Lunario siciliano* [*Sicilian Almanac*] because he considered that journal indicative "of what can happen when a country is oppressed by a dictatorship, when civilization is overthrown."[16]

In other words, self-commentary is never for Consolo an end unto itself; nor is it merely a means for directing reading by means of auto-exegesis. Consolo's ekphrastic *nóstoi*—collaborative volumes that combine photographic documents of disappearing and decaying Sicilian landscapes and urbanscapes—are motivated by the desire to allegorically recover material signs of Sicilian history and civilization, the olive trees mentioned above. As can be said of his efforts to valorize the dialect as a language of culture and literature, they evince an allegorical mode of creation: emblems of a process of decay are reappropriated and represented in a way that enables them to interact in a transformative way with the present so as to influence the future.[17] Recollected fragments, disjoined from their original context, become part of genuine experience, which depends on the reality of the past within the present. History regains the direction lost in the eternal present of postmodernity, because here the present contains within itself elements of both the past and the future. Consolo explains that, in taking his photographic walks through Sicily, he revisits "a Sicily of the past and a Sicily of 'just yesterday' . . . in the illusion . . . that my land, and its history, in a desired, future Springtime, can rise up from the darkness of today's winter, from the lowest depths of Hell" (Consolo 1990a, 5).

In *Cefalù* Consolo and the photographer Giuseppe Leone go to together on an archeological jaunt among the architectural treasures of Sicily's north-central shore (Consolo 1999a). Leone recovers lost images from the past of a "city of memory *retrouvé*," while Consolo tells of his search for a "narratable, historical Cefalù, that would give clues as to how the Sicilian mindset formed over the centuries[18] following the Arab conquest of the Island in 827 (Consolo 1999b, 212). Two other important examples of such collaborative efforts at an integral representation of the past are *La pesca del tonno in Sicilia* [*Tuna Fishing*] (Consolo 1986)[19] and *'Nfernu veru. Uomini & immagini dei paesi dello zolfo* [*Real Hell. Men and Images of Sulphur Towns*] (Consolo 1985b). All the essays included in the former are accompanied by graphics (old drawings, maps); photographs (of places, fisherman, tuna massacres); documents (such as balance sheets, bills of laden); and artifacts. The same can be said of the latter, which depicts the "real Hell" of the sulfur mines with photographs of the tools used by the miners.

These ekphrastic documentaries—and the same can be said of Consolo's "re-reading" of Laura Gonzenbach's nineteenth-century rendering of traditional Sicilian folktales—are for Consolo, and for his reader, "itineraries of consciousness, knowledge and love that follow long paths through history" (Consolo 1994a, 143) which "restore to our awareness that which was too close for us to see" (Consolo 1999c, XI). Consolo retraces the path of tourists like Gonzenbach and Goethe to ascertain if the concept of voyage of discovery is still viable in a period of time when "we are only allowed the obligatory 'beaten path' [*via unica*] of the already known and foreseeable," when postmodern citationism does little more than repackage the *dejà lu*, and when the mass

INTERLUDE: VINCENZO CONSOLO'S POETICS OF MEMORY   167

media pushes us "toward the stasis . . . of a world made of an uninterrupted sequence of images that flash before our eyes."

Goethe, particularly, represents for Consolo all nineteenth-century travelers whose Grand Tours took them through Sicily for the purpose of gaining knowledge of the self and knowledge of the other: "even while not seeing, or, better, misinterpreting [*stravedendo*] many aspects of Sicilian reality, they gave *visibility* to that *evidence* that, according to Sciascia, was previously invisible to Sicilians (Consolo 1988a, XVIII).[20] Consolo uses the example of the Grand Tour while availing himself of the decentered testimony of word and image in order to render a mode of observation that is participatory, but not emotional. For their part, the readers of Consolo's ekphrastic works are invited to collaborate intellectually with the content of what Consolo and the photographers have documented.

In this way Consolo succeeds in gaining distance from the object of narration, while avoiding the constitution of a strong center of narrative subjectivity.[21] In fact, Consolo's ekphrastic projects are animated by the desire—that carries over into his prose fictions, as we shall see presently—to provide not an objective, or dispassionate point of view, but an objectifying plurality of subjectivities:

> We have always gone throughout Sicily looking for the key . . . to understanding our cultural essence. We went to see, describe, depict. The portrait (the drawing, the watercolor, the etching) corroborated the word. However, like the word, the graphic was subjective. It was often emotional, mythic, preconceived, ornamental. But when one moves from the subjective to the objective, in passing from the etching to the "photogenic design," or to the photograph, it would seem that there would no longer be room for emotion. But instead, how much subjectivity, how much emotion is found in the first photographs of Sicily. . . . No, the photograph is not objective. And this is especially true on an island like Sicily, which is so full of nature and of history, and of contrasts. (Consolo 1985c)

Parenthetically, Consolo is less than kind with graphic artists who would adopt the posture of dispassionate observer. One such case is the photographer who, in *Le pietre di Pantalica* [*The Stones of Pantalica*], parachutes into a Sicilian town shaken to its core by the Allied invasion. The photographer, a Hungarian who has taken a French name and citizenship and has donned an

American army uniform, trusts that his camera's objective will record what his "ironic glance" (Consolo 1988b, 28) chooses not to see: a town where the dense tapestry of acquaintances, customs, loves and hates, of daily travails and of celebrations had been completely unraveled . . . by bombs, dispersal, and fear (Consolo 1988b, 23). In point of fact, his still photographs of the victims of violence—like all war photography, as Sontag has noted—portray people who, "even though they are not the 'enemy,' are regarded only as someone to be seen, not someone (like us) who also sees" (72). Viewers can view them with the detachment necessary for believing themselves completely unaccountable. By allowing others to kill for them, feelings of guilt or responsibility are transferred or deferred from them, giving them a sense of autonomy from events that are out of their control (Marcuse, 65). When the front advances the photographer disappears as quickly as he arrived, after recording events he believes do not involve him, only to be blown up, a decade later, in Indochina, while photographing another war.

In any event, the decentering or doubling of the narrating *I* is realized in the narrator himself before being put into effect in his writings. In the autobiographical *I linguaggi del bosco* [*The Languages of the Woods*] Consolo tells of his allegorical recovery of two photographs from his youth, which he reads, or reconstructs, as if they were archeological finds from his past. To tell his story he must graft together "two entirely different, irreconcilable languages, that of the photograph and that of literature (Consolo 1988b, 148).[22] Another allegorical *recherche* underpins *Il Teatro del Sole* [*The Theatre of the Sun*]. Here, the iconography condensed in a Parisian crèche causes Consolo to restore to narrative life an image of his childhood through the weaving of personal and collective history. Writing of the artist allows Consolo to speak metaphorically of himself: "of the ability, and need, to recreate, to represent, intact, an entire world that has come undone, a heap of bits and pieces, of corruption, of losses, [to tame] all rage and violence, [to make] loyalty from deception, order from chaos, [and give] limpidity and harmony to life" (Consolo, 1999e, 17–18)

When Consolo provides the verbal illustration for a collection of drawings of the Orvieto Cathedral by Fabrizio Clerici (a major twentieth-century artist who, according to Consolo, seeks to portray the "offense, the deep wound of history, the anguish of events that are both remote and incumbent, the melancholy of the time, and compassion for our destiny" [Consolo 1996a, 11]), the novelist reciprocates the painter's having provided the cover art and illustrations for the first edition of *Retablo*, a novel conceived when the novelist accompanied the painter on a trip through Italy in search of ancient ruins (Pagano 2002, 208). This "return to the traces of the past left on the surface of the world and in the poetic imagination" (Dombroski 2005, 220) takes the shape, in *Retablo*, of a "broad, hyper-literary linguistic research" in which the author experiments with new formal structures borrowed from the plastic arts.

The title, *Retablo*, refers to a triptych or series of three painted panels that recount episodes of a continuing story. It is indeed true, as Farrell writes, that "each fragment covers the same, or at least contiguous, ground but is told from the perspective of a different character. There is no absolute truth to be had, only the accumulation of various points of view" (71). The stories of the plebians Isidoro and Rosalia surround the tale of the painter Clerici (who, in the fiction, is converted into a Milanese antiquarian from the Age of the Enlightenment who sets out to travel in Sicily) and undermine what the painter might argue is a naturalistic rendering of the reality of the Island. To explain, the first panel, Isidoro's tale, is divided into two laisses. The first serves as antecedent to Clerici's story, the second as sequel and summation. Rosalia comes forward at the very end to give her version of "the truth." The juxtaposition of decentered narrative perspectives reflecting diverse, fragmented subjective truths prevents the reader from adjudicating the veracity of any one narration with respect to another. Yet, from this multiplicity of witness emanates a historically accurate portrayal of class society in Sicily in the eighteenth century.

Ultimately, Clerici decides who should be voiced into presence, and how. Within his own recounting, Clerici allows fellow bourgeois characters don Carmelo Alòsi and don Sciavèrio Burgio to tell their stories in the first person (89 and ff.; 130 and ff.); in contrast, the speech of the lower classes must pass through the verbal filter of Clerici's free, indirect discourse. Rosalia Granata is written into presence only because Clerici is forced to continue his diary on the back of the sheets on which she confided her most intimate secrets after his own "candid sheets" of paper are stolen (58). This Rosalia may or may not be the same young lady vindicated by Vito Sammataro after she was deceived and corrupted by a "depraved [*vizioso*] monk" (79); it certainly does not matter to Clerici, whose travelogue takes precedence over the young woman's privacy. In any event, both Isidoro's[23] and Sammataro's Rosalia resemble Teresa Blasco to the extent that both Vito and Isidoro mistake Clerici's portrait of Teresa for the objects of their affection, causing images of all three women to blend together in the reader's mind. To add to the confusion of identities, Isidoro in his 'sequel' blasphemously mistakes the sarcophagus of Saint Rosalia, patroness of Palermo, for that of his beloved (19). Thus, paraphrasing Dombroski, we may say that in *Retablo* the extension of the name Rosalia to many different textual referents results in the glossing over of the distinct individuality of the various women all of the same name. This state of affairs ultimately prevents the reader from finding a "focal point for meaning and understanding" (Dombroski 1998, 264).

For this reason we must also stress, with Farrell, the fact that the composite nonsubjective point of view contains "an insistent, if veiled and allegorical, probe into the history and condition of the island" (71). This condition, we must add, concerns the creation and perpetuation into the present in Sicily and in southern Italy of a mind set and patronage system that may be described as postfeudal. It can be said that the title and structure of the work reflect the class structure of the times because the principle narrating voice, that of the Milanese painter Fabrizio Clerici, occupies the large center panel. It is preceded by Isidoro's first-person recounting of his life—whose title, "Oratorio," anticipates Clerici's 'oratorio' or poetic-musical "peregrination" of expiation of his love for doña Teresa Blasco through the epic, lyric and dramatic genres—prior to meeting Clerici and after their return to Palermo. The third panel of the triptych is 'painted' by the object of Isidoro's affections, Rosalia, who swears she is telling the truth when she tells how she will soon enter a convent. The reader has no way of verifying if, in fact, Rosalia remained chaste—despite the fact that her mother was a courtesan—throughout her wanderings or if she encourages Isidoro to return to his monastery to get rid of an unattractive, penniless suitor. But what matters is that, unlike *Il sorriso*, none of the characters in this work can be considered a spokesperson for the author.[24]

This dichotomy between the author and his characters contributes to the projection, through art, of an imaginary world, which implicitly reveals a desire to escape from an unbearable reality: In [*Retablo*] the desire to travel to remote places and dream about extinct civilizations is considered always in dialectical opposition to the real world, characterized by profound inequities, which even a detached observer like Clerici cannot overlook" (Pagano 2002, 211). It is not reality, but an illusion, a Quixotic *retablo de las maravillas* [*altarpiece of wonders*] in its own right. Similarly, for the character Clerici traveling is a metaphor for dreaming (Pagano 2002, 211), a means of escape from his present. For Consolo, as we have seen, it is a way of revisiting history, and of speaking metaphorically of our present. As Clerici tells Teresa, he has set out to see

> the traces [*le vestigia*], the remains of the past of our culture and civilization. But the real reason is our discontent with the times in which we live, with our lives, with ourselves, and the need to gain distance from it, die from it, and live in the dream of ancient, by-gone [*trapassate*] eras, that from this distance we can imagine were golden, poetic, as is always the case with the unreality of dreams, by which I mean the substance of our desires. . . . And writing is even more a way of dreaming; to write remembering the past as a suspension of the present of daily life. And, finally, to write of a journey, of a journey to the land of the past is a supreme form of dream. (70)

As Pagano indicates, the character Clerici is a product of the Enlightenment. He is impressed by the beauty of Palermo immediately upon arrival, "but this dreamlike image is replaced almost immediately by the sight of the instruments of torture and capital punishment, symbols of a regime still based on feudal privilege" (2002, 211–12). Indeed, Clerici's awakening is reinforced by the brutal treatment reserved by a local noble (the son of Clerici's host, Cavalier Ludovico Soldano) for the lower classes (Consolo 1987b, 43) and for women (52). We may say, following Sciascia, that the young man's feudal *forma mentis* can be traced back to the end of Arab domination of the Island, after which Sicilian life became "historicizable" and a "Sicilian way of being" was instated (Consolo 1999b, 212). Consolo's reader will remember that it is precisely this event, the expulsion of the Arabs and the installation of a feudal economy, depicted in the altarpiece described by Clerici in his travelogue: "Here among you passes, on his white charger and with the standard of our Redeemer Jesus Christ in hand, followed by fair and bold, by the most courageous Norman knights, the magnificent Count Roger of Altavilla, the great commander who freed the Island from the yoke of the Saracens . . . Here he is granting feuds, castles, farmlands . . . Here he is investing dukes, barons, knights" (47–48). Indeed, the villagers see portrayed the creation of the local nobility whose violent disregard for the lower classes still governs their lives centuries later. However, they are duped by the *retablo*, a worthy predecessor of our modern-day cinematic special effects, into exchanging illusion for reality and into projecting their own shortcomings onto the triptych. They fail to see what lies implicit in Rosalia's tale of "truth": the real, lived effects of class and gender oppression. And so while observing the triptych and its effects, Clerici cannot help but ask himself if the essence and purpose of all art is not that of providing an escapist illusion (46) for its audience, those who are willing to pay the artist "a small fee" (50). If this were the case—Consolo would, of course, contend that it is not—then the reader, at the novel's end, would have to agree with Rosalia's contention, that like her protector, all creative artists, "those who want to represent this world, the musician, the poet, the singer, the painter, are all so many *castrati* . . . who occupy the margins, the sides of the street; who look, express, and, sometimes, with envy, with a languishing nostalgia, stretch out their hand to touch the life that rushes past" (152).

What remains undetermined is the narrative artifice: since Clerici contends he has no intention of publishing his notes (24), the reader is left wondering who bundled Clerici's testimony with those of Isidoro and Rosalia. There is no pretense here of a found manuscript as there is in many of Eco's fictions. Here the reader is confronted with a collaborative representation of eighteenth-century Sicily. Clerici's intended interlocutor, Teresa Blasco, and Consolo's readers must decide whether to read Clerici's tale without interruption, skipping over Rosalia's story to perhaps return to it later or not at all; or whether to read the texts exactly as they appear in the book, in alternation. One can only wonder how Teresa Blasco might have responded to the sad plight of a woman more her less her own age but from a much less privileged background. When all is said and done the reader is confronted with three epistles that expect no response. For Clerici, and perhaps for Isidoro, writing is a means for placing memory and external reality in a dialectic relationship; it is a means for elaborating the past, so that the writing *I* may live in the present and future. Teresa is merely a sounding board, an unattainable object of desire, a discursive site in which he and his memories are reflected. For her part, Rosalia writes in the hope that Isidoro will return to the cloister, never to disturb her again.

But since the narrative artifice is indeterminate, what can and must be pursued is not the intentions of the writers, but instead the query first raised ekphrastically by the author—the modes of reception that inhere in the act of reading—and then emphasized by Consolo when the character Clerici uses of the rear of the sheets onto which Rosalia Granata has poured her darkest secrets. The text is a palimpsest, but it is first and foremost a tool utilized by the author to induce reader collaboration in the rewriting of the testimonies of an individual whose class of origin wrote history and also of the two marginalized figures whose first-person testimonies have now been retrieved.

4
Antonio Tabucchi

BACK TO THE FUTURE: ON TABUCCHI'S POETICS OF A "POSTHUMOUS" LITERATURE

FOR ANTONIO TABUCCHI, WRITING IS A FORM OF SOCIAL ENGAGEment; narrators, by definition, make explicit society's collective, anthropological dreams (Borsari, 29). Although they write for themselves, their work must have exchange value, and collective relevance. So they write for others, and for the reflection of themselves they see in others. Writing enables them to restore to the present the 'detritus' of the past. They "insert us more intensely in the present" by evoking "our memories and nostalgias" (Borsari, 5–6). Therefore, the act of writing is an important tool for understanding and defining our existence. It allows us to deal, in a positive way, with the "fragility of existence" and that which "oppresses our civil conscience": the awareness that the "evil" that motivated the Holocaust is still among us, and that another Hiroshima can put a sudden end to the world. But most importantly, writing serves as a bridge to the future, to posterity: "when we write we project into the future, whether it be a near future that we can somehow possess, or a distant and unreachable future" (Borsari, 5–8).

Thus, we find in Tabucchi an intense commitment to the present that is not synonymous with a Sartrean *engagement* or with political militancy. Rather, it is the posture, borrowed from Blanchot, that

> the intellectual is all the closer to action in general, and to power, for not getting involved with [politicians]. In standing back from politics, [the writer] does not withdraw from it, he has not retired from it, but rather attempts to sustain this space of retreat and this effort of withdrawal [*retirement*] so as to take advantage of this proximity at a distance and install himself there (in a precarious installation), like a

look-out who is there solely to keep watch, to remain watchful, to wait with an active attention, expressive less of a concern for himself that of a concern for others. (Blanchot 1984, 207–8)[1]

At the same time, Tabucchi is aware that writers are public figures and, as such, are often called on to express views on non-literary topics affecting the commonweal. However, the fact that he believes that writers operate outside the political arena does not mean that he underwrites Vittorini's distinction between politics and culture (the former operates on the short wave of chronicle, while the latter provides the long wave of history). In fact, the relative autonomy of writers from contingent issues gives their words a different weight, and saddles them with a different responsibility (Tabucchi 1997c). This stance comes in polemical response to interventions by Lyotard—who defined intellectuals as "thinkers who identify themselves with a subject endowed with a universal value" (Lyotard, 3) and, are therefore, committed to the discovery and dissemination of disinterested knowledge above social conflict—and with Umberto Eco—who contends that intellectual work should not aim at social incisiveness in the present, but should content itself with influencing the future.[2] The premise for Tabucchi's commitment to living in and historicizing the present is the "supposition that the literary vocation is in itself, intermittently, a commitment to explore political and ethical problems" (Smith 102, 103).

Tabucchi's commentaries on the state of the polis—in editorials published in Italy's leading dailies, and in important journals such as *Micromega*—gives a clearer picture of the nature of his engagement. He typically uses as pretext the various incongruities of Italy's anomalous political system[3] to denounce an overall "process of degradation of human existence and of nature" that is tailored to fit the dimensions of the "happy consciousness" characteristic of a period in which the wealth among certain strata of the population of the West has dulled the collective intellect, cooled our sense of social solidarity, inhibited personal relationships, and lessened our respect for the planet (Bodei, 128). He traces the "vulgarity that hovers over contemporary Italy"[4]—a country that in the 1980s attained a level of economic well-being that entitled it, perhaps too suddenly, to full membership in the capitalist mainstream—back to the failure of the Unification of Italy, and the failure of the governing class to instill in the populace the traditional values of European culture and civilization (Tabucchi 1999b).[5]

Tabucchi has stated that his perspective on Italy has been broadened by the acquisition of a second homeland, Portugal (Gumpert 41). He has used that country and its former colonies as the setting for fictions, and, more importantly, to gain the necessary distance for discussing contemporary Italy (Petri 1997).[6] In other words, pre- and post-Salazarist Portugal, like Sciascia's Sicily, is a metaphor for Italy, a country in which democracy itself is at risk.[7] Portugal provides a distance from contingency that augments the text's capacity for provocation. Portugal as metaphor allows the author to attempt a more realistic and complex understanding of fascisms and police states, not as the embodiment of a metatemporal category of Evil, but as historically specific "examples of human experience critically examined within their own context." When seen as the site of the uses and abuses of the political legal systems (Corral, 1), Portugal restores to the reader's present precise examples of aggression and the will to power, forcing us to consider the fragility of freedom and of human dignity.

After an early phase of development—which includes his first two novels, *Il piccolo naviglio* [*The Little Ship*] and *Piazza d'Italia* [*Italy Square*]—and as a result of Tabucchi's analyses in the early 1980s of the heteronyms of the Portuguese Modernist poet Fernando Pessoa and Tabucchi's translations of works by Pessoa, the subject of Tabucchi's narrations see themselves from the vantage of (an)other. However, it must be made clear that Tabucchi defines the other not only as what is alien and potentially hostile to the self, but also as "the part of you that you already are, or that you would like to be, the projection of the desire of that which we are lacking" (Gumpert Melgosa, 158). Thus, the reflection occasioned by Tabucchi's studies of Pessoa—on the internal plurality of the ego, as manifested in the heteronyms, and a retrieval of Pessoan alloglossia[8]—makes possible Tabucchi's entrance, in the 1990s, into full maturity as a creative artist. To explain, the narrating voice of *Notturno indiano* [*Indian Nocturne*] (1984) and the protagonist of *Il filo dell'orizzonte* [*The Edge of the Horizon*] (1986) are both 'autobiographical'[9] characters (Tabucchi 2003a, 11) who seek self-understanding through identification with an alter ego. Beginning with *L'angelo nero* [*The Black Angel*] (1991d) the subject of narration in Tabucchi is no longer prevalently autobiographical, nor is he someone who looks for himself in another. Instead, the subject of narration begins to examine himself from the vantage of (an)other. This process is brought to completion when Tabucchi writes *Requiem* in Portuguese and achieves a desired "sense of alterity," something that in turn makes possible the sensation of perceiving himself as someone else: this ideological translation into another's language, to use Bakhtin's phrasing, permits the overcoming of cultural otherness (365). In other words, writing, for Tabucchi and *pace* Barthes, is not an intransitive but a reflexive verb: to write is to write oneself [*scriversi*] (Tabucchi 2003a, 91); but since the self is other, *scriversi* is transitive. For this reason, beginning with *Sostiene Pereira* [*Pereira Declares*], Tabucchi's fictions may be described as "other people's autobiographies" (Tabucchi 2003a, 11).

This move further outside the self enables Tabucchi to identify with and examine diversities from a perspective that is not his own (Tabucchi "1996a, 121). It allows him to write from the points of view of a plurality of disparate immanent narrators. What remains constant over his entire career as a writer is a view of literary commitment as "a question of becoming one's own alter ego without ceasing to be oneself" (Tabucchi 1990a, 7). In other words, following Bodei we may say that through all Tabucchi's work the subject of narration gives sense to his existence by "searching to connect oneself to the spectrum of life situations already experienced by others (112). This sets in motion a process of maturation and development beyond the narcissistic monadic ego—that separates "me from not-me"—toward the attainment of a "relational ego" defined by the understanding of that which connects the self to myriad other myselves (Chodorow). Therefore, the innovations in narrative strategy adopted in Tabucchi's more recent prose fictions do not constitute a change in direction, but instead anticipate "the possibility of a new mode of existence where individuals overcome repressive forms of identity and stasis to become desiring nomads in a constant process of becoming and transformation" (Best and Kellner 1991, 77).

Tabucchi's increasingly refined attempts to identify with the other precludes the assumption of a posture of serene detachment or nonparticipation that characterizes, for example Calvino's Mr. Palomar whose epistemological project was predestined for failure by his refusal to act until he arrived at a bedrock of certainties (Francese 1997, 96–106).[10] In contrast, Tabucchi's ontological project aims at instilling uncertainty in the reader by raising questions he feels that as narrator he is not obligated to answer. For example, disquietude is interjected when the reader is forced to deal with one writer's multiple poetics (in the subtitle to this volume [*poetiche a posteriori*], Tabucchi uses the plural "poetiche" where the singular "poetica" might be legitimately expected) elaborated only a posteriori, an oxymoron that denotes both the hindsight of reflection and the future-oriented tension inherent within the creative process (Binni 8).

Thus, the paradoxical subtitle of the volume *Autobiografie altrui* [*Other People's Autobiographies*] forewarns the reader that clarifications and guidance from a strong author will not be forthcoming. Instead, unreliable reconstructions of what may or may not have figured in the artistic rendering are to be expected. In other words, the cover of the volume makes clear that there will be no pretense of giving witness to or insights into the creative process. Instead, the subtitle undermines any truth value the reader might be tempted to attribute to the essays collected in the volume wherein Tabucchi presents himself as someone who does not recognize himself completely in the plural past selves who wrote his fictions. Moreover, readers are forced to confront the possibility that this collection of *poetiche a posteriori* is part of Tabucchi's fictional enterprise, that is to say, that *Autobiografie altrui* is not a work of nonfiction. Instead, it may very well be a falsehood that poses a challenge to the "boundary between reality and fiction" (Tabucchi 2003a; 12, 115, 122), which is, after all, the theme that runs through and unites the volume.

Bertone, following Genette, explains that "the pact for reading is established" in the paratext, the cornice that surrounds the main body of the text, or in her own words, the "intermediate zone between the body of the text and what lies outside it," such as introductions, epigraphs, and afterwords (33): and titles and subtitles, we may add. However, she contends, Tabucchi does not use the paratext to anticipate what will be found in the text, to indicate how to read it, "to establish a zone of clarity and of textual intelligibility," nor to control, direct and guide the act of reading (35). If this is indeed the case, and I believe it is, then we must ask ourselves if the poetics a posteriori that comprise *Autobiografie altrui* are not written with the same intent as the other paratexts that envelope all Tabucchi's prose fictions, that of advancing "contradictory and incongruous" (self)interpretations (Bertone, 36).

The epigraph that precedes *Autobiografie altrui*, taken from Joseph Conrad, contains an explicit warning from the author to not give excessive credence to the chapters that follow: "First one creates the work, and only later reflects on it. And this is an idle [*ozioso*] and egoistic activity that benefits no one and that often leads to false conclusions" (9). Tabucchi continues to toy with the reader in the paratext—further devaluing the practice of writing a poetics after the fact while undermining the truth value of the essays collected in this volume—in what I might be tempted to call the introduction to the book, had the author not titled it "Post-preface (After, therefore, before)" (11).

In this afterword-*cum*-foreword, a text written with authorial hindsight but placed at the beginning so as to condition reading, Tabucchi lets it be known that these essays are "vagabond, nomadic, highly arbitrary hypotheses, unfit for any sort of philology" (12). So why, the reader asks, did the author commit his ruminations to print? And why should readers bother with them at all? After all, these glances backwards are, by the author's own admission, "tendentiously illogical, lacking deontology, filled with false memories and false will, bearers of a meaning that we pathetically force ourselves to give, after the fact, to something that happened before" (12, 120). So to what extent is the paratext a snare set by the author, "a stairwell into which we unwittingly plunge" (122).

To make the conundrum even more complex, *pendant* to Tabucchi's unreliable author is his unreliable reader. As Bertone indicates, "There are readers who skip right over the paratextual elements, and those who go back to them only after completing their reading of the principal text. In point of fact, those who read the paratext, read the principal text differently than those who do not" (33). In addition to these readers, there are others who dutifully read dedications and epigraphs, introductions and afterwords, and then, once they begin to advance into the text, set what they have read in the paratext aside and project their own desire for coherence and legibility onto the text. Of course, in doing so, they create a writer in their own image, even though, as Tabucchi admits, "It is not very easy for a writer to reflect on his own work, and above all speak about it, because for the writer a book ends where it ends. One can attempt to propose some thoughts and considerations, which may or may not be of worth" (85).

Indeed, one cannot help but be struck by the fact that the apparent sincerity of such disclaimers generate the opposite effect: Tabucchi's earnest acknowledgment of the unreliability of his remembrances seems intended to reaffirm the truth value of his testimony, which is curiously authenticated by the non-professional reader's intertextual acquaintance with his other fictional works by the same author. The scholar may just as easily be induced to underwrite the veracity of affirmations that seem to find substantiation in another equally important paratextual bridge to the extratextual: the footnotes.[11] The enigma is further complicated because, as Tabucchi points out, while on a deep level "all autobiography is fiction" (37), his fictions, including his *autobiografie altrui,* are not autobiographical. In other words, while autobiography works to restore the ego's integrity, utilizing linear time as "an ideal external support for . . . individual time and identity" (Pike, 330), Tabucchi's ontological enterprise strives to deconstruct the ego. There is no presumption here of traveling back through time to the origins of the psyche; there is only its semblance.

Those who read *Autobiografie altrui* with the anticipation of finding chronology reversed are disappointed by the paratext. To explain, as set out in the table of contents, the chapters of *Autobiografie altrui* follow time backward—the first is "On *Requiem*"; the second "On *Pereira*"; this is followed by a section titled "On *Il filo dell'orizzonte*" and then another "On *Donna di Porto Pim*" [Woman of Porto Pim]—giving the appearance of a writer engaged in auto-exegesis, intent on leading his reader backward, book-by-book, to the origin of his career as a writer. However, as the end of the volume draws near, Tabucchi changes direction and uses the final chapter to return almost to the present, to what was, at that time, his most recent work of fiction, *Si sta facendo sempre più tardi* [It Is Getting Later and Later]. But here too he remains elusive: this final chapter is not "on" but "In the Vicinity of *Si sta facendo sempre più tardi.*" Even in what seems to be the most movingly personal essay of the volume—"Un universo in una sillaba" [A Universe in a syllable], which is subtitled "A wandering *around* a novel" ([*Requiem*] my emphasis)—Tabucchi leaves at least one layer of opacity between the more intimate details of his life and his reader. He warns us, lest we take his remembrances literally, that his "evocations" (20) of the dead have their source in his autobiography, but come forth through the filter of a novelistic pact [*patto romanzesco*]—or "fictional agreement," to use Eco's term—between all writers and readers whereby "readers know that what they are reading comes from the life of the author, but are at the same time cognizant of the fact that those life experiences have been transformed into fiction, that is to say, into a novel" (21).

In fact, in the eponymous section, "Autobiografie altrui"—which takes its impetus from yet another letter, this one from a reader who recognized himself in one of the missives that structure *Si sta facendo sempre più tardi*—Tabucchi, following Blanchot, admonishes his reader against looking for him in this epistolary novel, since writers die the moment their work comes into existence, and enter a literary space where the writer's story ceases to be his own and becomes that of others (102), that of readers who, unbeknown to writers like Tabucchi, see their lives reflected in fictions (12). Therefore, Tabucchi affirms, all of his books are the life stories of others: writing grants him access to a "literary space" where "the writer is no longer himself, he is nobody" (92). He is both a Ulyssean *oûtis* [anyone] who affirms and asserts his identity through negation, and an Everybody who, like the autobiographical Spino, participates in a circular quest for self-comprehension in the reciprocal sharing of the plight of his alter ego, "Carlo Nobodi." The other whom Tabucchi and his protagonists seek "is perhaps nobody. Or better, the person the protagonist is seeking is perhaps the very person who is doing the seeking" (Tabucchi 2003d, 174).

So what are we to make of these (auto)biographical glances backward at texts that today seem—to Tabucchi—to be the work of someone else, a past self?[12] It would appear that, despite the disquieting self-contradictions and tautological re-iterations of an unabashedly unreliable testimony, at some level Tabucchi feels compelled to explain and justify, to others and to himself, the motivations behind the genesis and the psychological plausibility of his characters. For example, he feels obliged to explain why the decision of Lucas Eduino, in *Donna di Porto Pim*, to kill his lover with a harpoon rather than strangle her is not "unnecessarily complicated" [*macchinoso*]. He also defends the laugh that closes *Il filo dell'orizzonte*, arguing that Spino thus acknowledges and denies the bonds of empathy linking himself to Hamlet—who came to see the interconnectedness between his own suffering and that of Hecuba (54, 59)—and those linking Spino to Nobodi in an open-ended "(in)conclusion" (to use Tabucchi's own term) that coincides with Spino's understanding that the sense of Nobodi's life, and Spino's own, cannot be known because life is "not biographable"; it cannot be synthesized (56, 59).

Tabucchi's reader is disquieted because whenever the author seems to be on the brink of making things clear, he interjects perplexity. For example, proceeding *à rebours* in *Autobiografie altrui*, to the "Post-preface," Tabucchi swears that "in truth" Spino is an autobiographical character; that his protagonist is animated with his "myself of that period, a man with a funereal pessimism" (11). This description of the author is implicitly corroborated by the immanent narrator of "Autopsia" (66), who explicitly refutes Tabucchi's assertion when he—the immanent narrator of "Autopsia"—claims that he, not Tabucchi, was the model for Spino, a man who found himself in (Carlo) Nobody when he saw himself reflected in Everybody. Of course, the issue cannot be resolved because the logic necessary to unravel the mystery follows a strange loop resembling a Möbius strip that doubles back on itself. Autobiographical readings that contradict "Autopsia" are 'confirmed' by remarks made by Tabucchi to several interviewers, to the effect that *Il filo dell'orizzonte* marked the beginning of a "black period" of almost five years in which he produced very few examples of prose fiction. However, more striking than this admission, is the repeated omission of the details of the causes of the remorse that presumably caused all the gloominess, and of the process by which Tabucchi worked his way out of it.

As we shall see in a subsequent chapter, *Il filo dell'orizzonte* does indeed mark the beginning of the middle period of Tabucchi's career as a writer, one dominated by the study and appropriation of the heteronymic theory of Pessoa. It is a period in which the subjects of his narrations attempt to understand themselves in the reflections of themselves they see in their alter egos. Following Lacan, we may say that their experiences in front of this narrative mirror force them, and their author, to come to grips with their subjectivity, and to develop a sense of themselves as individuals. Self-identification catalyzes the direct, dialectical confrontation of inner and outer realities, necessitating a lengthy period of self-interrogation. In other words, Tabucchi takes from Pessoa critical but "disquieting criteria for understanding one's relationship with oneself and with others, individuality and inter-individuality, sociality and privacy" (Tabucchi 1990a, 21). However, the Pessoan model is superseded when Tabucchi uses those criteria to look outside the self and reaffirm objectifying, extraindividual diachrony over the monadistic synchrony characteristic of Pessoa's poetic inquiry.

The section dedicated to *Il filo dell'orizzonte* is the only one in *Autobiografie altrui* composed entirely of previously unpublished essays. Accompanying the subchapter on the genesis of this novel—"Ma cosa ha da ridere il signor Spino?" [What does Mr. Spino have to laugh about?], a previously unpublished 'letter' whose dedication, to Mavi and Luigi Surdich, the latter a literary scholar whose study of the poet Giorgio Caproni was 'presented' by Tabucchi (1990c), corroborates the truth value of the other letters collected in the volume by providing a verifiable extratextual link to Tabucchi's nonfictional writings—is one that deals with the novel's reception. This subchapter, titled "Autopsia" [Autopsy], appears to be a letter written by a fleeting acquaintance made by Tabucchi during the period in which he wrote *Il filo dell'orizzonte*.

A note to this text leads the reader to believe that Tabucchi (the writer of the footnote is unidentified) chose the title for this subchapter, his translation into the Italian of a letter written in English by a former colleague at the University of Genoa, who now resides in New York, to Fernando Lopes, the Portuguese director of the cinematic version of *Il filo dell'orizzonte*, which was made in French, and subtitled in English for the Bard College audience of which the letter-writer was a part. The reader is not made privy to Tabucchi's rationale for choosing this title, which seems to refer to the morgue technician Spino, not to the ostensible writer of the letter, who is not a coroner like Spino, but a radiologist specializing in CAT scans, which the narrating *I* describes as "machines for simulation" (63), a depiction that is equally applicable to the literary texts, hence to the raw material used by Tabucchi to make his livelihood as writer and scholar. Tabucchi does not justify his decision to serve as translator of this essay, an unusual choice given his refusal to translate his own *Requiem* from Portuguese, a language he knows much better than English[13]. In other words, "Autopsia" raises more questions than it answers, especially if we assume that Tabucchi wrote the note on page 61 and chose the title given the letter, "Autopsia."

The 'author' of this letter claims he recognized himself in Spino and then takes Tabucchi to task for deflecting his own inadequacies onto characters based on acquaintances such as the writer of this 'letter' (66). However, the letter is, to use a term dear to Tabucchi, incongruous. Although its writer uses it as a pretext to send an article he wrote in art criticism to Lopes, the letter appears to have no other discernible purpose than to allow its signatory—whose signature is omitted "for obvious reasons" by the author of an explanatory footnote (61)—to vent his frustration with Tabucchi.[14]

The letter's narrating *I* claims that upon meeting Tabucchi in the early 1980s he warned the ingenuous writer of the activities of radical political militants. He then declares that he is of the opinion that at that time Tabucchi seemed to be under duress due to suspicions that the University of Genoa was a haven for terrorists (65). The letter-writer then proclaims: "non vorrei che Tabucchi avesse sospettato che nell'università ci fossero degli infiltrati di quell'organizzazione" (65), which translates into English as "I would not want [now] that Tabucchi might have suspected [then] that within the University there were moles from that organization," an unusual turn of phrase, due to the use of the present conditional (*vorrei* [I would want]) when the imperfect (*volevo* [I wanted]) might be reasonably expected. The temporal disjunction of the sentence is a signal of its writer's present regret—for having raised suspicions in the mind of the "cowardly," therefore untrustworthy, Tabucchi (66), who transferred his tribulations and shortcomings onto a character, Spino, a transmogrification of the letter-writer—and his implied fear that members of the unnamed terrorist "organization" might now equate the letter-writer with the imprudently curious Spino, rather than with Tabucchi "who had gotten it into his head" to get to the bottom of various unsolved mysteries (65).

Thus, this letter confirms the paradox at the base of these poetics a posteriori, as put forward by Tabucchi in the "Letter to a Friend" excerpted in the Post-preface. To wit, the act of writing transforms the writing *I* into its other while transforming that other into yet (an)other. To phrase it a bit differently, I = Nobody = Everybody.

The letter writer—while denying any similarity to Tabucchi, other than suffering, in the early 1980s, from a "mal di testa e di universo [a head- and universe-ache]—claims that Spino is both his own doppleganger and Tabucchi's autobiographical protagonist. Of course, the letter tells us more, implicitly, about its 'writer' than about Tabucchi, who does not explain why he decided to include the letter in the volume, leaving the reader to assume that the letter's function is to provide an 'objectifying' view of Tabucchi. Moreover, while intertextual references seem to corroborate the content of the letter (the title evokes Spino's morgue, and the smell of fried food that permeates Tabucchi's place of employment is reminiscent of the editorial offices of Pereira's *Lisboa* [64]), the truth value of the letter's testimony is undermined because it implicitly confirms what Tabucchi seems to deny: that Tabucchi himself is the writer of the letter.

In sum, "Autopsia" propels the reader onto a journey over another strange loop of inter- and intratextual self-corroborations of factuality and paratextual assertions of the fictionality of the book. At the same time, it confirms the only certainty the writer is willing to place at the reader's disposition, the paradoxical caveat inherent in the novelistic pact: when the fiction that presides over literature transforms autobiographical information into unreliable fictionalized memory "the reader must believe the writer when he says that he is a liar" (Tabucchi 1990a, 27).

Since the act of reading implies acceptance of a novelistic pact that recognizes the translation of autobiographical data into fiction, then we must assume that the seemingly autobiographical narrating *I* of *Requiem* is not Antonio Tabucchi, but a fictional character (Tabucchi 2003a, 37) that Tabucchi "calls 'I'" (Tabucchi 1992a, 7). Thus, the subject of narration effaces the boundary between fiction and nonfiction: in both the fictional *Requiem* and in the nonfictional *Autobiografie altrui* the subject of writing is a metaphor. In other words, in both volumes the *I* is not a person, but an esthetic configuration, the imaginative and skillful manipulation of autobiographical material.

In the "hallucinatory" *Requiem*, esthetic resolution is achieved by altering and rearranging details from the author's life so that art, not life, dictates the various contiguities and convergences that give the work structural and esthetic cohesion (Bailey, 81–82). The same can be said of *Autobiografie altrui*, whose ambiguous paratext—the cover takes care to avoid labeling the book a work of either fiction or of nonfiction—does not specify if the reader is to respond to the narrating *I* as a fictional person. And yet, as Tabucchi has argued, if we believe that Pessoa, in creating his heteronyms, becomes his own alter ego, and if we must consequently feign to believe the flesh-and-blood *fingidor* Pessoa was the imitation—with the same biographical data—as an impostor-hortonym[15] Fernando Pessoa who was identical to himself (Tabucchi 1990a, 12), then it follows that the 'author' of *Autobiografie altrui* is not Antonio Tabucchi, but his hortonym.

Tabucchi's hortonym deals with Spino's "funereal pessimism" and elaborates his own remorse through allusions to recurring metaphorical figures such as Tadeus, Isabel, and the Father: allegorical images à la Montale—*senhals* much larger than themselves—of people and events from the past. Therefore, remorse does not necessarily refer to specific occurrences from the author's life, but is instead a metaphor for the impossibility of changing what has been and for the need to modify behavior in the future (Gumpert Melgosa 153).

This remorse is a metaphor for what Kristeva has called a "malady of the soul" or of the psyche, which in her definition constitutes the nexus between the speaking being and the other and is therefore endowed with a therapeutic and moral value (4). Remorse in this context is a means of engaging both the other and the future through the symbolization of traumas (9), that is to say, by providing desire with a narrative, by making drives come forth through discourse.

At the same time, Tabucchi's 'autobiographical' backward looks rewrite the past, sending the reader out on more strange loops, because they necessitate rereadings that forestall definitive interpretations of his fictions. As is the case with betrayal—the only human action that can modify experience, as Tabucchi, following Jankélévitch, affirms (Tabucchi 2003a, 79)—rereadings of Tabucchi's fictions in the light of self-exegeses such as *Autobiografie altrui* betray earlier interpretations of the texts and of the *senhals*. Matters are further complicated when the writer assumes the mantle of a latter-day Pessoan *fingidor*, a writer whose "greatest truths" come forth when he lies to readers who appreciate his penchant for fabrications. The *fingidor* is the writer who falsifies and simulates what is intimately personal by projecting emotions and sentiments onto his artistic creations, the depersonalized subjects of his narratives, to broach interpersonal, shareable truths.

According to Tabucchi, *Si sta facendo sempre più tardi* is all about betrayals that rewrite the past (*Autobiografie altrui* 87). Betrayal is also the stock in trade of the "Sublime Accomplice" of "Futuro anteriore" [Future Anterior] (*Autobiografie altrui* 107–12), a brief narrative that retrospectively undermines the integrity of *Si sta facendo sempre più tardi*,[16] hence all exegetic readings of that work. At the same time "Futuro anteriore" also developes intertextually the protagonist-*senhal* of "Staccia Buratta" (Tabucchi 1991b, 51–70), the protégé who is intent on writing her autobiography in a way that renarrates her past, and that of her elderly accomplice.[17] "Futuro anteriore" betrays all previous readings of the letters that comprise *Si sta facendo sempre più tardi* while undermining future readings of that work because "Futuro anteriore" serves to warn that some day other works by Tabucchi may also be rewritten by a living writer or by documents to be discovered posthumously (as was the case with Pessoa) in another *baule pieno di scrittori* [chest full of writers] preserved by Antonio Tabucchi in Vecchiano. "Futuro anteriore: una lettera mancante" [Future anterior: A missing letter], the frame-tale for "Futuro anteriore," contains a summary by the author of the lapsus that prevented the publication of the narrative within the volume for which it was intended,[18] and an explanation of its unconscious motivation: he was unwilling to transform events that had "really existed" into something twice or "hyper-real." That is to say, he did not want to transform lived experience into something apperceived and de-personalized, having happened to someone else: a narrating *I* (71). Belated publication of "Futuro anteriore" in a subsequent volume would therefore indicate that he succeeded in "taming that disturbance" by consigning the task of narration to his hortonym—a person at one remove from himself—who, of course, also signs his work "Antonio Tabucchi."

"Un universo in una sillaba" also develops another recurring figure who is also associated with the process of elaborating remorse, that of the father.[19] Scholarly references give this essay— in which details of events leading to the father's death and of his interaction with the narrating *I* are rewritten—the semblance of an exercise in non-fiction. However, when empathy for the elder character's suffering reaches the intensity of *"pietas"* the narrating *I* abruptly changes tack, and begins to expound on the intellectual aspects of his own plurilinguism, specifically his uncanny utilization, in writing *Requiem*, of a non-native language that had acquired psychological, or affective, status for him (see Shanon). The subject of narration then further distances himself from the personal by bringing into play the author's public self-image, that of a writer who, like Pirandello, "convokes ghosts" (24, 25, 47)—characters who visit him while he is half-asleep—and then, following the example of Pessoa's hortonym, sets their stories to paper "as if in a trance" (Tabucchi 2003a, 34, 35, 47, 104; see also Tabucchi 1990a, 29).

These paeans to the automatic writing of the surrealists are yet another *senhal*, this one of the creative process to which the writer refers metaphorically as dreams; "dreams that you know you are dreaming, whose truth consists of their being both real and outside reality" (Tabucchi 1987, 40). When writers dream, they simulate; they become another so that their solitude, Blanchot's term for referring to what is intimately the writer's, can be shared. In *Sogni di sogni* [*Dream of Dreams*] Tabucchi "dreams the dreams of other" writers in order to gain access to "their 'heart,'" that is to say the shareable solitude writers project outward into their works (Mauri). In so doing, Tabucchi loses or immerses himself in the first-person narration of lives that are not his own. Similarly, in *Autobiografie altrui* a hortonym dreams the dreams of Antonio Tabucchi, effacing yet another boundary, one that in previous fictions by Tabucchi separated first- and third-person narration. In *Autobiografie altrui* the *I* is other and the other is now *I*; the process of identification with (an)other, begun in the early 1980s, is complete.

Parenthetically, *Sogni di sogni* is literally a collection of *autobiografie altrui* that deal specifically with the creative process, or the restoration of "signifying images" from the past (Tabucchi 1992c, 26). Here the dream is a metaphor for the mining of the raw material necessary for new esthetic endeavors, and Tabucchi's *sogni* are dreams of dreams, of "past lives that had still yet to be" [*la sua vita passata che doveva ancora essere*] (51).[20] "Dreams," he avers, "are life not only because they are verisimilar, but especially because they are real when they deal with visions of emotions, for example the dreams of the artist, which are always real even when they seem fantastic" (Tabucchi 2000, 22). They are fictitious testimonies, or allegories in the Benjaminian sense: "vicarious narrations" carried forth for the dead.

Moreover, if "writing to the dead," as Tabucchi claims, is "the quickest way to write to ourselves" (Tabucchi 1987, 74), then the evocation of the Father has the same scope of psychotherapy, that of examining the past with the goal of modifying behavior in the future. So, when the narrating *I* becomes his own descendant [*postero a se stesso*] through interaction with the ghost of the Young Father in "Un universo," the objectifying vantage so gained allows the subject of narration to see himself as other and understand how a dialectical relationship with posterity enables him to interact with the present. In other words, the oneiric restoration of the past provides the fulcrum between past, present, and future, necessary for giving a sense, or direction to history.

To close the parenthesis, what is also striking about these glimpses into the hortonym's unconscious is what they peremptorily conceal: they present the psychoanalytic process as completed: the revelation and explanation of lapsus truncates all discussion (107).[21] At the same time, the possibility of an ex post facto addition of a nineteenth letter to *Si sta facendo sempre più tardi* undermines narratological definitions of the text as a self-contained 'open work' that can be read without regard for its *hic et nunc* and the biography of the author who 'dies' after consigning it to press.

Instead, the literary text, and literature for that matter, are not closed, self-sufficient, self-referential systems, but—as is the case with mathematics, as Gödel's incompleteness theorems have shown—must look outside themselves to history for validation. For this reason, Tabucchi contends that writing is the telling of our public, collective, anthropological dreams: and "precisely in this sense literature is synonymous with social commitment" (*Conversazione con Antonio Tabucchi*, 29). Furthermore, while precluding definitive readings and encouraging new readings, the "future anterior" rewriting of a previously published text by a no longer dead, but 'reincarnated' author, reasserts the writer's presence within that text while paradoxically forestalling any reaffirmation of an authorial pretense that might direct reading.

Since writing fixes the ephemeral as a presence in time, as

Blanchot maintains, this particular rewriting transforms *Si sta facendo sempre più tardi* into a collaborative effort: 'dead' author, reader, 'reincarnated' author, rereader. Furthermore, the letter titled "Futuro anteriore" gives substance to the paradoxical presence of absence—it is both recognition of the self, and cognition of the self-as-other (that is to say, of the *I* who becomes Nobody in order to embrace the fate of Everybody). When writing "makes what is ungraspable inescapable," it forces both author and reader to never cease reaching for the unattainable (Blanchot 1955, 30–31). And if—as the epigraph, from Rilke, to the section "near" *Si sta facendo sempre più tardi* avers—the future enters into us, to transform itself within us, far before it comes to be, then writing is indeed, a "foretelling of the past that occurs posthumously" (103); and books for their part are "small universes in expansion" (98). They are both a discovery/recovery of what existed in the past and locus of dialogue, in absentia, with the future.

Since, as Tabucchi claims, writing is a way of extracting "what 'really happened' from non-cognition and bringing it into existence through the act of textualization" (104), then the writing of "other people's autobiographies" brings us into a literary twilight zone bereft of borders: between reality and imagination; between truth and falsehood. The fictitious is universally true because it transcends what is specific or particular to the individual; there is no singular Truth, but multiple, individual truths whose boundaries are defined by truth's complement (94), the "mendacity, voluntary or involuntary," that inheres in the novelistic pact (12). The border between text and extratext is also erased: the "story" told by the cover image leads outside the text—it is cited in both the "Post-prefaction" and on the back cover—while its insertion on page 114 creates another link between the text and the paratext and, from there to a translation (judging from the differences in type,[22] layout, and number of words in the photograph reproduced on the cover of *Autobiografie altrui*) of *Si sta facendo sempre più tardi*.[23]

Gone also are all distinctions between genres: when the writers of letters, like the keepers of diaries, write *dialoghi mancati*, monologues that do not anticipate a response, they, like all memorialists, can be said to write books—for themselves and for posterity—that are both their own biographies and "other people's autobiographies" (93, 102).

Thus, following Pirandello, writing can be seen as a means for giving manageable boundaries to inchoate life (86); but more importantly, it enables us to put ourselves "In rete" ([Tabucchi 2003a, 85–88] a term that in Italian can mean online or on the Internet; but also in the net or network of individuals that recognize their own lives reflected in Tabucchi's (auto)biographies.[24] Each (auto)biographical essay brings us far beyond the borders between fiction and nonfiction; and when they come together in the volume, as so many mosaic tiles, or "syllables," they transform into an expanding universe (98) of "other people's life stories" to be recounted in books that can be housed in a library where they will be catalogued not with a Library of Congress designation, but with an icon, that of a "little man with an enormous headache" (101).

Indeed, *Si sta facendo sempre più tardi* was composed with the intention of providing the reader with a "huge headache" [*un'enorme cefalea*] (Tabucchi 2003a, 101–2), comparable to that suffered by Tabucchi's Minotaur, who is beset with a condition known to "only the unhappily privileged few," people like Fernando Pessoa, who described his own disquietude as a "mal di testa e di universo" (Pessoa 1988, 14). The writer, a latter-day Dedalus in this view of things, pursues the trail of his own Minotaur by dreaming dreams that are more than verisimilar, that are indeed "synonymous with life itself" because they "are visions of emotions, true even when they seem fantastic." For Tabucchi, when writers dream dreams that introduce a necessary chaos into our lives, they contribute to our comprehension of the universe, and to our understanding of the Infinite (Tabucchi 2000, 21–22).[25]

Back to the Present: The Self as Other in Tabucchi's "Ekphrastic" and Theatrical Writings

As we have seen, after writing two debut novels, *Piazza d'Italia* and *Il piccolo naviglio*, Tabucchi entered what we have called an intermediary phase characterized by the investigation of narrative possibilities using Fernando Pessoa's heteronyms as his model. The brief narratives collected in *Il gioco del rovescio* [*The Reverse Game*] (1981), and in *Piccoli equivoci senza importanza* [*Small Misunderstandings of No Importance*] (1985) were examples of this experimentation.[26] However, he published no book-length work of prose fiction between *Notturno indiano* (1985) and *Il filo dell'orizzonte* (1986),[27] and *L'angelo nero* (1991). During this interval, which he has described as his "black period" (Hernández 26),[28] he wrote two one-act plays, published together as *I dialoghi mancati* [*Failed Dialogues*] (Tabucchi 1988c), important examples of his experiments with "non-descriptive prose," that is to say monologue or soliloquy. He also published several works[29] that one might be tempted to call ekphrastic because they were first published juxtaposed to visual texts that treat similar subject matter from a diverse perspective, that of the figurative artist. However, these brief narratives are not "verbal representations of visual representations" (Mitchell, 152). Rather, they stand independently of what surrounds them. Indeed, one of these brief narratives, "Voci portate da qualcosa" [Voices Brought by Something], was re-published several years later as the first story in *L'angelo nero*.[30]

The placement of autonomous writings next to figurative art installs a dialectic of collaboration and resistance that forces readers to question their own horizon of expectations in accordance with the decentered perspective they gain by virtue of the hybrid work. The narratives in question all deal in some way with the act of observation: of the other, of the self, and ultimately, of the self from the point of view of the other. Together they chart a path for Tabucchi's narrating voices beyond the acquisition of self-understanding through empathy for the other—attained in *Notturno indiano* (1985) and *Il filo dell'orizzonte*—to the ability to elaborate the past from the non-autobiographical perspective that underpins *L'angelo nero* and subsequent fictions.

Tabucchi has called *L'angelo nero*, the work that brought his five-year hiatus to a close, a milestone in his career, the book with which he achieved "adulthood" as a writer (Van Eekhout, 22–23). Indeed, *L'angelo nero* is the first work by Tabucchi in which the subject of narration begins to demonstrate the ability to observe himself as other. In *Requiem*, written almost at the same time, that is to say between January and October 1991 (Tabucchi 1999a, 22), the protagonist uses the externalized monologue characteristic of *I dialoghi mancati* to confess, the same device that will structure the one-sided epistolary dialogues of *Si sta facendo sempre più tardi* (2001). In *Si sta facendo* the desire to confess or engage the past in dialogue in order to elaborate remorse is frustrated by the silence of the addressees. Nonetheless, the acknowledgment of remorse to a single, deceased 'interlocutor,' a projection of the interiority of subject of narration, and the narrating voice's attempt to engage in conversation the addressee of his communications creates a *dialogo mancato*, a state of affairs wherein soliloquy and dialogue are synonymous.

Through these conversations with the 'dead,' or reflections/projections of himself, the subject of narrative comes to see himself from the vantage of (an)other. This further weakens a center of narrative gravity already challenged by Tabucchi's investigation into the possibilities of theatrical form and his experimentation with collaborative, hybrid texts. The result is his entrance, in the 1990s, into a period of artistic maturity, defined precisely by works whose subject of narration utilizes a diverse, less subject-centric point of observation from which to observe the self.

In *Sogni di sogni* (1992), the work that helps mark the advent of the new phase of development to which we have referred, Tabucchi succeeds in dreaming the dreams of others by "putting [him]-self in their shoes as he would with any fictional creation" and by "confess[ing] obliquely" (Mauri). By this he means by writing about himself in a nonautobiographical mode, from the perspective of others. In other words, in this collection of brief narratives, Tabucchi attempts to narrate from the perspective of artists who really existed rather than assume the perspective of fictive characters that are the projection of his own imagination.

This narrative strategy will subsequently be utilized by the author in *Sostiene Pereira* and *La testa perduta di Damsceno Monteiro* [*The Lost Head of Damsceno Monteiro*] to envision protagonists whose 'dialogues with the dead' will spark in both cases what Gramsci calls a "catharsis," or passage from the egoistic-economic to the ethical-political that in turn generates in both Pereira and Firmino the desire to engage posterity in dialogue. In other words, at opposite ends of this trajectory we see Spino, who in *Il filo dell'orizzonte* [*The Edge of the Horizon*] seeks self-understanding through an alter ego; at the other are Pereira and Firmino who seek affirmation by attempting to influence those who will follow.

We will return to this topic further on. For now it is important to stress how the juxtaposition of word and image in parallel texts causes two artistic messages to imbricate and interact in the mind of the reader/observer. The polyvocal message not only provides a more objective representation of experience, but the collaboration of writer and figurative artist, by raising the issue of the conventional divisions between art forms, calls into question how meaning is created in the work of art. As Jameson (1975) has argued, the reciprocal understanding between artists and public that makes reception possible is based on and conditioned by on the artist's formal choices. When the form into which the writer organizes experience deviates from what is known and expected, inherited strategies of reading are challenged and the reader's horizon of expectation is modified. This is particularly the case with the brief hybrid narratives written by Tabucchi in the late 1980s and early 1990s because they stand in a relationship of autonomy and of parity with a figurative text. Since neither word nor image is subordinate to the other, possibilities of interpretative freedom are augmented, and the audience is transformed into active participant in the signifying process (see Benjamin 1955b, 204–12).

The ekphrastic work installs a triangular relationship between the figurative artist, the writer, and the reader-beholder. The written text conditions reception of the image when it "sutur[es] discourse and representation" (Mitchell, 69). The same effect is achieved when the verbal text comes to the audience through the filter of a privileged reader: the illustrator whose drawings supplement the verbal text, conditioning reception.[31] In contrast, the brief narratives written by Tabucchi during the period in question do not supplement the image. For this reason, they are not ekphastic works, but may be more accurately described as parallel texts or as elements of hybrid works in which word and image complement each other and interact with audience expectations in a nonprescriptive way.

When writers speak for or interpret pictures, they translate, or convert silent objects into narratives (Heffernan 20, 23, 30).[32] This is the case with an earlier work by Tabucchi, "La traduzione" [The translation] (Tabucchi 1987, 62–64), wherein a sighted person translates or describes a painting for a vision-impaired companion.[33] The same can be said of the eponymous tale of *I volatili*. Here too the image supplements the word in telling of the creative process by evoking several paintings by the Renaissance artist Fra' Angelico. Strictly speaking, these two texts do not serve as mere enhancements; it is more precise to say that they call forth an unattainable object of desire, figurative texts that are not there. When these ekphrastic stories are contrasted to the parallel texts of the late 1980s and early 1990s we see how the presence of the figurative text allows Tabucchi's contributions to hybrid projects to challenge the locus of constitution of human subjectivity: the dialectic of word and imaging (see Mitchell, 24).

When the relationship of image and the text is characterized by an "independence or coequality that permits collaboration in a truly composite form" modes of perceiving are challenged (Mitchell qtd. Heffernan). When the hybrid text challenges readers' horizons of expectation, it enables Tabucchi to approach his goal of supplying his reader with a "salubrious dose of disquietude" (Tabucchi 1983, 7; Gumpert 104). The reader/spectator must look beyond a subjective representation—be it the two-dimensional unified perspective of a painting or univocal verbal text—toward a more objective reflection of the variety of the world. The audience thus gains access to a spectrum of possible meanings that vary according to the various points of observation and of reception which in turn forestall the installation of any one authoritative reading. Indeed, Tabucchi's participation with brief narratives in works that combine his words with others' images provides the audience with a repertoire of sensations "whose sense is not given by the individual figures, but by the way they are put together" (Calabrese, 15); first by those who collaborate to create the various volumes, and then in the mind of the reader/observer whose global impressions are the result of the interaction of multiple stimuli.

The disquietude provoked by these challenges to unifying perspective carries an implicit caveat: to use the phrasing of a character in *Notturno indiano*, the photographer Christine, "*Méfiez-vous des morceaux choisis*" [beware of selected pieces] (Tabucchi 1984, 102). Her enjoinder is against the framing or isolation of what is represented from the surrounding context. Interpretation—translation—is always and at best an approximation of the intent of an author or artist, a transposition from one culture—a *forma mentis* that has developed over time with a specific history and traditions in interaction with myriad internal and external, social and natural, forces—to another. However, the decentering of perspective that takes place within the hybrid text (re)kindles audience awareness that, inherent in the act of reading/observing, is an "infidelity" or unavoidable "tendency to mis-understand" or "misinterpret" what is in fact the intrinsic semantic ambiguity of the artistic work (Costanzo 48, 51). In turn, cognizance that this broader, objectifying perspective brings into play something that is not represented, the out-of-field, to use Deleuze's term (1983), encourages the reader/viewer to become a producer of meaning.

For this reason, in a review published approximately at the beginning of this period of formal research (to be precise, in late 1988, shortly after the appearance of *I dialoghi mancati*[34]), Tabucchi applauded Daniele Del Giudice's novel *Nel Museo di Reims* [*In the Reims Museum*], attributing the felicitous artistic rendering of the novel to the enigmas, "lacunae, meanings to be expanded upon, and other interrogatives" left by its author for the reader to resolve. The "elliptic, allusive" character of Del Giudice's novel is enhanced by reference to paintings that, in Tabucchi's opinion, do not merely illustrate the text, but "speak on their own behalf." Instead, by refraining from defining the images, the verbal text traces "an interrogative way of . . . narrating." It does so by "making aware and communicating, while avoiding the pitfall of becoming caption and explanation" (Tabucchi 1998e). The end result is "a story in which a situation is given in its essential elements which must be elaborated by readers, who may deduce their own meanings and conclusions."

In contrast, the out-of-field is purposely ignored by the protagonist of "Vivere o ritrarre" [To Live or to Portray], one of the hybrid texts published by Tabucchi in 1989, as part of a collection of drawings of intellectuals, writers, and artists by the noted caricaturist Tullio Pericoli. Tabucchi's Film Director contends that the preservation of the "purity of his art" coincides with the creation of re-assuring filmic presentations of the already known. He is described as having taken one eye into his hand and placed it over the other. The Director believes he can "see better" through this "bi-occhio." Instead, this "double-eye" deprives him of his capacity for depth perception; more importantly, it transforms what he sees into something twice real, tautologically true because each eye confirms the other's perceptions. Consequently, those who audition for him—writers, such as Dostoyevsky and Joyce, and intellectuals such as Benedetto Croce and Freud—are not real, three-dimensional individuals who live in time, but flat, unrealized characters. They are true cameos whose performance reflects and corroborates what the Director already knows: their static public image. Ultimately, because he is incapable of understanding that artistic portrayal is a means for interacting dialectically with life, the Director is overtaken by what he has set in motion; that is to say, he becomes, like his walk-ons, a larger-than-life character, living authentication of the public image he has created for himself.

The process of artistic maturation and development we are tracking comes into relief when a narrative such as "Vivere o ritrarre" is compared to those that compose *Sogni di sogni*, which was written shortly after this period of five years in which Tabucchi interrogated the ramifications of the decentering of visual perspective and of the word; that is to say, the effects of observing oneself and speaking oneself from an external vantage, that of (an)other. Unlike the Director of "Vivere o ritrarre," the subjects of the oneiric narratives of *Sogni di sogni* are real people who lived in history, and whose creative work cannot be separated from the rest of their lives (Gumpert Melgosa 196), a fact underscored by the writer's arrangement in chronological order of their stories, and of their biographies, which are appended to the volume. The exception to this pattern is the dream of Sigmund Freud. Freud's biography merits special consideration—and is therefore placed in relief at the end of the volume—because Freud uncovered the modalities of the artist's creative dialectic, the transformative dialogue with the unconscious, the disturbing "*parte oscura*" or dark recess within each of us that artists must have the courage to explore (Tabucchi 1992c, 66–67).

That dark recess, as Tabucchi makes clear in the epigraph to *Sogni di sogni*, may be gained when we dream the dreams of another, that is to say, when we see the world from the intimate perspective of someone with whom we have identified. This empowers us to write of our life as if we were narrating so many *autobiografie altrui*, as did Freud, in Tabucchi's view, when he wrote of Dora, Hans, and the Wolf-Man.[35] Indeed, we may describe the process of maturation of Tabucchi's poetics from the mid-1980s through the early 1990s by paraphrasing what Blanchot said of Freud's discovery of transference: first, he plays the role of another; then he is other [*l'autre*] before becoming another [*autrui*] (1993, 231).

Whereas in such works of the early and mid-1980s, as *Notturno indiano* and *Il filo dell'orizzonte*, the point of reference for what we can 'know' is internal to the self, in the later period of creativity marked by works such as *Sogni di sogni*, the point of departure for self-understanding is external. However, it must be made clear that, even in this earlier period, self-understanding is not achieved through a radical turn inward, as is the case with Pessoa, but through self-(re)cognition, of knowing oneself anew (Steiner), which is accomplished when the subject of narration identifies with and comes to know himself through (an)other. Indeed, the protagonist of Tabucchi's "La Battaglia di San Romano" (Tabucchi 1987, 54–57) can be described as truly loving a woman "because he loved her in the most authentic of ways, because he loved himself in her" (55). This definition of love as reciprocity reflects but supersedes the view of the Pessoan heteronym Ricardo Reis—who contends that 'no one loves another; we only love what we see, or believe we see, of ourselves reflected in another' (Tabucchi 1990a, 96)—because the protagonist's quest for self-understanding in *Notturno indiano* does not exclude the world, and Spino's self-love in *Il filo dell'orizzonte* does not forestall consideration of *agape*, love for all humanity: Spino can laugh into the darkness of uncertainty when, following Hamlet, he understands the compassion for Hecuba simulated by Yorick.[36]

However, after this five-year period of formal research, self-comprehension in Tabucchi's work is no longer contingent on identification with (an)other, but on the ability to see oneself from the perspective of the other. Indeed, the great innovation of Tabucchi's fictions of the 1990s is to be found precisely in the decentralization of the subject of narrative, whose end result, as we shall see presently, is that of seeing oneself from the perspective of posterity.[37]

Tabucchi attains the capacity to look at himself nonsubjectively, "as if in a mirror" while at a public showing of the cinematic version of *Notturno indiano*, which debuted in 1989. Tabucchi explains that watching the film as a member of the audience permitted him to overcome his trepidation at seeing himself as others see him, an accomplishment that allowed him to gain a diverse form of awareness of his own subjectivity, and develop an enhanced sense of himself as a creative artist (Tabucchi 1990b). To facilitate this process of externalization in his narratives, Tabucchi assumes an alienated posture to write of himself (Palmieri, 27). For example, he writes *Requiem* (1992a) in his adoptive language, Portuguese, setting in motion a process of estrangement that forces him to see himself as other: in this case he assumes the stance of his first reader, or translator (see Tabucchi 1990a, 34; Tabucchi 1998b, 19; Tabucchi 1991c, 65–66).[38] In other words, writing in Portuguese grants Tabucchi a desired "sense of alterity" that in turn makes possible the sensation of perceiving himself as someone else.

By inverting the roles of writer and translator, he liberates the voice of an internal other (see Orengo) so that writer and translator both infiltrate and overcome the uniqueness and singularity of each other. Thus, following Steiner, we may say that writing in a language other than his native Italian is for Tabucchi a means of self-critique, of recognizing the other and the self" (Steiner, 8–10).[39] The attainment of this more objective vantage, whence Tabucchi perceives himself as other (in Lacanian terms, *se voir se voir*: he sees himself see himself), in what Kilborne calls a "dialectics of seeing" (wherein the subject imagines herself being seen and not being seen by the other), enables him to view his "own Desire in relation to the other, through the observation of observation," and attain analytic consciousness (Ragland-Sullivan, 93–94). In other words, he (re)cognizes his language and belief system as they are known in someone else's language and belief system.[40]

During the middle phase of Tabucchi's career as a writer—which coincides roughly the early 1980s, beginning with the publication in 1981 of *Il gioco del rovescio* (a collection of brief narratives characterized by experimentation with diverse narrative points of view) and ending with *Notturno indiano* and *Il filo dell'orizzonte*—his studies of the work of Pessoa helps Tabucchi address a crucial aspect twentieth-century literary inquiry, one that is at the core of his own work during this period, the question of otherness and alterity (Tabucchi 1998b, 18–19). During this poetic phase, the quest for self-knowledge carried forth by Tabucchi's protagonists and narrating voices follows a path evoked by the "strange loop" contemplated by Xavier Janata Monroy in "La frase che segue è falsa. La frase che precede è vera" [The following sentence is false. The proceeding sentence is true] (Tabucchi 1987, 42–53). Monroy suggests a way of knowing that may be visualized as a sort of Möbius strip—going off in one direction, then turning over, then back on itself and then over again, back to its point of departure—outside the self toward the Other, and then inward, backward in time through the formation of the unconscious to the moment of birth, the *"place d'effroi"* [place of terror] where one moves from nonbeing to being.

Critical for Tabucchi's poetic inquiry during this middle period is the question of how "Pessoa examines the alterity he carries within himself" through the creation of heteronyms, "independent and autonomous personalities that live independently of their author." The heteronyms are explicit manifestations of multiple internal others, each of whom are distinct and self-sufficient individuals, poet-characters invented down to the most minute detail, biography, somatic features, aesthetic preferences, cultural background and even idiosyncrasies, each of whom manifests his own poetics, esthetics, worldview, and creative style (Tabucchi 1990a, 25). Through the exploration of these heteronyms Pessoa's quest for self-knowledge goes in only one direction, inward.[41] Tabucchi explains in his essays how the heteronyms expose the artificial nature of the autobiographical I (Cannon 2001, 101; 106), and he stresses that the need to bring such investigation to artistic resolution leads Pessoa to contemplate the metatheatrical "Shakespeare Problem," which concerns an author who watches his double or alter ego "recite while he [the author] recites" (Tabucchi 1975, 144).[42]

The poet's attempt to identify the means by which Shakespeare was able to bring the real theatricality of life to the fictional reality of the theater is at the heart of Pessoa's Shakespeare Question (Tabucchi 1975, 151, 152). Like Shakespeare's Hamlet, Pessoa's heteronyms are exteriorizations of the writer's internal reality. Pessoa contends that Shakespeare projected a Hamlet who finally empathized with Yorick who identified with Hecuba, whose real suffering is feigned in the theater by the actors so that it might be 'relived' by the audience. This furnishes the Portuguese poet with the means and the justification for his radical turn within, away from "the crushing and massive presence" of reality (Tabucchi 1975, 153): the heteronyms provide the writer with the means for "feigning to believe real that which truly is real" (145, 151). Similarly, Pessoa's *poeta fingidor*[43] analyzes his own psychic torment with ironic detachment, and deludes himself that his anguish is not his own but emblematic of a metahistorical human condition manifested by his heteronyms. However, unlike Pessoa's *poeta fingidor*—whose "therapy of solitude" brooks dialogue only with the self—the subject of narration in the fictions of Tabucchi's middle period seek self-knowledge externally. Self-understanding is predicated on empathy for the other which, once achieved, reverses onto the self, casting into full relief the necessary reciprocity of autotelia 'self-knowledge' and heterotelia 'knowledge of the other.'

For this reason, we may say that in the 1980s Tabucchi uses the "essential solitude" of writing as a source of strength. The loss of self inherent in the act of writing of oneself in the third person, as if the I were another (Blanchot 1955, 28) allows Tabucchi to avoid the incommunicability characteristic of Pessoan introspection, and to exact reader participation. The work, the site of the writer's solitude, affirms the writer's presence-as-absence and provides the reader with a point of access into the writer's solitude. Then, after his five-year period of formal research into the potentialities of the theater and of ekphrasis, Tabucchi begins to "write 'as if' [he] were (an)other;" he writes in a manner of an "actor who transubstantiates" and embodies the 'truth' of the theatrical fiction by identifying with the suffering, the rancor, the melancholy, the irritability, the desperations and the triumphs that Shakespeare felt for Hamlet (Tabucchi 1998a).

In fact, Tabucchi has contended that of all the arts, acting most closely resembles writing: "the actor is he who feigns being, who puts himself in another's shoes, who creates characters and interprets them. This is why the actor is very much like the novelist who creates, invents, and breathes life into his characters and his fictions. Indeed, the actor is a metaphoric portrait of a writer, of a creator" (Gumpert Melgosa, 174). In writing *I dialoghi mancati* Tabucchi builds on his formal investigation into the capabilities of more traditional or "Joycean" interior monologues utilized in such works written at the advent of what we have indicated as his middle period as "Lettera da Casablanca" [Letter from Casablanca], "Dolores Ibarruri piange lacrime amarc" [Dolores Ibarruri Cries Bitter Tears], and "Il piccolo Gatsby" [The Minor Gatsby] (in Tabucchi 1981, 25–41, 102–8, 109–23). In *I dialoghi mancati* Tabucchi experiments "with a form of writing that," in his own words, "falls somewhere between monologue and dialogue" by presupposing "an absent antagonist" or interlocutor. The evocation of Pirandello in one of the plays is the external "projection of a desire," while the soliloquy directed at the deceased brother in the other serves to elaborate remorse (Gumpert Melgosa 173).

In order to develop his ability to write for the stage, Tabucchi had to pretend he was an actor. He 'recited' or 'performed' his soliloquies as failed, one-way conversations or *dialoghi mancati*. Rather than set pen to paper, he began to "speak aloud and to record the monologue that rose from within." To use his own phrasing, he performed a sort of "puppet theater [*teatro de guiñol*] for [him]self." He cast himself as actor/puppeteer, character/puppet, and audience, and used this experience to modify his writing" (Gumpert Melgosa, 175).[44] This equation of soliloquy (exteriorized monologue) and dialogue enabled Tabucchi to move into a new stylistic phase, and, after *I dialoghi mancati*, the subject of his narration no longer splits in two, into self and other, to pursue a strange loop toward self-knowledge.

After the period in question, the subject of narration is—and this must be stressed because it marks a sea change in perspective—tripartite: the subject of narration is now actor, character and spectator. He speaks aloud—"throwing" his voice outward—through the character to himself as spectator. By exteriorizing monologue, the subject of narration—of the *Dialoghi mancati*, but also of *L'angelo nero, Requiem, Sostiene Pereira*, and *Damasceno Monteiro*—sets in motion a dialectic of inner and outer realities whose express purpose is to elaborate the past. The implied, silent interlocutors are the dead, who serve as a metaphor for repressed sources of remorse.[45] Like Barthes's mute angel (1977, 79), they inscribe something indefinable within the subject of narrative, contemporaneously stimulating and frustrating desire. This new strategy allows Tabucchi to set aside the autobiographical tensions that animate *Notturno indiano* and *Il filo dell'orizzonte* and install what he calls a "novelesque pact" [*patto romanzesco*] where the reader knows that episodes from the author's life have inspired the narration but have been transformed into fictive form (Tabucchi 1999a, 7–8).

For this reason, after the close of the middle phase of Tabucchi's career as a writer—one characterized by investigation of Pessoa's heteronymic theory—*Requiem* helps mark the beginning of a new phase of development of his poetics. Tabucchi, by delivering *Requiem* in a language other than his own, positions himself as other to himself, a strategy that enables him to identify with both with the dead and with the audience, those who will read and respond to his work. This process frees his decentered subject of narration from the binds of the Möbius strip that contains the search for self-knowledge within the boundaries of the past and present. The subjects of narration during this later stage of poetic development hope to fill an absence, and make reparation. But since the past cannot be modified, they must commit to the present and begin to look toward the future for self-definition. Indeed, beginning with *Sostiene Pereira* the subject of narration evaluates his actions using the criteria he anticipates will be imposed by posterity, those who will be called to deal with the consequences of action (or inaction, in Pereira's case) in the present.

Pereira's "testimony"[46] may be described as the transcription of a soliloquy, whose implied interlocutor is neither the ghost of his wife nor that of his young acquaintance, Monteiro Rossi, as has been conjectured in the critical literature dealing with this work. It may indeed be the case that Pereira is testifying to the police, or undergoing psychoanalysis, as has been hypothesized. However, one cannot help but wonder how long the secret police would allow Pereira to spare himself the humiliation of answering questions about his personal life (Tabucchi 1994b, 21, 27). Similarly, a psychotherapist would at some point encourage Pereira to confront the issues raised by the content of his dreams (108) in the improbable event that Pereira would seek counseling after successfully elaborating the loss of his wife, thanks to the salubrious presence of Monteiro Rossi and the help of his physician Dr. Cardoso. At the same time, it is highly possible that in testifying the veteran journalist Pereira is speaking aloud, to himself and to his remorse—which we can define as "the impossibility of modifying that which has been" (Gumpert Melgosa 187)—using the narrative device of the self-interview.

Pereira is motivated to give witness by the assassination of his young friend. This pivotal event causes Pereira to understand that there must be a future in death, for Monteiro Rossi, and, therefore, for himself. In fact, Pereira's "testimony" has value—for Pereira and for the reader—only if intended as his legacy, "a message in a bottle he hopes someone will gather up" (Tabucchi 1994b, 78). Like the narrating voices of "Voci portate" and *Requiem*, Pereira need not address a specific "someone" who records (Brizio-Skov, 129); rather, he may very well speak to a something, a tape recorder that in all likelihood closely resembles the one used by Tabucchi while composing his *Dialoghi mancati*. Thus, Pereira ceases to converse with the dead—his wife and the authors he would have had Monteiro Rossi honor with obituaries and commemorations[47]—and "assumes a 'posthumous' stance," one that offers a testimony of the present for posterity (Tabucchi 1996a, 121, 125).

Il filo dell'orizzonte is also informed by a 'dialogue with the dead,' but Spino's 'conversation' with The Kid is not future-oriented. Rather, Spino's goal, as we have seen, is that of achieving a better understanding of himself in the present, of his identity and place in society and the world. The same can be said of the narratives united in *I volatili del Beato Angelico*, whose subjects of narration follow a strange loop that traces an unending effort to reconstruct and locate the determining influences on one's individual and social identity.

In sum, if prior to the period in question self-understanding is sought in the image of an "inverted myself who looks back at me" (Tabucchi 1987, 45–46), in the 1990s Tabucchi's subjects of narration see themselves reflected posthumously in an other myself who looks back at them from the future. This new phase of artistic development is made possible not only by his inquiry into the potentialities of the theatrical word, but also by his investigation of multiple narrative points of view inherent in the hybrid work.

The strange loop that informs the works of what we have called Tabucchi's middle period is at the center of the first experiments with hybrid works. "Vagabondaggio" [Vagabondage] (Tabucchi 1986b), depicts a scene from the life of the poet Dino Campana, an unwilling example of radical introspection when his life's work was lost and he was forced "to spend the rest of his days searching his memory for the poems he had written" (Gumpert Melgosa 150). Similarly, the 1992 narrative "Sera di pioggia su una diga d'Olanda" [A Rainy Evening on a Dam in Holland] (Tabucchi 1992d), which is included in a collection of paintings by José Barrías titled *Tempo* [Time], a left-over from this middle period, also depicts a strange loop uniting significant others, a man and a woman who see each other after several decades of separation. He, a well-known, elderly photographer, travels from Switzerland to Holland to see a retrospective of an artist whose work both he and she have long admired. There he chances on her, a former companion who now lives in Paris and they engage each other in a sort of *recherche à deux* of their shared past. From their conversation it would appear that her memory is more precise, at least as far as a chronology of shared events is concerned, because she has kept a written record, a diary. However, there are lacunae in what she recalls—she claims she prefers to rely on "the eye of memory" and leave her visual memory unbridled—which can be filled by his photographic record of what transpired.

An analogous Möbius strip progression is traced by the protagonist of the 1988 "Tanti saluti" [Greetings] (Tabucchi 1988d), a short story published within a collection of watercolor postcards by Pericoli. Here, a widower with the uncommon name Taddeo, is mired in the present. The protagonist, a character study for Pereira, discusses with his deceased wife's portrait the many trips to exotic locales they planned, but never took. Suddenly, and inexplicably, this unrealized character breaks with routine, and leaves the home he has occupied his entire life, determined never to return. He arrives at the local rail station—intending to board a train that is to take him to Rome, then Fiumicino, whence he is to fly to undetermined points on the South American continent—and chances on an adolescent street vendor, also named Taddeo, who, like the protagonist, wishes to travel the world. After a brief conversation, the senior Taddeo inexplicably experiences an epiphany, gives his postcards with their dream destinations to his young friend—who we may assume is to take these trips in the older man's stead—and returns home.

By contrast, Pereira can break free from the strange loop that keeps Taddeo from expanding his horizons because the decentralized, nonautobiographical narrating voices of *L'angelo nero* and of *Sogni di sogni* have opened the door to the author's theatrical "transubstantiation." Pereira can do so because he is the product of a newer phase of artistic development in which Tabucchi becomes his characters, who are thus enabled to elaborate their past.

An explanation as to why they are able to accomplish this is foreshadowed in Tabucchi's "Letter" to Tullio Pericoli (Tabucchi 1991a), another brief parallel text published in a catalogue of a retrospective showing of Pericoli's work for the years 1982 through 1991. Here the writer congratulates the figurative artist for having re-created reality "in a way reminiscent of the theater." He comments that Pericoli's representations are not realistic but verisimilar; they reproduce reality using a technique of narrative: they present the audience with a collage of images that, when taken together, provide a summary of the salient events of the subject's life.[48] In other words, Pericoli condenses the past into an accumulation of Deleuzian time-images, an irrational or nonchronological grouping of memory or sensory impressions. As Tabucchi phrases it, Pericoli "feigns that real fiction, which consists of recounting to others the stories that our characters have lived for us" by telling the life of his subject in a way that demand the viewer's collaboration: Pericoli's narrations are filled with gaps, a state of affairs that forces the audience to structure the recounting of the events by placing them in a narrative hierarchy. Therefore, following Tabucchi, we can say that Pericoli's drawings are "multiple fictions" that, as is the case with Pasolini's "cinema of poetry," "narrate poetically through images." Pericoli—as was the case with Robert Louis Stevenson, the subject of one of Pericoli's drawings—looks outside himself and narrates what he sees: that which is "other, diverse, and alien" (Gumpert Melgosa 68).

The reference to Stevenson is of particular importance for several reasons. After publishing *Requiem* Tabucchi made clear that he felt he had absorbed Pessoa, and believed it was time to move on (see Orengo), presumably to the work of Robert Louis Stevenson, whom Tabucchi has said is his favorite writer (Petri 1994, 75). Whether or not this is the case, Tabucchi's treatment of Stevenson in his fictions makes evident the change in perspective consequent to the five-year period of relative silence. Prior to 1987 Tabucchi's characters were concerned primarily with the relationship of the self and the other, and the dialogue with the dead was an inquiry into the relationship of being and nonbeing. Consequent to this period, narrative inquiry centers on the nature of having-been from the perspective of being. In other words, the primary concern and source of self-knowledge for the subject of narrative is a dialogue with posterity.

To clarify, in *I volatili del Beato Angelico* the past is composed or better, recomposed in letters that examine the influence of the past ("that which, having to be, has already been" [Tabucchi 1987, 31]) on the present (depicted as a "dimension of darkness in which the future is already here" [23]): since it is impossible to find what has been lost within the past, time, people, one's image, History, the past must be recomposed" (see "Passato composto. Tre lettere" [Past perfect. Three letters], Tabucchi 1987, 23–39). In contrast, in *Sogni di sogni* Robert Louis Stevenson reinstates his "past life" into a present "che doveva ancora essere" [that still had yet to be] (Tabucchi 1992c, 51). In other words, the creative act, the metaphorical "dream," provides the lynchpin between the past and the future, giving a sense, or direction, to history. Therefore, when writers, artists, and intellectuals transform their atemporal 'dreams' into historical, textual materiality they become "posthumous" to themselves; the transformative power of the act of narrating "makes happen that which has yet to happen" because "to narrate means to extract the existent from the non-existent, to suggest to reality that which it must do" and what become (Tabucchi 2001b).

By objectifying interiorities through external monologue, Tabucchi's subjects of narration come to elaborate past sources of individual and collective remorse from diverse, nonautobiographical perspectives.[49] The dialogue with the dead begun in "Voci portate" is pursued in *Requiem* where the "addio" placed at the end of the volume marks a very tangible turning of the page beyond Pessoa and into a new poetics.[50] After *Requiem* the quest for self-understanding is future-oriented: the act of writing is seen as the locus for dialogue in absentia with posterity.[51] Just as the decentering of the subject of narration grants agency to the dead—dialogue with them is a way of allowing them to influence our behavior (Petri 1994, 71)—writing is an act of self-assertion by the dead author whose posthumous, future-oriented subject of narration must adapt his behavior according to the criteria by which he anticipates posterity will judge him.

Fragments of the Discourses of Lovers and Other Strangers

Tabucchi claims that *Si sta facendo sempre più tardi* is a collection of seventeen letters whose authors are overwhelmed by "impossible regrets," regrets for what cannot be rectified: "regret for that which could have been, and never was; and regret for that which we could have done and did not do" (Sancis Antonio). The narrating voices come forth in randomly ordered autos-da-fé that readers are free to "bring together [*colligere*] as they wish." The chorus of narrative perspectives that informs the work gives tangible form to Tabucchi's desire to create an "all-encompassing panorama of life," a historicizing "typology" or cross section of contemporary Italian society (Gumpert, 70–71). Furthermore, a poetics defined by an extremely clear vision of the roles of art, literature, and the intellectual in society emanates from from *Si sta facendo sempre più tardi*. As was the case with *L'angelo nero*, this recent book is more than a collection of brief narratives; it is a mosaic, a unitary work with an internal design (Gumpert Melgosa, 143): its multitude of narrating voices forms a polycentric, novelistic universe of fragments of amorous prose. Through their contemplation of the relationship of love to life and death, the letters actively interrogate the book's readers, who are called to rethink their lives and examine instances of incoherence and contradiction in their own behavior.

Si sta facendo sempre più tardi is a collection of "bizarre stories," *poémes en prose*, and dense, one-sided dialogues[52] whose narrators are overwhelmed by their need to somehow make amends for the past. Like Pereira, they feel a vague need to repent for, perhaps even repudiate, a life they fear has served no purpose. The book is also a record of its author's disappointment with recent developments in Italian society, particularly its failure to meet the challenges and fulfill the legacy of the Resistance. And like Mello Sequiero, the attorney in *La testa perduta di Damasceno Monteiro*, the characters in this book put messages in a bottle, so to speak, and wait for responses in the form of "letters from the past that might explain a period in our lives that we have never understood, that might provide some explanation capable of helping us grasp the sense of the many years that have passed, of what got away from us back then" (128). Emblematic in this regard is the narrator of the epistle "Forbidden Games," a man who writes because he is overcome by melancholy, but does not know how to articulate his affliction, specifically his nostalgia for a time when he and his fellow university students used to "dream of possible worlds" (Tabucchi 2001a, 43). Now, no longer capable of rethinking the past, he is overwhelmed by the inevitability of the future: "the games of Being, as we all know, are prohibited by that which, having to have been, has already been. It is the minuscule yet insurmountable Forbidden Game forced on us by our Present" (50).

4: ANTONIO TABUCCHI

Tabucchi's civic engagement informs all his fictions, beginning with his first novels, *Il piccolo naviglio* and *Piazza d'Italia*,[53] and provides Tabucchi with the means for approaching a definition of the "physiognomy," or social character of contemporary Italians. As he told an interviewer, he believes that his countrymen have a short memory, and occasionally need to be reminded of their history (Hernández 24). Vague reminiscences of community gnaw at the egoism and the moral and ethical torpor of the narrators of *Si sta facendo sempre più tardi*, who refer back to "our Nation" [*il nostro Paese*] and its civic holidays.[54] Indeed, the reinvigoration of an atrophied civic memory is several instances the force that propels the reawakening of the individual narrators.

In "Buono come sei" [How good you are] the narrator offers his ex-wife morphine to alleviate the suffering of the man for whom she left the narrator. This affords them a way of facing the illness together, despite his lingering resentment and animosity, in "a Nation such as ours where 'pain therapy' for those afflicted with terminal infirmities is not considered" (133). This follows the reawakening of civic memory in the appropriately titled "A cosa serve un'arpa con una corda sola?" [What Use is a Harp with Only One String?] The narrator's turbid memory is jogged by an encounter with a fruit vendor, the elderly grandson of Italian emigrants to Egypt who wishes to keep active a "bond with his country [*paese*] of origin" (112) by subscribing to an Italian daily. This sets in motion a series of personal reminiscences that are intimately linked with major events in the life of *la Patria*. The thought of Italy quickly fills the narrator with "shame" for when he abandoned his own "*paese d'origine*" in Northern Italy and his childhood love to begin, in Naples, what he thought would be that of a successful concert harpist, but instead can be described more accurately as "a life that took on the semblance of death" (112).

The harpist writes over forty years after the his emigration, at the beginning of the Tangentopoli investigations (which he ignores), and he remembers that his departure coincided with the rebirth of Italy, the plebiscite on the Republic, a time when he thought that he too was "being born again into a new life" but instead had hid from it (112). Hindsight reveals to him that the nostalgia of his Neapolitan neighbors and that of his Greek landlady was a means of elaborating their suffering and of mourning on the one hand, and, on the other, a nostalgia for a better life in the future (113). He had accompanied them with his harp but remained oblivious to their life situations, changing name, language and country of residence as soon as he became too attached to them. News read in a fruit vendor's paper, that the narrator's old love will visit Alexandria, causes him to remember the remark that prompted his abrupt departure from his childhood home: "what use is a harp with only one string, when all the others are broken?" (120), a rebuke for his failure to demonstrate friendship and solidarity to those who had lost their loved ones in the war. This causes him to ask himself if it is possible that "the sense of your life is, senseless, in looking for lost voices, and even perhaps one day believing you have been found them" and that "you have lived your entire life for that illusion and you think that this gives sense to all the senselessness" (121).

Tabucchi examines civic questions through an externally directed introspection whose intent is to give voice not to his own concerns, but those of others (Tabucchi 1998c, 39). His narrating voices "doubt their existence as unique individuals, and see themselves," to use Bodei's term, "as 'dividuals,'" internally divided individuals.[55] Here, Tabucchi again takes as his model Pessoa's multiple internal others, each of whom manifests his own poetics, esthetics, world view, and creative style. Pessoa's heteronyms are distinct and self-sufficient individuals, poet-characters invented down to the most minute detail, biography, somatic features, aesthetic preferences, cultural background, and even idiosyncracies. As Tabucchi explains, "The heteronyms are not merely alter egos. The alterity that Pessoa carries inside himself, as do we all, finds in the heteronyms an incarnation that it so strong and so defined that it projects itself to the point of existing in total autonomy. The heteronyms are *des autres que lui-même,* independent and autonomous personalities who live outside their author" (Tabucchi 1998b, 24–25).

The self-knowledge gained from his exploration of the otherness within enhances comprehension of everything that is external, and therefore potentially antagonistic, to the self. Recognition of the forms of mutual determination linking the internally plural self and the other allows for interaction, thus strengthening social bonds. In Tabucchi's fictions, the complementarity of self-knowledge and mutual understanding is predicated on what Benjamin has called the reciprocity of the gaze. According to

Benjamin, that which returns the gaze "conjures up" the past and restores the *mémoire involontaire* to the present (1955a, 188). In other words, seeing and being seen by the other—Tabucchi would not distinguish between internal and external—reinstates in consciousness latent remnants of the individual and collective unconscious. The reciprocity of the gaze returns to the present what has been written out of history. Literature is therefore both a form of collective memory and a means for recovering and preserving the past; it transforms society when the "complicity of text and reader" (Costanzo) inherent in literary communication modifies the reader's horizon of expectation.

Because literature is found precisely at the intersection of private and public, it allows and compels writers to link the personal with the social, and to insert themselves, and their readers, in contexts larger than themselves. Thus, from all Tabucchi's fictions emanates the premise for an ethical democracy grounded in the belief in the importance of human consortium, and of love intended both as agape and as the bond between two individuals. Love-for-the-self, love-for-a-significant-other, and love-for-the-social-other define, imbricate, and complement each other.

In novels such as *La testa perduta di Damasceno Monteiro* and *Sostiene Pereira* commitment in the polis is prompted by respect for and identification with the memory of a violated, deceased other. This compassion is of a piece with the protagonists' self-love, which extends to all the other (my)selves of which humanity is composed. *Il filo dell'orizzonte* and *Requiem* depict processes of self-analysis that lead to identification with the external, and result in strengthened social linkages. *Si sta facendo sempre più tardi* depicts this same process, but on a more intimate scale, when the search through memory for lost loves spark repentance for time wasted in egoistic solitude.

The development of this concept of reaffirming and strengthening social bonds through the examination of the relationship between self, internal other, and external other raises the question in Tabucchi's fictions of how to become, or identity with, (an)other while remaining oneself. Tabucchi has stated that creating characters who are very different than he is, but who interest him and involve him in their fate, allows him to see the world with eyes that are not his own, but continue to be his own (*Conversazione con Antonio Tabucchi*, 18). He first attempted to enter his fictions as a character in an early work, *Il gioco del rovescio*, but was not fully pleased with the result (Gumpert Melgosa, 145). Subsequently, Joyce's *Dubliners* provided him with a model of an author who "entered into his characters while not becoming one of them." That is to say: "Joyce simultaneously personalized and depersonalized his stories, almost as if he were a prestidigitator who is on stage one minute and suddenly disappears, surrounded in a cloud of smoke, hiding himself in the pocket of someone in the audience, whence he can spy on everything that happens around him" (Gumpert, 67).

Tabucchi has since begun to apply this "great lesson in writing" to his own stories, attempting to "hid[e] in a corner, so that the reader could not be sure where the real narrator [is] hidden," so that "not even the presence of a character that uses "I" in a first-person can eliminate the sensation that there is another narrator hidden somewhere else in the story (Gumpert, 67). In other words, his goal is not to create a voice he can claim is not his own, but to project onto a character, as if he were an actor, a voice that makes manifest a previously unknown or concealed aspect of his own personality. Following this line of reasoning, Tabucchi came to understand that when writers become (an)other, they enable themselves to "transcend the constraints not only of identity, but also of historical determination and of the "unforgiving passing of time" (Sancis Antonio).[56] More importantly, it allowed him to avoid asking the reductive question "who am I" and question instead "who are we," "because the individual is always plural, multi-faceted, and internally diverse."

It must be stressed that the concept of writer as actor is defined by Tabucchi in terms that differ dramatically from those used by Calvino in the latter's well-known essay, "I livelli della realtà in letteratura" [Levels of Reality in Literature]. Like Tabucchi, Calvino has argued that authors project their internal reality onto their narrating voices. However, for Calvino this allows the author to obscure his true identity: "It is always only a projection of himself that the author puts into play when writing; it can be the projection of a real part of himself or the projection of a fictitious I, a mask" (Calvino 1978, 317).[57] In this way, Calvino creates the (auto)illusion of empirical writers who sever all ties with their texts, and abdicate responsibility for them, when in fact, what is projected onto the page reflects in mutated form some aspect of the empirical author's psyche. In contrast, Tabucchi aspires to create narrative universes "Where the 'I' is not 'I' but a Magellenic cloud of momentary energies always in the process of fission" (see Steiner, 100–1).[58] George Steiner's image of a "cloud" whose component parts are in continuous movement restates metaphorically the concept of the "confederation of souls" discussed by Pereira's psychotherapist who explains that all individuals house a "hegemonic I" that imposes itself on, and defines the norm for, but does not suffocate "the incommensurable plurality" of the Ego (Tabucchi 1994b, 123).

Tabucchi also finds in the work of Steiner a definition of translation as (self-)critical reading, based on the reciprocal perception of writer and audience.[59] For Steiner literary understanding is a form of remembrance that—when it reinserts the past into the reader's present—catalyzes "recognition and discovery (to recognize is to know anew) of the other and of the self" (8–10). If indeed, as Steiner claims, translation is a "journey toward a work" and therefore toward (an)other, for Tabucchi it is also a journey inward, a journey of discovery and understanding of the "linguistic schizophrenia" or "alloglossia" that causes him to occasionally express himself in a language other than his native Italian, as he did in *Requiem*.[60] Tabucchi claims that writing in a second language helps bring to the fore aspects of his own personality that are not part of the conscious ego but are hidden by a 'hegemonic I' whose different aspects must not be reconciled or homologated, but accepted in their diversity (see Tabucchi 2003d, 171–72).

His desire to interrogate the internal other leads Tabucchi to underwrite the necessary reciprocity (Gramsci) linking literature to society, and I to other. This, in turn, precludes his subscribing to any postmodern crisis of representation that would circumscribe the act of writing within a purely literary world.

For this reason Tabucchi recently argued in print with Umberto Eco, who claimed that intellectuals should speak only within their field of expertise (Eco 1997d), and Jean-François Lyotard, who argued that the social role of the intellectual is that of administering, transmitting, and giving normative status to knowledge, not that of transforming it" (Lyotard 1983; Tabucchi 1998c, 37). After stating that Eco's definition of the intellectual should be broadened to include artists and writers—because "the act of intellectual cognition is also a creative act" (Tabucchi 1998c, 36)—Tabucchi underscores the "cognitive function" of art that in his opinion allows us to revisit those past events that have brought us to where we are today "with a logic that does not follow a conformist sequence of reality," but instead provides us with the courage to speak of what is not known (Tabucchi 1998c, 28). In other words, he is opposed to a linear reading of history that reduces the past to a function of the present and diminishes the present to the unavoidable consequence of the past. In this way Tabucchi is responding to Eco's appropriation of the distinction between politics and culture proposed after World War II by Elio Vittorini, for whom politics is a "chronicle" of the quotidian while culture defines the long trends of history.

According to Eco, intellectual work may prove to be socially incisive in the future, but rarely in the present (Tabucchi 1998c, 41). Therefore, the intellectual should not work to transform the present, but to consider it the antecedent of a yet-to-be-determined future. In fact, Eco's prose fictions are all told as flashbacks; the premises for narration are his novels' conclusions. Their diegetic progressions explain and demonstrate the—seemingly ineluctable—causes of known effects; past and present validate each other tautologically: things are they way they must be.

Tabucchi counters that the bonds between culture and politics make necessary a commitment to act in our present. Then, in contrast with Lyotard's description of the intellectual as little more than a "cultural bureaucrat" (37) and Eco's contention that the role of the intellectual is that of political administrator and organizer of culture (López 47, 48), Tabucchi develops Blanchot's idea that the intellectual is called on to produce "novelties" (36), that is to say, to recover to our present what has been excluded or written out, that which Benjamin calls the "detritus of history." To use Tabucchi's own phrasing, the function of the intellectual "is not to 'create' crises, but to *put in crisis* something or someone who is not in crisis, but is instead very convinced of his views" (Tabucchi 1998c, 32; his emphasis). In other words, the function of art is bipartite. First, it compels its consumer to contemplate what might have been, had the active engagement of other intellectuals in the past created the conditions necessary for a different configuration of our present; second, it helps foresee futures that are not the logical consequence of current patterns of development (Tabucchi 199c, 28–29). When writers examine and express their own internal reality, they restore to our present the forgotten and/or repressed past, so that it might serve as a model for collective analysis of the disquietude of contemporary society.

When literature takes us beyond introspective interior monologue, it absolves its role as a means of self-analysis and self-understanding for both the individual and the larger community. It makes public the writer's most intimate thoughts, but in an opaque way, and in transmogrified form. Therefore, critique must look beyond the writer's biography and refrain from reading works of literature as manifestations of the return of the repressed of authors about whom there is always much we cannot know with certainty, and who are unavailable for the crucial element of the psychoanalytic process, transference. However, since the practice of art is always to some extent "an activity whose aim is to assuage unappeased wishes" for both the artist and the person who enjoys it, and a means of reconciling conflicting forces of desire and prohibition (Sterba 257–58), the collective interrogation of individual desires and dreams enables Tabucchi's reader to "seek out the essence of our humanity." Self-analysis interacts dialectically with interrogation of the Other so that we may "look for ourselves in others" (Gumpert Melgosa, 41).[61]

Tabucchi describes his own prose fictions as "so many stages of a self-reflection" (Gumpert, 25), carried forward in the hope of shedding light on our shared human condition. The externalization and textualization of ephemeral individual experience absorbs, attenuates and objectifies the subjectivity of the author and provides a common locus for understanding characteristic human traits and problems such as love, hate, good, and evil. Love, as he defines it, is synonymous with desire—but not necessarily with the "visceral, erotic" desire used as a marketing tool in the mass media—and must be seen in relation to other equally important aspects of our lives. Moreover, representations of physical love are not as interesting from a literary perspective as "the phantasm of love; that is to say . . . love as yearning, as disquietude, as a constant and incorporeal presence." When understood this way, love provides a secular response to the loss of religious sentiment (Gumpert, 74). When utilized as literary material, it provides the basis for a dialogue directed at finding an ethical common ground, a modus vivendi for coexistence. To use his own phrasing: "I am not religious; I am not a Catholic. But I believe that there are rules that we must respect, rules that, after all, were invented by religion. There is a religious ethics, based on the Ten Commandments, that was fundamental to all the ethics that followed, even those that were not inspired by religion. The Ten Commandments maintain to this day their seductive power over me" (Gumpert, 102–3). These ethical principles, along the values of the French Revolution, liberty, equality, and brotherhood, suggest a utopian vision, whose application, in Tabucchi's view, is incumbent on secularized societies. They inform an ethical democracy that in turn shapes the literary dialogue he proposes fill the gap in our existence in the absence of shared belief in a metaphysical end to history. To use his own words, "When we lost the belief that someone was watching us, our lives lost finality" (Gumpert, 98).

These values are of a piece with the "civil function" of literature, which is not synonymous with the "facile populism" and grands récits of certain literary (neo)realisms, nor is it necessarily a way of publicly taking a stand" (Gumpert, 26). Instead, the role of literature is that of providing the tools for seeking out "practical truths," useful for excogitating individual responses to historical contingency, which raise as many questions as they answer. In this way, Tabucchi interrogates his readers, who receive for their efforts a small but salubrious dose of disquietude (Gumpert, 104), a "lucid extolling of our *mal de vivre*" (Tabucchi 1979, 7–10). By refusing to offer answers, he encourages reader participation in the production of the text while eschewing abdication of authorial responsibilities.

Thus, Tabucchi's insistence on provoking the reader leads him to voice his opposition to escapist literature, particularly the postmodernist use of pastiche that collapses the literary past into the eternal present of the text. He contends that when literature remains at a level of "play" it is no more than "a melancholy artifice" similar to a "set of Legos" the writer utilizes to reproduce the predictable, and assuage the reader with what is already known, the déja lu (Tabucchi 1998a). While Tabucchi would not deny the importance of the ludic quality of art, he is quick to assert that it can also be a serious game of "intelligence, research, tactics and strategy" involving reader and writer (Gumpert, 59).[62]

David Harvey, following Benjamin's comments on the Parisian arcades of the nineteenth century—specifically that they seemed designed to induce nirvana rather than critical awareness—addresses the issue of the eternal present installed in postmodernity, according to which "'there is no alternative,' save those given by the conjoining of technological fantasies, commodity culture, and endless capital accumulation" (2000, 168). In contrast to the state of affairs Harvey describes and analyzes, Tabucchi builds on the "metaphysical nostalgia" of the Pessoan heteronyms Àlvaro de Campos and Bernardo Soares to excogitate a means of resisting our shared condition of postmodernity. Soares's thoughts on the universe, metaphysics, and death, evoke a painful [*cuisantes*] "nostalgia of the possible," or of what might have been. Tabucchi then gives a positive connotation to this "oblique" or "reverse" nostalgia, and to the regret inherent within it, when he acknowledges how it can catalyze a rethinking of the past (Tabucchi 1998b; 73, 40). In this way Soares's inertia is transformed into a "nostalgia of the future," a tension to live in the world accompanied by the desire to influence what is yet to be. In this way Tabucchi moves beyond both the synchrony of Pessoa's "nostalgia to the second degree"—wherein the Portuguese poet's heteronyms live exclusively within the moment of poetic creation (Tabucchi 1998b, 31)—and the eternal present of postmodern pastiche, which reconstructs a world that we already know in order to condense and install the literary and historical past into the reader's present.

In describing his translation of Pessoa's *O Marinheiro* [*The Sailor*], Tabucchi notes the difficulties encountered in dealing with a drama written in the pluperfect of the subjunctive, a tense that in Portuguese indicates an unreal action in the past. Tabucchi applies this concept in writing *Si sta facendo più tardi*, whose component texts ponder the dubitative: remembered pasts "which maybe we have not had" and real pasts "which we might not have had," had its participants behaved differently.

The nonchronological recovery of the past found in Tabucchi's fictions allows us—following Rodowick's exegesis of Deleuze's writings on the cinematic image—to say that Tabucchi's work depicts the direct, qualitative image of time: time is independent of movement. For example, in *Si sta facendo sempre più tardi*, diegetic progression is catalyzed not by action, but by memory. Irrational juxtaposition of sensory images restores the out-of-field. The nonchronological division and irrational regrouping of diegetic progression destabilizes and overturns the subordination of time to movement-in-space. In *Si sta facendo sempre più tardi* memory appears as a force from the past that continuously breaks up and multiplies the present into unpredictable past and future trajectories. This narrative strategy, as is the case with Deleuze's cinema of time, produces an image of thought as a nontotalizable process and upsets the concept of a stable truth. History has a sense, but it is one characterized by discontinuity and unpredictable change.

As is the case with the characters in Pires's *O delfim* [*The Heir Apparent*], the lives of the narrating voices of *Si sta facendo sempre più tardi* are marked by "stasis and decay, a break in diachrony." They are living "cadavers" who suffered an ontological death, that is to say, removed themselves from historical becoming. Pires's characters look to the past, not the future, and deny "the dialectical rapport between the individual and the events of the individual" (Tabucchi 1992b, 8, 9). Tabucchi's reading of Pires leads him to conclude that in a period of time such as ours without shared absolute truths, or agreement on the question of metaphysical death, historical death—death in time—can perhaps provide us with a key for survival (Tabucchi 1992b, 14). For this reason, the narrating voices and readers of *Si sta facendo sempre più tardi* are called back to historical time at the novel's end when they are confronted by death.

The concept of identity has been linked in Tabucchi's fictions with that of death at least since *Il filo dell'orizzonte*, but not in the sense assigned to it by the ancient Greeks, for whom death irrevocably sealed an individual's identity.[63] In Tabucchi's fictions meditations on death are a means of establishing and maintaining a dialogue with the past: "The dead need to be remembered because there must be a future in death, a causal link to posterity. The living, for their part, need to bring the dead back to life through remembrance" (Petri 1997, 62), another source of disquietude. This is certainly the case with Tabucchi's "Ritratto d'autore" [Portrait of an Author] (1996) wherein his "answers" to a deceased mentor inform an autobiographical self-portrait of himself as author.

At any rate, the constellation of narrations that animate *Si sta facendo sempre più tardi* reflect the disappointment and failure of a generation of men whose lives and loves are out of harmony with what surrounds them. Confronted with life's great events, mysteries and absurdities—births, deaths, suicides, insanities—

they failed to give "a sense to the senselessness" (Tabucchi 2001a, 121). When faced with smaller questions—disappointments, frustrations, abandonments and betrayals, roads not taken, renunciations, the life choices thrust on them—they abdicated from their responsibilities. When death appears on their horizon, they repent, and narrate themselves in an attempt to engage their lost loves in epistolary dialogue.

Indeed, *Si sta facendo sempre più tardi* has two unifying themes, as we have seen, death and love, understood as frustrated desire. The narrators hope to make reparation, and fill an absence. They send out messages to addressees whose primary, perhaps only function is to serve as sounding boards. Indeed, they catalyze in the writer a dialectic of inner and outer realities, and allow the narrators to begin to elaborate their past and to live in the present. But responses are not forthcoming, and in this the addressees are reminiscent of Barthes's mute angel, who inscribes something indefinable within the person who desires (Barthes 1977, 79).

In fact, Tabucchi's letters constitute an amorous discourse à la Barthes; the goal of their writers is to reach an unobtainable object of desire. The chorus of letters that compose the volume constitutes a site of extreme solitude; each addressee—the incarnation of desire for an absent being (Barthes 1977, 15)—is a discursive site who shrouds herself in silence. Nonetheless, the letters are also a locus of affirmation for writers whose lover's discourse always anticipates a response. Therefore, their writing, *pace* Barthes (1984), is always transitive. Indeed, the addressee's absence confirms the sender's presence. As Barthes puts it, "absence can exist only as a consequence of the other" (1977, 13).

Following the example of Barthes, who claims that writing begins precisely where the other is not (1977, 100), in *Si sta facendo sempre più tardi* the other's silence creates an exhausting languor: the writers are unable to complete the transition from narcissistic libido to object libido. They wish to confront (an)other, who does not speak, often because she cannot: she is dead. Thus, love and death intertwine. In fact, for Tabucchi the purpose of writing is to see "ourselves reflected in others, our contemporaries, but also our dead and our memories of them, and also to see ourselves reflected in posterity, in the illusion that they will be willing and able to listen to us." This enhanced temporality "inserts us more intensely in our own present," in the seemingly immobile flow of time while allowing us to project ourselves into the "after of existence," into the "future that will follow our demise" (*Conversazione con Antonio Tabucchi*, 5–6).

Frustration with one's own failings followed by repentance motivates the letter writers to renarrate themselves. Each would like to be the object of another's desire. Unfortunately, *si sta facendo sempre più tardi*, it is getting later and later, while the narrators (and readers) await their mailing from the Anthropos, the Fate whose duty is to cut the thread of life. Like Pereira, who finally understood that "it has grown late" and saw the need to become an active participant in the happenings of his time (Tabucchi 1994b, 178), the narrators *Si sta facendo sempre più tardi* also see that the time has come to repent and to atone with decisive action. As Anthropos explains, we share a common destiny shaped by the inevitability of death and a final rendering of accounts. "Unforgiving" time is running out "for understanding that we have failed to understand." And, as Tabucchi contends, "we may not know with certainty who the addressee [of each letter] is, but each of us has a letter of our own waiting to be written, one that we do not have the courage to write" (Sancis Antonio).

Who's Zoomin' Who? in *Tristano muore*

What was implicit in *Si sta facendo sempre più tardi*, Tabucchi's disappointment with the Italians' failure to live up to the hopes and expectations of social renewal raised by the Resistance, is explicit in *Tristano muore* [*Tristano Dies*]. The work metaphorically calls to task a large segment of the country's governing leadership, whose willingness to sacrifice national sovereignty in order to safeguard against the threat of Communist expansion cost Italy unique opportunities to explore alternatives for economic and social development in the half-century following World War II.

The past is recovered nonchronologically in *Tristano muore*, but in a way that is perhaps best described as the obverse of what takes place in *Si sta facendo sempre più tardi*. In *Tristano muore* the division and regrouping of recovered memories into a halting diegetic progression give a picture of the past that is almost complete, with the significant exceptions of those crucial events the narrating voice, who in a sense embodies the collective drama of Italy as it enters the new millennium, wants to keep concealed. The voice engages a writer who is charged with editing and reconstructing the past to fit present desire. For this reason, whereas we have described *Autobiografie altrui* as a work composed of autobiographical fictions charged with undermining certainty, *Tristano muore* is a fictionalized autobiography. Here the subject of narration would impose his own stable, coherent Truth while setting a predetermined direction for the future, the one whose original impetus was put in motion by his (mis)behavior during the Resistance. He would like to "predict," in the etymological sense of the word, "that which, having been, can no longer be changed" (154). In other words, there is a subtle cynicism subtending the narrating voice's reminiscences that would indicate his satisfaction that posterity is on its way to following the infelicitous path his actions have traced.

The voice is something of a Faustian character whose image of his place in the polis is quite unlike that of the writer, Tabucchi, who again feigns himself an actor, in this case one who is cast in a role that calls on him to deliver a soliloquy conveying the suffering, rancor, melancholy, anger, and irritability of a man who sees death approaching and rues the fundamental life choices he made a half-century ago. But unlike other *dialoghi mancati* we have had occasion to consider in preceding chapters, in *Tristano muore* there is no decentering of the subject of narrative. Instead we see the desire of the narrating voice to impose his univocal point of view. And while the soliloquies of *I dialoghi mancati* and *Si sta facendo sempre più tardi* express the elaboration of remorse (the various 'confessions' constitute attempts to engage the past in dialogue, to repent for misdeeds, and to make reparation) in *Tristano muore* the subject of narration expresses nothing other than regret, for a plan gone awry.

The narrating voice, a Tuscan, was born out of wedlock at the outset of World War I to bourgeois parents who married when the voice was already a "little boy" (71). Nuptials were postponed until after the father's return, several years after the end of hostilities, from a prisoner-of-war camp in Austria where he recovered from the Spanish flu epidemic of 1918. The father, a research biologist and lover of American jazz, is denied a university appointment presumably because of his anti-fascist views.

He makes plans to emigrate to the United States, but death soon overtakes him (41). Little is known of the mother, other than she left the narrating voice "a small black book" of "complicated recipes"—which the voice may have used to cook snails *à la provençal* for Marilyn, an American undercover agent who participated in Resistance alongside the narrating voice during the war (21). The cookbook, the voice's only relic of his mother, was written in French, the language he uses to converse with Daphne (23), the Greek woman who competes, so to speak, with Marilyn for the voice's affections. The mother marries the father in a civil ceremony—perhaps out of conviction, perhaps in deference to her father-in-law's anticlericalism—but invites the local pastor to the reception out of respect for social convention. In any event, her son is never baptized (71). And, for reasons unknown to the reader, primary parenting responsibilities are assumed by the grandfather—an ex-*garibaldino*, gentleman farmer, and astronomer—and the paternal grandmother, who sings lullabies to the narrating voice (48) and probably dies when the narrating voice was still very young: his only description of her is that of a *"volto senza volto"* [a face without a face] from his earliest childhood (152). While in elementary school the voice is made to take weekly language lessons from a young woman his own age who the grandfather imported from Germany for this sole purpose. Although the voice's profession is never made clear, he is a polyglot and an intellectual whom his farmhands address as "Professor" (29).

Neither is it clear, as we shall see, if Tristano is truly the name given to the narrating voice by his mother to evoke his absent father (71); or if it belonged to his father and was adopted by the voice as a battle name during the Resistance. His childhood nickname, Ninototo, might indicate that the voice's given name was Antonio. In any case, by calling himself Tristano the voice makes reference to the fact that he is a tragic character, *nato triste* [born to unhappiness], and must fulfill the destiny his name assigns him. Misfortune is also portended by the name of his love, Daphne,[64] who hangs herself from an orange tree (135, 147), and by the title of the literary review on which they collaborate, *The Pages of Hypnos*, named for the mythological twin brother of Death.

Tabucchi has stated that the name of his title character was taken from the last of Leopardi's *Operette morali*, the *Dialogo di*

Tristano e di un amico [*Dialogue of Tristan and a Friend*] (Teroni 2004).[65] While this may very well be the case, the name also evokes for the reader and then perverts the image of the tragic hero of the epic *Tristan and Iseult,* a tale that embodies the medieval values of faith and constancy, loyalty, and honor that triumph over human passions and illicit love. In fact, Tabucchi's characters transmogrify the legend when they behave in a manner more in keeping with that of Scarlett O'Hara and Rhett Butler, the protagonists of a film to which the voice repeatedly makes reference, fictional characters who—as Rhett tells Scarlett while bringing her from Atlanta to Tara—were made for one another and could love each other because they are "both of the same sort," without principles, ideals, or scruples.

A month after taking to bed (42) with an advanced case of gangrene that has destroyed his leg, the narrating voice, a decorated hero of the Resistance, summons to his estate a writer of some note who has already published a novel on heroism whose plot closely parallels the voice's wartime exploits (102). The voice had occasion to read and appreciate this work of fiction (97), and so he engages the novelist to ghost-write his autobiography. To do so the writer must cull information conveyed in semicoherent stream-of-consciousness fragments through a morphine-induced delirium. In fact, the narration can be more accurately described as an exterior monologue or *dialogo mancato*. The writer never speaks, nor is his presence ever corroborated in any way.

It is quite possible that the writer may be no more than the manifestation of the voice's frustrated desire to make the unconscious conscious without the benefit of psychotherapy; and that the writer has been 'summoned' by the voice's imagination because the voice would like to somehow make a connection between past and present, and to somehow remedy his withdrawal from emotional relatedness to everybody (see Karon 2003, 111).[66] However, since no dialogue takes place, there is no therapeutic healing. Therefore, the voice's self-recriminations are no more than sterile regret, which never gives way to remorse and redemption, that is to say the initiation of a mechanism for improving his behavior.[67] Indeed, the voice's regret is not future oriented; from his deathbed his engagement of posterity is predicated on the wish to deride and mislead. As we shall see, the narrating voice, having lost control of his spiritual inheritance to those to whom he had entrusted it, is content to sneer at the

Italians who will survive him and deceive them with his falsified historical testimony.

The voice's caretaker, the Frau (ironically, given the voice's hopeless condition, named Renate, *reborn* in both German and Italian), is also an absence. Her speech is referred through the narrating voice who provides almost no physical description of her, other than telling of the angelic "bun of white hair that circles her head like a halo" (30). However, he attributes behavior to her that raise the suspicion that through the Frau a split, nurturing/malevolent, mother imago is made manifest: it would seem she is another blank screen onto which the voice projects his emotions. Indeed, she appears to know what he is thinking, making speech superfluous at times, anticipating and evaluating his needs before he articulates them (50). She also beleaguers him with a *"tormentone,"* a coinage that may be translated as "enigma," but is in fact the augmentative of *tormento,* which signifies torment or agony. The voice uses this term to refer to the fragments of poems he recalls from their Sunday evening readings, which he attempts to utilize as clues to solve a riddle whose answer is buried deep in his early childhood—in the "dreams" Ferruccio admonishes should never be told, because "it is like giving away your soul" (31)—and is of a piece with his ambivalent feelings for the mother, whom he fails to mention in describing what he claims was an "extremely happy childhood" (131).

The Frau is a cross between servant and a wisdom-dispensing philosopher (106), and a perfect match for the "philosophizing" subject of narration (93, 106). The voice at times sees her as affectionate, like Daphne, a loving nurturer (96): indeed, the Frau often acts as if she were the voice's mother (17). However, she can also be treacherous, like Marilyn. He describes her as "sententious" (10) and peremptory: when he protests that one of her Sunday poems sounds too much like a lullaby, she tells him to "be quiet and listen" (30). He believes she doubles his dose of morphine when it suits her (46); but at other times is "spiteful"—reducing his dose of pain killers at whim—and therefore untrustworthy (9, 17, 50, 77). Even though the narrating voice is almost eighty years old, she still addresses him as *"signorino"* (21, 102), little master. It is not clear why she never married, thus remaining sexually available to the voice for nearly three-quarters of a century, especially since the voice believes she has very strong maternal instincts, and would have liked very much to have children (111).

Daphne claims to intuit that while the Frau may seem emotionally distant, that is not the case: Daphne surmises that the Frau, like many Germans, is a person who "can cry on the inside without crying on the outside" (17, 46). This is why Daphne would forgive the Frau for the consequences of the Second World War, were there no linguistic barriers between them (17). However, the narrating voice, who is able to converse in both German and Italian with the Frau, never conveys these sentiments, allowing us to assume that his silence may belie his mute resentment for maternal abandonment.[68]

When the father dies, the son is still young enough to enjoy playing with his grandfather's sword. The father's absence during his son's childhood precludes his serving as a model for gender identification, a role filled by the grandfather. Projective identification becomes one of the child's defenses; he becomes his grandfather's son. In fact, he will tell Marilyn that Tristano was not his father's name, but his brother's (63).

Indeed, where the grandfather was a volunteer soldier and the father a combatant, the voice is a pacifist (149), a reluctant warrior who stares with incredulity at the rifle he used to kill a German soldier in Greece (154); who is drawn inadvertently into the Resistance; and who hopes that the end of hostilities will mark the beginning of an era of peace: [Tristano] sang our fatherland is the entire world, our law is liberty,[69] and in him life began again . . . of life-bloods [*linfe*], after all that bellicose adrenaline, massacres and blood" (107).[70]

Although it is not made clear when the mother dies, repressed feelings of helplessness associated with the separation from his parent(s)[71] are relived by the voice in Plaka. When he sees a defenseless Greek boy killed in cold blood, his "instinctive" reaction (14) is to avenge the murdered youngster. This proves to be an overwhelmingly emotional experience "for a boy of his age" (23), an odd self-description for someone who, in the early 1940s, would have been in his late twenties. Daphne protects him from reprisal and, once danger subsides, has him escorted to Corinth, and then up into the Peloponnesian Mountains. The voice never speaks of his decision to participate in the Greek Resistance, rather than quickly return home via the port of Pireus to contribute to the Italian anti-Fascist movement. Only when he sees himself abandoned by another father figure—the king who on September 8, 1943, "left all Italians in the lurch"—does he return to his *patria*, and to his patrimony, his ancestral home, where he again goes into hiding (25–26). In other words, in this phase of his life—the period prior to his becoming the hero Tristano—the voice behaves in a manner quite unlike that demonstrated by his heroic friend Mario, who in 1939 had begun "his own Resistance beforehand" (12).

The narrating voice returns home and, after he grows tired of his hiding place "underneath the straw" (45), goes off into the mountains, alone, defenseless, with no intention of joining the conflict. His only arm is a relic of his grandfather, but it is not the sword. He takes instead his grandfather's telescope, an instrument that will allow him to look away from the *patria-patrimonio* and toward the heavens (38, 46). There he is drawn reluctantly into the Resistance—when he mistakes Marilyn for his beloved Daphne, whom he left behind to fend for herself in Greece. Because the voice underwrites a traditional definition of heroism—equating it with aggression, domination, and risk-taking (see Spielberg 1993, 174)—he discounts the killing of the German soldier in Greece as unheroic: it was a reflex action (14). He will instead consider heroic his conversion of passive experiences of loss (for example, Marilyn's infidelity) into active experiences of inflicting loss—for example, his killing, singlehandedly, an entire squad of Germans.[72] This act earns him the right to insist that he be addressed using the name of his grandfather's son and heir, Tristano.

Thirty-odd years later, he will lose this heroic identity when he is forced to relive the childhood trauma of helplessness when he is caught completely unaware by the death of his stepson, blown up while planting a bomb for a right-wing terrorist group (96). The voice's inability to foresee danger and to protect his stepson from annihilation costs the voice that which he held most dear, the possibility of passing on his inheritance. This repetition of the childhood experience of object loss is "accompanied by observable signs of overwhelmed helplessness and disorganization of ego processes" (Hurvich 316). Put differently, the death of Ignacio shatters the voice's self-image, causing him to fall victim to a mental disorder: he ceases to be Tristano and begins to refer to his past self in the third person (104).[73]

The voice's loss of identity is foreshadowed in his representation to the writer of an exchange with Marilyn, who at one point believed that her romantic involvement with another man, the secret agent Cary, had caused the voice to "lose his sense of identity" (67). In his delirium the voice also confuses Mario (a prewar friend from Turin) and Antheos (a Greek partisan) with Ghiannis, a taxi driver the voice meets when he returns to Greece in 1953 (12, 152). More importantly, Daphne (46) blends in his mind with Marilyn (he calls the latter "Mary Magdalene" [45], perhaps in the hope that she will change her promiscuous ways, and be faithful to him) into the conglomerate figure of the Francophone Giuditta (Judith), female counterpart to the voice's Giuda (Judas). In sum, for both the narrating voice and the reader, the glossing over of the distinct individualities forestalls the establishment of a focal point for meaning and understanding.

The loss of identity is also anticipated by the voice's projective identification with his dead father. In other words, the voice takes from his grandfather, who participated in the creation of the Italian nation, the equation of *patria* and patrimony, and the expectation that the voice regain the inheritance that Fascism had usurped from his father's generation. Thus, Tristano's contribution to extinguishing the "Republic of Salò—that [had] proposed, with insolent arrogance, that it serve again as arbiter of the fate of all Italians" (12)—permits the voice to see himself as the avenger of his father and of all Italians (78). Like the grandfather who had contributed to the birth of a liberal regime as a member of Garibaldi's *Mille*, the voice sees himself as a true patriot.

As Tranfaglia points out, for the Liberals who had exercised their hegemony over the Italian government during period following Unification and particularly during the two decades preceding the March on Rome, "Fascism [had] served the indispensable function of breaking the ability to resist of the mass workers' parties who after World War I intended either to overthrow Italy's liberal capitalist system or at least dictate their conditions for integrating themselves into that system." Once Fascism had accomplished this, the bourgeoisie had every interest in restoring the Liberal State and those institutions that had in the past guaranteed the noncoercive administration of Italian society and return as quickly as possible to constitutional normality (Tranfaglia 1973, 121).[74]

And just as the voice's failure to return to Italy is consistent with that of the Liberal Party's negligible contribution to the Resistance prior to the deposition of Mussolini as prime minister July 25, 1943 (Ginsborg 1990, 16), his participation after Italy's surrender to the Allies reflects the Liberals' belief that the war had given initial impetus to the closing—albeit with a delay of twenty years—of what they saw as a "parenthesis" in the development of the Liberal State.[75] For Tristano, the end of the Fascist regime signifies the restoration of the *patria-patrimonio* to its rightful heir, the father with whom he identified consequent to his own inability to elaborate his father's death.

When the father dies, the voice is too young to tolerate the painful affects and the work of grieving. As is the case with the deaths of his mother and grandparents, the death of the father is never explicitly addressed in this monologue. In other words, the narrating voice is at no point able to acknowledge the finality of these deaths and work through his grief. Instead, he seeks to deny the reality of the loss of this 'abandonment'[76] (a reenactment of the father going off to war, which however, ended happily with the father's return). In fact, the only family photograph the writer is shown—it is in a black, ebony frame, indicative of ongoing, incompletely decathected mourning—depicts the father who, although he is coming to marry the mother and retrieve his son, has turned his back to the camera, "as if he were saying 'goodbye'" (162). Elaboration of mourning is impeded further by the grandfather who assumes for his grandson the guise of the father: the elderly man becomes the lover of all things American his late son once was, and commences to 'sneak' the voice into the father's study (the two pretend the father is still alive, intent on examining specimens under his microscope) so that they can listen to and appreciate the dead man's record collection.

The conflict of the contemporaneous disavowal and acknowledgment of the reality of the death (the cognizance that he is to become his father's successor implants in the narrating voice a sense of obligation that he must replace the father and continue in the path the grandfather had intended for his own son) an unsustainable tension in the voice to recover and safeguard the inheritance of the Liberal State the grandfather had helped create as one of Garibaldi's *Mille*, which had been usurped from the father's generation by Fascism. Identification with the father comes at the expense of the voice's own personality: it is not by pure coincidence that the young boy who once played with his grandfather's *garibaldino* sword refutes the name by which only Marilyn addresses him, Clark (102), which is based on a spurious identification with the male lead in the film *Gone With the Wind*.[77] Once he becomes a war hero, he insists on being addressed by his father's name, Tristano: "Don't call me Clark, Tristano replied, I already told you, I am no longer Clark, now I am Tristano . . . Don't call me Clark, he said, I'm no longer Clark, I told you, I am Tristano, that's what I like, now my name is Tristano" (61, 63).

However, the voice's resentment of having thrust on him the duties and responsibilities associated with the inheritance by the absence of a father who studied micro-organisms before dying prematurely is revealed through Ferruccio, who "always used to say that inferior organisms possess a greater vitality than more evolved ones. This must be the theory of someone who died young; people who think this way must die young, if for no other reason than to be consistent" (147). Ferruccio's identity is never clarified. However, the derision of the father implicit in this statement and the knowledge of contemporary literary theory that emanates from other statements attributed to Ferruccio, along with the name's evocation of Ferruccio Parri[78] and the name's ability to suggest a diminutive but resistant, "iron-like" [*ferrigno*] character of a man who succeeded where the father had failed by surviving into old age, would justify speculation that Ferruccio may be the real name the narrating voice refuses to reveal. Furthermore, Tristano's onanistic refusal to have children may be interpreted as a repudiation of his father's heritage. The adopted son would have perpetuated a line that goes back directly through the narrating voice to the grandfather, circumventing the father.[79]

The murder of the Greek boy recalls from memory what his grandfather had told him—"in life you must love life, and remember you must always love life, Fascists like death" (41)—and he rebels. He refuses to absolve his patriotic obligations and deserts the army. He discards his army jacket for pragmatic reasons, but more importantly because "he no longer wanted to be Italian" (22). The voice neglects to mention what he did with his rifle, a "gift of the military" [*dono d'ordinanza*], but it seems it disappeared together with his jacket: to explain to Daphne what he had just done, he must use his thumb and index finger to mime a weapon (22). When he first sees Daphne, she too is helpless and unarmed—he describes her as he would Vanda, "a lost little animal" [*un animaletto sperso*] (22)—and shields him from danger. He tells her that Italy's invasion of Greece has caused him to reject both *patria* and patrimony—finally resolving oedipus while in his late twenties—and to assert the validity of a perspective that is distinct and autonomous from those of his grandfather and father. In other words, he tells her that both his father, who "studied life up close, with the microscope," and his grandfather, who "sought life very far away, with his telescope," had been mistaken. Life is not to be observed through lenses; it is to be "discovered by the naked eye—neither too close nor too far away—but at a human dimensions" (41). Indeed, he tells her that he "doesn't want to spend his life in a university classroom nor his nights in an observatory searching the sky, why? to discover other worlds, isn't this one, and the way we've ruined it, enough?" (75). This is why he defines his heir as someone who "would have continued [his] look [*sguardo*]" (95). The voice's heir would emulate a grandfather who appears through the screen of memory as kind and indulgent, and unable to observe the sky unaided (136) by learning what the voice taught himself using the self-help manual *How to Guide Yourself by the Stars* (159). The heir would also oversee the family land once the voice, like his father, was blinded by death. Indeed, the voice attempts to develop his vineyards and olive groves because he equates the bequeathal of real estate with the preservation of the memory of the deceased; he tells Daphne: "bring me to Crete, I want to see the house you were born in, you cannot leave it abandoned, it would be as if your father and your mother died twice, I will be the one who re-opens that door, you will enter with me" (75). In sum, this definition of the heir, as someone who would perpetuate the voice's vision of the sky and land, explains his eccentric mourning ritual when the stepson's death demonstrates to the voice that he is helpless against fate: ". . . He would go out into the garden at night, wander through the fields and vineyard, lie down on the naked soil, cover his face with clumps of sod as a show of mourning uniquely his own, and would put a bit of dirt in his mouth too, he would look on high at the firmament, stretched out immobile in the middle of the fields, cadaver-like, even though at times he would raise his arms and stretch them toward the moon" (95).

A symbol of the helplessness that overtakes the voice as he lies defenseless against death is the horsefly that is trapped with him in his room (13, 17, 30, 34, 77).[80] Indeed, while obeying the order to clean his dead stepson's room, the voice explicitly equates his frustrations as an adult, the fly, and the riddle from his infancy embodied by the Frau: ". . . and I saw my whole life contract in an insect, a minuscule, complicated instrument for flying and hibernating, the buzzing of his anger, and the fragile beating of his elitrons, his filthy paws, and I threw everything into the sewer, crumbs of rubber and smell of burnt plugs is all that binds me to the world . . . You understand what I am talking about, it was that riddle [*tormentone*] of the Frau" (115–16). The voice fears that the fly—a disguised representation of his fears, such as his loathing for a body that old-age, illness and drug dependency has rendered once again supine and helpless—will have the last laugh, and mock him by landing on his mouth after he dies and is no longer capable of fending it off (161). Indeed, the voice says of the insect, "there is a horsefly hitting up against my mirror who is looking for the exit, a stupid horsefly, who like me cannot find the exit, who needs morphine like me, me who is here who is talking, but why insist on unburying times past?" (106).

What the fly 'talks about,' in the voice's moments of waning lucidity, is not clear. It is clear, however, that the morphine administered by the Frau plays an integral role in the voice's delirium (see Maddocks 1996): indeed, in telling of his refusal to have his infected limb amputated, the voice reproduces almost verbatim the plea of a similarly afflicted Confederate soldier during the siege of Atlanta in *Gone With the Wind*. Ostensibly, the voice takes morphine to lessen the pain associated with his gangrene, but he never explains how he contracted this affliction, or why he allowed it to spread so dramatically, given the pain and stench that would have begun to quickly emanate from the mortified area. Indeed, in declaring the voice mentally ill (68), the doctors of the local public health office provide a physical description of him that resembles that of a drug addict, a suspicion not refuted by their refusal of his request for laudanum, a preparation of opium dissolved in alcohol (130–31) nor by his claim that the Frau laces his drinking water with hops (28), the active agent in beer and slang for opium. In sum, the voice's dependence on morphine raises and leaves unresolved the possibility that this exterior monologue is little more that the ranting of a drug addict who has projected himself into a book he read several years ago—a hypothesis validated when the voice imagines himself the protagonist of a novel on heroism written by the writer he 'summons' to compose his biography (see 102), a novel in which the voice sees himself confused not only with Rhett Butler, but with the title character of the classic Western *Shane* (105), the retired gunfighter who, at the film's culmination, walks into Grafton's saloon and takes precise aim on rear-guard cattlemen and gunslingers to apply summary justice, and then tells the young son of the homesteaders who had taken Shane in, "There's no going back . . . everything is going to be all right . . . there are no more guns in this valley."[81]

Whether or not the writer is physically present is less important than how the voice utilizes the writer to reenact emotionally laden experiences from his childhood, but in the role of parent, thus making manifest his "identification with the aggressor," to use Anna Freud's phrase.[82] In other words, the voice seems to have appropriated aspects of the behavior of his disciplinarian grandfather, who insisted that the voice sit idly and patiently every Sunday for precisely fifteen minutes prior to his German lesson ("he did not compromise when it came to tardiness: 'because of tardiness,' he used to say, 'there were those who missed the boat for Calatafimi' [26][83]). Indeed, the voice treats the writer with an arrogance similar to that used by the grandfather, a haughty man [*un uomo burbero*] (159), in dealing with his shepherds and sharecroppers. The voice installs and reiterates his social supremacy when he expresses his displeasure at the writer's tardy arrival and reminds the writer that it was he, the voice, who summoned the writer (11, 19, 32, 34, 47, 82, 87, 101, 134). And when irritation gets the best of the voice, he commands: "listen and write; write and keep quiet; are you ready?" (43; see also 81). Later on, when exhaustion and anxiety set in, he lashes out again: "You're no help at all; you don't say one word; you ask no questions. It's true that you obey the instructions I gave you when I summoned you: *zitto e mosca*[84] I told you; you come here *zitto e mosca* . . . but now you are obeying too much." (66)[85] In other words, the voice projects inner realities onto the writer. However, we may also infer from the voice's vulgar euphemisms that he does not hold in high regard corroborating witnesses—exegetes such as the writer—and that he esteems only protagonists, men like himself who fight wars and write poetry (35). People like the writer are followers, or to be more precise disciples [*zebedei;* Italian slang for testicles] (131), people of secondary importance. This is why he tells the writer, "I don't want anything from you, I don't need your help, I can take care of myself" (67).

This power relationship will be overturned, or at least modified, when the final session draws near and the voice realizes that he is dependent on the writer's complicity if he is to survive as the "dead author," in the Barthesian sense, of his own life story (159, 160). He asks the writer's permission to quit using the "disrespectful," familiar form of address and begin using the formal *Lei,* because in the absence of witnesses and given the difficulty of contradicting the dead, as the epigraphs point out, the writer is free to render his own edited view of the past, one that may or may not conform to the voice's memory.

In the course of asking the writer to edit historical memory, the voice equates his past complicity with foreign agents with Judas's betrayal—the Risorgimento, after all, was fought to free Italy of foreign domination—and extends that request to those who sacrificed themselves "for good cause" [*a fin di bene*], but in so doing may have found themselves on the losing side in the Resistance (157). The rehabilitation of those who 'mistakenly' fought for the Republic of Salò would, of course, wash away his own betrayal of the *patria.*

The writer is suited for this task because he has insisted on calling the Resistance a civil war, a definition that subtracts from the idea of the Resistance as a war of liberation.[86] Liberation would mean acknowledging that the country had been occupied by the Germans and invaded by the Anglo-Americans. The writer's stance, that the Resistance was a civil war, represses this awareness, and implicitly validates revisionist attempts to rehabilitate Italian Fascists, who in this scheme of things are equal in destiny to those who died ridding Italy of Mussolini and his followers in a settling of accounts that was somehow separate from the war between the Allied and Axis powers.[87] The advancement of the image of the Resistance as primarily a civil war and not one of liberation, permits the depiction of the *repubblichini* as equal to the partisans in a fratricidal conflict in which each side saw itself incarnating good and the other evil, a position that in turn justifies each side's attempt to annihilate the other. In contrast, the idea of liberating the Peninsula from foreign oppression, according to Umberto Eco, encapsulates the moral and psychological significance of the Resistance for Italians: they did not passively wait for others to free them but took their destiny into their own hands (Eco 1997b, 27).[88] In addition, the writer's definition of the Resistance as a civil war not only resonates in the voice's fascination with the reactionary encomium of the United States' Old South proposed by *Gone With the Wind*, but it also attenuates blame for his role in the death of the partisan commander: "we shot at both enemies and friends," he says (13), transforming a premeditated killing into a harbinger of the new millennium, the euphemism "friendly fire."

For Tabucchi this sort of historic revisionism—in Italian at times referred to with the depreciatory term *dietrologia*, which conveys the idea that the past can be rewritten in function of present political expedience—is contradicted by its very premise, the idea that time is somehow reversible, because the study of what we believe is behind us, the *dietro*, "is already here, *in front of us*" in the guise of the neofascist party *Alleanza nazionale* and its partners in the Italian government and in the current attempts to re-present the past so as to valorize them (Tabucchi 1997e, 3–4).

Reference to the contemporary revisionist histories of the Holocaust and the Resistance makes a bit less cryptic the epigraph, from Ferruccio, that "it is difficult to contradict the dead" (7): after all, it is not impossible to reinterpret them. In fact, the historiographer has a relatively free hand in emplotting the past, that is to say, reordering events in a hierarchical structure of relationships which are then subsumed into an integrative whole that narration endows with meaning (Hayden White). Consequently, in responding to the other epigraph to *Tristano muore* (from Paul Celan)—"who testifies for the witness?" or, to rephrase, who need corroborate the witness's testimony?—Tristano affirms, "no one" (156). In the absence of material evidence the witness's testimony needs no corroboration because it is 'objective,' self-validating, tautologically true: "the world is made of acts, actions . . . concrete things that pass [. . .] permanence is in words, that continue to make the action exist, that testify for it. It is not true that *verba volant*. *Verba manent*. Of all that we are, of all that we were, the words we said remain, the words that you are now writing, writer, and not what I did in a specific place and a specific time. Words remain . . . mine . . . but above all yours . . . the words that testify" (155).[89] So in opting not to narrate, but to be narrated (161), the voice entrusts himself to the printed word—which, as Ferruccio reminds him, serves for "future memory" (158)—because it will take the place of the stepson, the deceased heir who, had he lived, was to serve as a "prosthetic device" that would have enabled the voice to "prevail over the prison of existence" (109).

The substitution of the writer for the stepson in the voice's mind becomes evident when the voice asks the writer the time: "*È già la una, come dite voi del Nord?*" [Is it one o'clock, as you Northerners say?] (110).[90] In this brief laisse the uncharacteristic gentleness of tone and request for empathy are incongruously combined with the attribution to the writer of a colloquial usage not in keeping with his status. Furthermore, the unique indication of an aspect of the writer's identity, his provenance, raises the suspicion that the voice, through his delirium, is in fact addressing his Northern stepson, who spoke Italian with a Spanish inflection.

While Italian is the voice's native tongue and German is a language of affect, Spanish is associated with early childhood through the step son. In fact, repressed, filtered material returns uncannily to consciousness through lapses in language when the voice speaks of young, victimized boys. The Greek lad in Plaka goes to his death carrying an aluminum mess kit that the voice calls a *gamella* (14), a Spanish derivative, rather than using the more common *gavetta*. While speaking of his own childhood, the voice remembers taking *siestas* (17), not *pisolini*, after having fallen asleep "*a las cinco de la tarde*"—the same hour the Frau held her poetry readings—to the singing of cicadas, whose music remind him of castanets and cymbals (17, 105), sounds that are more congruous with a childhood spent in Castile, than in the voice's native Tuscany.[91] Furthermore, the voice reports how, while "navigating in oneiric space," he would create a "semi-incomprehensible, fantastic zoology" that includes *gambusinen*—an admixture of Spanish *gambusin* (a freshwater prawn) and the German plural—which he fished with Daphne.

These returns of repressed material confuse traumatic situations lived as an adult and recollections of experiences of anxiety and helplessness in early childhood, particularly those caused by abandonment and death. For example, after killing the German in Plaka, the voice identifies himself to Daphne using his childhood nickname, "Ninototo" (22; see also 136 and 159). When Tristano and Marilyn first meet and fall in love he sings her lullabies. He sings another while burying Vanda.[92] In fact, while traveling to Spain to kill the man he believes responsible for the death of the stepson the voice sings "a sort of nursery rhyme" [*filastrocca*] (150). Furthermore, while lying in wait outside a "fairy-tale house" [*una casetta da fiaba*] (44) to kill the German platoon he hears a woman sing "a strange melopoeia with strange words, a lullaby as ancient as the timber of the voice that sang it."[93] The lyrics of this lullaby—"*Fate la ninnananna*," which his grandmother used to sing to him, tell of betrayed love.[94] The rhythm of its music mimes the rocking of a cradle, causing Tristano's surroundings begin to rock back and forth as if he were in a cradle being lulled by a woman who cannot be seen, but only heard as she sings of a man who is held captive by love. At the same time, the German platoon appears to be mysteriously bewitched by the uncanny return of the first poem the Frau ever read to the narrator— about a siren, Lorelai, whose voice seduces sailors, causing them to shipwreck, a nursery rhyme the narrating voice still knows by memory (26–27)—giving the 'hero' Tristano the time necessary to shoot all the Germans without a single shot being returned.

This motif of betrayal resonates throughout Tristano's act of 'heroism.' It was the voice who revealed to Stefano, who turns out to be a Fascist collaborator, the whereabouts of the partisan commander, effectively signing the commander's death warrant (47, 123). What remains unclear—either because the voice deliberately chooses silence or because the answer is buried in the depths of the unconscious—is his motive for discussing the location of the hideout with someone who was not a member of his brigade. Also unknown to the reader is whether the voice knew that Marilyn spent her nights in the hideout, betraying his love. The voice does not clarify why he spent that night sleeping outside the farmhouse where the Germans ambushed the commander (rather than with the rest of unit—with whom he was scheduled to participate in an offensive action early the next morning—in the cave near the river, as was his habit [45]). It may perhaps be the case that the German platoon was his means for eliminating the commander, who was seen by the narrating voice as an enemy in the civil war for control of the future of Italy (155).

There are other questions the voice dares not ask, and the Pythia he consults fails to pose. For example, was Marilyn in collusion with the Germans? She knew the commander would be alone that night (138), and may have told them so. She was, after all, the daughter of a Sicilian gangster brought back to Italy from Brooklyn after the Allied invasion to ensure against Communist hegemony, at the expense of Fascist continuity (64). Why the Germans allowed her to leave the farmhouse unscathed also remains a mystery (did they neglect to search the house after killing the commander and his bodyguards risking their being shot in the back while exiting?). Equally murky is the reason the voice and Marilyn accuse the other of duplicity. In any case, since her role in the death of the commander—the only person who knew the voice's true identity (137)—cannot be ascertained, it is not clear why the voice lets her escape, especially because it puts her in a position whence she may embarrass or blackmail him later on: "one shot and you will be vindicated and the only witness to what really happened will disappear, and you will be a perfect hero" (155).

The voice justifies his role in the death of the commander by comparing his actions to those of "Judas, who betrayed out of loyalty" (158). This would give credence to the hypothesis that his tragic destiny is that of a man whose love for his country led him to collaborate with the same foreign secret services who will enact severe limitations on the nation's internal sovereignty, after acceptance of Marshall Plan aid dictated Italy's subservience to its Atlantic allies in foreign affairs (see Duggan and Wagstaff). The voice's betrayal is, at first, "transitive" (97), and later "reflexive," because once it has been unleashed, its scope and magnitude can no longer be controlled, and it turns on its perpetrator, Tristano (99). In other words, the cost of closing the Fascist parenthesis and preventing the installation of a "classless society that suffocates the individual" in Italy[95] is the acceptance of Anglo-American interference in Italy's domestic affairs. The unforeseen consequence of this action is the covert funding of the domestic political parties who provide a shield for the black and white terrorism responsible for Ignacio's death, and who used the Marshall Plan as seed money for a free economic market that fosters social disparities, the necessary humus for the rise of the inelegant type resembling Italy's current prime minister (127) who uses his monopoly of *"pippopippi,"* television, to limit and condition Italians' freedom, right, ability, and duty to think.

The voice begins to lose control of his betrayal in 1948, at a time that coincides with the outbreak of the Cold War. He believes he "found" [*ritrovò*] Marilyn at this time (28), but his role in arranging the encounter is a much more passive than his choice of verb would indicate. Marilyn inexplicably appears, almost out of thin air, after in all likelihood identifying and locating him surreptitiously. She invites him to go with her to an inexistent town she calls Pancuervo[96] for a briefing on the West's plans for postwar Europe. They travel together to Spain, but he loses his resolve, gets distracted, and misses the train to Pancuervo: "kaputt" (62). And so, "With a wide and liberal gesture Tristano embraced the horizon. I should defend liberty . . . the liberty that I sought and that is so dear, but to tell you the truth I begin to not know what it is, I've gotten myself involved in an adventure that doesn't concern me, I don't know why, during the war everything was so clear, or it least it seemed so, and now nothing is clear any more, and I want to understand" (66). In other words, the milepost for this critical juncture in his life is a nonchoice, a refusal of protagonism.

He will return to Greece in 1953, but he is "a parody of Ulysses," a man who "had taken the wrong streetcar" (56–57). To make matters worse, once there he learns that during his absence Tristano's erstwhile allies, the Anglo-Americans had intervened, using military force to impose their own solution on that country's internal affairs:[97] "The English and their younger cousins have two types of democracy, the good one, reserved for internal consumption, and the spoilt one that was left to grow mold in the warehouses of time, the one they export to poor nations, after all, the poor will eat anything" (56). He determines that someone had "gone back on his word," and, in his opinion, "to break a deal means to betray" (99), and to betray, as Tabucchi has written elsewhere, is to edit, rewrite or modify the past (Tabucchi 2003a, 79). However, the narrating voice does not give specifics of the deal, or what he had assumed they were, nor does he state who had broken it. But in his opinion, what had been betrayed was the anticipated restoration in Italy of the constitutional Liberal State, and the promulgation throughout the world of governments resembling Italy's model democracy. At least this is what he assumed had been tacitly promised him when he sided with Marilyn and the West. He tells the writer as much—with bitter irony bordering on cynicism underscored when he appends to his statement the refrain from an anarchist hymn learned, perhaps, during the Resistance: "Writer, the spread of liberty, which is capillary, arrives to its beneficiaries throughout the world, our fatherland is the entire world; our law is liberty" (101).

The voice—who had been accustomed to seeing things in black and white (10), much like the postwar newsreels that told Italians of his bravery (78) and particularly the script of the texts that immortalized him by dividing the world into good and evil, right and wrong (91)—is shaken by the cognizance that there may have been other possible futures for Italy. When confronted by the possibility that he may have incorrectly assumed he was faced with an either-or proposition between East and West he begins to suspect there may have been other options than following Marilyn and her choice of freedom, especially since his binary opposition of liberty and equality failed to consider the need to temper both with justice (100): "Tristano was at a crossroads, and the problem branched off precisely in the sight of his rifle, squeeze the trigger in one direction and you have chosen a classless society that suffocates you, you squeeze it in the other direction and the world goes on as it always has, with rich and poor, but, hey, you have chosen liberty" (90). And so he withdraws from the spotlight reserved for the nation's war heroes (149), many of whom were elected to Parliament, when he is overtaken by the knowledge that there is no going back; he is a prisoner of his own past: he had lent his rifle, and, after the war, his public image to the cause of continuity, to the bridging of Fascism and the Republic.

As Ginsborg points out, after the war Anglo-American forces swiftly disarmed Italian partisans and installed absolute military authority. They also moved to ensure that economic conditions would not deteriorate and provoke social unrest, while working to forestall any profound institutional break with the past (Ginsborg 1990, 70–71).[98] Duggan adds that

> failure [by the Italians] to tackle squarely the issue of responsibility for fascism had far-reaching consequences. It resulted in a curiously schizophrenic climate in Italy in the late 1940s and 1950s, in which

calls for change and a renunciation of the immediate past jostled uneasily with many indications that a large part of the country's former political baggage—both material and ideological—had simply passed unchanged into a new constitutional wrapper. Many liberal intellectuals felt that fascism should be regarded as an historical "parenthesis": the philosopher and historian Benedetto Croce claimed the inter-war years had been simply a digression from the country's otherwise steady path of liberal progress since 1860, an "illness" that had temporarily laid low a fundamentally healthy body." (3–4)

For his part, Tristano places himself squarely at the center of this collective denial of Italy's fascist past when he elevates himself to synecdoche of all Italians: Tristano "committed that act of heroism, but he is not he, he is like the Unknown Soldier, he represents all Italians, even we presidents and generals who did not participate in the Resistance, he represents all of us because the Italians were never a Fascist people" (78). Thus, by sharing his glory he transfers responsibility for his actions. In hindsight, his evocation of the "self-evident truth," his opting for liberty, serves to rationalize and justify his treachery. He did not physically kill the partisan commander, the Germans did. But he made that killing possible, acting in the name of all those who believe that civil liberties are sacrosanct. And the end would have justified the means, had the course of events not taken a few unexpected, tragic turns, such as the bombing of Hiroshima and Nagasaki, NATO's cohabitation with Francisco Franco, and liberist consumerism's exploitation and manipulation of the masses.

The elevation of Tristano to Everyman is cast in relief through the writer, an intellectual whose worldview resembles that of the narrating voice: "At times it seems that you are a part of me" (82), he tells the writer at one point, and then adds further on:

> the book that you wrote using Tristano as your main character, someone who writes the life of someone else in the first person as if that life were his own, when all is said and done has written something resembling a fictionalized biography. Why did you write about me in the first person? To you perhaps it seems normal, but, you know, it's not. Why did you become Tristano? Why did you put yourself in his place? ... and in any event what does your life have to do with Tristano's, why did you identify so closely within him? (104)

The identification of the writer and Tristano metaphorically extends the drama of Tristano's choice in time through the Cold War and the collapse of the Berlin Wall and the Soviet empire, beyond the narrating voice's death to the preventive wars of the twenty-first century:

> You had to kill one or the other, and Tristano has to choose. And you know what he chose, because you know what liberty is, you are a liberal intellectual, and ideas are important to you . . . in fact, you are the one who points the rifle, chooses the direction, aims, shoots. Pum. You chose democracy. Bravo. You made the same choice as Tristano, and that is how you got inside him, but what mimetic abilities, you are Tristano in the flesh, in my opinion you are Tristano. I don't know why I am telling you about him, you are Tristano, . . . you suffered his dilemma, you lived it in the first person. (90–91)

Thus, the identification of voice and writer absolves Tristano from responsibility for his choice which resulted in the perpetuation, "in the name of liberty" (90), of civil and social injustices and the grotesque transmogrification of his concept of individual freedom into the freedom of someone who, like Vanda, is "buried in sand up to his neck" (132). This identification transfers responsibility to the writer, and to all who participate in the wealth of the developed world. It does so by shifting accountability for the text from the soon-to-be-literally dead narrator to the metaphorically 'dead' author, and ultimately, to the reader (161), those whose freedom is conditioned by the choices made by Tristano over a half-century ago.

Thus, the voice arrives at the postmodern realization that truth is not based in material reality, but in narratives: "only when written do things become real" (146): "Naturally, it didn't happen this way, you must have realized by now. But you write it as if it were true, because for Tristano it was truly real, and what matters is what he imagined his whole life, to the extent that it became one of his memories" (25). This is especially the case in the absence of living witnesses or physical evidence that might contradict the dead author; as the Frau reminds him, there is "no trace in the river of where [he] once swam with a woman" (10). The postmodern understanding that only the editing of events by the writer can give his life sense, or meaning (49), and that only textualization give them permanence (155) frees him to declare that everything is relative, including the values of the Resistance (13), which in turn releases the voice, and the *repubblichini* he asks the writer to rehabilitate, from historical accountability. More importantly, it justifies his production of a document that is neither a forgery or a counterfeit, to use Eco's terms, but a fictionalized (auto)biography, a paradoxical term that, in this case, denotes purposeful deception, a false document. It does not seem to matter that, following the voice's own logic, such modifications of the past and betrayals are synonymous because, like the protagonist of *"La trota che guizza"* (Tabucchi 1991b, 91–106), he would absolve himself before 'sinning.'[99] Because it is an original testimony, the reader is paradoxically obliged to assume authority over and responsibility for a narration whose many lacunae exact reader collaboration and answerability: "so take a look around, if you don't believe me, and ask yourself why, no, ask yourself 'for what,' for whose benefit did Tristano go up into the mountains with a telescope on his shoulder? . . . do you think that maybe Tristano wanted to look at the stars because his country was a sewer? And how is your country? Do you like it?" (46).

5
Epilogue. Something's Burning: A Mysterious Flame

IN JUNE 2004, ONLY A FEW MONTHS AFTER THE PUBLICATION OF Tabucchi's *Tristano muore*, a new novel by Umberto Eco, *La misteriosa fiamma della Regina Loana* [*The Mysterious Flame of Queen Loana*], was in print. Because both novels represent a dialectic of microcosm and macrocosm that summarize the second half of the twentieth century—the former expressing disappointment for paths not taken, the latter revisiting the choices that contributed to the unfortunate state of Italy's current affairs—they invite a comparison that, hopefully, clarifies and reinforces the distinctions drawn and arguments advanced in our introduction.

Both Tristano, and Eco's protagonist, Giambattista Bodoni, claim to find themselves in a state of sublime detachment from the events of the day. As we have seen, Tristano attributes his "ataraxy" to his awareness of the imminence of death. Bodoni is recovering from amnesia;[1] therefore his main concern is not the present, but retrieving a lost past. Although Eco's protagonist is a full generation younger than Tabucchi's Tristano, Bodoni was raised on Italian translations of books written in the 1920s (142) the same books Tristano read as a lad; hence many of their experiences overlap. As a result, both provide us with an intimate overview of Fascism, the Resistance, and Italy's First Republic.

However, unlike Bodoni, whose story ends in 1991, Tristano is very much concerned with the path taken by the Second Republic, forged by the judicial purges of Italy's political leadership in the early 1990s. As Tristano awaits death, his thoughts go toward his country: specifically the role he played in its reconstitution during and after World War II. It is his fate to live in a consumerist Italy that has forgotten its traditional values. He is disturbed by the realization that in Italy solidarity and the ability to believe in causes larger than oneself are things of the past: the Italy in which he lives does not correspond to the one he thought he was constructing while combating Fascism. In contrast, Bodoni's medical condition causes him to be preoccupied exclusively with his past. He wants to recover his autobiography, and understand the events that made him the man he was prior to almost falling underneath a moving vehicle. For example, he wants to recall to consciousness the modalities of the "infantile schizophrenia" that led him, first, to eschew the "exaggeratedly heroic [*eroicizzante*] rhetoric of the Fascist regime," and then underwrite— "more because of instinct than because of ideology" (67)—an anodyne progressive political stance. As stated, the *recherche* represented in *La misteriosa fiamma* ends in 1991—the time of *Tangentopoli* and the fall of the Berlin Wall, events Bodoni never mentions—with the protagonist in a coma. So, he does not worry himself with thoughts of what may happen to and in his country after many of Italy's most prominent politicians and business leaders are indicted by the "Clean Hands" investigators.

Bodoni's tale culminates in a return home, a *nóstos* (this is the title given by the author to the third section of the novel, dealing with Bodoni's relapse). However, Bodoni's voyage takes place entirely within his mind, with a radical turn inward: the coma that separates him from the outside world precludes all interaction and dialogue. In contrast, the social compunction of Tristano is palpable: he describes his various returns home as parodies of Ulysses' *nóstos* (he was a man who always seemed to take "the wrong streetcar" [56–57]). Parenthetically, Consolo's writings also make explicit reference to Ulysses' *nóstos*, which in the Sicilian author's parlance connotes the future-oriented expiation of remorse for errors committed in the past, possible only within a civil consortium and within the flow of history, metaphor for an understanding of one's place and role in the polis.

In other words, all three writers historicize our times by depicting the dialectic of microcosm and macrocosm; but in Consolo and Tabucchi the social influences the way the individual experiences the past, whereas in *La misteriosa fiamma* the opposite is the case: interior reality "colonizes," to use Jameson's term, the past. Indeed, one cannot help but ask if Eco is not satirizing those individuals such as Bodoni, whose believe their life's story does not take place in society, and inside whom we cannot see reflected the story of a people.

By situating his novel in 1991, Eco can avoid engaging Italy's present, which is defined to a large degree by the changes wrought by the dismantling of the Soviet bloc and the upheaval caused by *Mani pulite*. In fact, as far as Bodoni is concerned both events remain out of sight and out of mind. This allows Bodoni to avoid any sort of self-criticism and justify, through hindsight, his life choices. Bodoni's retreat inward allows him to edit his past in function of the present. In other words, unlike Consolo and Tabucchi, who have placed their work at the center of a nucleus of social issues—particularly, the rise of a prime minister whose privatization ideologies have successfully formed "a coherent project for political and cultural dominance" (Ben-Ghiat)—drawing artistic strength from them, the protagonist of *La misteriosa fiamma* dispenses the comfort of a stroll down Italy's memory lane, hinting that though it may be flawed, this is the best of all possible worlds.

Bodoni's retrieval of the historical past accurately reflects what Jameson, in his seminal essay, labeled the "postmodern nostalgia mode," the "cannibalization of the past, which is recombined into new, overstimulating ensembles" (66). The restructuring of the past, through the pastiche of memories, projects individual memory onto a collective and social level (Jameson 1984). One need only read the review of Eco's novel by such a perceptive critic as Remo Ceserani to see how *La misteriosa fiamma* comes to constitute—for Eco's and Ceserani's generation—"the privileged lost object of desire." In other words, individual memory conditions how society assimilates the past into collective experience.

At the same time, the work's utilization of ekphrasis, the incorporation into the text of visual documents—posters, book and magazine covers, photographs, war documents, record dust jackets, and other memorabilia—from the period in question, transforms the relived years into a once lost and now recovered heroic period that subjects successive generations to the "esthetic colonization" of the perspective shared by contemporaries of the narrating voice. In other words, for all, those who are Bodoni's age and those who are not, the trivial pursuit of an edulcorated past allows the author to "lay siege" to the "present and immediate past" of readers of all ages. Present reality is approached through "the pastiche of the stereotypical past" and through the language of the image. The pastness conveyed by the image is without historical depth, which has been leveled into the eternal present lived by the narrating voice in his amnesia and coma. Thus, the reader's present is endowed with "the spell and distance of a glossy mirage" (Jameson). The present, having lost the past as its referent, becomes, in its turn, immune to genuine historical analysis.

When used in tandem with the nostalgic reevocation of the past, ekphrasis directs reading. The visual document corroborates the text, tautologically providing material documentation of 'what really happened' (145). The visual images eliminate the haziness of reader memory and the lacunae in what the reader can know. The images remove all doubt and ambiguity. Things must have been—and still be, now and forever—as the author documents them. In other words, the illustrations set definitive boundaries for 'common sense' readings; they substantiate the univocality of verbal text that then, in its turn, sets forth the parameters for interpreting the visual text. In sum, Bodoni's reconstruction of the past cannot be questioned.

Thus, Eco's use of the nostalgia mode constitutes a very astute development of his poetics of the Model Reader. It not only allows him to determine how the text is to be consumed, but it allows him edit history. It also, perhaps more importantly, broadens his appeal to an incredibly wide demographic, comprised not only of Italians of his own generation, but of the multitudes of youthful television addicts raised on the Italianized versions of American game shows whose stock in trade are fairly useless, disconnected tidbits of information.

As is the case with *Il pendolo di Foucault*, the protagonist of *La misteriosa fiamma della Regina Loana* is Eco's contemporary. He was born in 1931 (11), at Christmastime, "like the Baby Jesus," whose birth is symbolic of new beginnings. Indeed, Bodoni awakes from his coma on April 25, Italy's Day of the Republic (11), the annual occurrence that marks the Peninsula's liberation from Nazi-Fascist oppression. But Bodoni does not see his reawakening in patriotic terms. Instead, like Casaubon, Bodoni remembers the Resistance as a grand, confused mix of Black Brigades; royalists (the *Badogliani*); anarchists; the socialists and communists of the *Garibaldini* brigades, and Catholics.

5: EPILOGUE. SOMETHING'S BURNING

Like Casaubon, Bodoni also remembers that during the Resistance the only person who was truly pure of heart (other than, of course, the narrating voice, who like all Eco's protagonists succeeds in absolving himself from blame, as we shall see) is the parish priest, who is apolitical but willing to put his life on the line to protect his flock (356).

As Bodoni remembers things, he was an innocent lad; before his accident he was a philandering, yet loving husband, and a good provider for his family. Like Tristano, Bodoni believes that both the *Badogliani* and the *Garibaldini* were "all fighters for liberty" (361). He sidesteps the issue of the historical responsibilities for the rise of Fascism, hinting that his parents went along with the Regime because of their desire to achieve economic independence from his paternal grandfather. Bodoni recalls that in the 1940s, even though Italy's paterfamilias, the king, betrayed his country (a second time; the first occurring after the Black Shirts marched on Rome), the *Badogliani*, the partisans who did not rebel against the king, when compared to the Reds, seemed to be the lesser of many evils (365). While Bodoni had no direct contact with the *Garibaldini*—he remembers them mainly through the prism of a unit of Cossacks who had fled to Italy to escape Stalin's purges—he aligns emotionally with the *Badogliani*, hence with the king, and therefore with the Anglo-Americans, repressing knowledge of who betrayed Italy by opening the door to twenty years of dictatorship.[2] In so doing, he positions himself to participate in the spoils of the centrists' assumption of leadership after the war.

Bodoni's political choices are consistent with his upper-middle-class upbringing (32). His greatest childhood influence, the paternal grandfather, was active in the Socialist Party before the March on Rome. During the Resistance the older man hid fleeing subversives in the attic of the family estate from the *repubblichini*, and gained his heroic reputation by repaying in kind the Fascist who humiliated him in the 1920s by forcing him to drink castor oil. Indeed, the only lesson Bodoni takes through life from the Resistance is summarized by Amalia, the housekeeper of his country estate at Solara: politics is a dirty business, best left to others (383). This lesson is driven home by his recollection of the one time he was involved in politics, his "night of terror." Bodoni remembers how that night he learned once and for all to love the fog that kept him from being seen while escorting a platoon of Cossacks from danger, and, more importantly, prevented him from seeing (since he could not identify any of those who were with him that night, he could not be called on to testify, unlike his friend Gragnola who committed suicide for fear of betraying his comrades in arms [383]).

His politics coherently reflect a personality that is quite indifferent to the humanity that surrounds him: an antiquarian book dealer by trade, Bodoni loves books more than he loves people (66–67). Those closest to him serve only to help unlock the mysteries of his ego. His daughters are no more than cameos; at no time does Bodoni ask them of their lives, homes or spouses. He can relate to his grandsons only by recounting to them the plots of adventure books he had read as a child; but he does so autobiographically, that is to say as if the events he reports happened to him, and not to fictional characters (162–63). Bodoni's best friend, Gianni, exists as a function of this latter-day Narcissus: Gianni is summoned to fill gaps in Bodoni's memory, but quickly dismissed whenever he would "pollute" Bodoni's "tabula rasa with his own memories" (167–68).

Bodoni's amnesia does not deprive him of "implicit" or muscle memory: he can drive, write, and perform other physical activities just as before (16); he also retains one of two kinds of "explicit memory," the cognitive kind that enables him to speak and to remember facts. However, his amnesia has deprived him of autobiographical memory of his affective life. He can remember the books he has read, but nothing with a personal, emotional valence (19); this is precisely the past that must be reconstructed (20).

Because he is preoccupied with recovering the past, he is "scarcely interested in the present" (215); he is more than happy to review the events of the last two thirds of the twentieth century from the most egocentric position possible. In this way, the *recherche* takes on the patina of a disinterested intellectual exercise, like other research projects from Bodoni's recollected past, carried forth with an absolute minimum of emotional investment (179). To use his own words, "Memory is a haphazard solution used by humans, whose time flows, and what passes has passed. I, however, enjoyed the marvel of a re-birth *ab ovo*" (224). And yet his research methodology seems flawed: the reader cannot help but ask why no attempt is ever made to contact his best source of information of his early past, his sister Ada.

His amnesia and coma allow him to view himself with the detachment necessary for believing himself completely unaccountable for whatever may have happened in the past, events that are now out of his control. Following Kilborne, we may say that Bodoni's step outside himself allows him to manage his appearance anxiety, the way he believes he appears to others. If, as Kilborne maintains, seeing and being seen are the basis of the social bond, then in this—and perhaps in all Eco's novels—counter-love, the experience of an important person looking and loving back, is reflexive: Bodoni, the quintessential narcissist, looks at and loves only himself while forcing all others to pay attention only to him. In other words, the novel is the story of a man who seeks to reappropriate his appearance or self-image—his belief in his own political and social correctness—by imposing his fantasy-construction on the one who looks, the reader. Any act of which Bodoni is less than proud may now be blamed on nurture, his upbringing at the hand of his paternal grandfather and his parents, or on nature, instincts, which, of course, is a way of assigning responsibility to uncontrollable stimuli, and, therefore, of absolving oneself for blame.

In any event, Bodoni's amnesia forces those closest to him, if they wish him well, to look only at him, to set their own needs aside—at least until he recovers—to indulgently remember events from his past, to allow themselves to be reduced to a function of his ego.[3] Similarly, Bodoni's amnesia demands that he look only at himself and reexamine his past. In contrast to Tabucchi's protagonists, who identify with and love the other, Bodoni, like all Eco's protagonists, love themselves as if they were other; they abstain from looking outward. Thus, in *Regina Loana* narcissistic autoeroticism reaches its culmination: the external world is absorbed into the vortex that is the narrating voice's ego.

In a manner of speaking, Bodoni is his own child: his name, Giambattista, John the Baptist, "seals his fate" by deeming him his own precursor. The concern of postamnesia Bodoni with his predecessor, preamnesia Bodoni, provides Eco's protagonist with an excuse for redirecting the "self-love which the real ego enjoyed in childhood" not to an offspring, but to himself.[4] This allows him, for example, to compliment himself for his precocious ability to avoid falling prey to the nationalistic propaganda of Fascism, and to ignore the subtle manner in which he absorbed class prejudices that identified good with the *Badogliani* and other protectors of the status quo such as the protagonists of his comic books, who always triumphed over evil.

Evil in Bodoni's mind had paternal attributes. His friend Gragnola taught him that all wickedness may be blamed on God the Father (67). According to Gragnola, God's demands for obedience and obeisance are reflected in an age-old aspect of human nature, which Gragnola calls "eternal Fascism" (346–48). And because Bodoni's amnesia has placed him outside the flow of time, Bodoni believes that this equation of evil, dictatorial behavior and *patria potestas*, paternal authority, makes him innocent of the 'sins' of previous generations, both those of the domineering patriarch—the grandfather who failed to prevent Fascism from seizing power—and of those who acquiesced—men like his father.

However, cognizance of his father's shortcomings does not lead Bodoni to rebel. Instead, he feels filial piety for his father, who never succeeded in achieving financial independence from the grandfather, and was therefore parsimonious with the family budget. In fact, the only teenage memory left intact by the amnesia is that of his father turning down Bodoni's request for a motor scooter: the father explained that only spoiled youngsters owned them. Bodoni accepts what his father tells him, but sees through the justification to the underlying frugality. Nonetheless, Bodoni does not question the hypocrisy of the less-than-forthright answer, but utilizes it in learning to be a skeptic. And, in surrendering his dream of owning a Vespa—which now becomes, in his eyes, tantamount to sinning (408): a Vespa was the "solar and foggy proof" of "what could happen when you took off with an Amazon sitting behind you" (409); you might acquire forbidden carnal knowledge—the young Bodoni learns to repress and sublimate sexual desire.

As a result, he takes to venerating his own "private divinity" (416), a "creative and organizing Will" (389):[5] "the eternal feminine" whose memory will spark a "mysterious flame" whenever he remembers his adolescent fantasies for the comic book heroine Queen Loana. So, to help himself suppress his craving to physically possess "the eternal feminine," he reads, an activity that allows him to transgress a prohibition when he possesses, with his mind, the naked form of the many virgin-prostitutes that inhabit his adolescent readings (391): "I read, and I burst into flames, all in my head. . . . I need not confess this to Father Renato. It is literature, and I can partake of it, even if it tells me of perverse nudity and androgynous ambiguities. It's far enough from my experience so that I can avoid its seduction. It's word, not flesh" (397). When he approaches what he is not supposed to see, Mother's prohibited female sexuality, the mysterious flame of the eternal feminine is rekindled. To explain, the sanctum sanctorum in which the flame is preserved is found at Solara, where the "forbidden kingdom" (126) of his illicit childhood readings has been stored for some forty years.[6] There, as a child, he would read incessantly—much to the chagrin of a father who was "a bit disappointed by that son who spent his days ruining his eyesight" (389)—until he entered a "uterine fog" (399), one that would allow him to dream of idealized women such as Lila Saba, the unreachable object of his desire, more a fantasy than a real person, born less from lived experience than from the book that caused his first ejaculation (402).

On the positive side, Bodoni's teenage fantasies of Lila allowed him to repress memories of the one time in his life that he was called on to be a protagonist: his "night of terror." Somehow, his unrequited love for her restores his love for life, and allows him to make his peace with an unhappy childhood.[7] However, Lila's unexplained disappearance causes him to turn away from the world once again: "On the one hand, I escaped into a comfortable and promising knowledge (I graduated with a thesis on the *Hypnoerotomachia Poliphili*, not with a history of the Resistance); on the other, I met Paola" (411-12)—his future wife, at the time a "defenseless high school girl" (20) whom he "seduced" shortly after the deaths of his parents and of his grandfather (events that shook his sense of identity; undermined his confidence in the continuity of his life; and caused him to understand that there was no one left to look out for him). Paola becomes the surrogate mother figure who indulgently looks away from the sexual peccadilloes of her Latin *maschiaccio* [wild boy] (46), uses her training as a psychologist to nurture him as would a perfect mother, and allows him to utilize her sexuality when she "deflowers him at sixty years old" (78).

Bodoni's last infidelity, more mental than physical, is Sibilla, whose name predestines her to close the circle as pagan *pendant* to the protagonist: she is Sibyl to his John the Baptist, his chaste but sexually available mentoree in book collecting and in economic rapacity.[8] For Bodoni's Sibilla is both "immaculate virgin" (54) and "whore" (57); she is a Polish "black pearl" (59) of an immaculate blackness" (55). When Bodoni realizes Sibilla's fantasy—discovering an original edition of Shakepeare's works—the excitement sends him into his coma (306), metaphor for his *nóstos* or return home to the confines of his mind.

Entrance into the coma reminds him that regaining access to the cantinas at Solara had symbolized for him "the reception of the maternal uterus, with its amniotic humidity," "airiness," and "healing warmth" (121). In the coma, in the complete absence of interlocutors, Bodoni can "think, feel, remember, outside the flow of time" (307). There, he can simply "be, full of bliss, in an eternal present" (313). He can live "with himself and for himself" (308), far from social consortium, and concern himself only with himself, his past, and the books he has read (324). Moreover, he can avoid thinking of the civilization in which he was able to live without feeling any discontent because he made a habit of exercising his negative freedom, the freedom from attenuating some his own instinctual drives for the good of civil society. Hidden from view—behind the visual texts he uses as a sort of literary Novocain—are the consequences of his selfishness, a country besieged by all the social ills, injustices and inequities of modern industrial nations. But since his autobiography is the story of an escape from life, neither he nor the reader need think about how we got where we are or about where we are going.

Notes

Chapter 1. Introduction

1. In analyzing "socially symbolic acts," namely literary texts, I will examine the poetics of authors in question, which Binni defines as the site where the "moral, intellectual and cultural force of authors, their historicity-humanity, is transformed into art" (8).

2. In fact, Lilli Gruber, in resigning her post as anchor of Italy's most prestigious evening newscast, the RAI's TG1, decried the pressure to "homologate" information exerted by the political parties currently in the national government and criticized the de facto expropriation of a public broadcast service charged with reflecting the variety of political positions and ideas in the country and in Parliament (Gruber 2004). For an attentive analysis of the rise of Silvio Berlusconi to power, see Ginsborg 2004.

3. Eco explains that when citizens delegate to one person the rights to which they are entitled in a representative democracy, they effectively surrender their freedom to identify and select alternatives to that leader. When this occurs, 'the people' continue to exist, but as an abstract concept. In other words, 'the people' ceases to be a quality—wherein each possesses individual rights and responsibilities, and can govern by forming majorities—and becomes a quantity, a monolithic entity whose will can be shaped and manipulated by the media. He adds that when the media are able to aim in a predetermined direction public opinion, by selecting 'representative samples' of 'common citizens' whose emotional, visceral responses to the issues of the day, circumventing the slow proceedings of representative democracy, freedom is threatened (Eco 1997b, 44–47).

4. This locus of meaning is equated in Eco's novels to God and is defined as "a space that is not there" (Eco 2000, 433) and as "all and nothing," an "absolute availability" (Eco, 1980; 503, 496).

5. In order to give the greatest possible resonance to his opposition to the involution of Italian politics and society, Tabucchi ran in 2004 for the European Parliament as a member of the Portuguese *Bloque de izquierda* [*Leftist Bloc*] (Cotroneo). The platform of the *Bloque* included a plank against the war in Iraq and a denunciation of terrorism. This movement has gained great visibility in Portugal, where its representatives in parliament are vociferous advocates of gay rights and the legalization of abortion (Sostieni Tabucchi).

6. However, it must be said that after the Soviet invasions of Eastern Europe in 1956, Calvino moved to establish himself as a sort of 'rational eye suspended

over the world,' but found over time that free thinkers *au dessus de la mêlée* often fell prey (this is certainly the case with his Mr. Palomar) to a pessimism stemming their inability to act until they succeed in thinking—that is to say cognitively mastering—the world. Contaminated with the malaise of postmodern perplexity, thinkers such as Mr. Palomar can only contemplate, and with "bitter serenity," their rationalist utopias (for Calvino see Francese 1997 and Francese 2001).

7. Eco stated that when a house catches fire the intellectual can to no more than "try to act as a normal person of good sense, like everyone else" and "call the fire department," and adding that those who look to the intellectual to explain the cause of the metaphorical fire "is acting like a hysteric." Intellectuals should not try to teach principles of humanity to xenophobes who are unwilling or unable to learn them, but should invest their efforts in attempts to influence the future by acting within their area of expertise, by re-writing the text books used in the middle schools attended by the grandchildren of those xenophobes.

8. This, of course is on a societal level. On an individual level, Tabucchi explains, "Dante would use the word 'desìo' [*longing*]. When we look closely at life, we cannot help but think about all that has passed, but also about all that could have been but was not. And about all that we could have done and did not do" (Parazzoli 1998, 80–83).

9. Consolo recently created a stir when he announced he would attend, but not accept government sponsorship for his appearance, a Parisian book fair. He justified his decision by calling the government headed by Silvio Berlusconi anticulture and antidemocratic. In response to Consolo's call for a boycott, Tabucchi also let it be known that he would attend, not as a representative of the government, but as a private citizen who paid his own expenses. Eco, after being brought into this dispute by a government minister, distanced himself from all parties, saying that he would attend, as always, that is to say as a representative of himself and of Italian culture, not of any Italian government and would stay, as is his custom, at five-star hotels at the expense of his publishers (Presa di distanza dalla protesta di Consolo e Tabucchi).

10. The rapid advances of information technology redefined the modalities of resistance to capital accumulation. As Harvey writes, "workers' movements have been better at commanding power in places and territories rather than in controlling spatialities with the result that the capitalist class has used its superior powers of spatial maneuver to defeat place-bound proletarian/socialist revolutions . . . The recent geographical and ideological assault on working-class forms of power through 'globalization' gives strong support to this thesis" (Harvey 2000, 38).

11. For Cvetkovich and Kellner globalization is a "legitimating ideology for the westernization of the world" (1–2) because it justifies a world market system that worsens unequal relations of power and force (4). At the same time, they point out that "culture is an especially complex and contested terrain today as global cultures permeate local ones and new configurations emerge that synthesize both poles, providing contradictory forces of neocolonization *and* resistance, global homogenization *and* new local hybrid forms and identities" (8; their emphasis). In other words, global culture raises issues of identity

that may be exploited: "as a form of resistance, emphasis on national and individual identity has emerged as a response to homogenizing global forces" (9). And so we are forced by global culture to rethink identity, and redefine the polis: "Rethinking identity requires openness to new forms of global identity or citizenship. If democracy is to play a genuinely progressive role globally, nationally, and locally, new ways must be created for citizens to participate in the different levels and dimensions that constitute their lives" (12). Of course, globalization does not automatically allow us to assume the notion of a universal culture that can be analyzed through investigations of specific local cultures: "This strategy has too often produced problematic versions of multi-culturalism that have no way of explaining the relations of power that connect different cultural contexts" (Cvetkovich and Kellner 19). However, as Harvey reminds us, "universality always exists *in relation to* particularity: neither can be separated from the other even though they are distinctive moments within our conceptual operations and practical engagements" (241).

12. Kellner explains that media culture is organized industrially, on the model of mass production, and produced for a mass audience. Its products play on a broad range of emotions, feelings and ideas that are intended to shock, but not to delude audience expectation. In other words, it is a form of commercial culture whose stock-in-trade are commodities that attempt to attract private profit to giant corporations interested in the accumulation of capital. (Kellner 1995, 1–2).

13. For the passage from a qualitative vision of time to a quantitative one, see Maiello.

14. Mari (2001) argues that our inability to orient ourselves in time, caused by the flattening of the temporal dimension into the 'eternal present' installed by postmodernity, and our lack of a unitary and global vision of the sense, or direction, of history may be restored when space is redescribed as without limits, global, but at the same time geographically defined and centered, from the perspective of diverse individuals. Such a relativistic view of events would reflect both the plurality of peoples and individuals and the universality of multiple societies who come into contact and conflict with each other, above all geographic determinisms. In response to the annihilation of space by technological globalization on the one hand, and, on the other, to the ever-increasing acceleration of our experience of time, and postmodernity's lack of a telos, a unitary or global history may be retrieved from the connections that we are able to see and comprehend—between facts, single events, and histories—and our narrations/explanations of them.

15. Marcuse would argue that public reaction to George H. W. Bush's sanitized, videogame war in the Persian Gulf clearly demonstrated the extent to which the instincts, particularly Eros, have been colonized by media culture. The liberalization of sexual taboos within a repressive society which has succeeded in using sex as a salable commodity results in either the elimination or the subduing of those forces and features that, according to Freud, made sexuality and Eros a truly liberating and socially dangerous force. In the condition of repressive desublimation installed by media culture, destructive and competitive instincts gain ascendancy over the instinctual need for privacy, for quiet, for tenderness, for solidarity, for peace on a scale hitherto unknown.

Moreover, "in technological and aggression and destruction the satisfying act is transformed from the human agent to the mechanical, electronic, or nuclear agent. That is to say, the objective power of a thing separates the human person from his target, and executes, as a thing, the satisfaction of his needs. Consequence: the weakening of individual responsibility—the apparatus did it, or the machine did it" (92).

16. An odd state of affairs in a country whose current president has not moved to protect domestically the "God-given right" to vote we are willing to wage war for abroad by acting to prevent reoccurrences of the irregularities that marked his election and re-election by calling for federal election standards for a unitary voting system, and for uniform enforcement of those standards by the attorney general.

17. For Marcuse this does not entail a simple liberation of instinctual drives and their sensuous manifestations, lest we fall further victim to the norms of a repressive society wherein Eros is no longer administered by the Father, the erstwhile representative of the reality principle, but by media figures outside the family (athletes, rock and movie stars), the role models who make adolescents aware of the renunciations and restrictions necessary for living in society through public-service announcements. (Marcuse 2001, 138).

18. However, since the scope of this study is limited to modes of narration and of historicizing our present, analysis of the demographics of who buys Eco's novels and who reads them will be deferred to sociologists of literature, and the question of why this is so to social psychologists. For our purposes it will be sufficient to note that when Eco's popularity as a novelist lags, it is not because he has altered the marketing formula discussed in our chapter on "The Poetics of the 'Model Reader.'" It is due to the fact that Eco does not follow it. *L'isola del giorno prima* [*The Island of the Day Before*] and *Baudolino* are not as 'successful' as *Il nome della rosa* and in *Il pendolo di Foucault* [*Foucault's Pendulum*] because their author fails discuss intellectual issues in way that is palatable to his preferred readership by striking a proper, amenable balance of *docere et delectare*.

19. This, in effect, is what Eco's prose fictions accomplish when they point the reader's gaze in a direction of Eco's choosing. For example, in the introduction to *Il nome della rosa* Eco refutes the critic Beniamino Placido's assertion that Eco's protagonist, Adso da Melk, is not a historically verifiable personage. However, the main thrust of Placido's review falls very far from contesting that Adso existed, as Eco would lead his reader to believe. Placido proposes that Eco's writings, even some of his nonfictions, are autobiographical recountings à clef of Eco's intellectual itinerary. Placido claims that all biographical novels are "self-justifications of the author," who unavoidably holds up his own life as an example for others. In Eco's case, the reader is confronted with an apolitical overachiever who uses "every refined narrative expedient" in his arsenal to convince Italy's youth to set aside their political activism and redirect their energies to their studies. It is not for us to say whether or not Placido's reading is accurate. At the same time, the critic must be given credit for having painted an accurate picture of Eco's protagonists, all good boys who never complain; are "quiet and obedient, full of health and joy," who eagerly do their all to please the Father (Placido 1977).

20. The plot of *Il sorriso dell'ignoto marinaio* is built around a painting, the *Portrait of an Unknown* by Antonello da Messina, as is *Lo spasimo di Palermo* (1998), inspired by the eponymous canvas by Raffaello, which formerly decorated the Church of Santa Maria in Palermo and is now in the Prado.

21. See Consolo 2003b in this regard.

22. As Pagano has indicated, "images not only play a fundamental role in the genesis of [Consolo's] texts, but . . . re-enforce the narrative discourse, endowing his writing with a visual force uncommon in contemporary letters" (Pagano 1999–2000, 84).

23. It must be made clear, before moving on, that this "topographical knowledge" is by no means synonymous with an epistemology of place, "possible only from the place of Benjamin's 'victor,'" of the barbaric history" that has brought us to where we are (see Dainotto).

24. Following Dainotto's analysis of "the literature of place," we may say that Consolo's Sicily is not a "purported origin of being and thought," nor a regionalist reaction to the "fear of placelessness brought on by globalization," nor "a means of restoring 'concrete geographical identity.'" Sicily in Consolo's work is not "the figure of an otherness that is, essentially, otherness *from*, and against, history," nor is it a move outside of history, outside the present to a place that remains "eternally the same," but "a hypothesis of what *could* have existed and *could* be realized again in the future" (Dainotto 2000, 2, 3, 17, 9).

25. Pagano writes that in *Retablo* Consolo creates "a narrative context in which the themes and images of the contemporary Milanese painter [Fabrizio Clerici] are freely developed. His fictional transposition is another way to 'speak for pictures,' different from the kind of *ekphrasis* practiced by art criticism, and certainly more loosely connected to the original, but more dynamic, and thus capable of making us perceive Fabrizio Clerici's art in a new light. . . . This 'intertextual' approach to art is typical of allegory." . . . In [*Retablo*] the desire to travel to remote places and dream about extinct civilizations is considered always in dialectical opposition to the real world, characterized by profound inequities, which even a detached observer like Clerici cannot overlook" (Pagano 2002, 210-11).

26. Dombroski contends that Consolo is perhaps the only modern Italian writer who has fully understood that in order to strike at the heart of what was once an enlightened "culture of privilege, while preserving the potential for liberation contained in its discourses," one "must return to the foundations of his people via a route opposed to all forms of foundational-ism" (Dombroski 2005, 234). In *Il sorriso*, for example, Consolo interrupts the discourse of his enlightened, economically privileged narrator with discursive fragments taken from multiple, contrasting voices who represent the oppressed classes so as to energize the subaltern perspective by re-writing it "in a language of mobility, transgression and power" (Dombroski 2005, 234). In *Il sorriso* Consolo "dismantles" the traditional linear structure of narrative, filling the "fractures" between the chapters—and exacting reader collaboration—with "historiographic inserts," documents, that connect those gaps.

27. Tabucchi has written, "In a society founded on the cult of the personality, on private initiative, and on individualism, what is more valid than collective

creation, than direct . . . collaboration, for meeting one's fellow humans?" (Tabucchi 1971, 30).

28. For example, those of Calvino and the *Oulipo* group, whose games, "do not bother anyone" (Tabucchi 1998e).

29. See Pessoa's poem "Autopsicografica": "O poeta é un fingidor. / Finge tão completamente / que chega a fingir que é dor / a dor que deveras sente" [The poet is a faker. He / Fakes so completely, / He even fakes he's suffering / The pain he's really feeling. // And they who read his writing / Fully feel while reading / Not the pain of his that's double / But theirs, completely fictional]. (Pessoa 1986, 139).

30. For Tabucchi, Pessoa's heteronymic system is the drama of a man "in conflict with himself who is desperately seeking an unobtainable self." The heteronyms are the actors-interpreters of a dramatic action that the poet has set up so that they might share responsibility for his disquietude (Tabucchi 2003).

31. In the preface to *La struttura assente* (Eco 1958) Eco contends that since reality is not knowable in its totality, the manipulation of falsifications allows us to better contemplate "the mysterious Origin of this contradictory reality that evades us" (XI). Reality is contradictory because it is a "binary calculation," an Absolute that is both Absence and the Fullness of Presence (XII). Once we accept "the concept of binary oppositions as a metaphysical principle we are forced to abolish the notion of [fixed] structure," which is not the same as saying that there is no Code of Codes. It is to say that this *Deus absconditus* cannot be known, because the "original Game . . . at the root of all possible communication" "is not a Code, but the absence of all codes" (XXXIII). However, the nature of this absent code can be gleaned if we observe the critical junctures where it is transformed, the falsifications just mentioned. Reality is transformed when we set in motion "a dialectic between God and Nothingness, between Presence and Absence" (XI–XII). This is accomplished when we move toward an indeterminate "elsewhere" by interrogating and informing ourselves" through language, "the Origin of every possible structure." Indeed, we do not speak language, Eco affirms, we are spoken by it. Linguistic structures define Presence, a system of probabilities that in turn orders chaos, the non- or yet-to-be codified. The dialectic of the codified and the not-yet-codified catalyzes transformations of the system and, therefore, "is the *source* of all possible information of reality" (XIX). In order to understand what has not yet been absorbed into the code necessitates excogitating a theory of probability. Language, then, constitutes "an original locus," and our speech an "interrogation of Being" (XXIV). A theory of probability or of "play" that considers linguistic simulation, paradoxes and falsehoods, for Eco, is an intellectual exercise in metaphysics that contemplates an indeterminate Origin and an unreachable End—which is to say the lost Fullness of Presence or eschatological end to history that have been lost in postmodernity.

32. As he told an interviewer, "to lie is not to say something that is false; it means to say something you know is false. When Ptolomy said that the Sun revolved around the Earth, he made a false statement but he wasn't a liar. When my Baudolino fabulates, he places blind faith in what he says. 'Inventing' is his way of being; it is the motor of his existence" (Padovani).

33. Behind Baudolino's fabrications are unconscious motivations that Bau-

dolino—and Eco, it would seem—prefer the audience disregard. For his part, Eco enjoys talking and writing about his work, and how he writes, but refuses to talk about why he writes: "I have no intention of discussing here the motivations (how should we describe them? existential?) that led me to write my first novel. There were many reasons, probably it was a combination of them, and I believe that to simply assert that I was taken with the desire to write a novel should suffice" (Eco 2002, 330). As we shall see, just as Eco draws a line between what is fair game for critics and what is not, his characters refuse to acknowledge any of the insights that might be made available to them by psychological investigation.

34. And since Eco's Model Readers (see above, note 17) are those who follow Eco's instructions for use and rely on the reliability of conscious, stated intentions for divining the author's textual strategy, they willingly assume accountability for and authority over the "open work."

Chapter 2. Umberto Eco

1. Respect for the literal sense means "You may infer from texts things they do not explicitly say—and the collaboration of the reader is based on this principle—but you cannot make them say the contrary of what they have said." (Eco 1984, 92; see also Eco 1998, 52). Yet what to make of humor and lapsus, such as Ronald Reagan's jocular announcement, made while testing a microphone and then quickly denied, that the United States had begun bombing the Soviet Union? When the reporters present, based on their knowledge of Reagan and his policies, took the President literally, the administration's 'spin doctors' immediately set out to convince a terrified public that Reagan was "only joking."

2. According to De Lauretis, in Eco's so-called open work "writer and reader do have interpretative 'freedom' (the term is Eco's), but that freedom is conditional and overdetermined: for the writer, by the (historically specified) universe of discourses available, which Eco calls at different times 'the world of the encyclopedia' and 'the format of the semantic space'; for the reader, it is overdetermined as much by the reader's codes and frames as by the text's own project" (De Lauretis 1987, 60). In this chapter De Lauretis also broaches the topic of "the theory of the lie" in Eco's semiotic writings (53–54)

3. For the manner in which Eco sets the limits on reading, see De Lauretis (66–67) who defines the role of the reader in the text as a "semantic-pragmatic mechanism of textual strategies" (66) whom Eco provides with "the norms and the semiotic instruments for analyzing the reading of texts and for interpreting them correctly" (68). In her view, Eco succeeds in this way in giving readers credit for creating the open work while limiting interpretation and controlling them (75–76). Elam contends that in *Il nome della rosa* "the act of love is committed both for and with the manuscript itself . . . The romance *of* the text is the romance *with* the text. What we find in romance, according to Eco, is what reading and writing (what narratives) are all about—if writing once was thought to be a way to change the world, now it is simply positioned as a form of romance, an act of love, which give the writer and the reader pleasure and consolation" (29).

4. Capozzi writes, "As we know, [Eco's] ironic and postmodern metafictions make extensive and explicit use of intertextual references . . . to most of his own theoretical studies" (226). He claims that "*Il nome della rosa* confirmed how well Eco combines in a most clever fashion his theoretical and creative writings" (226).

5. Mc Hale claims that cognitive fiction is "organized in terms of an epistemological dominant." Its "formal strategies implicitly raise issues of the accessibility, reliability or unreliability, transmission, circulation, etc., of knowledge about the world" (146) On the other hand, postmodernist fiction is "organized in terms of an ontological dominant, fiction whose formal strategies implicitly raise issues of the mode of being of fictional worlds and their inhabitants, and/or reflect on the plurality and diversity of worlds, whether 'real,' possible, fictional, or what-have-you." They ask the "post-cognitive question" "Which world is this?" (147). He goes on to argue that *Il pendolo* is an ontological "experiment in self-conscious world making" (173).

6. That Eco intended to flatter the reader of *Il pendolo di Foucault* is made quite explicit at the very outset by the epigraph that precedes the narration: "Solo per voi, figli dell dottrina e della sapienza, abbiamo scritto quest'opera. Scrutate il libro, raccoglietevi in quella intenzione che abbiamo dispersa e collocata in più luoghi; ciò che abbiamo occultato in un luogo, l'abbiamo manifestato in un altro, affinché possa essere compreso dalla vostra saggezza." [Only for you, children of doctrine and learning, have we written this work. Examine it, find yourselves in that intention that we have dispersed and gathered throughout: that which we hid in one place, we have revealed in another, so that it might be understood by your wisdom.]

7. Available on line at the time of writing at http://www.dsc.unibo.it/dipartimento/people/eco/CURRICUL3.htm

8. It should be noted that Eco at age thirteen joined the political organization *Gioventù italiana* [Italian Youth], the youth association of *Azione Cattolica* [Catholic Action], the most important of the Roman Church's many parallel organizations among the Italian laity. He told an interviewer that the group's "democratic-social" orientation for social reforms and advocacy of the oppressed made it comparable ideologically to the liberation theology movement of South America and he characterized his *liceo* [high school] years as a time of "great political commitment and religious fervor." After his second year of university studies he was invited to join the group's national committee in Rome. However, in 1954 the conservative policies of the national parent group caused his resignation. This event coincided roughly with the completion of his studies, his transfer to Milan, and the beginning of a profound philosophical and religious crisis that was resolved only in the early 1960s. However, this does not mean that the importance of a transcendental dimension has disappeared completely from his thought. In his own words, "He who has lived a religious experience can lose God, but does not lose the religious dimension. Once you have experienced metaphysics, you undoubtedly remain bound to it" (Stauder 1989, 9–10).

9. In a recent debate, Eco, a proponent of "weak thought," claimed that although there is no metaphysical "end to history," we must maintain our ability to give history a direction (Martini and Eco 11), a stance similar to that

assumed by Vattimo, who recently argued that in the absence of an idea of a unitary meaning of history (the idea that history has a general, comprehensive direction that individuals might adopt as a norm on which to model their behavior [Vattimo et al., 9, but see also Vattimo 2000]), we must cultivate our ability to think the future in a nonprophetic way (see Mari 1998). For Eco this means that loss of religious faith does not exempt from loving the present and "believ[ing]—with charity—that there is still room for Hope" (Martini and Eco, 11).

10. In *Kant e l'ornitorinco* [*Kant and the Platypus*] (Eco 1997c), as Antonello points out, "Eco is ostensibly arguing in favor of a pre-linguistic stability of reality which precedes language and finds the very possibility of meaning."

11. Capozzi attributes Eco's "uncontrollable temptation" to "expound (with plenty of footnotes and bibliographies) on everything he writes" to a desire for contextualization and to rule out of bounds what the author considers are "blatantly unacceptable interpretations" (qtd. Capozzi, 224). Yet what is this "desire for contextualization" if not a move by Eco to make the text comprehensible within the text's here and now, and an overt attempt to reassert writer authority over the text?

12. See Shumway, who outlines the strong parallels between celebrity and the academic star systems. For our purposes, we can limit ourselves to underlining similarities in the way show business and literary-academic audiences response to stars: "identification and desire." Identification can be important, in that it leads to emulation, but perhaps more important is the installation of the star as object of desire and the consequent desire of the fan for the star's approval.

13. As opposed to an "objective-denotative" concept of language (a "dictionary," in his terminology [Eco 1983a, 74]), that is to say, a strong semantics that presents itself as a "system of rules" which attempt to "express the internal structure" of the language (Eco 1983a, 54).

14. In Eco's opinion, reality is much simpler and comprehensible than what adherents to the "Syndrome of Suspicion" would have us believe "Surely there are conspiracies, but . . . they shed their cloak of secrecy after no more than five days . . . Conspiracies remain secret for a short while. Then History arrives" (Adornato 96–98).The "Suspicion Syndrome,' he argues, "is not research into the meaning behind things, but the practice of unlimited slippage of meaning" (Adornato, 99). He tells the reader that "the true theme" of *Il pendolo di Foucault* is in fact this "neurosis of interpretation," the defining condition of contemporary literary criticism and political analysis, "a barbarization and a primitivization of thought" common to all forms of radical politics. To use his phrasing, it is a "form of undisciplined interpretation that can generate Nazism or other ideologies that can involve both the Left and the Right." It prevails because its theoretical counterpart, "hermetic semiosis"—which he defines as "a meta-historic model of thought" and distinguishes from Peircian unlimited semiosis—has acquired excessive currency. Eco also argues that Derrida misreads Peirce; for Peirce unlimited semiosis does not imply infinite interpretation: "While unlimited semiosis allows the initial sign to be better known and understood, infinite interpretation allows for the passage from one analogy to another, and a each passage the preceding step is forgotten. There is the con-

tinuous loss of sense to be had in drifting through the labyrinth. To my mind this is the sickness of infinite interpretation, 'The Secrecy Syndrome' (Stauder 1989, 7).

15. Eco performs a similar operation in *Il pendolo* by lumping together political and intellectual *engagement* with political extremism and the religious fanaticism of the occultists. Another example of this rhetorical strategy is an editorial written by Eco during the 2001 parliamentary campaign. Eco contributed to charge led by the Roman daily *Repubblica* in favor of the neoliberal coalition by demonstrating the stylistic similarities between the propaganda of Silvio Berlusconi, right-wing candidate for Prime Minister (who feigned to decry the "permanent plots" against him by a demagogic magistracy) and those of Palmiro Togliatti, an historic leader of Italy's Communist Party. Both, according to Eco, used the "vetero-communist" (in other words, Stalinist) rhetorical model that served very well the hooligans who gave rise to the civil unrest that has marked Italian life of the past half-century, the same "*sessantottardi*" from whose ranks rose the Red Brigades (Eco 2001a).

16. Capozzi contends that Guglielmo is the protagonist and Adso is at most the coprotagonist of this recounting of his initiatory journey.

17. Should anyone question the veracity of the text, a very empirical Umberto Eco is quick to smite. In the introduction to *Il nome della rosa* Eco engages in polemic Beniamino Placido, a reviewer of Eco's manual for Italian university students, *Come si fa una tesi di laurea* [*How to Write a Dissertation*], first published in 1977. Eco does so to distract his reader from the main thrust of the review, the claim that *Come si fa una tesi di laurea* is less a manual on writing a thesis and more an autobiographical novel à clef in which Eco proposes his own life as an exemplum for Italy's youth and an admonition to his country's rebellious university students to avoid politics. Eco completely sidesteps the gist of the review in order to object to the reviewer's questioning of the historical veracity of Adso and the Abbot Vallet, Adso's seventeenth century French editor. In anticipation of our reading of *Il pendolo di Foucault*, it is interesting to note that Eco's reviewer points out how the protagonist of *Come si fa una tesi di laurea* runs through life "never stopping to smoke a cigarette, have a coffee, or look at a girl." He asks out loud why Eco would advance such an "example of Stakhanovism" and then answers his own question by asserting that Eco wants to serve as a model for Italy's youth, many of whom supported or participated in the Student Movement of the late 1970s at the expense of their studies. "Think how great it would be," goes the review," if [Eco] were successful. What peace in our Universities. No one protesting; no one striking; or even mumbling. Everyone quiet and obedient, full of health and joy, busy writing their theses." This, of course, is a perfect description of Casaubon, the protagonist of *Il pendolo di Foucault*, as we shall see presently.

18. For example, "Pulchra enim sunt ubera quae paululum supereminent et tument modice, nec fluitantia licenter, sed leniter restricta, repressa sed non depressa" (233); la ragazza gli apparve "valde bona" (247); "anche questa mulier mi apparve bellissima" (244).

19. His obsession with these events not only mark their importance in his life, but his decades old inability to elaborate and move beyond them. Adso returns to the site of his entrance into the adult world many years later. Upon

arrival he throws away the possessions he had brought with him on his journey and refills his two large bags with reliquia of the fire. Only after contemplating this "poor treasure" for a very long time can he bid a sad farewell to his childhood, elaborate and resolve the trauma caused by events, mourn his losses, and set his confession to paper (501–3).

20. While analyzing a much more modern form of public confession, one with which the media expert Eco would probably have familiarity, Samuels found that although the perverse activities exposed on television talk shows "appear to be based on a desire to transgress the social order, . . . what we actually find in them are constant attempts to create a *law* of enjoyment." Those who confess attempt to regulate their transgressions by symbolizing them in an intersubjective discourse. Samuels finds in the pervert a neurotic distinction between social law and private desire; public discourse allows subjects to normalize private desires that the larger social order consider abnormal.

21. To quickly cite a few examples, Adso believes Nicola da Morimondo is "humiliated" by the latter's inability to make suitable reading lenses (216) but is spared further "humiliation" by Guglielmo who graciously accepts a poor substitute the smith eventually produces. (279). The head of the Franciscan delegation, Adso recalls, promises not to "humiliate" the Pope's pride, if the latter will promise to refrain from humiliating the Franciscans' positions (298). The Inquisitor Gui defeats the heretic Dolcino when he succeeds in "humiliating" his opponent (479). In fact, the narrating voice of Eco's *L'isola del giorno prima* will also quote as epigraph a proclamation of the pride derived by protagonist Roberto de La Griva from his humiliations (*L'isola,* 5; 8–9).

22. In Melanie Klein's terminology, a "combined parental figure" is a father who metaphorically contains the mother's breast or the whole mother. I will use this term in reference to Guglielmo, because of the nurturing, almost maternal posture the mentor assumes in relation to his pupil.

23. Nonetheless, Adso disobeys Guglielmo twice and is punished both times. When a "strange fire" that "burns in his heart and guts" causes Adso to venture into the Library alone, he uncannily recalls watching a Franciscan monk burn at the stake because traitorous women had falsely accused him of heresy (234–35). Later, "burning with curiosity," Adso disobeys Guglielmo's explicit instruction to not abandon Severino to his fate, leaving the door open to "so many other misfortunes" that might otherwise have been avoided (355).

24. The reader will remember that Adso was assigned a pallet on which to sleep in an alcove adjacent to Guglielmo's cell the first night they spent in the Abbey.

25. The root of *sacerdote* is *sacerdos,* a priest or someone who has the authority to make holy; from *sacer* [holy] and *dos* [to give].

26. Carnal appetite, the enemy of reason, is repeatedly referred to by both Adso and Guglielmo as "il demone meridiano" [the mid-day demon] (see 143, 250, 284, 312, 325). The euphemistic utilization of "mid-day" to refer to the genitals builds on one of the first lessons imparted by Guglielmo to his youthful charge, a shared Northern European distaste for the religion and the politics of Italy (127 [a corroboration of what Adso had learned as a novice in Melk [57]) and for *il Mezzogiorno* and 'Mediterranean personalities' in general (350). These

lessons provide Adso-narrator with a filter that will lead him to recall Italy's churches, including that of the Abbey, as inferior (48).

27. He tells his reader that he was a "fanciullo" when he met Guglielmo (23), and a "humble and innocent child" in the presence of the Abbot (38, 42). He feels compassion for the other novices, other "fanciulli," because they too were sent away from home at an excessively tender age (458) to deal with the improper advances of sodomitic elder monks (143).

28. However, he is not at all concerned with what the woman said to him prior to sex. Although he does not understand her dialect, he "perceived [*mi avvidi*] from the tone of her voice she spoke sweet words, and it seemed to him that she said something like, 'You are young, you are beautiful'" (247).

29. *Mondo*, from *mundus*, a clearly defined, closed, integral, sacred space, fit for human residence; an area defined by God who set limits and defines authority.

30. As Franco Masciandaro reminded me while I was working on this chapter, Roman and Etruscan cities were separated from the *immondo* by the *pomerium* (the bare strip of land inside and outside the city walls).

31. When seen in this light, the young woman bears a striking resemblance to Amparo, a character in *Il pendolo di Foucault*, as we shall see.

32. Thus availing himself of the opportunity to be among those with whom the mother is unfaithful to the father. See Richard Sterba, "Equation of Mother and Prostitute" (Sterba 1968, 29–30). To use Ubertino's phrasing, the Church, "transformed into a prostitute, and softened by comforts, . . . rolls herself up in lust" (69).

33. See Sterba "A Contribution to the Theory of Sublimation" (Sterba 1987, 20–28).

34. See his letter of June 20, 1898 in ibid, *The Origins of Psychoanalysis*, 255–57; Sigmund Freud, "Family Romances," *S.E.*, 9: 237–41; and Linda Joan Kaplan, 187.

35. Anthony has written of how oedipus functions unconsciously in the parents: "the hostile feelings of parents toward their children are often powerfully stimulated and reinforced by the unconscious process that identifies the child with the parents' own parents, so that there tends to be some similarity between the parent-child relationship of one generation and the parent-child relationship of the earlier generation" (10).

36. Canuto, from the Latin *candidus* (white) and *candere* (to be of a glowing white [accendere, incendere = to set on fire (candle, incense)] and from "canities" and "canutus" (both derive from "canus" = having very white hair, venerable, etc.)

37. The virgin smell that attracts the unicorn is probably a veiled reference to menstruation which, while not proof of virginity, on some level of the unconscious is associated 'through the screen of memory' "with the mother's freedom from pregnancy, which by implication means that her child-suitor has no competitors, either in the form of nascent siblings or of the pregnancy-creating father" (Mohacsy 1984, 396).

38. Guglielmo knows that the search for absolute certainty leads to the opposite extremisms of doctrinaire orthodoxy and heresy (203). He believes there is an order to the universe that is however incomprehensible to us. God, who

created it, understands it from the outside; from within God's creation we can neither see nor comprehend an overarching plan governed by chaos theory (210).

39. Ubertino, at sixty-seven, is a full generation older than Guglielmo (47, 225).

40. When they meet, the elder man caresses his cheek with a "hot, almost burning hand" (60). During subsequent encounters he will take Adso by the hand (224), caress his head (234), and hug him tightly (396). Adso comes to enjoy the sweetness of the elder man's breath (225, which he can compare to Salvatore's "very bad breath" [223]).

41. Mohacsy argues that that "the unicorn's tale [is] an allegory of the transition into the phallic period" (1984, 395).

42. When Ubertino teaches Adso to sublimate his heterosexual impulses, he leaves Adso with only two venues for his sexual drive, masturbation or sodomy. After assuming a position of power in his order, Adso-narrator tells the reader that he struggles to repress his homosexual impulses and an attitude of dominance toward a homosexual object: "Can I, when all is said and done, hide from myself the fact that even my old age is still today upset by the *demone meridiano* when I happen to let my glance linger, while in chorus, on the beardless face of a novice, pure and fresh like that of a young girl? (143). See Gold and Weiner in this regard. The resultant emotional conflict is resolved through an auto-eroticism that presumably causes his neurasthenia—a state of excessive fatigue and irritability. However, lest his reader believe Adso less than a man— since years of masturbation may in a later age impair potency—Adso takes great care to make evident his firm grasp of the lessons on herbal therapy taken from his master, Guglielmo, who knew which herbs increase sexual potency (24, 74, 116, 455).

43. As we shall see, Roberto de La Griva, protagonist of Eco's *L'isola del giorno prima,* also eliminates his sibling as contender for the parents' affection by bastardizing him. As Freud indicated, the material necessary for family romances comes "generally from the lower social order of female servants" and they are "made all the easier if the seducer herself was a servant" (Freud *The Origins of Psychoanalysis,* 255). Freud also argued that the family romance figured in the liberation of the individual from family authority (237). The boy, who is usually more inclined to feel hostile impulses toward the father (238), "tends to picture himself in erotic situations and relations, the motive force behind this being his desire to bring his mother (who is the subject of the most intense sexual curiosity) into situations of secret infidelity and into secret love-affairs" (239).

44. See Sigmund Freud, "Group Psychology and Analysis of the Ego," 125, qtd. in Anthony 9.

45. In German, in the original

46. In 1983 Socialist Education minister Alain Savary introduced reform proposals aimed at securing more secular control of French private (for the most part Roman Catholic) schools. The measures were the result of a compromise between President Mitterand and the head of the Roman Church in France, Jean-Marie Lustiger. After months of contention, such a bill passed the parliament in May 1984. Religious opposition sought to outflank the Cardinal, by

demonstrating on June 24; supporters responded with their own march ("Battle of the Books").

47. For the P2 lodge and the involvement in it of current prime minister Berlusconi see Ginsborg 2004, 30–32. See also "La grande congiura di Gelli."

48. See Cipriani et al. for a synthesis of these politically charged years.

49. A similarly heroic image of the parish priest will figure in *La misteriosa fiamma della Regina Loana* [*The Mysterious Flame of Queen Loana*].

50. As is the case with Belbo, the skeptic Diotallevi is described as "miscredente" (152). For the identification with Diotallevi, see 15 (Was it possible that only I—Jacopo Belbo and Diotallevi and I—had intuited the truth?") and 494–95 ("I did not know about Diotallevi then, but now I do").

51. The most significant example of self-projection is Casaubon's determination that Belbo's "sense of the ridiculous," a corollary to Casaubon's incredulity, allowed Belbo to calmly face death (629).

52. This incident will be retold, mutatis mutandis, in *La misteriosa fiamma della Regina Loana* (Eco 2004).

53. In addition to his yearnings for Cecilia, Belbo also developed a crush on an older girl, who is involved with Remo, during his stay at ***. Belbo is jealous of the older boy, but does not pursue this love interest, even after the latter has been executed (521–22). Curiously, Belbo's computerized texts do not investigate his failure to do so.

54. See Sterba, "The Equation of Mother and Prostitute." In a computerized *rêverie* Belbo equates his first love, Cecilia, with "Mary the Most Holy." He then refers to her as "Mommy," and then as "Marilena," or Mary Magdelene (65–67).

55. The files constitute his final testament "to himself, to Abulafia, to [Casaubon] or to whoever else was both willing and able to crack his password (601). Of course, no one but his alter, Casaubon, would care enough to invest the time necessary to crack the password.

56. In a file titled "Doktor Wagner" (and subtitled "The Diabolical Doktor Wagner. 26th Episode" [245–50]) Belbo affirms that Wagner "killed" him by revealing what Belbo truly wanted, but feared to desire (246). When Wagner speaks of divorces motivated by unconscious desires, Belbo, who comes to disdain psychoanalysis (598), mistakes other (what is external to the ego) for Other (what is internal, but non-ego within the unconscious), and begins to pursue Lorenza in earnest.

57. As Eco has stated, his "philosophical novels" cannot avoid the question of our mortality (Stauder 1996, 8, 10): since "man is the only living being to know in advance that he will have to die. . . . This 'being for death' is a significant experience" (Viegnes 73).

58. Eco writes, "That which I have defined as a 'lay ethics' is in truth a natural ethics, something that is recognized by the non-believer also. Is Natural instinct, when allowed to mature and become self-knowledge, not a foundation that provides sufficient guarantees? We can certainly think that it is not a sufficient stimulus for virtuous behavior. In fact, the non-believer can maintain that no one looks on him from on high; no one will be aware of the evil that I am committing. Therefore, precisely for this reason he also knows there is no one who can forgive him his misdeeds. He knows he has done wrong, his solitude

will be limitless, his death desperate. He will seek, more than the believer, the cleansing of the public confession. He will ask his fellows to forgive him. Otherwise, how do we explain the fact that remorse is a sentiment felt by the non-believer?" (Martini and Eco, 75–76).

59. Casaubon considers the oneiric narrative titled "Il ritorno di San Germano" [*The Return of Saint Germano*] a postmodern collage of "citations, plagiarisms, and borrowings," a means of "escape from the disquietude of History" for Belbo who "had written, using writing as a third party mediator to revisit life" (524). That "third person"—the narrating voice utilized by Belbo to tell this story—is the Count of San Germano, a pseudonym of Agliè. Within this dream, Cecilia (the object of Belbo's adolescent infatuation) and Lorenza, "Vestal and Megera," blend together; Lorenza wears Cecilia's "androgynous blue jeans" (527), and appears as a "splendid mulatta" (527). This is noteworthy, not only because the text provides no physical description of Belbo's love interest, but also because it fits Amparo, who was of mixed Dutch and African origin with a Spanish surname (175).

60. After this apex there is a chapter break and an epigraph both inserted, readers must assume, by the empirical author. The purpose of the epigraph, we must also assume, is to demonstrate the scientific precision of the narrative (which with Eco's vaunted "cinematographic exactitude" [Eco 1983b, 514; and Adornato] forms the basis of his enhanced realism). In any event, the epigraphs inserted at beginning each of the book's chapters point the reader toward a specific reading, one the empirical author strives to predetermine. Chapter titles, in contrast, are specified in the table of contents, but missing from the text. While this strategy reinforces the impression of a stream-of-consciousness narration, it raises, then leaves unresolved, the question of who composed the "Table of Contents"? Casaubon? the Model Author? the empirical author?

61. However, Casaubon learns his lesson, and leaves Lia home when invited by Agliè on an out-of-town excursion (339).

62. The reader will remember that Agliè, having recognized Casaubon's talents in the field of occultism, twice tries to take the younger man under his wing (228–29, 292–93).

63. The root of Belbo's unease, of course, is both mental and physical. "It is true," Belbo writes, "I have fornicated (or I have not fornicated): but God is the one who has not resolved the problem of Evil" (559). But the tension is resolved when Belbo recognizes his limitations, that is to say, his lack of "genius,' or creative imagination (635–36]), and he can submit to the Father.

64. The reader will remember that Belbo's execution occurs in the section of the novel titled "Hod" ("Majesty"). After watching his friend die, Casaubon makes his escape through the nether regions of the Parisian sewer system. He emerges and, in "Jesod" ("Foundation"), returns to Italy by airplane where he uncovers the "Key Text" to understanding how Belbo learned to sublimate his frustrated sexual desires. Having done so, Casaubon achieves the inner peace necessary to await Agliè in "Malkut" ("Kingdom").

65. Below this surface, Casaubon's nonparticipation and active voyeurism combine to allow him to achieve his own "victory" (605): his empirical understanding of Belbo's behavior permits him to forego questioning of the motives behind his own.

66. Lia's methodology is reminiscent of the exclusion of psychoanalytic theory from semiotic investigation outlined by Eco in "The Subject of Semiotics" (Eco 1976c, 314–18). Here Eco maintains that any "attempt to introduce a consideration of the subject into the semiotic discourse would make semiotics trespass on one of its 'natural' boundaries." Doing so would transform semiotics into "the study of [the] creative activity of a semiosis-making subject, and [intend] this subject not as a phenomenological transcendental Ego, but a 'deep,' profound subject" (315). In other words, since semiosis is the theory of codes, and not of sign production (316), it must avoid consideration of the "'deep' individual origins of any 'wish to produce signs'" within the subject (315).

67. I would like to note in passing the similarities between Amparo, Casaubon's gender and racial other, and Sibilla, a character in Eco's *La misteriosa fiamma della Regina Loana*. Sibilla, as we shall see, although decades younger, serves as mentor in financial covetousness to the protagonist of that novel, who considers her both "immaculate virgin" (54) and "whore" (57). Moreover, even though she is Polish, he describers her a a "black pearl" (59), and of an "immaculate blackness" (55)

68. As Casaubon points out: "In some way Lorenza was a creature invented by Agliè, Agliè was a creature invented by Belbo, and Belbo no longer know who had invented him" (593). Belbo's inventor, of course, is Casaubon. As is the case with Casaubon, Belbo occupies his own idiosyncratic world. For example, see 582: "Belbo typically sought forms of revenge to which he was the only witness. He did not do so because of modesty or shame [*pudore*] but because he lacked faith in the testimony of others."

69. See Eco 1983b: "There is no doubt that the modern novel has tried to sought to diminish amusement resulting from the plot in order to enhance other kinds of amusement. I am a great admirer of Aristotle's *Poetics*, and so I have always thought that, no matter what, a novel must also amuse through its plot" (525–26), and Eco 1990: "Forgive the aesthetic crudeness of my statement; I'm one of those who still [or again] maintain that enjoyment is reason enough to read a story" (156).

70. For a few examples, see 5 ("The letters do not say . . ."); 9 ("as best as I can gather [*intuisco*]"); 11 ("this is my decision: I will try to decipher his intentions and them I will use terms that are familiar to us. If I am incorrect, patience: the story does not change"); 26–27 ("Perhaps I am weaving together a story from insufficient evidence . . . And so the best thing to do is to open things up to fantasy and imagine how things might have happened"); 276 ("That which follows is of uncertain nature").

71. As Bouchard indicates, we are dealing with an "obtrusive" "twentieth-century narrator" (358) who is not concerned with the present, which he can transform, and the future he can influence, but with forces beyond his control that transformed him from virtuality to reality.

72. In the "fictional universe" that is *L'isola*, the "authorial entity," to use Eco's term, provides "a set of reading instructions" to assist Model Readers in their "quest for the model author [that] is an Ersatz for that other quest, in the course of which the Image of the Father fades into the Fog of the Infinity, and we never stop wondering why there is something rather than nothing" (Eco 1994, 116). That "other quest," as we have seen, is not future oriented; it implies no

desire to transform the present, nor does it seek to give direction to the future, because unlike Jacopo Belbo in *Il pendolo di Foucault*, the narrating voice of *L'isola* looks for a beginning, a transcendental signifier, or an eternal father that will give meaning to everything that has followed. Moreover, because the narrator believes himself an exceptional, God-like person to whom ordinary rules do not apply, he can refuse to accept the reality principle. Indeed, he writes to provoke fate and expose to possible discovery information about himself that he would prefer be kept hidden (see Jacobson 137, 139, 147). So he projects that information onto his protagonist, who, as we shall see, chafes under but submits to oedipal laws, and responds with an asceticism that allows him to atone for his own 'sins' and those of his parents.

73. Those forces, as we shall see, cause in Roberto feelings of guilt for incestuous desires, resentment for the stifling of those oedipal strivings, and culpability consequent to his aggressive responses to his offended narcissism.

74. Roberto will respect this etiquette even while on the *Daphne* (60).

75. Immediately after the death of Saint Savin, Roberto thinks he sees himself in a mirror. However, the experience does not make him aware of his own subjectivity because upon closer examination the mirror turns out to be a window, and his image that of his 'evil twin' Ferrante (58–59). In fact, the reader is at no point provided with a physical description of the protagonist. In sum, the displacement onto Ferrante of all the negative traits of his parents and himself prevents Roberto from developing a sense of his own individuality, moving into what Lacan calls the symbolic order, and placing in direct confrontation his inner and outer realities.

76. The verse "God of the Heavenly Armies is with Us; The Lord of Ya'akov is a Fortress Protecting Us, Selah" appears twice in Psalm 46 (Psalms 46:8 and 46:12). The Midrash on Psalms [text-a 9] connects this theme, the identification of God with a fortress or high place, with the opening words of this Psalm: "For the leader, of the sons of Korach, on Alumot, a song." When Korach leads a rebellion against Moses and Aaron (Numbers 16:1–17:5), God causes the earth to miraculously open up and swallow him, his two hundred fifty followers and their families. The sons of Korach, on the other hand, warned the righteous ones, (Numbers 16:32) and did not die (Numbers 26:11).

77. Indeed, the narrator does so by making an intertextual reference to same God praised by the narrating voice of *Il nome della rosa* who refers to the Benedictines' "privileged relationship with the Lord God of the Armies" (414), a divinity whose authority is funneled through the Abbot, the Benedictine patriarch whose power Adso patiently waited to inherit. Adso, the reader will remember, associates the nameless young woman metaphorically to the administration of the divine retribution meted out to those who challenge the patriarchs when he describes her—three times—as "as terrifying [*terribile*] as an army lined up for battle" (248, 280, 430), in contrast to his own inept attempts to serve as a "soldier of Christ" (168, 176).

78. Roberto's ambivalence toward his parents derives from unresolved oedipal issues, which are the result of his fear that his affection for his parents is not fully reciprocated. He avoids the anxiety associated with questions of whether or not he is loved by regressing to the pre-oedipal time when he could believe that he was the exclusive object of their affection. Instead of asking if he should

be allowed to demand his parents' love, he represses the oedipal guilt and fears of paternal retaliation for his incestuous wishes and desexualizes a mother whom he suspects had a child with someone other than his father, and is therefore available to all men, including himself (Sterba, "Equation of Mother and Prostitute," 30). As Linda Joan Kaplan points out, within the family romance there is often the fantasy of an illegitimate brother sired by a man with whom the child has grown up (173).

79. This allows him to reach a compromise resolution that forestalls oedipal guilt; at the same time, the prospect of a past sexual transgression ascribable to his mother frees him from dreading a sexually pure, hence metaphorically castrating mother (see Karon 1970). Since the impure mother is available to all men, Roberto's desires for her are not forbidden, and he need not fear Father, whom Roberto kills twice.

80. This passage suggests that sexual arousal met at a deep level with repressed castration anxiety, attributable to his terror of reprisal for oedipal desires at the hands of a sexually pure, idealized, mother. For illuminating pages on the young male's terror of mutilation by the mother as castrator, see Karon 1970. As Karon has argued, while the fantasy of the father as castrator is consistent with the classical Freudian view of oedipal dynamics, the deeper and more frightening fear is of the mother.

81. See, for example, page 164: "Roberto saw in her smile the acceptance of all the letters he had sent her."

82. Soon after arriving on the *Daphne* Roberto takes refuge in his nocturnal vigils "as if in a maternal uterus" and "recreates his Signora on paper, so as not to lose her; [although] he knows he has not lost much more than what he already had" (10). During their only conversation Roberto "tacitly recites among the [theater-going] public his role as a lover" and leaves to the woman to propose advancing beyond an otherwise imaginary relationship (166).

83. Following Karon, we may say that Roberto uses the father imago to resolve, through the repression of instinctual derivative, the pre-oedipal split of the mother. As Karon has argued, the evil of she who would murder or castrate pretenders for her affections is displaced onto the father. This duplicitous image of the loving, yet persecutory mother is imperfectly healed. Subsequently, the mother's potential for evil will be removed through Roberto's denial of instinct.

84. The narrating voice of *L'isola del giorno prima* depicts Lilia as "blinded" [*abbacinata*] when looking at Roberto (149). This is the same adjective used by the narrator of *Baudolino* to describe the way the mother of his protagonist looks at her son after he returns home a success.

85. See Scaglione, who, in writing of courtly love, has argued that "Love outside of socially-acceptable boundaries" is kept "pure and perfect by not performing the final, lowly physical act."

86. As is his failure to describe in any detail the age, appearance, or deportment of the Carmelite's unnamed servant, who spent three months a year with his master at the La Griva estate (23).

87. See 141: "It may seem incredible to the disinterested reader, but a castaway, lost in brandy, and alone on a ship, if he finds one hundred clocks that in near unison tell the story of his time, thinks first of the story and not of its author."

88. The narrator tells us that Roberto thought "he would be able to construct a story, of which he was not protagonist, because it would not take place in our world, but in a Land of Novels. And the events described would run parallel to the world he was in, and never meet or overlap" (340–41). The narrator, with hindsight, can see the trap into which Roberto was falling: "the Art of the Novel, even though we know deals with fictions, opens the door to the Palace of Absurdity. If we are not careful, it will close shut behind us" (343). And, as the narrator ironically points out, this is exactly what happens to Roberto, who "after initially imagining a Land of Novels completely extraneous from his world, finally began to bring together these two universes. He did so effortlessly, confusing their laws" (460).

89. Moreover, she adds, "the fabula and the diegesis of this novel appear to fulfill the performative intent of a cautionary tale, the 'moral lesson' of 'Colophon,' marshalling Eco's Pragmatic semiosis as opposed to an Hermetic one, and illustrating the importance of 'reasonable' semiotic practices; interpretative adventures which, as one section of Semiotics and the Philosophy of Language puts it, are provisional, yet settle in 'local' . . . systems of knowledge" (359).

90. Page numbers without further specification refer to the novel *Baudolino* (Eco 2000).

91. Following Kilborne, we may say that he does so with an averted gaze, "a defense against the annihilation anxiety triggered by the infant's looking to the mother for a response that is not there" (65).

92. Following Brown and Bosson we may advance the hypothesis that Baudolino's self-loathing may be based largely on his relationships with his caregivers and be attributable to a deficient child-parent relationship during the preverbal stage.

93. From the present-day Italian *aula* (from the Latin *aula*, in turn from the Greek word for the residence of a sovereign), which can be a synonym of *reggia*, royal palace.

94. Baudolino's departure from home just before the onset of puberty precludes oedipal conflict and resolution. Subsequently, he will covertly resent, rather than challenge, paternal authority, and then feel remorse for having done so. Indeed, he will repeat the pattern outlined in previous chapters of avoiding conflict in the hope of inheriting what belongs to Father.

95. The reader learns indirectly, from the narrating voice, that Niketas noticed Baudolino's "hands were large, and when he folded them on his lap one quickly noted his knotty knuckles. Peasant's hands, better suited for a hoe than for the sword" (18).

96. Baudolino's failure to resolve oedipus retards drive development: the ego and the superego fill the void typically filled by the libido, causing a reluctance to grow up and out of the latency period, reinforcing Baudolino's self-image of the good son, considerate to his mother and submissive to his father (see in this regard Anna Freud 1958, 272).

97. See Anna Freud 1966; 266, 269.

98. After Frederick is almost killed in combat, Beatrice leaves no doubt as to the primary object of her affection: "Beatrice saw Frederick approach in the distance. She went toward him sobbing and hugged him with passion. He told

her that he was alive because of Baudolino, and then she noticed that Baudolino was there also. She turned red, then pale, and cried. She stretched out only her hand and touched his heart, and begged the heavens to repay Baudolino for what he had done, calling him son, friend, brother" (210–11).

99. In addition to Brown and Bosson, and Kilborne, who has written illuminating pages on "oedipal shame," see Potash who differentiates between guilt (which for Freud is experienced primarily in the aftermath of the oedipal situation) and, therefore "can be circumscribed and atoned for," and shame, which is learned during the pre-verbal period and "is a central feeling state within the self." According to Potash, "Shame originates through the parent's reproach of the 2-year-old's activities. Small children lack the cognitive defenses necessary to deflect powerful criticism, and they do not have the verbal skills needed to differentiate between doing a bad thing and being a bad person." Therefore, "To feel shame is to experience that one's totality is inherently and permanently defective" (254).

100. According to Klein, the fear of the phallic mother (the mother who has permanently incorporated the father's penis into her body in permanent coitus) gives rise to the greater fear of the mother as castrator, and "the displacement of feelings of hatred and anxiety from the father's penis to the mother's body" (Klein 189). Klein also contends that "at its period of maximal strength the child's sadism is centred round coitus between his parents. The death-wishes he feels against them during the primal scene or in his primal phantasies are associated with sadistic phantasies which are extraordinarily rich in content and which involve the sadistic destruction of his parents both singly and together." See also Karon's illuminating pages on this topic (1970).

101. She tells Baudolino that she and her peers "accept this humiliation only because they must continue to exist, and to redeem the world from [the] error of male domination of women," overturning the roles assigned to women by an author Eco knows quite well, Thomas of Aquinas, who spoke of "woman as merely 'a necessary object . . . needed to preserve the species" (qtd. Mohacsy 1988, 89).

102. She explains: "Opposites compose themselves and find reciprocal harmony in God. But when God beings to emanate outward, the ability to control the harmony of the opposites is lost, and they break up and begin to struggle against each other" (435).

103. In an essay titled "Quando i figli divorano i padri" ["When Sons Devour Their Fathers"] (Eco 2001b) Eco uses the idea of parricide to broach the topics of history and the history of ideas. He contends that in the Middle Ages it was possible to oppose the Father without metaphorically killing him, but by simply mocking him [*irriderlo*]." Parenthetically, this describes certain behavioral tendencies of Baudolino, who submits to his fathers but dupes them into acting in ways Baudolino believes is in their "best self-interest." Eco then goes on to argue that prior to Descartes, the Schoolmen did not openly rebel against their elders. Instead, "they committed the most dramatic parricides by demonstrating that they were repeating exactly what their masters had said, but that they believed to possess, thanks to the masters, clearer ideas." Following this line of reasoning, Eco maintains that we need not embrace the relatively modern idea of parricide, because true revolutionaries were and are those sons who

do not kill fathers, but stand on their shoulders in order to see farther, like so many dwarfs on the shoulders of giants. In other words, we would do well to set aside the prospect of revolution or social upheaval in the name of a *trasformismo* or generational reformism, a stance that coincides with his postmodernist aesthetic, which is grounded on the belief that there is nothing new under the sun: everything we do, say and write is a citation and re-arrangement of what has already been done, said, and written.

104. The narrator augments the audience's "automatic transfer of emotions" cast in relief by Brecht by explicitly and repeatedly referring to Baudolino and his traveling companions as "our friends" (see for example, 82 and 480).

105. The reader will remember that Pafnuzio is the creator of the prodigious devices and trick contrivances such as those that characterize the castle of Ardzouni (see 294, 511)

CHAPTER 3. INTERLUDE

1. See *Italy's "Southern Question"*—especially the essays by Rosengarten and Dombroski—for an application of Said's arguments to southern Italian writers.

2. Consolo considers Sciascia one of Italy's preeminent "civil writers." See Consolo 1999b, 186; Consolo 1987a; Consolo 1994b; Consolo 1990b; Consolo 1991a; and Consolo 2000.

3. The industrialization of western Sicily fostered "a new way of being Sicilian, a new humanity. From sulfur and for sulfur came a new political and social history" (Consolo 1993b, 30). The sulfur miners rejected the "archaic, traditional peasant culture" of fatalistic resignation that remained characteristic of the working classes and the writers of Eastern Sicily (Sanna 17, 30), while writers from the other half of the Island, for example Pirandello and Sciascia, are typically more rationalist (Consolo 1993b, 15).

4. He avoids "absolute themes such as life, death and love" and favors "temporal themes that are relative to a precise political and social setting (Genovese 37); he eschews the psychological analysis of his fictional characters so that he might explore their interactions in the polis (Sanna 17). Consolo also abstains from postulating on absolute truths and eschatological ends to history, and from speculating on utopias because he prefers to deal in relative truths: humanity in its here and now, in both its private and public, civic, and historical dimensions (Consolo 1993b, 64).

5. Consolo explains, "We have all contributed to the unleashing of wars, the creation of death camps, ethnic cleansings; we let the large majority of humanity starve. . . . Therefore, penitential journeys are no longer possible. Ithaca is unreachable. In my opinion, this is what today's writer today must write about" (Consolo and Nicolao, 21).

6. See also Consolo 1993a: "My writing increasing tends to move from prose to a poetic rhythm. I feel the need to do so because I believe that the language of narrative must re-consecrate itself ([*risacralizzarsi*] but certainly not only through the external expedient of rhythm); it must find its lost dignity.

Language today has no identity of its own, it is so flat, 'burnt out' on a daily basis by the media, to the point where it finding a language suitable to narration is difficult" (53).

7. The intention of Consolo's contribution to a collaborative, ekphrastic project titled *La terra di Archimede* [*The Land of Archimedes*], "La Dimora degli Dei [Home of the Gods]," is to allow the reading public to become acquainted with "the historical and artistic characteristics" of the province of Siracusa—one of the few places that "still remains, in this period of cancellation and of forgetfulness, one of evocation of the past, of reconciliation [even] in the face of "transformations, destructions, losses;" the destruction wrought by "invasions, wars, epidemics, earthquakes, [and] industrialization" (Consolo 2001a,13, 16).

8. Consolo contends that Verga's mimesis of the dialect makes manifest his surrender of the text to the characters, a strategy that is synonymous with a defeatist retreat into the past (Consolo 1999b, 30): "It is as if Verga impressed a positive Italian valence on its negative dialect counterpart, reproducing lexicon and syntax. The thoughts and the speech patterns are those of the populace of the Catania province. Those patterns are not straightforward, but circular, closed, that is to say, entrusted to an illogical, superstitious way of thinking" (Consolo 1999b, 119).

9. In Marcuse's own words, "The super-ego as represented by the authoritative father is weakened and the moral imperatives, once imposed upon the child by the super-ego, are being replaced by the imperatives of the mass media. They tell the child and the adolescent, and without the innumerable conflicts formerly involved in the quest for identity, exactly who he is and who he is supposed to be" (89–90).

10. In a recent editorial Consolo makes reference to Pirandello's theater in order to address again the damage to contemporary society caused by media culture, particularly television. He explains that the theatrical masks used in the theater of Ancient Greece made clear to the Sicilian Nobel laureate—who saw the loss of the self as the result of the clash of being and appearance, of reality and fiction, and of life and form—the conflict of self-perception and the way the self is seen by others. It is Consolo's contention that television transmogrifies "Pirandello's theater of characters and masks, of actors who were also spectators," a theater based on the dialectic interaction of actors and public, and turns it into an "an axiomatic, peremptory, imposed monologue, a theater of only characters. The mask no longer signifies the way in which others sees us," but refers only to the image projected outward. What used to be an open-air theater "is now held in an enclosed space . . . and in the darkness of single homes." In sum, "the television mask transforms millions of viewers into absolutely passive, mentally and physically immobile receivers" who are unfaithful to the Greek etym "*drào*, which means to do and to act, the static, petrified, by the Medusa mask" (Consolo 2003a).

11. For closer analysis of this aspect of Consolo's prose see D'Acunti.

12. According to Consolo, "It is necessary to write in any case, but to write using a non-dialogic form—reducing the dialogic, communicative part—and move ever closer to expression, to the monologue of poetry. . . . This is why my prose is organized rhythmically, as if it were verse" (Consolo 2001b, 12). He

continues, "I believe that today's writer has been expelled from society and therefore is no longer capable of communicating with it. Therefore, the tendency is toward aphasia; the relationship between literary text and situational context has been broken. . . . Since I believe that the literary text . . . can no longer find its referent; can no longer find its audience . . . I believe that what we commonly refer to as 'the novel,' narration, can only be practiced as a poetic form. Communicative writing is no longer practicable; one can no longer serve as messenger—which is what the writer once was—who narrated and, while narrating reflected on the act of narrating. . . . The writer intervened with his authority and commented on what he was narrating. Today it is no longer possible to tell stories . . . I believe that this Socratic, reflexive, and communicative spirit is no longer possible. I believe that it is possible to narrate only in poetic form and therefore in a way that is the least merchandisable and communicative possible" (Consolo 2001b, 11–12).

13. Eco, a founding member of *il Gruppo '63* also labels his own work experimental, and not avant-gardist, because it does not provoke for the sake of provocation. Rather, his linguistic experimentation seeks to delude expectation, but does so "with a pedagogical intent, and in order to reach a consensus" and acceptance among "a wide reading public," and to "become the norm" over time. So, while seeking to modify the horizon of expectation of his reader, Eco takes care to not make his work inaccessible: literary art, reading pleasure, and marketing success go hand in hand (Eco 98).

14. In the opinion of Cesare Segre, Consolo's brand of experimentation develops a theme that circulated consequent to the social uprisings of 1968, that economic and political oppression perpetuates itself linguistically (79). He writes: "Consolo's ideological discourse is, in fact, enunciated, on another plane, that of narrative structure (the relationship between documents and authorial text; the relationship between protagonist—whose profession of faith in the sixth chapter [of *Il sorriso*] coincides with that of Consolo himself—and the deuteragonist). The style fulfills the discourse because it subsumes in its materiality all the forms of expression present in Sicilian society—its idioms and stylistic registers—and therefore includes also those classes who have yet to acquire to right to make themselves heard" (86).

15. *Museo mandralisca* provides a 'virtual' tour of the museum where Consolo found the inspiration for *Il sorriso dell'ignoto marinaio*. In addition to Consolo's essay—"Viaggi dal mare alla terra," to which are attached close-up photographs of the portrait by Antonello and a portrait of the Baron of Mandralisca—the volume contains sections on the art gallery, the archeological collection, and the malacologic collection, all which are complemented by drawings and photographs of artifacts preserved in the museum.

16. In his own words, it is "a precious historical and literary document" from the late 1920s and early 1930s (Consolo 1999d), evocative of an historical period that resembles to one in which we live (Bibulas, 14). The same can be said of Consolo's participation in another collaborative, ekphrastic *nóstos* intended to document the actuality of the Renaissance of the Val di Noto, in southeastern Sicily, whose cities were razed by earthquake in 1693 and then quickly and completely restored to Baroque splendor as recorded in Giuseppe Leone's photographs. This volume implicitly contrasts the failure of a series of Italian govern-

ments over several decades to rebuild the Valle del Belice after the earthquake of January 15, 1968, leveled the southwestern corner of the Island (Consolo 1991b).

17. See Pagano 2002 for a very interesting discussion of Consolo's use of allegory.

18. What holds true in the nonfictions can also be said of the fictions. According to Neri and Segneri, in Consolo's narratives "historical events are never just part of the setting; they are actors who influence the direction of plot" (98).

19. Consolo's contribution to this volume, "La pesca del tonno" can be found in Consolo 1999b (35–66).

20. Parenthetically, the central character of *Retablo*, Fabrizio Clerici (a twentieth-century artist and Consolo's friend who is converted in the book into an eighteenth-century Milanese painter and antiquarian), will follow in the footsteps of Goethe and Gonzenbach, traveling to Sicily to elaborate an infelicitous love affair. While there he sketches the classic ruins distributed throughout the Island and reports on aspects of the Sicilian landscape that go unnoticed by the natives, the Arab castles, the Greek ruins at Selinunte, the Norman churches, the Phoenician and Carthaginian ruins.

21. As Dombroski has explained, "Consolo's archeological project, rather than directed toward the creation of a premodern world, is one that opposes those forces of technological progress that have buried that world deep within its own ruins, destroying its customs and languages, and therefore its unifying myths (2005, 234).

22. In earlier works, such as the brief fiction "Un giorno come gli altri" [A Day like all others] (Consolo 1981), Turi's canteen is an allegorical trace of his ancestors and of a pre-historic Sicily. In Consolo's debut novel, *La ferita dell'aprile*, the past is depicted metaphorically as a road rolled up like a ribbon, that [the narrator] can unwind (Consolo 1963, 3).

23. The reader will remember that Isidoro's love served as model for the painting of "Veritas" in the oratory of San Lorenzo (19), whence the title and theme of Rosalia's version of events. Indeed, this particular Rosalia effaces her identity when she changes her name to Ortensia so as to gain access to a new life on the stage.

24. At the same time, what Farrell says of *La ferita dell'aprile* may also be *Retablo*: "Consolo never permits himself any level of knowing or superior irony over the life he depicts" (62).

Chapter 4. Antonio Tabucchi

1. In this regard, see Tabucchi, 1997d.
2. See Tabucchi 1998c, 15–18; and Eco 2003.
3. In contemporary Italy "there are no blind trusts. No meaningful guidelines on conflict of interest. No culture of divestment. No legal reason for a Prime Minister even to consider divestment" (Kramer, 96). And so the owner of the country's largest private television networks oversees his primary competitor, the public television networks.

4. "La sempiterna Italia dei furbi e dei servi," to use the phrasing of the philosopher Norberto Bobbio.

5. Tabucchi sees himself writing in a country dominated by a petite bourgeoisie that did not see the denunciation and prosecution of widespread government corruption as an opportunity to "turn the page" that is to say, give amnesty to all who would pledge to never permit similar crimes in the future (Tabucchi and Borrelli). What the press called "Tangentopoli" [Graft City]—a major overhaul of Italy's governing class wrought by the magistracy in the early 1990s when over nine hundred leading politicians, bureaucrats, and businessmen were indicted on charges of corruption (Kramer, 98) did not spark any examination of the collective conscience; politics and business went on 'as usual,' creating a situation, as Tabucchi writes, where "everyone is blackmailable" (Tabucchi 2003b).

6. In his editorials Tabucchi speaks of a nation headed by a prime minister, Silvio Berlusconi, who publicly insults and attacks those magistrates who would force reforms onto a recalcitrant executive and who unabashedly uses the mass media, which is evermore under his own personal monopoly, to intimidate all opposition. Although "immunity for Italian lawmakers was largely revoked after the corruption scandals of the early 1990s brought down the political establishment, new laws passed in June 2003 reinstated immunity from prosecution for the President of the Republic, the Prime Minister, the Speakers of the two houses of Parliament, and the Chief Justice ("Parliament in Italy Passes Immunity Law for Berlusconi").

7. Italy is today a country beset with racisms and xenophobias that have found representation in Northern League (paradoxically, a secessionist party and member of the governing coalition) which advances the cause of "a mythical 'white' Italy": it would ban immigration and require southern Italians to obtain passports for travel to points north of Rome (Kramer, 103). The third party in coalition with Berlusconi's "Forza Italia" group is a neofascist party that refuses to break with its past, nor to admit and honestly evaluate the responsibilities of Italian Fascism. In fact, it has repeatedly promoted revisionist visions of the Second World War that minimize or deny the participation of the Italian Fascists in the Holocaust, and for the death and destruction of the war, in the name of a process of national reconciliation which is tantamount, as Tabucchi has pointed out, to an erasure of memory (Corral, 1–2).

8. Pessoa, raised in South Africa, was bilingual; one of his heteronyms, A. A. Crosse, wrote in English.

9. As will be made clear presently, I use the term "autobiographical" advisedly, given the intrinsic factual unreliability of his *Autobiografie altrui* (Tabucchi 2003a).

10. Indeed, Tabucchi has stated his antipathy for this novel whose "enlightened impetus" (Tabucchi 1988e) pretends to explain and interpret the world rather than interrogate it (Gumpert 92). Hence his preference for works such as Del Giudice's *Nel Museo di Reims* [In the Museum of Reims], whose author is "too preoccupied following the inexplicable flow of events to attempt explanations" (Tabucchi 1988e).

11. In *Autobiografie altrui* references to the works of authors and thinkers other than Tabucchi are carefully noted (11, 54, 56, 57, 91, 91, 93, 94, 100), as are

other works by Tabucchi, who uses the notes to validate a reading of *La testa perduta di Damasceno Monteiro* which he affirms provided him with the cue for his own reflections (105): in other words, a scholarly treatment of one of his novels provided the impetus for a poetics a posteriori that does not necessarily coincide with the poetics that informed that novel a priori. The footnotes also facilitate the reading of "Ma cosa ha da ridere il signor Spino" by providing the reader with specific page references to *Il filo dell'orizzonte* (51, 52). The author also utilizes the notes to step outside himself and assume the guise of "Editor" who clarifies the reflections of the "Author" of "Autobiografie altrui" (89).

12. The "a priori" dedication of *Autobiografie altrui* provides yet another disquieting paratextual riddle: when were the essays dedicated? before he wrote them? before he collected them in the volume? But since many of them had already in print should the dedication not be "a posteriori"?

13. As evidenced by his idiosyncratic use of the adverb "anywhere" (104), where "somewhere" might have been expected, and by the misprints in the epigraph from Dickinson (103), which should read, "The Riddle we can guess / We speedily despise. / Not anything is stale so long / As Yesterday's surprise." Tabucchi does, however, modify the idiosyncratic spelling of "Any where out of the world" of *Piccoli equivoci senza importanza* [*Small understandings of no importance*] (Tabucchi 1985b, 71–81) and exempts himself from translating Emily Dickinson (25). At the same time, he provides his own translations from the Portuguese (55, 77), and of Diderot (33). And although he utilizes others' translations of Bergson and Rimbaud (56–57), he corrects what he believes is an imprecise rendering.

14. Indeed, it is not clear why its writer, who does not want to "bore" Lopes with a discussion of Lopes's film, believes Lopes would find interesting unknown aspects of the man whose novel Lopes transformed into a film (62).

15. Pessoa's hortonym is the heteronym whose name coincides with that of his creator. As Tabucchi explains it, the hortonym "is a poetic realization . . . a character that actively participates in the heteronymic system [while] Pessoa is the mind who constructs that system." Tabucchi goes on to compare the hortonym to an actor who "impersonates the playwright and participates in the dramatic situations that take place on stage, engaging all the other characters in dialogue, while the flesh-and blood author—the author of the himself who is portraying him [the author] at the very moment—observes the show as part of the audience" (Tabucchi 19975, 144). See also Tabucchi 1998b, 27.

16. The reader is forewarned by the epigraph, from Emily Dickinson: "The Riddle that we guess / We speedily despise—/ No anything is tale so long / as yesterday's surprise."

17. Readers of Tabucchi will remember that "Staccia Buratta" immediately precedes, within *L'angelo nero*, "La trota che guizza fra le pietre mi ricorda la tua vita" [The trout that darts through the stones reminds me of your life] (Tabucchi 1991d, 91–106), which tells of a posthumous betrayal and, in its turn, develops the relationship between the protégé and her elderly mentor previously established in "Le persone felici" [Happy people] (Tabucchi 1987, 65–71).

18. Tabucchi does not specify where he would have inserted the narrative, thereby undermining readings predicated on some sort of diegetic progression within the work.

19. Events preceding the Father's death are remembered in "Un universo" in a way that diverges from those depicted in "Gli archivi di Macao" [The Archives of Macao] (Tabucchi 1987, 72–75) and then in *Requiem* (Tabucchi 1992a, 58–63).

20. Tabucchi's Beato Angelico considers himself no more than spokesperson for the dream apparitions that return from the repressed to impose themselves on him (Tabucchi 1987, 16). In contrast, the dream metaphor of *Sogni di sogni* provides the necessary means for moving beyond the "composite past" of *I volatili del Beato Angelico*, a "dimension of darkness in which the future is already present" (Tabucchi 1987, 23]) and in which the possibility of engaging in dialogue is precluded. Like the denizens of *Inferno* X, the protagonists of *I volatili* may do no more than predict and live "that which, having to be, has already been," while defenselessly facing, the "empty terror of eternity" (Tabucchi 1987; 31, 33).

21. Repeated references to remorse are never accompanied in Tabucchi's fictions by the public confession one would expect. In other words, the subject of narration neither requests forgiveness—because that would necessitate his making known the causes of his regret—nor, apparently, is any needed: the issue has been resolved. Details as to how and when remorse was elaborated are never forthcoming; deeper understanding of the psychic process and enhanced self-understanding are forestalled (see Horney, 296–97).

22. While the type is centered on cover of *Si sta facendo sempre più tardi*, it is flush right the cover of the volume reproduced on the cover of *Autobiografie altrui*.

23. The cover photograph is also the point of departure for another strange loop through reality and fiction: it is impossible to verify if the embrace it depicts is spontaneous or staged (115).

24. Given the image of the river around which Tabucchi's essay is constructed, this is the more plausible of the two interpretations of this title.

25. We may reasonably assume that the final redaction of *Autobiografie altrui* gave its author his own "cephalea," which he claims is "not a migraine, nor a headache. Those things go away with a pill. It is much more, and very different" (Tabucchi 2000, 27). According to the "Notes to the Texts" on pages 123–24 of *Autobiografie altrui*, the essays that compose this volume go back at least until 1994: "Apparizione di Pereira" [Apparition of Pereira] was first seen in print in September of that year, approximately eight months after the novel's publication in January. "Un universo in una sillaba" was set to paper in "Paris, February 1998. In the same places where *Requiem* was written" (39). This propensity for specifying the time and place of composition is furthered in the texts, where we learn that the cover design for *Si sta facendo sempre più tardi* was resolved between February 2001 (117) and publication of the volume in March. "Storia di un'immagine" [Story of an Image] was written after 2 August 2002 (121) in Comporta, a small coastal city approximately 30 miles south of Lisbon and completed later that same month (122), four months after Tabucchi began correcting the proofs, that is to say in April 2002. The publisher hoped to see "this book," presumably *Autobiografie altrui*, in print "before the summer" (119). Instead, *Autobiografie altrui* was in press for over a year: the colophon bears the date of May 2003. Interestingly, an "incomplete version" of "Futuro

anteriore" was published in April 2002 (124), and "Autopsia," one would assume, could not have been incorporated into the work prior to 20 December 2002, the day Fernando Lopes sent a photocopy of the letter in question to Tabucchi (61). In sum, autobiographers of Tabucchi's life (lives?) can only wonder what the proofs on which Tabucchi was working in April 2002 looked like, unless they have access to Feltrinelli's files. Or to Tabucchi's *baule pieno di scrittori.*

26. See Brizio-Skov for a chronology of this period and relative bibliography.

27. *I volatili del Beato Angelico,* a collection of brief narratives, was published close to the beginning of this period (in November 1987). Tabucchi considers this book a document of the advent of this "very difficult time." As he told an interviewer, "I published it just as if I were exorcizing a ghost, because I wanted to get out of this very difficult relationship with life and with everything that life was dealing me. More than an involution, I would describe it as a period of incommunicability. At a certain point in time, the channel between me and what surrounded me broke down. I ceased communicating with the external, and the external no longer succeeded in communicating with me. I believe every writer goes through periods such as this, times when everything seems deaf and mute. It [*I volatili*] is a paradoxical work, because in it I tried to somersault over an obstacle: I tried to give voice to something mute by writing about it" (Botta, 95).

28. In this regard see Gumpert Melgosa ("The publication of *L'angelo nero* marked the end of a period of almost five years in which I wrote practically nothing, and reached the awareness that I had reached the age in which one begins to grow old" [177]), but especially Tabucchi's recounting of the dream of his late father in Tabucchi 1999a.

29. Tabucchi's experimentation with hybrid projects is not exclusive to the period in question. As best as I have been able to ascertain, the first instance is from 1985, "Uma conversa no Outono del 1935" [A Conversation in the Fall of 1935] (Tabucchi 1985a) a study for the *dialogo mancato Il signor Pirandello è desiderato al telefono* [*Mr. Pirandello is wanted on the telephone*]. Subsequent to the period in question Tabucchi contributed a short story to a collection of watercolors by Giancarlo Savino ("Il pittore e le sue creature" [The Painter and His Creations] [Tabucchi 1994a]), and in 1995 "Il mistero dell'annuncio cifrato" [The Mystery of the Coded Message] (for which I refer the reader to chapter 4 note 33). The ekphrastic narratives published during this period are "Messaggio dalla penumbra" [Message From the Shadows] (in Tabucchi 1987), "Tanti saluti" (Tabucchi 1988d), "Fiamme" [Flames] (1989c), "Voci portate," "Le mappe del desiderio" ([Tabucchi 1989b] possibly a study for the *sogno* of Robert Louis Stevenson), and "Vivere o ritrarre" (Tabucchi 1989a). A resolution is reached in his 1991 "Lettera a Tullio Pericoli" [Letter to Tullio Pericoli], included in the catalogue of a show of the work of the noted Italian caricaturist. Unfortunately, I was not able to find a copy of Tabucchi's 1991 "Lettera a Salgot [Letter to Salgot]," which was published in the catalogue of an exhibition held by the director of the film version of *Donna di Porto Pim.*

30. See Dibattito con Antonio Tabucchi 161–62 in this regard. The original setting for the short story was *Las tentaciones. Un pintor, Jerónimo Bosco. Un escritor, Antonio Tabucchi* [*Temptations. A Painter, Jerónimo Bosch, A Writer, Antonio Tabucchi*].

31. This is the case with "Irma Serena" (Tabucchi 1980) when it first appeared in a book for young children.

32. It would seem with Tabucchi's "Le mappe del desiderio" [Maps of Desire] the opposite is the case, due to the commercialized setting among fashion photographer Barbieri's glossy publicity shots for the high-end jewelry company who figures as author of the composite work.

33. The supplementarity of the esthetic effects demands reader participation by invoking that which the narrator can see, but the audience can only imagine. Indeed, narratives written by Tabucchi after the period in question will encourage reader participation by giving rein to the work's "power of suggestion," which is unleashed when the writer uses devices such as limiting the physical descriptions of characters and failing to give names to his narrating voices (Gumpert Melgosa, 118–19).

34. The colophon of *I dialoghi mancati* bears the date September 1988.

35. See Gumpert Melgosa 194, 196–97. Tabucchi claims that Freud's clinical studies "can be read as ingenious novels" (Tabucchi 1992c, 86) because they are first and foremost self-projections and self-analyses: in writing of his patients and their dreams, Freud told of himself (Tabucchi 1992c, 76). Freud's great deductive abilities are a tribute to his exceptional powers of imagination, the primary characteristic of all great novelists (Gumpert Melgosa, 193).

36. For *Il filo dell'orizzonte,* see Francese 1992, 136.

37. According to Dombroski, "The subject of narrative is generally construed as the locus of consciousness, the point of view or vision of reality that organizes the world of phenomena and interacts with it. In literature, the subject has always occupied a position of extreme cognitive and epistemological importance as bearer of meanings. In modern and contemporary Italian fiction, its function, although varied, has been to identify and define a kind of problematic which, through the process of writing and structuration, it brings under the control of its authority. Whether we are reading Manzoni, Svevo or Gadda, writers of extremely different narrative styles and disparate ideologies, our first critical impulse is to locate a controlling consciousness, i.e., the subject of narrative whose purpose it is to subject the reader to its meaning" (1990, 7).

38. "Uma conversa" (Tabucchi 1985a) marked a first attempt in this direction because two distinct copies of the narrative—a reproduction of the original, hand-written, signed text and its type-set version—precede Brito's drawings. Both versions of Tabucchi's narrative are in Portuguese.

39. This strategy—of observing another observe him in the manner of Velásquez's *Las meniñas* (Gumpert, 50)—resulted in *Gli Zingari e il Rinascimento* [*The Gypsies and the Renaissance*], a "reportage of another's reportage," a diary Tabucchi kept while accompanying a journalist who visited a reality already known by Tabucchi, a gypsy encampment on the outskirts of Florence. This "series of notes taken while observing a person [he] already knew (or believed [he] knew)" allowed him to see and recognize himself through the eyes of another (Tabucchi 1999b, 7).

40. See "I morti a tavola" [The Dead at the Dinner Table] (Tabucchi 2002), a brief fiction in which the subject of narrative, a former secret agent used to identifying and observing an "Objective" is surprised to learn that the most intimate details of his private life had been observed and catalogued by the intelligence agency for which he had worked.

41. As Tabucchi explains, with the heteronyms "the subject becomes its own object; it becomes its own alter ego; the Other is no longer; there is only the alter ego, the heteronym" (*Un baule pieno di gente* [A Chest Full of People] 29–30; 35).

42. This situation will be realized dramatically in *Il signor Pirandello* when the actor pronounces, "I am Pessoa who feigns to be an actor / who this evening interprets Fernando Pessoa" (Tabucchi 1988a, 16).

43. For the *poeta fingidor* see "*Autopsicografia*" [*Autopsychography*]: "The poet is a faker. He / Fakes so completely, / He even fakes he's suffering / The pain he's really feeling. // And they who read his writing / Fully feel while reading / Not the pain of his that's double / But theirs, completely fictional." (Pessoa 1986, 139)

44. Tabucchi further refined his capability in this area of "non-descriptive prose"—the exclusive use of monologue and dialogue at the expense of descriptions of the characters and their environs—in the 1997 play for radio, *Marconi se ben mi ricordo* (Tabucchi 1997a). Here, resistance to the evoked visual element—and the resulting tension between verbal and visual ways of knowing—is both resolved and exacerbated when the ambivalent figure of the appropriately named fortune teller, Miss Scriblerus, uses the "verbal representation of visual representation" to "make us see" (Mitchell, 154) when she "reads the future" in her crystal ball (Tabucchi 1997a, 30–34). Tabucchi maintains that these techniques, along with the limited physical descriptions of his characters and his propensity to leave many of the characters in his fictions unnamed, are intended to stimulate and encourage reader participation (Roelens, 162–63; Gumpert Melgosa, 118–19).

45. For Tabucchi's "conversations with the dead," see Agostinelli; Mattei; Botta, 95–96; Décina Lombardi.

46. "A Testimony" is the novel's subtitle.

47. The assassination of Monteiro Rossi makes clear to Pereira that literature does not "deal only in fantasies" (30), distinct from the 'truths' published in newspapers (37), but with "fantasies that tell of truths" (37). So when Pereira testifies he uses professional habits developed over his thirty-year career as a reporter, and cites documents—the writings submitted by Monteiro Rossi—that certify the truth value of what Pereira has to say (51). Pereira reinforces the semblance of journalistic objectivity for his audience by speaking of himself in the third person, and by distancing himself from and depersonalizing everything he writes—including his obituary of his friend Monteiro Rossi—by habitually omitting his first name from all references to himself.

48. "Il pittore e le sue creature" [The Painter and His Creation] (Tabucchi 1994a), published within a volume of watercolors by Giancarlo Savino (who makes word and image collide by including long-hand captions onto his watercolors), extends the metaphor of the figurative artist as narrator who is visited, or dreams, his creations in a manner of Pirandello, who wrote of Sunday visits in his study by aspiring characters in search of an author. This brief narrative superseded the depiction of the creative process in "I volatili del Beato Angelico" in a manner consistent with our hypothesis: in "I volatili" the artist's creations are external manifestations of an idiosyncratic, interior monologue (Tabucchi 1987, 13).

49. See Francese 1997 in this regard.

50. Indeed, it is more than a simple act of compliance to the wishes of the book's Portuguese editor, as Tabucchi claims (Gumpert Melgosa, 189–90).

51. In Tabucchi's own words, "We write for ourselves, for others, for the reflection of ourselves that we see in others, for our dead, for our memories, and even for posterity, because we believe they can listen to us" (*Conversazione con Antonio Tabucchi*, 5).

52. In the original Italian, *Si sta facendo sempre più tardi* is, for Tabucchi, "un romanzo 'contenitore,' dove buttar dentro storie bizzarre, dialoghi, spezzoni narrativi, poemi in prosa, lacerti" (Orengo).

53. Indeed, Tabucchi's affirmation, "That which, without a doubt, links my first book to my last is their political, civic nature" (Petri 1994, 69) is easily underwritten. A recent conversation with Francesco Saverio Borrelli (the chief magistrate of a pool of prosecuting judges who, in the early 1990s animated the investigation of the protection racket of Italian politics resulting in thousands of indictments of Italy's top government officials, politicians and economic leaders, commonly called *Mani pulite*, the "Clean Hands" operation) presents an image of the average Italian as "reactionary" [*forcaiolo*] wanting to see others punished while his own crimes against the collectivity are tolerated, and "not respectful of civic value" (Tabucchi and Borrelli, 66), and the source of the "vulgarity that hovers over contemporary Italy." In another intervention Tabucchi contends that Italy is a country defined by a petit bourgeoisie that is unashamed of its everyday compromises and tawdry agreements, and is "the quintessence of a Nation that was poor and suddenly became rich, without taking on the social attributes of the bourgeoisie that defined European civilization" (Tabucchi 1999b, 8).

54. See, for example, references on pp. 109, 112, 133, 158, and 179 to "il Paese" and "la festa della Repubblica."

55. As Bodei writes, "To create characters who evolve into autonomous variations on the ego is to invent imaginary interlocutors who are surrogates of the principal subject, the author of poems and novels or of the creator of fantasies" (120–21).

56. As he puts it, we may very well be "prisoners of our time and our body," but writing allows him "to freely peruse [his] personal time, to be a man today and a baby tomorrow" (Sancis Antonio).

57. See Benedetti 1998 for an interesting analysis of Calvino's attempts at evading identification with his work.

58. Tabucchi has claimed that "literary criticism is useful if gives points of orientation and counsel. I read Steiner's *Real Presences*; it was a breath of fresh air" (Orengo).

59. In Steiner's own words, "Translation comprises complex exercises of salutation, of reticence, of commerce between cultures, between tongues and modes of saying. A master translator can be defined as a perfect host. So far as it analyzes the conditions of awareness and of intelligibility between the ego and the other, between the one and the many, so far as its means are those of question and response, of proposition and examination, philosophy systematizes intuitions, impulses of both encounter and valediction" (145).

60. In this regard see Borsari, 7.

61. See also Tabucchi 1991c, 39–40.

62. This sort of socially significant, heterotelic exchange must take place in the world, not as an internal monologue within an isolated, idiosyncratic subject, as is the case with Pessoa's heteronyms. For example, the hortonym Fernando Pessoa thinks and lives exclusively within the immanence of his writings, outside the flow of time (Tabucchi 1998b, 9–10, 31). Another heteronym, Ricardo Reis, also lives in an eternal present where everything exists now, in "an immobile time, in a world that knows neither aging nor deterioration (Tabucchi 1998b, 33–34). Their modernist ineptitude, that is to say their propensity to think and to write about life rather than live it, foreshadows its postmodern radicalization: they retreat to a purely metafictional existence wherein writers do not think about life, but write about the act of writing.

63. For the concept of death giving synthetic meaning an individual's life, see Pasolini's discussion of the last four lines of Sophocles' *Oedipus rex* in his "Observations on the Sequence Shot" (Pasolini 1972, 233–37).

64. Daphne's mythological namesake abhorred the thought of loving, and when pursued by her lover, Apollo, was transformed into a laurel tree.

65. Leopardi's Tristano was harshly criticized for his critique of contemporary society, and in this dialogue pretends with great irony to have changed his opinions so as to conform with the fact that people prefer illusions to truth and the disquietude associated with the critical analysis of reality.

66. The voice may very well suffer from borderline schizophrenia, a shattering of the mind that splits from reality, not the formation of a second personality (see Karon and VandenBos 223; and Karon 2003, 111).

67. See in this regard Potash, for whom remorse can serve the same function as rebukes from others. Because it is a form of guilt, it is redeemable: it is primarily a mechanism for improving one's behavior (252–53).

68. The voice's bitterness is reflected in the Frau's refusal to speak German, which may suggests the loss of the object of affect, the mother. The Frau, as already mentioned, came to Italy at a very young age and alone, never to return home. For the Frau—as can be said of Paul Celan, the poet evoked in the epigraph who lost his mother in the Holocaust—the use of the *Muttersprache*, the German mother tongue, would serve only as a very painful reminder of her loss(es) (119).

69. I would like to thank Charles Klopp for pointing out to me that "Nostra patria è il mondo intero / nostra legge è la libertà / ed un pensiero / ribelle in cor ci sta" [Our fatherland is the entire world / our law is liberty / and a rebellious thought / is in our hearts] is the refrain from the anarchist hymn *Stornelli d'esilio* [*Songs of Exile*].

70. The voice states repeatedly that he would like to return to "the origin of the world" (31), which he equates with the maternal archetype (28). He tells the writer he would like "so much to have a uterus, . . . to be a woman, a young woman, beautiful and fecund, with life-blood circulating throughout her body, it would be great . . . to be one that is raised up by the moon like the tides, a woman who was the origin of the world" (82).

71. According to Hurvich, Freud emphasized that the infant who at birth is faced with unmasterable levels of stimulation constitutes the prototype for a traumatic situation, one in which the person is faced with a quantity of stim-

ulation (inner and/or outer) that he or she cannot discharge or otherwise master. Hurvich goes on to explain that "In traumatic anxiety, Freud was emphasizing massive, unwanted, painful affect, free of psychic content, that was automatically generated (i.e., without ego participation) as a result of the economic conditions (overwhelming stimulation)." As the child matures, s/he moves "from a passive state of current overwhelmed helplessness (traumatic anxiety) to an active state of anticipating future danger that could be avoided," which Freud calls "signal anxiety" (312).

72. The same can be said of the murder of the *Omaccio*, the person responsible for the stepson's death. The *Omaccio* may perhaps a nickname for Cary, "lo zio d'America [The uncle from America]," who after World War II moved to Irún (113–14), a town in Northern Spain.

73. The onset of the mental disorder is marked the arrival of cephalalgias, whose physical symptoms are reminiscent of those used in "Le cefalee del Minotauro" [The Minotaur's cephalalgias]. In this brief narrative Tabucchi attributes a more spiritual quality to these intense headaches, defining them as part of "a condition in which only the unhappy privileged few can participate, those who, as a poet once wrote, are familiar with "il mal di testa e di universo" [aches of the head and of the universe] (26). The poet to whom Tabucchi refers here is Pessoa, who uses this image to signify an existential discomfort not unlike the voice's "existential tiredness," as diagnosed by Dr. Ziegler (117). However, in contrast to cephalalgias of the narrating voice of *Tristano muore*, those suffered by Tabucchi's Minotaur are a summons to link microcosm and macrocosm, a call to the individual to participate in and feel empathy for the fate and suffering of the collectivity.

74. According to Eugenio Garin, in the period leading up to the March on Rome Liberals such as the historian and philosopher Benedetto Croce failed to conduct a serious critique of the "Italian Liberal State to whose preservation [Croce] had contributed." Garin hypothesizes that Croce's theory of Mussolinism as an "an invasion of the Hyksos [a nomadic people that invaded Egypt 1700–1580 c. BC and were able to wrest control of Egypt from the Second Intermediate rulers of the 13th Dynasty, inaugurating the 15th dynasty] might be seen as an elegant way of absolving the liberal world from its great responsibilities before the advent" of the Regime (12).

75. Croce argued that with the Unification and the success of the patriotic cause came independence, unity, and liberty. The full realization of a liberal regime during the first decade of the twentieth century solved "the problem of order and government" while safeguarding the civil and political liberty that had come with Unification. In his own words, "the liberals upheld social order and the authority of the Government"; at the same time "they recognized the new needs by giving free play to the competition of economic forces among both employers and employed, and by directing their attention towards social organization" (310). The Liberal State represented the general interest "above and beyond class interests" and showed that "Italy could only be governed by liberal and parliamentary methods" (314) by defusing the subversive elements within the workers' movement after "the reactionaries had failed, both in theory and practice, in their attempts to constrain social forces by violence and police methods" (310).

76. I am indebted here to Palmer's interesting analysis of Tom Sawyer's early parent loss, which follows Sigmund Freud's *Mourning and Melancholia*. Mourning, as Freud argues in *Mourning and Melancholia*, is the reaction to the loss of a loved person, but it can also characterize the loss of some abstraction which has taken the place of a person, such as fatherland (125). In mourning, typically, libido is gradually withdrawn after a period of hypercathexis during which "Each single one of the memories and hopes which bound the libido to the object is brought up" (126) and then elaborated, or decathected. In Freud's own words, "The testing of reality, having shown that the loved object no longer exists, requires forthwith that all the libido shall be withdrawn from its attachments to this object. . . . The normal outcome is that deference for reality gains the day. . . . Each single one of the memories and hopes which bound the libido to the object is brought up and hyper-cathected, and the detachment of the libido from it is accomplished" (126).

77. The identification is based on a scant physical resemblance: even though the voice's hair is not jet black (95) and he has no mustache [63], as did Clark Gable, the voice and Marilyn seem to believe that he and Rhett Butler share the same "malicious smirk" (88). *Gone With the Wind* makes appearances throughout the narrations as a metaphor for the progressive tainting of the voice's outlook. To explain, Daphne gives him a director's chair for his birthday, and writes on it Scarlet O'Hara's phrase "Tomorrow is another day" (33); further on, the voice remembers that the projection of the newsreel that showed him as a hero of the Resistance was followed by a showing of this "emotionally-charged American feature-film" in which Scarlet's optimistic catch phrase, "tomorrow is another day," is delivered against "a blood-red sunset" and the postbellum South, a background similar to that of postwar Italy (78); finally, it is remembered in conjunction with *pippopippi's* obverse "Nirvana," which the voice equates with freedom from thought: "that is what awaits you tomorrow, dear writer, because 'tomorrow is another day,' as Scarlet said" (135).

78. Parri, the first prime minister of liberated Italy (June-November 1945), was an exponent of the Resistance formation, *Partito d'azione* [*Action Party*], which "took its name from Giuseppe Mazzini's party during the *Risorgimento*" and brought together "various groups of radical and democratic anti-Fascists." The *Partito d'azione* "was composed initially of young men and women from the Italian professional classes, . . . who were committed to establishing a new democracy based on greater local autonomies and, while accepting the framework of capitalism, . . . wanted to correct its distortions and injustices" (Ginsborg 1990, 15)

79. If we consider this aspect of Tristano's behavior in the light of Genesis 38 we see that for both Tristano and Onan coitus interruptus was a means for controlling the devolution of the inheritance. Onan was "wicked in the Lord's sight" because by refusing to fecundate Tamar and spilling his semen on the ground, Onan insured that his position as head of the clan of Judah would not be jeopardized by a child who would have been considered his elder brother's heir. For the figure of Onan, see Jeffreys who contends that Onan's behavior was considered "wicked" because it was socially, and not biologically, offensive.

80. As is often the case with schizophrenics, rather than deal real problems directly, the voice deals with symbols such as the horsefly (see Karon and VandenBos, 225; See also, Karon 2003, 109).

81. Shane's victory marks the end of the open range that characterized old West, and a new beginning, of a rule of law similar to the one auspicated by the narrating voice for Europe after the defeat of Nazi-Fascism.

82. Karon explains that Anna Freud emphasized the use of this behavior as a defense against experiencing unpleasant affects and unacceptable impulses. She claims it is enacted with the specific unconscious motive that the object of transference "will not be devastated by this sequence of interaction," which would be the subject's reaction to the aggression. According to Karon, there is a type of transference in which the patient treats the therapist not as if the latter were his father or mother, but as if the therapist were the patient and the patient reenacts the role of mother or father. This usually occurs when the therapy session seems irritating, exhausting or anxiety-provoking; this is particularly frequent with borderline and schizophrenic patients (Karon 1984, 345–47).

83. The Sicilian city where, on May 15, 1860, Garibaldi cried, "Here we make Italy—or die!"

84. The eminent linguist Giulio Lepschy advances the hypothesis that the expression *zitto e mosca* is an exclamation that may be linked to the expression *che non si senta volare una mosca* so that the phrase may be translated as "Silence! May not even a fly be heard" (personal correspondence).

85. The voice also blindly obeys the command of the anonymous voice who, prior to informing him of Ignacio's death, tells him to "shut up and listen" (114). The voice also does as the Frau tells him—"keep quiet and listen"—when he objects to a poem that sounds like a lullaby (30).

86. One of the letter writers of *Si sta facendo sempre più tardi* refers to the present as a period characterized by "negationism and revisionism according to which the cadavers in the common graves of concentration camps, the mountains of shoes and eyeglasses still visible today at Auschwitz are no more than smoke from the chimneys of the imagination of sectarian historians" (Tabucchi 2001a, 90–91)

87. The anti-Fascist partisan fighter Claudio Pavone acknowledges that the diffidence of his comrades-in-arms to refer to the Resistance as a civil war is fueled by the fear that doing so would confuse the two factions, erasing all differences between them. This, in turn, might ultimately serve to attribute to all combatants a common judgment—either of absolution or condemnation—as members of two warring factions fighting for control of the Nation. He explains that "to affirm that the Resistance was also a civil war . . . means that we must strive to understand how three analytically distinguishable aspects of the struggle—patriotic, civil, and class—were often found within the same individual and collective subjects" (221). In other words, since there is no single, luminously clear position that defines any historical subject, we may still make a heuristic distinction for the purpose of analysis. See *infra,* Chapter V, note 2.

88. This essay quoted here, Eco's *Cinque scritti morali* [*Five Moral Essays*], was written 1995—that is to say after the reassertion of the right, in a period

when Communism was no longer the primary target of the center and center-left—and represents a reappraisal by Eco of the view of the Resistance presented in *Il pendolo di Foucault*. In this same essay, Eco contends that while the Resistance was also a civil war, and therefore a period of division whose memory needs to be kept alive, the sort of national reconciliation augured by the narrating voice of *Tristano muore* would repress the memory of what happened and could lead only to a collective neurosis (Eco 1997b, 29). Following this line of reasoning, it may be able to see in Eco's *La misteriosa fiamma della Regina Loana* a revision of the politics discernible in previous works of fiction by him, such as *Il nome della rosa* and *Il pendolo di Foucault*. It would seem that the protagonist of *La misteriosa fiamma*, Giambattista Bodoni, attempts to justify, in a very subtle way, his lifelong alignment with the political center and support for those responsible for the sorry state of affairs into which Italy fell in the 1980s, by presenting it not as a choice made freely and spontaneously, following the enlightened self-interest of his social class, but as one of having been forced into opting for the lesser of many evils.

89. "And if you write the life of Tristano, this is the truth, the whole truth, and nothing but the truth . . . But, writer, if you would rather write that which you would have written of your own imagination if you had known of the episode earlier, you are free to do so. You choose; after all, who could ever prove you wrong?" (57).

90. The lack of elision in the feminine article followed by vowel (LA+VOWEL instead of the standard L'+VOWEL) is not uncommon (see Lepschy and Lepschy, 78, 103) outside of Northern Italy. According to Giulio Lepschy (personal correspondence) the form without elision seems to be gaining ground, particularly at a lower, more demotic level.

91. Charles Klopp reminds me that "*a las cinco de la tarde*" is the refrain of "La cogida y la muerte [The Goring and the Death]," the first canto of García Lorca's *Llanto por Ignacio Sánchez Mejías* [*Lament for Ignacio S.M.*], a bullfighter whose goring wound turned gangrenous before he died. See the *ricorrenza* written by Tabucchi commemorating the one-hundredth anniversary of García Lorca's birth (Tabucchi 1998d).

92. He tells the writer that he does not know if he did so to lull [*cullare*] Vanda toward her nothingness, or to lull himself and Marilyn, who had tried to breast-feed the dog back to health, or to lull his dreams, that is to say his preverbal memories (20–21).

93. Karon and VandenBos explain that one of the symptoms of schizophrenia is hallucinations, whose primary modality is auditory, such as hearing voices (see Karon and VandenBos 1998; and Karon 2003, 108).

94. "Fate la ninna nanna" [Sing a lullaby] tells of a small, gray-haired horse that would gaze at the moon and was not lucky in love. The little horse was tied to a rope that would get tangled as he walked around, just like the man who is in love. It also tells of a woman whose mother-in-law encourages her son to stay with his wife while she finds him another, prettier woman. The refrain tells of a little boy [*cittino; citto* in rustic Tuscan is a boy], who loves his grandmother (Vettori, 70–71).

95. See pp. 88–89 for the voice's negative views of Eastern European popular democracies.

96. According to the Information Department of the Spanish Government's Tourist Office in Chicago, there is no such locality as Pancuervo in Spain (private correspondence). This is keeping with the covert nature of Marilyn's trip there, while the name of the locale, which translates as "raven's bread" is in keeping with the lugubrious connotation assigned to it by Tristano.

97. See Ginsborg 1990: "When Churchill met Stalin at the Kremlin in October 1944, they successfully carved up Europe between them. There were some countries, Yugoslavia and Greece especially, where the issue was not clear cut" (39). However, in "December 1944, after the Greek partisans had liberated Athens, the uneasy truce between Communists and Monarchists disintegrated into civil war. Here [unlike in Yugoslavia, where Tito, whom the British had supported, escaped their control] the British decided that immediate military intervention was called for, and an expeditionary force was dispatched to Athens to support the Monarchists. By 11 January 1945 the Greek Communists were forced to sign an armistice and evacuate the capital" (42).

98. Ginsborg also maintains that during this interim, "The British were . . . the predominant external influence in Italy, and a résumé of their attitudes does not make comforting reading" (Ginsborg 1990, 40). Duggan explains that "the British were eager to prevent the existing machinery of state from disintegrating for fear of opening the door to a Communist takeover; and although the Long Armistice of 29 September 1943 stipulated the 'arrest and internment of fascist personnel,' no serious purge was ever conducted. In fact, the Royal Government, fully supported by the Allies, was led by Mussolini's ex-Chief of Staff, Marshall Pietro Badoglio, and among the ministers were a number who had served in earlier fascist cabinets. When the Resistance hero Ferruccio Parri tried, as Prime Minister, to seriously conduct a purge of Fascist personnel in November 1945, his government fell" (2–3).

99. For the recurrence of this theme in Tabucchi's prose (which plays on the infelicitous destiny of Guido da Montefeltro in *Inferno* XXVII, 118–20: "ch'assolver non si può chi non si pente,/né pentere e volere insieme puossi/ per la contradizion che nol consente" [He who does not repent cannot be absolved. Nor is it possible to sin and repent at the same time; the contradiction does not allow it.] (see *infra,* Chapter IV, note 17).

Chapter 5. Epilogue

1. Bodoni is left with a mild form of amnesia when his wife prevents him from falling underneath a moving car (302) and dying in a manner eerily reminiscent of his parents, who were killed when the father crashed the family car. It is never made clear to the reader—and so we will not pursue this line of inquiry—if Bodoni hit his head, or if his amnesia is occasioned by a brush with mortality that causes him to fall victim to a form of hysteria that transforms unconscious conflicts into physical symptoms, pushing him back into the fog he associates with his "night of terror," the night in which he led a group of disbanded Cossacks from his town, sparing his fellow citizens a possible German reprisal.

2. While the Resistance, as was specified in the previous chapter, was a war of liberation, the term does not suggest that Italy was simply oppressed and sought freedom: Fascism had been brought to power by the Italian people. For Asor Rosa (2005), it was part of a "deep process, grounded and ramified throughout the more significant strata of [Italian] society."

3. In writing of instincts and their vicissitudes, Freud considered narcissism an instinct, that of loving oneself, composed of scoptophilia—the active desire to look—and its passive reverse, exhibitionism, the desire to be observed. See Freud *On Narcissism*; Freud *Instincts and their Vicissitudes*; and Kilborne.

4. For this, see Freud *On Narcissism* 115: "If we look at the attitude of fond parents toward their children, we cannot but perceive it as a revival and reproduction of their own, long since abandoned narcissism." The baby "is really to be the center and heart of creation, 'His Majesty the Baby,' as once we fancied ourselves to be."

5. In the Italian, the substantive phrase "volontà creatrice e ordinatrice" is feminine.

6. Solara also preserves, intact, his grandparents' and parents' bedrooms. However, after the deaths of his dear ones, Bodoni refused to visit the family estate—until forced to do so by his wife (36)—because every step that brought him closer to the "temple of temples" (224) gave rise to "the sensation of committing a sacrilege," of viewing the primal scene, a feeling intensified by the fantasy of observing his own conception (99). Bodoni would discount the primal scene as no more than an invention of Sigmund Freud, even he remembers his mother discussing his father's sexual prowess with her friends (363).

7. Bodoni, by his own admission, was a "melancholy child" who spent the better part of his time alone with his books and his reveries (328) because reading was his only escape from a "feverish and solitary adolescence" into a "less desperate reality": a world of prohibited sexuality inhabited by "bitterly virginal temptresses" (382). While at Solara he would hide in the chapel, ostensibly to read, but also to punish his parents for ignoring him, and to give them the opportunity to find him (Kilborne has written of the "shame-laden feelings" related to "pain over not being noticed" [100]): in this light Bodoni's retreat into a world inhabited by books, not people, is a mechanism against future injury. Since the parents are now dead, Bodoni can control how the reader perceives the parents, making them appear and disappear according to his own desires. At the same time, he seems incapable of mourning them; preferring to make vanish those who ignored and then abandoned him through death. His inability to elaborate the past is a consequence of a repression, "the primary defense against trauma and shame of being seen to be injured" (Kilborne 130) by the heedlessness of parents (just as his refusal to underwrite a belief system—his skepticism—defends him by allowing him to control how he appears to the world, and regulate his feelings). He is unwilling to talk about their death (36); he claims he cannot remember what they looked like (124); and he blames his "damn aunt and uncle" (325) for destroying photographs and other memorabilia after their death, even though he was already a young man and might have intervened. When the parents figure into his recollections—in, for example, the story of the unbreakable glass—they are never more than the objects of Bodoni's agency, or a screen that allows Bodoni to express his resentment of the

overbearing paternal grandfather, "gay *viveur* without financial cares, crowned in glory for his political past and for his vendetta against the [the Fascist] Merlo" (304).

8. Sibilla aids, abets, and condones his tax evasion and his rapacious business methods (52, 59).

Reference List

Adami, Valerio. 2000. *Opere 1990–2000*. Ed. Paolo Fabbri, Milano: Skira.
Adornato Ferdinando. 1988. Il mio piano. *Espresso* (October 9): 92–107.
Agostinelli, Alessandro.1992. La mia anima incongrua. *Unità*. (April 5): 17.
Alexander, V. K. 1956. A Case Study of Multiple Personality. *The Journal of Abnormal and Social Psychology* (52): 272–76.
Alexandre O'Neill, Made in Portugal. 1979. Ed. A. Tabucchi, Milano: Guanda. 7–10.
Anthony, E. James. 1980. The Family and the Psychoanalytic Process in Children. *The Psychoanalytic Study of the Child* (35): 3–34.
Antonello, Pierpaolo. The Myth of Science or the Science of Myth? Italo Calvino and the "Hard Core of Being." *Italian Culture* 22 (2004) 71–91.
Arpaia, Bruno. 1999. Il Bene e il Male secondo Eco. *Repubblica*, (November 11): 44.
Asor Rosa, Alberto. 1965. *Scrittori e popolo*. Roma: Samonà e Savelli.
———. 2005. Noi, figli della Resistenza. *Repubblica*. (May 7): 39.
Bailey, Peter. 1981. Notes on the Novel-as-Autobiography. *Genre* 19: 79–93.
Bakhtin, Mikhail. 1981. *The Dialogic Imagination*. Ed. Michael Holquist. Trans. Caryl Emerson and Michael Holquist. Austin: University of Texas Press, 1988.
Barina, Antonella. 1987. Io, nessuno e forse centomila. *L'Europeo*, (October 31): 122–25.
Barrias, José. 1992. *Tempo*. Verona: Colpo di fulmine Edizioni.
Barth, John. 1984. *The Friday Book Essays and Other Non-fiction*. New York: Putnam.
Barthes, Roland. 1968. The Death of the Author. In Barthes 1984, 49–55.
———. 1977. *A Lover's Discourse. Fragments*. Trans. R. Howard. New York: Noonday Press, 1978.
———. 1984. *The Rustle of Language*. Trans. R. Howard. New York: Hill and Wang, 1986.
———. 1984a. To Write: An Intransitive Verb? In Barthes 1984.
Battle of the Books. 1984. *The Economist* (June 16): 43–44.
Benati, Davide. 1989. *Davide Benati*. Modena: Cooptip.

Benedetti, Carla. 1998. *Pasolini contro Calvino. Per una letteratura impura*. Torino: Bollati Boringhieri.

———. 2002. *Il tradimento dei critici*. Torino: Bollati Boringhieri.

Benedict, Helen. 1992. *Virgin or Vamp. How the Press Covers Sex Crimes*. Oxford: Oxford University Press.

Ben-Ghiat, Ruth. 2004. Politics and Media Power as a Toxic Mix for Italy. *New York Times*. (August 25).

Benjamin, Walter. 1955a. *Illuminations. Essays and Reflections*. Ed. Hannah Arendt. Trans. Harry Zohn. New York: Schocken Books, 1968.

———. 1955b. L'autore come produttore. In *Avanguardia e rivoluzione*. Torino: Einaudi. Translated by Anna Marietti. 1973.

———. 1998. *The Origin of German Tragic Drama*. New York: Verso.

Bertone, Manuela. 1988. Antonio Tabucchi. Il gioco del peritesto. *Gradiva* 9, 2: 33–39.

Best, Stephen. 1992. Creative Paranoia: A Postmodern Aesthetic of Cognitive Mapping in *Gravity's Rainbow*. *The Centennial Review* 36: 59–89.

Best, Steven, and Douglas Kellner. 1991. *Postmodern Theory. Critical Interrogations*. New York: Guilford Press.

———. 1997. *The Postmodern Turn*. New York: Guilford Press.

———. 2001. *The Postmodern Adventure. Science, Technology, and Cultural Studies at the Third Millennium*. New York: Guilford Press.

Bibolas, Noemí. 1996. El mensajero de la melancholia. Entrevista con Vincenzo Consolo. *Quimera* 47 (1): 12–18.

Binni, Walter. 1993. *Poetica, critica e storia letteraria e altri scritti di metodologia*. Firenze: Casa editrice Le lettere.

Blanchot, Maurice. 1955. *The Space of Literature*. Trans. Ann Smock. Lincoln: University of Nebraska Press, 1989.

———. 1984. Intellectuals under Scrutiny: An Outline for Thought. In *The Blanchot Reader*. Ed. Michael Holland. Oxford: Blackwell, 1995, 206–27.

———. 1993. The Speech of Analysis. In *The Infinite Conversation*. Minneapolis: University of Minnesota Press, 230–37.

Bodei, Remo. 2001. Giochi proibiti. Le "vite parallele" di Antonio Tabucchi. In *Dedica a Antonio Tabucchi*, 117–39.

Bondanella, Peter. 1997. Interpretation, Overinterpretation, Paranoid Interpretation and *Foucault's Pendulum*. In *Reading Eco*, 285–99.

Borsari, Andrea. 1991. Cos'è una vita se non viene raccontata? Conversazione con Antonio Tabucchi. *Italienisch–Zeitschrift für Italienische Sprache und Literatur* (November): 2–23.

Botta, Anna. 1991. All'ascolto di 'rumori di fondo' fatti scrittura. *L'anello che non tiene* 3: 83–97.

Bouchard, Norma. 1997. Whose "Excess of Wonder" Is It Anyway? Reading the Tangle of Hermetic and Pragmatic Semiosis in *The Island of the Day Before*. In *Reading Eco*, 350–61.

Brecht, Bertoldt. *Brecht on Theatre. The Development of an Aesthetic*. Ed. and trans. John Willet. New York: Hill and Wang, 1992.

Brito, José João. 1985. *Uma conversa no Outono del 1935*. Lisbon: Imprensa nacional—Casa da Moeda.

Brizio-Skov, Flavia. 2002. *Antonio Tabucchi. Navigazioni in un arcipelago narrativo*. Cosenza: Pellegrini.

Brown, Ryan P, and Jennifer K. Bosson. 2001. Narcissus Meets Sisyphus: Self-Love, Self-Loathing, and the Never-Ending Pursuit of Self-Worth. *Psychological Inquiry*. 12, 4 (October): 210–13.

Brownmiller, Susan. Women Fight Back. In *Against Our Will*, New York: Simon and Schuster, 1975, 375–404.

Calabrese, Omar. 1995. Prefazione. In Pratt 1995, 13–19.

Calvino, Italo. 1957. *Il barone rampante*. Torino: Einaudi.

———. 1978. I livelli della realtà in letteratura. In *Una pietra sopra*. Torino: Einaudi, 1980, 310–23. Now in *Saggi*. 1995, 381–93.

———. *Saggi. 1945–1985*. 1995. Ed. Mario Barenghi. Milano: Arnoldo Mondadori.

Cannon, JoAnn. 1992. The Imaginary Universe of Umberto Eco: A Reading of *Foucault's Pendulum*. *Modern Fiction Studies* 38 (4): 895–909.

———. 2001. *Requiem* and the Poetics of Antonio Tabucchi. *Forum Italicum* 35: 100–109.

Capozzi, Rocco. 1997. Interpretation and Overinterpretation: The Rights of Texts, Readers and Implied Authors." In *Reading Eco*, 217–34.

Ceserani, Remo. 2004. Così Umberto Eco gioca a mosca cieca con i lettori. *il manifesto*. (June 26).

Chodorow, Nancy. 1980. Gender, Relation, and Difference in Psychoanalytic Perspective. In *The Future of Difference*, 4–19.

Cipriani, Gianni, G. De Lutiis, and A. Giannuli, *L'Italia dei misteri e delle stragi. Servizi segreti. Dal dopoguerra a Firenze (maggio 1993)*. Supplement to *Avvenimenti* 21.

Coletti, Theresa. 1992. Pinball, Voodoo, and "Good Primal Matter": Incarnations of Silence in *Foucault's Pendulum*. *Modern Language Notes* 107: 877–91.

———. 1997. Bellydancing: Gender, Silence, and the Women of *Foucault's Pendulum*. In *Reading Eco*, 300–311.

Consolo, Vincenzo. 1963. *La ferita dell'aprile*. Torino: Einaudi, 1977.

———. 1976. *Il sorriso dell'ignoto marinaio*. Torino: Einaudi, 1992.

———. 1981. Un giorno come gli altri. In *Racconti italiani del Novecento*, 1429–42.

———. 1985a. *Lunaria*. Milano: Mondadori, 2003.

———. 1985b. *'Nfernu veru. Uomini & immagini dei paesi dello zolfo*. Roma: Edizioni lavoro.

———. 1985c. *Sicilia. Immagini del XIX secolo dagli Archivi Alinari. Con uno scritto di Vincenzo Consolo*. Firenze: Fratelli Alinari. 1996.

———. 1986. La pesca del tonno in Sicilia. In *La pesca del tonno in Sicilia*. Palermo: Sellerio.

———. 1987a. Blasone di Palermo e blasone di Milano. *Linea d'ombra* 18, 42.

———. 1987b. *Retablo*. Milano: Arnoldo Mondadori.

———. 1988a. L'idea della Sicilia. In Vincenzo Consolo, Atanasio Mozzillo, Emanuele Kanceff, Massino Ganci, and Carlo Sciolla, *La Sicilia dei grandi viaggiatori*. Ed. Franco Paloscia. Rome: Edizioni Abete, XIII–XVIII.

———. 1988b. *Le pietre di Pantalica*. Milano: Mondadori. 1990.

———. 1989. L'ora sospesa. In *Ruggero Savinio, con uno scritto di Vincenzo Consolo e un testo dell'artista*. Palermo: Sellerio, 9–10.

———. 1990a. *La Sicilia passeggiata*. Fotografie di Giuseppe Leone, Torino: Edizioni Rai.

———. 1990b. Il cavaliere, la morte e i corvi. *Linea d'ombra* 45: 19–20.

———. 1991a. Lo scrittore di pensiero. *Linea d'ombra* 56: 39–40.

———. 1991b. Un cielo livido. In Vincenzo Consolo and Giuseppe Leone, *Il Barocco in Sicilia. La rinascita del Val di Noto*. Milano: Bompiani.

———. 1991c. Viaggi dal mare alla terra. In Vincenzo Consolo, Vittorio Orlando, Amedeo Tullio, and Teresa Viscuso. *Museo Mandralisca*. Palermo: Edizioni Novecento, 8–13.

———. 1992. *Nottetempo, casa per casa*. Milano: Arnoldo Mondadori.

———. 1993a. *Fuga dall'Etna. La Sicilia e Milano, la memoria e la storia*. Roma: Donzelli.

———. 1993b. La mafia nella letteratura siciliana. *Italienisch* 30: 2–8.

———. 1993c. Il regime dei proci. *Linea d'ombra* 84: 55.

———. 1994a. *L'olivo e l'olivastro*. Milano: Oscar Mondadori, 1999.

———. 1994b. Letteratura e potere. Attualità del caso Dreyfus. *Linea d'ombra* 97: 47–49.

———. 1995. Postfazione. In *Narrare il Sud. Percorsi di scrittura e di lettura*. Ed. Goffredo Fofi. Napoli: Liguori, 81–92.

———. 1996a. I Corpi di Orvieto di Fabrizio Clerici. In Fabrizio Clerici *I Corpi di Orvieto; Con un testo di Vincenzo Consolo*. Firenze: Bezuga, 7–20.

———. 1997. Per una metrica della memoria. In *Parole di scrittore. La lingua della narrative italiana dagli anni settanta a oggi*. Ed. Valeria Della Valle. Roma: Edizioni minimum fax, 117–28.

———. 1998. *Lo spasimo di Palermo*. Milano: Arnoldo Mondadori.

———. 1999a. La scoperta di Cefalù (Come un racconto). In *Cefalù*, Vincenzo Consolo and Giuseppe Leone. Bruno Leopardi editore.

———. 1999b. *Di qua dal faro*. Milano: Arnoldo Mondadori.

———. 1999c. Presentazione. In Laura Gonzenbach, *Fiabe siciliane. Rilette da Vincenzo Consolo*, Ed. Luisa Rubini, Roma: Donzelli, xi–xiv.

———. 1999d. Presentazione. In *Il Lunario ritrovato. Ristampa anastatica del "Lunario siciliano" 1927–1931. L'avventura culturale di Francesco Lanza e Nino Savarese presentata da Vincenzo Consolo*. Enna: Editrice Il Lunario.

———. 1999e. *Il Teatro del Sole. Racconti di Natale*. Novara: Interlinea Edizioni.

———. 2000. Leonardo Sciascia. Siniestras galerías del crimen. *La Nación. Cultura* (January 16): 1-2.

———. 2001a. La Dimora degli Dei. In Vincenzo Consolo, Giuseppe Voza, and Salvatore Russo. *La terra di Archimede*. Fotografie di Mimmo Jodice. Palermo: Sellerio, 13-16.

———. 2001b. Internet è un luogo assolutamente misterioso per me nel quale per la prima volta mi inoltrerò. http://www.italialibri.net/interviste/consolo. January-March.

———. 2002. *Oratorio*. Lecce: Manni.

———. 2003a. Italia—La maschera e il potere. *l'Unità*. (October 11).

———. 2003b. Risorgimento and Literature: The Post-Risorgimento Novel in Sicily. *Italian Culture* 21 (2003): 149-63.

Consolo, Vincenzo, and Mario Nicolao. 1999. *Il viaggio di Odisseo*, Milano: Bompiani.

Consolo, Vincenzo, et al. 1993. *Requiem per le Vittime della Mafia*. Palermo: La Palma.

Conversazione con Antonio Tabucchi. Dove va il romanzo? 1995. Ed. P. Gaglianone and M. Cassini. Roma: Il libro che non c'è.

Corral, Pedro. 1997. El nombre de los verdugos. *La Nación. Suplemento Literario*. (July 27): 1-2.

Costa, Marithelma, and Adelaida López. 1985. Entrevista con Umberto Eco. *Revista de Occidente* 52 (September): 117-30.

Costanzo, Mario. 1991. *Appunti e postille per un Seminario di Storia della critica letteraria*. Roma: Bulzoni.

Cotroneo, Roberto. 2004. Mi candido in Portogallo per un mondo senza conflitti. *l'Unità* (April 8).

Croce, Benedetto. 1970. Liberalism and Idealism in the Giolittian Era. In *Italy from the Risorgimento to Fascism. An Inquiry into the Origins of the Totalitarian State*. Ed. A. William Salomone. New York: Doubleday. 306-38.

Cvetkovich, Ann, and Kellner, Douglas. 1997. Introduction: Thinking Global and Local. In *Articulating the Global and the Local. Globalization and Cultural Studies*. Ed. Cvetkovich and Kellner. Boulder, CO: Westview Press, 1-30.

D'Acunti, Gianluca. 1997. Alla ricerca della sacralità della parola: Vincenzo Consolo. In *Parole di scrittore. La lingua della narrativa italiana dagli anni settanta a oggi*. Ed. Valeria Della Valle. Roma: Edizioni minimum fax. 101-16.

Dainotto, Roberto. 2000. *Place in Literature. Regions, Cultures, Communities*. Ithaca: Cornell University Press.

De Caro, Roberto. 1994. Finché Pereira diventò un altro. Colloquio con Antonio Tabucchi. *Espresso* (January 28): 98-99.

Décina Lombardi, Paola. 1991. Tabucchi in nero. *Tuttolibri* (March 2): 3.

Dedica a Antonio Tabucchi. 2001. Edited by Claudio Cattaruzza, Pordenone (Italy): Associazione Provinciale per la Prosa.

De Lauretis, Teresa. 1981. *Umberto Eco*. Firenze: La Nuova Italia.

De Lauretis, Teresa. 1987. *Technolgies of Gender. Essays on Theory, Film, and Fiction*. Bloomington: Indiana University Press.

Deleuze, Gilles. *Cinema I. The Movement-Image*. 1983. Trans. Hugh Tomlinson and Barbara Habberjam. Minneapolis: University of Minnesota Press, 1997.

Delueze, Gilles, and Felix Guattari. 1972. *Anti-Oedipus. Capitalism and Schizophrenia*. Trans. Robert Hurley, Mark Seem, and Helen R. Lane. Minneapolis: University of Minnesota Press, 1983.

Del Giudice, Daniele. 1988. *Nel Museo di Reims, con sedici dipinti di Marco Nereo Rotelli*. Milano: Arnoldo Mondadori.

La strage. L'atto d'accusa dei giudici di Bologna. 1986. Ed. Giuseppe De Lutiis. Roma: Editori Riuniti.

Dombroski, Robert S. 1990. Antonio Pizzuto and the Subject of Narrative. *Italica* 67: 1–16.

———. 1998. Re-writing Sicily. Postmodern Perspectives. In *Italy's "Southern Question,"* 261–76.

———. 2005. Consolo and the Fictions of History. In *Risorgimento and Modern Italian Culture*, 217–37.

Duggan, Christopher. 1995. Italy in the Cold War Years and the Legacy of Fascism. In *Italy in the Cold War*, 1–24.

Eagleton, Terry. 1981. *Walter Benjamin. Or Towards a Revolutionary Criticism*. London: Verso.

———. 2003. *After Theory*. New York: Basic Books.

Eco, Umberto. 1962. *Opera aperta*. Milano: Bompiani, 1976.

———. 1964. *Apocalittici e integrati*. Milano: Bompiani.

———. 1968. *La struttura assente. Introduzione alla ricerca semiotica*. Milano: Bompiani. 1991.

———. 1971. Sulla possibilità di generare messaggi estetici in una lingua edenica. *Strumenti critici* 5, 11 (June): 135–51.

———. 1976a. Un bugiardo di duemila anni fa. *Corriere della sera*. September 22.

———. 1976b. L'intellettuale chiuso nella riserva indiana. *Corriere della sera*, September 30.

———. 1976c. *A Theory of Semiotics*. Bloomington: Indiana University Press.

———. 1977. *Come si fa una tesi di laurea. Le materie umanistiche*. Milano: Bompiani, 2002.

———. 1979. *Lector in fabula La cooperazione interpretativa nei testi narrativi*. Milano: Bompiani, 1998.

———. 1980. *Il nome della rosa*. Milano: Bompiani. I Grandi Tascabili, 1993.

———. 1983a. L'antiporfirio. In *Il pensiero debole*, 52–80.

———. 1983b. Postille a *Il nome della rosa*. In *Il nome della rosa*, 507–33.

———. 1984b. Consumo, Ricerca e Lettore Modello. In *Letteratura tra consumo e ricerca*, Ed. Luigi Russo, Bologna: Il Mulino. 97–113.

———. 1984c. *The Role of the Reader.* Bloomington: Indiana University Press.

———. 1987. L'irrazionale ieri e oggi. *Alfabeta* 9, (101) (October): 36–38.

———. 1988. *Il pendolo di Foucault.* Milano: Bompiani.

———. 1989. In principio era il rebus. *Espresso*, (November 25): 82–86.

———. 1990. *I limiti dell'interpretazione.* Milano: Bompiani, 1999.

———. 1992. Reading My Readers," *Modern Language Notes*, December: 819–27.

———. 1994a. *L'isola del giorno prima.* Milano: Bompiani.

———. 1994b. *Six Walks in the Fictional Woods.* Cambridge: Harvard University Press, 1998.

———. 1997a. Il primo dovere degli intellettuali. Stare zitti quando non servono a nulla. *Espresso.* (April 24): 226.

———. 1997b. *Cinque scritti morali.* Milano: Bompiani, 2001.

———. 1997c. *Kant e l'ornitorinco.* Milano: Bompiani.

———. 1997d. Il primo dovere degli intellettuali. Stare zitti quando non servono a nulla. *L'Espresso*, (April 24).

———. 1998. Intentio lectoris. The State of the Art. In *Recoding Metaphysics.* 29–43.

———. 2000. *Baudolino.* Milano: Bompiani.

———. 2001a. Perché in Berlusconi si nasconde un communista. *Repubblica*, (April 3): 1ff.

———. 2001b. Quando i figli divorano i padri. *Repubblica*, (July 19): 1ff.

———. 2003. Il rischio del ricatto. *l'Unità.* (November 8).

———. 2004. *La misteriosa fiamma della Regina Loana. Romanzo illustrato.* Milano: Bompiani.

Elam, Diane. 1992. *Romanticizing the Postmodern.* London: Routledge.

Esplorazioni sulla Via Emilia. Scritture sul paesaggio. Ed. Giulio Bizzarri. Milano: Feltrinelli, 1986.

Fairbairn, W. Ronald. 1954. *An Objects-Relation Theory of the Personality.* New York: Basic Books.

Farrell, Joseph. 1993. Vincenzo Consolo. Metaphors and False History. In *The New Italian Novel.* Ed. Zygmunt G. Barański and Lino Pertile. Edinburgh: Edinburgh University Press, 59–74.

Federman, Raymond. 1993. *Crtifiction. Postmodern Essays.* Albany: State University of New York Press.

Ferretti, Gian Carlo. 1983. *Il best seller all'italiana.* Milano: Masson, 1993.

Foucault, Michel. What Is an Author? In *What Is an Author?* Trans. J. V. Harari. Ithaca: Cornell University Press, 1979. 141–60.

Flamigni, Sergio. 1996. *Trame atlantiche. Storia della Loggia massonica segreta P2*, Milano: Kaos edizioni.

Francese, Joseph. 1992. L'eteronimia di Antonio Tabucchi. *Stanford Italian Review* 11 (1–2): 123–38.

———. 1997. *Narrating Postmodern Time and Space.* Albany: State University of New York Press.

———. 2001. Lo scrittore che non venne dal freddo. Il primo viaggio di Calvino negli Usa. *Allegoria* 10 (37): 38–61.

Freud, Anna. 1958. Adolescence. *Psychoanalytic Study of the Child* 13: 255–78.

———. 1966. *The Ego and the Mechanisms of Defense.* Madison, Conn.: International Universities Press, 2000.

Freud, Sigmund. 1953–1957. *The Standard Edition of the Complete Psychological Works of Sigmund Freud.* Trans. James Strachey. London: Hogarth Press, 1953–74.

———. A Special Type of Choice of Object Made by Men," In Freud, *Standard Edition,* vol. 9, 165–75

———. Family Romances. In Freud, *Standard Edition,* vol. 9, 237–41.

———. Some Character-Types Met With in Psycho-Analytic Work. In Freud, *Standard Edition,* vol. 14, 311–13.

———. 1954. *The Origins of Psychoanalysis. Letters, Drafts and Notes to Wilhelm Fliess, 1887–1902.* Ed. Marie Bonaparte, Anna Freud, and Ernst Kris. Trans. Eric Mosbacher and James Strachey. New York: Basic Books.

———. 1957. *A General Selection from the Works of Sigmund Freud.* Ed. John Rickman. New York: Liveright.

———. On Narcissism: An Introduction. In Freud, *A General Selection from the Works of Sigmund Freud,* 104–23.

———. Instincts and Their Vicissitudes. In Freud, *A General Selection from the Works of Sigmund Freud,* 70–86.

———. 1963. *General Psychological Theory. Papers on Metapsychology.* Ed. P. Rieff. New York: Collier.

———. Mourning and Melancholia. In Freud, *General Psychological Theory,* 164–79.

———. Negation. In Freud, *General Psychological Theory,* 213–17.

The Future of Difference. 1980. Ed. Hester Eisenstein and Alice Jardine. Boston: G.K. Hall.

Garin, Eugenio. 1997. *Intervista sull'intellettuale.* Roma-Bari: Laterza.

Genette, Gèrard. 1997. *Paratexts. Threshholds of Interpretation.* Cambridge: Cambridge University Press. Original title. *Seuils,* Editions du Seuil, 1987.

Genovese, Andrea. 1977. ". . . uscire fuori dal romanzo, fuori dalla letteratura, fuori dalla scrittura . . ." *Uomini e libri* 63: 36–37.

Gilberg, Arnold L. 1974. Asceticism and the Analysis of a Nun. *Journal of the American Psychoanalytic Association* 22 (2): 381–93.

Ginsborg, Paul. 1990. *A History of Contemprary Italy. Society and Politics, 1943–1988.* New York: Penguin Books.

———. 2004. *Silvio Berlusconi.* London and New York: Verso.

Gold, Gregg J., and Bernard Weiner. 2000. Remorse, Confession, Group Identity, and Expectancies About Repeating a Transgression. *Basic and Applied Psychology* 22: 291–300.

Gramsci, Antonio. 1975. *Quaderni del carcere.* Torino: Einaudi, 1977.
Gruber, Lilli. 2004. Informazione prigioniera. *Unità.* (April 28).
Gumpert, Carlos. 2001. La letteratura come enigma ed inquietudine. Una conversazione con Antonio Tabucchi. *Dedica a Antonio Tabucchi,* 17–105.
Gumpert Melgosa, Carlos. 1995. *Conversaciones con Antonio Tabucchi.* Barcelona: Editorial Anagrama.
Harvey, David. 1989. *The Condition of Postmodernity. An Enquiry into the Origins of Cultural Change.* Cambridge: Basil Blackwell.
———. 2000. *Spaces of Hope,* Berkeley: University of California Press.
Heffernan, James A. W. 1999. Speaking for Pictures: The Rhetoric of Art Criticism. *Word and Image* 15: 19–33.
Hernández, Domingo-Luis. 1998. No hay estética sin ética. Entrevista con Antonio Tabucchi. *Quimera* 134: 24–26.
Horney, Karen. 1942. *Self-Analysis.* New York: W.W. Norton.
Hurvich, Marvin S. 1989. Traumatic Moment. Basic Dangers and Annihilation Anxiety. *Psychoanalytic Psychology* 6 (3): 309–23.
Hutcheon, Linda. 1997. Irony-clad Foucault. In *Reading Eco,* 312–27.
Il pensiero debole. 1983. Ed. G. Vattimo and P. A. Rovatti, Milano: Feltrinelli.
Il poeta e la finzione. Scritti su Ferando Pessoa. Ed. Antonio Tabucchi. Genova: Tilgher, 1983.
Italy in the Cold War. Politics, Culture and Society 1948–58. 1995. Ed. Christopher Duggan and Christopher Wagstaff. Oxford: Berg.
Italy's "Southern Question." Orientalism in One Country. 1998. Ed. Jane Schneider. Oxford: Berg.
Jacobson, Edith. 1959. The "Exceptions." An Elaboration of Freud's Character Study. *The Psychoanalytic Study of the Child* 14: 135–54.
Jameson, Fredric. 1975. Magical Narratives: Romance as Genre. *New Literary History* 7: 135–63.
———. 1981. *The Political Unconscious. Narrative as a Socially Symbolic Act.* Ithaca: Cornell University Press.
———. 1984. Postmodernism, or the Cultural Logic of Late Capitalism. *New Left Review* 146: 53–92.
———. 1992. *Signatures of the Visible.* New York: Routledge.
Jeffreys, M. D. W. 1951. Onanism: An Anthropological Survey. *International Journal of Sexology* 5: 61–65.
Jennings, J. L., and C. M. Murphy. 2000. Male-Male Dimensions of Male-Female Battering: A New Look at Domestic Violence. *Psychology of Men and Masculinity* 1: 21–29.
Jensen, Viggo W., and Thomas A. Petty. 1996. The Fantasy of Being Rescued in Suicide. In *Essential Papers on Suicide.* Ed. J. T. Maltsberger and M. J. Goldblatt. New York: New York University Press, 131–41.
Kaplan, Harvey. 1987. The Psychopathology of Nostalgia. *Psychoanalytic Review* 74 (4): 465–85.
Kaplan, Linda Joan. 1974. The Concept of the Family Romance. *The Psychoanalytic Review* 61 (2) (Summer): 169–202.

Karon, Bertram P. 1970. An Experimental Study of Parental Castration Phantasies. *British Journal of Psychiatry* 117: 69–73.

———. 1984. A Type of Transference Based on Identification with an Abusing Parent. *Psychoanalytic Psychology* 1 (4): 345–48.

———. 2003. The Tragedy of Schizophrenia without Psychotherapy. *Journal of the American Academy of Psychoanalysis and Dynamic Psychiatry* 31 (1): 89–118.

Karon, Bertram P., and Gary R. VandenBos. 1998. Schizophrenia and Psychosis in Elderly Populations. In *Clinical Geropsychology*. Ed. I. H. Nordhus, G. R. VandenBos, S. Berg, and P. Fromholt. Washington, DC: American Psychological Association, 219–27.

Kellner, Douglas. 1995. *Media Culture*. London: Routledge.

Kilborne, Benjamin. 2002. *Disappearing Persons. Shame and Appearance*. Albany: State University of New York Press.

Klein, Melanie. 1949. *The Psycho-Analysis of Children*. Trans. Alex Strachey. New York: Humanities Press, 1969.

Klopp, Charles. 2001. The Return of the Spiritual, with a Note on the Fiction of Bufalino, Tabucchi, and Celati. *Annali d'italianistica* 19: 93–102.

Kramer, Jane. 2003. All He Surveys. *The New Yorker* (November 10): 95–105.

Kristeva, Julia. 1993. *New Maladies of the Soul*. Trans. R. M. Guberman. New York: Columbia Univerity Press, 1995.

Kuhn, Thomas S. 1962. *The Structure of Scientific Revolutions*. Chicago: University of Chicago Press, 1970.

La granda congiura di Gelli. 1984. *Repubblica* (May 10): 1–3.

Las tentaciones. Un pintor, Jerónimo Bosco. Un escritor, Antonio Tabucchi. 1989. Barcelona: Anagrama.

L'astromostro. Racconti per bambini. 1980. Ed. Antonio Porta. Milano: Feltrinelli.

Latrive, Florent, and Annick Rivoire. 2000. Eco: la cultura corre on line; chi non si adegua è perduto *Repubblica* (January 8): 13.

Le Goff, Jacques. 1989. Forcement médiévale et terriblement moderne. *Magazine litteraire* 262. 30–33.

Lepschy, Anna Laura, and Giulio Lepschy. 1977. *The Italian Language Today*. New York: Routledge, 1991.

López, Asbel. 1999. Antonio Tabucchi: A Committed Doubter. *The Unesco Courier*. (November): 46–50.

Luperini, Romano. 1999. *Il dialogo e il conflitto. Per un'ermeneutica materialista*. Roma Bari: Laterza.

Lyotard, Jean-François. 1983. Tomb of the Intellectual. In *Political Writings*. Minneapolis: University of Minnesota Press, 1993, 3–7.

Lynn, Steven Jay, Judith Pintar, and Judith W. Rhue. 1997. Fantasy Proneness, Dissociation, and Narrative Construction. *Broken Images, Broken Selves: Dissociative Narratives in Clinical Practice*, Ed. Krippner Stanley and S. M. Powers. Washington, DC: Brunner/Mazel, 274–302.

Maddocks, Ian, et al. 1996. Attenuation of Morphine-Induced Delirium in Palliative Care by Substitution with Infusion of Oxycodone. *Journal of Pain and Symptom Management.* 12 (3): 182–89.

Maiello, Francesco. 1996. *Storia del calendario. La misurazione del tempo, 1450–1800.* Torino: Einaudi.

Manacorda, Giuliano. 1996. *Storia della letteratura italiana contemporanea. 1940–1996.* Roma: Editori Riuniti.

Marcuse, Herbert. 2001. *Towards a Critical Theory of Society,* vol. 2, Collected Papers of Herbert Marcuse. London: Routledge.

Mari, Giovanni. 1998. *Postmoderno, democrazia, storia.* Pisa: Edizioni ETS.

———. 2001. *I vocabolari di Braudel. Lo spazio come verità della storia.* Napoli: Luciano.

Marramao, Giacomo. 1985. *Potere e secolarizzazione. Le categorie del tempo.* Roma: Editori Riuniti.

Martini, Carlo Maria, and Umberto Eco. 1996. *In cosa crede chi non crede?* Roma: Atlantide Editoriale.

Mattei, Paolo. 1991. Gli angeli che abitano il nostro tempo. *Il Tempo* (April 10): 8.

Mauri, Paolo. 1998. Io, Tabucchi sognatore e bugiardo. *Repubblica* (October 22): 28.

McHale, Brian. 1992. *Constructing Postmodernism,* London: Routledge.

Mitchell, W. J. T. 1994. *Picture Theory.* Chicago: University of Chicago Press.

Mitgang, Herbert. *Words Still Count with me. A Chronicle of Literary Conversations.* New York: W.W. Norton, 1995.

Mohacsy, Ildiko. 1984. The Legend of the Unicorn: An Illumination of the Maternal Split. *Journal of the American Academy of Psychoanalysis* 12. 387–412.

———. 1988. The Medieval Unicorn: Historical and Iconographic Applications of Psychoanalysis. *Journal of the American Academy of Psychoanalysis* 16: 83–106.

Neri, Francesca, and Giampiero Segneri. 2002. "Reshaping Memory: Bufalino, Consolo and the Sicilian Tradition," *European Studies* 18: 91–105.

Orengo, Nico. 1992. Tabucchi: Addio Pessoa. Ora fuggo con Stevenson. *Tuttolibri* 805 (June).

Padovani, Marcelle. 2002. Vi scrivo dal medio evo. Intervista a Umberto Eco. *Repubblica* (February 17).

Pagano, Tullio. 1999–2000. Metamorfosi dell'immagine nell'opera di Vincenzo Consolo. *L'anello che non tiene,* 83–97.

———. 2002. A World of Ruins: The Allegorical Vision in Fabrizio Clerici, Vincenzo Consolo, and Luigi Malerba. *Italica* 79: 204–22.

Palmieri, Giovanni. 1994. Intervista a Antonio Tabucchi. *Concertino* (June 30): 26–27.

Parazzoli, Ferruccio, ed. 1998. *Il gioco del mondo. Dialoghi sulla vita, i sogni, le memorie.* Cinisello Balsamo (MI): San Paolo.

Parliament in Italy Passes Immunity Law for Berlusconi. 2003. *New York Times* (June 18).
Palmer, Allen J. 1984. Tom Sawyer: Early Parent Loss. *Bulletin of the Menninger Clinic* 48 (2): 155–69.
Pasolini, Pier Paolo. 1972. *Empirismo eretico.* Milano: Garzanti, 1981.
Pavone, Claudio. 1991. *Una guerra civile. Saggio storico sulla moralità nella Resistenza.* Torino: Bollati Boringhieri.
Pericoli, Tullio. 1988. *Tanti saluti. Con un racconto di Antonio Tabucchi,* Milano: Rosellina Archinto.
———. 1989. *Woody, Freud and Others.* Munich: Prestel-Verlag.
———. 1991. *Attraverso il disegno.* Ed. Roberto Tassi. Milano: Fabbri.
Pessoa, Fernando. 1986. *Poems of Fernando Pessoa.* Trans. and ed. Edwin Honig and Susan M. Brown. New York: Ecco Press.
———. 1988. *Il poeta è un fingitore. Duecento citazioni scelte da Antonio Tabucchi.* Milano: Feltrinelli. 2003.
Petri, Romana. 1994. Uno scrittore pieno di gente. *Leggere* 61 (June): 68–75.
———. 1997. Tabucchi. Il mondo è tutto un Portogallo. *Avvenimenti libri* (September 17): 62–63.
Piccole finzioni con imporanza. Valori della narrativa italiana contemporanea. 1993. Ed. Nathalie Roelens and Inge Lanslots. Ravenna: Longo.
Pike, Burton. 1976. Time in Autobiography. *Comparative Literature* 28: 326–42.
Pires, José Cardoso. 1978. *O delfim. Romance.* Lisbon: Moraes. Italian trans. R. Biscetti. Milano: Feltrinelli. 1992.
Piromalli, Antonio, and Domenico Scafoglio. 1977. *L'identità minacciata. La poesia dialettale e la crisi postunitaria.* Messina-Firenze: D'Anna.
Placido, Beniamino. 1977. Quel falso manuale scritto da Umberto Eco. *Repubblica* (September 22): 11.
———. 2002. Dove iniziano i diritti dei lettori. *Repubblica* (February 17).
Potash, Herbert M. 1988. Remorse versus Self-Hatred: An Existential Analysis. *The Psychology Patient* 5 (1–2): 249–57.
Pratt, Hugo. 1994. *Avevo un appuntamento.* Roma: Edizioni Socrates. 1995.
Presa di distanza dalla protesta di Consolo e Tabucchi. 2002. *Repubblica.* (February 6): 46.
A Pretext to Literary Semiotics. 1997. Ed. Rocco Capozzi. Bloomington: Indiana University Press.
Racconti italiani del Novecento. 1983. Ed. Enzo Siciliano. Milano: Mondadori.
Ragland-Sullivan, Ellie. 1987. *Jacques Lacan and the Philosophy of Psychoanalysis.* Urbana: University of Illinois Press.
Reading Eco: An Anthology. 1997. Ed. Rocco Capozzi. Bloomington: Indiana University Press.
Recoding Metaphysics. The New Italian Philosophy. 1988. Ed. Giovanna Borradori. 1988. Evanston: Northwestern University Press.
Rich, Frank. 2004. Operation Iraqi Infoganda. *New York Times.* (March 28).

———. 2005. The White House Stages Its "Daily Show." *New York Times*. (February 20).

Richard Sterba. *The Collected Papers*. Ed. H. Daldin, Croton-on-Hudson, NY: North River Press, 1987.

Risorgimento and Modern Italian Culture. Revisiting the 19th Century Past in History, Narrative, and Cinema. 2005. Ed. Norma Bouchard. Madison, NJ: Fairleigh Dickinson University Press.

Rodowick, D. N. *Gilles Deleuze's Time Machine*. Durham: Duke University Press, 1997.

Rossi, Andrea. 1988. Il "contastorie" del bel tempo che fu. *Grazia*. (October 30): 19–21.

Rosso, Stefano, and Umberto Eco. 1991. A Correspondence on Postmodernism. *Zeitgeist in Babel. The Postmodernist Controversy*. Ed. I. Hoesterey. Bloomington: Indiana University Press, 242–53.

Rutenberg, Jim. 2004. Disney Forbidding Distribution of Film That Criticizes Bush. *New York Times* (May 5).

Samuels, Robert. 1996. The Culture of Public Confession: Talk Shows, Perversion, and Neurosis. *Journal for the Psychoanalysis of Culture and Society* 1 (1): 134–36.

Sancis Antonio, Emma. 2001. Tabucchi possiede il dono di una sapienza antica. http://www.cremonaonline.it. (August 9).

Sanna Salvatore A. 1987. A colloquio con Vincenzo Consolo. *Italienisch* 17 (May): 8–50.

Savino, Giancarlo. 1994. *Frame café. Con un testo di Antonio Tabucchi*. Naples: Electa.

Scafoglio, Domenico, and Geppina Cianflone. 1977. *Le parole e il potere. L'ideologia del vocabolario italiano*. Messina-Firenze: D'Anna.

Scaglione, Aldo. 1997. Petrarchan Love and the Pleasures of Frustration. *Journal of the History of Ideas*. 557–72.

Schneider, Jane. 1998. The Dynamics of Neo-orientalism in Italy (1848–1995). In *Italy's "Southern Question": Orientalism in One Country*. Ed. Jane Schneider. Oxford: Berg, 1–23.

Sciascia, Leonardo. 1979. *La Sicilia come metafora*. Milano: Arnoldo Mondadori.

Segre, Cesare. 1991. La costruzione a chiocciola nel *Sorriso dell'ignoto marinaio* di Vincenzo Consolo. In *Intrecci di voci: la polifonia nella letteratura del Novecento*. Torino: Einaudi. 71–86.

Shanon, Benny. 1991. Faulty Language Selection in Polyglots. *Language and Cognitive Processes* 6: 339–50.

Shumway, David R. 1997. The Star System in Literary Studies. *PMLA* 112: 85–100.

Smith, Jonathan. 2000. Tabucchi Echoes Lacan: Making an End of "Postmodernism" from the Beginning. *Annali d'italianistica* 18: 77–108.

Sobieraj, Sarah. 1998. Taking Control. Toy Commercials and the Social Construction of Patriarchy. In *Masculinities and Violence*. Ed. Lee H. Bowker. Thousand Oaks, Calif.: Sage Publications, 15–28.

Sontag, Susan. 2003. *Regarding the Pain of Others*. New York: Farrar, Straus and Giroux.

Sostieni Tabucchi: lo scrittore candidato alle Europee dalla sinistra portoghese. *l'Unità*. (March 23, 2004).

Spielberg, Warren E. 1993. Why Men Must Be Heroic. *The Journal of Men's Studies* 2 (2) (November): 173–88.

Stauder, Thomas. 1989. Un colloquio con Umberto Eco su *Il pendolo di Foucault*. *Il lettore di provincia*. September 21, 75: 3–11.

———. 1996. A colloquio con Umberto Eco. *Italienisch. Zeitschrift fur Italienishce Sprache und Literatur.* 18: 2–13.

Steiner, George. 1989. *Real Presences*. Chicago: University of Chicago Press, 1991.

Sterba, Richard. 1940. The Problem of Art in Freud's Writings. *The Psychoanalytic Quarterly* 9 (1): 256–68.

———. 1968. Remarks on Mystic States. *American Imago* 25, 1: 77–85.

———. A Contribution to the Theory of Sublimation. In *Richard Sterba*, 20–28.

———. The Equation of Mother and Prostitute. In *Richard Sterba*, 29–31.

———. Aggression in the Rescue Fantasy. In *Richard Sterba*, 121–23.

Surdich, Luigi. 1990. *Giorgio Caproni. Un ritratto*. Genova: Costa e Nolan.

Tabucchi, Antonio. 1975. *Piazza d'Italia*. Milano: Feltrinelli, 2001.

———. 1975. Interpretazione dell'eteronimia di Fernando Pessoa. *Studi Mediolatini e volgari*, 139–87.

———. 1978. *Il piccolo naviglio*. Milano: Arnoldo Mondadori.

———. 1979. La "verità pratica" di Alexandre O'Neill. In *Alexandre O'Neill, Made in Portugal*, 7–10.

———. 1980. Irma Serena—la sirena bambina. In *L'astromostro*, 120–23.

———. 1981. *Il gioco del rovescio*. Milano: Il saggiatore.

———. 1983. Nota introduttiva. *Il poeta e la finzione. Scritti su Ferando Pessoa*, 5–8.

———. 1984. *Notturno indiano*. Palermo: Sellerio.

———. 1985a. Uma conversa no Outono del 1935. In Brito, *Uma conversa no Outono del 1935*.

———. 1985b. *Piccoli equivoci senza importanza*. Milano: Feltrinelli, 2001.

———. 1986a. *Il filo dell'orizzonte*. Milano: Feltrinelli.

———. 1986b. Vagabondaggio. In *Esplorazioni sulla Via Emilia*, 169–78.

———. 1987. *I volatili del Beato Angelico*. Palermo: Sellerio.

———. 1988a. *Il signor Pirandello è desiderato al telefono*, In Tabucchi, *I dialoghi mancati*, 15–44.

———. 1988b. *Il tempo stringe*. In Tabucchi. *I dialoghi mancati*, 47–75.

———. 1988c. *I dialoghi mancati*. Milano: Feltrinelli.

———. 1988d. Tanti saluti. In Pericoli, *Tanti saluti*, 5–15.

———. 1988e. L'ultima menzogna davanti a Marat. *Corriere della sera*. (December 3).

———. 1989a. Vivere o ritrarre. In Pericoli, *Woody, Freud and Others*, 142–47.

———. 1989b. Le mappe del desiderio. Pomellato. *Le mappe del desiderio. Un viaggio raccontato da Antonio Tabucchi visto da Giampaolo Barbieri.* Milano: Idea Books.

———. 1989c. Fiamme. In Benati, *Davide Benati*. 5–6.

———. 1990a. *Un baule pieno di gente. Scritti su Fernando Pessoa.* Milano: Feltrinelli.

———. 1990b. Io, scrittore, come in uno specchio." *Repubblica.* (February 4).

———. 1990c. Presentazione. In Surdich, *Georgio Caproni*, 5–6.

———. 1991a. Lettera a Tullio Pericoli. In Pericoli, *Attraverso il disegno*, 114–17.

———. 1991b. *L'angelo nero.* Milano: Feltrinelli.

———. 1991c. *El siglo XX, balance y perspectivas: seguido de La novela, el problema: una conversación con Antonio Tabucchi.* Las Palmas: Viceconsejería de Cultura y Deportes, Gobierno de Canarias.

———. 1991d. *L'angelo nero.* Milano: Feltrinelli.

———. 1992a. *Requiem. Uma alucinação.* 1991. Italian Trans. S. Vecchio. Milano: Feltrinelli.

———. 1992b. *Introduzione.* In Pires, *O delfim*, 7–14.

———. 1992c. *Sogni di sogni.* Palermo: Sellerio.

———. 1992d. Sera di pioggia su una diga d'Olanda. In Barrias, *Tempo.*

———. 1992e. *Sogni di sogni.* Palermo: Sellerio.

———. 1994a. Il pittore e le sue creature. In Savino, *Frame café*, 6–7.

———. 1994b. *Sostiene Pereira. Una testimonianza.* Milano: Feltrinelli.

———. 1995. Il mistero dell'annuncio cifrato. In Pratt, *Avevo un appuntamento.* 307–15.

———. 1996a. Catullo e il cardellino. *Micromega* 2 (May–June): 121–25.

———. 1996b. Ritratto d'autore. *Micromega* 4 (October–November): 233–37.

———. 1997a. *Marconi, se ben mi ricordo. Una pièce radiofonica.* Rome: RAI.

———. 1997b. *La testa perduta di Damasceno Monteiro.* Milano: Feltrinelli.

———. 1997c. Prefazione. In Claudio Di Scalzo, *Vecchiano, un paese. Lettere a Antonio Tabucchi.* Milano: Feltrinelli.

———. 1997c. L'Ortese ammira la dignità di Priebke. E quella delle vittime? *Corriere della sera.* (January 19).

———. 1997d. L'albanese sono io. *Corriere della sera.* (April 7).

———. 1997e. Un fiammifero Minerva. *Micromega* 2 (Supplement): 1–13.

———. 1998a. I cambi di stagione della letteratura. Queneau e Calvino, due grandi giocolieri del secolo al tramonto. *Corriere della sera.* (January 15).

———. 1998b. *La nostalgie, l'automobile, et l'infini. Lectures de Pessoa.* Paris: Éditions du Seuil.

———. 1998c. *La gastrite di Platone.* Palermo: Sellerio.

———. 1998d. García Lorca, il poeta assassinato. *Corriere della sera.* (May 31): 27.

———. 1999a. Un univers dans une syllabe (Promenade autour d'un roman). *La Nouvelle Revue Française* 550 (June): 1–24. Now in Tabucchi, *Autobiografie altrui*, 15–39.

———. 1999b. *Gli zingari e il Rinascimento. Vivere da Rom a Firenze.* Milano: Feltrinelli.

———. 2000. Le cefalee del Minotauro. Diario cretese con le sinopie di Valerio Adami, *Opere 1990-2000.* In Adami, 21-29.

———. 2001a. *Si sta facendo sempre più tardi. Romanzo in forma di lettere.* Milano: Feltrinelli.

———. 2001b. Io, prigioniero del mio film. *Repubblica.* (May 27): 1.

———. 2002. I morti a tavola. *Micromega* 3: 178-87.

———. 2003a. *Autobiografie altrui. Poetiche a posteriori.* Milano: Feltrinelli.

———. 2003b. Il silenzio è d'oro. *Il manifesto.* (July 2): 1.

———. 2003c. Signor presidente. *Il manifesto.* (July 4): 1ff.

———. 2003d. Some Reflections on Translations. *Italian Culture* 21: 165-76.

———. 2004. *Tristano muore.* Milano: Feltrinelli.

Tabucchi, Antonio and Borrelli, Francesco Saverio. 2002. Sulla giustizia e dintorni. *Micromega* 1: 25-74.

Teroni, Sandra. 2004. Le voci di Tristano raccontate da Tabucchi. *Il manifesto.* (May 21): 14.

Tomkins, Silvan. 1963. *Affect, Imagery, Consciousness. Volume II. The Negative Affects.* New York: Springer Publishing.

Tranfaglia, Nicola. 1973. *Dallo Stato liberale al regime fascista. Problemi e ricerche.* Milano: Feltrinelli.

Van Eekhout, Fabienne. 1993. Sostiene Tabucchi. *Romanesche* 19, 3: 21-31.

Vassalli, Sebastiano. 1989. *Il neo-italiano. Le parole degli anni ottanta.* Bologna: Zanichelli.

Vattimo, Gianni. 2000. *Vocazione e responsabilità del filosofo.* Genoa: Il nuovo melangolo.

———. 2003. *Nichilismo ed emancipazione. Etica, politica, diritto.* Milano: Garzanti.

Vattimo, Gianni, et al. 1990. *Filosofia al presente,* Milano: Garzanti.

Vettori, Giuseppe. 1975. *Il folk italiano. Canti e ballate popolari.* Roma: Newton Compton.

Viegnes, Michel. 1990. Interview with Umberto Eco. *L'anello che non tiene* (Fall): 57-74.

Wolf, Mauro. 1992. *Gli effetti sociali dei media.* Milano: Bompiani.

Zamora, Lois Parkinson. The Swing of the "Pendulum": Eco's Novels. In Capozzi, *Reading Eco,* 328-47.

Index

Adornato, Ferdinando, 92, 261, 267
Agostinelli, Alessandro, 282
Alexander, V. K., 107
Alighieri, Dante, 254
Anthony, E. James, 264, 265
Antonello, Pier Paolo, 261
Aquinas, Tomas, 43, 272
Aristotle, 66, 72, 75, 268
Arpaia, Bruno, 54
Ashcroft, John, 27
Asor Rosa, Alberto, 162, 290

Badoglio, Pietro, 289
Bailey, Peter, 186
Bakhtin, Mikhail Mikhailovich, 177
Barbieri, Giampaolo, 281
Barina, Antonella, 159
Barrías, José, 204
Barth, John, 33, 116–17
Barthes, Roland, 34, 43, 58, 115, 177, 202, 219, 233
Benedetti, Carla, 40, 136, 283
Benedict, Helen, 113
Ben-Ghiat, Ruth, 28, 245
Benjamin, Walter, 32–33, 57, 157, 164, 189, 210–11, 214, 216, 257
Bergson, Henri, 278
Berlinguer, Enrico, 91
Berlusconi, Silvio, 17–18, 27, 28, 238, 245, 253, 254, 262, 266, 276, 277
Bertone, Manuela, 178–79
Best, Stephen, 23, 24, 114, 115, 177
Bibolas, Noemí, 164, 275
Binni, Walter, 178, 253
Blanchot, Maurice, 174–75, 181, 188, 190, 197, 201, 214

Bobbio, Norberto, 277
Bodei, Remo, 175, 177, 210, 283
Bondanella, Peter, 53, 95, 113
Borrelli, Francesco Saverio, 277, 283
Borsari, Andrea, 174, 283
Bosch, Jerónimo, 280
Bosson, Jennifer K., 271, 272
Botta, Anna, 280, 282
Bouchard, Norma, 118, 134, 268
Brecht, Bertoldt, 273
Brizio-Skov, Flavia, 203, 280
Borsellino, Paolo, 21
Brito, José João, 281
Brown, Ryan P., 271, 272
Browning, Robert, 29
Brownmiller, Susan, 113
Bush, George H. W., 22, 255
Bush, George W., 22, 23, 27–28, 256

Calabrese, Omar, 195
Calvino, Italo, 16, 19, 33, 40, 58, 177, 212, 253–54, 258, 283
Campana, Dino, 204
Cannon, JoAnn, 107, 200
Capozzi, Rocco, 43, 74, 260, 261, 262
Caproni, Giorgio, 183
Chodorow, Nancy, 177
Choniates, Niketas, 137
Churchill, Winston, 289
Célan, Paul, 234, 284
Ceserani, Remo, 235
Ciampi, Carlo Azeglio, 19
Cianflone, Geppina, 161
Cipriani, Gianni, 266
Clerici, Fabrizio, 31, 168, 169–70, 257, 276

309

Clinton, William Jefferson (Blythe IV), 22
Coletti, Theresa, 54–56
Conrad, Joseph, 179
Consolo, Vincenzo, 15–38, 156–73, 244–45, 254, 257, 273–76
Corral, Pedro, 176, 277
Costa, Marithelma, 53
Costanzo, Mario, 47, 196, 211
Cotroneo, Roberto, 253
Croce, Benedetto, 196, 240, 285
Cvetkovich, Ann, 22, 24, 254–55

D'Acunti, Gianluca, 274
Dainotto, Roberto M., 31, 158, 257
De Caro, Roberto, 36
Décina Lombardi, Paola, 282
De Lauretis, Teresa, 259
Deleuze, Gilles, 34–35, 52, 58, 114, 146, 217–18
De Lutiis, Giuseppe, 93
Del Giudice, Daniele, 196, 277
Derrida, Jacques, 261
Dickinson, Emily, 277
Diderot, Denis, 278
Dombroski, Robert S., 33, 169, 170, 257, 273, 276, 281
Dostoyevsky, Fyodor Mikhailovich, 196
Duggan, Christopher, 239–40, 289

Eagleton, Terry, 22, 25, 33, 34
Eco, Umberto, 15–38, 39–155, 164, 172, 175, 181, 213–14, 234, 242, 243–52, 253–56, 258–59, 259–73, 275, 276, 287–88, 289–91
Elam, Diane, 259

Fairbairn, W. Ronald, 88
Falcone, Giovanni, 21
Farrell, Joseph, 161, 169, 170, 276
Federman, Raymond, 39, 53
Ferretti, Gian Carlo, 42, 44, 54
Flamigni, Sergio, 93
Fra' Angelico (Guido di Pietro da Fiesole), 194
Francese, Joseph, 177, 254, 281, 283
Franco, Francisco, 240
Freud, Anna, 74, 121, 232, 271, 287

Freud, Sigmund, 59–60, 67, 76, 85, 110, 121, 126, 139, 196, 197, 255, 264, 265, 281, 284–85, 286, 290
Foucault, Michel, 39, 40, 55

Gable, Clark, 229, 286
Gadda, Carlo Emilio, 164, 281
García Lorca, Federico, 288
Garibaldi, Giuseppe, 227, 228, 287
Garin, Eugenio, 285
Gelli, Licio, 93, 266
Genette, Gèrard, 35, 178
Genovese, Andrea, 273
Gilberg Arnold L., 74
Ginsborg, Paul, 93, 94, 228, 239, 253, 266, 286, 289
Goethe, Johann Wolfgang von, 166, 167, 276
Gödel, Kurt, 189
Gold, Gregg J., 265
Gonzenbach, Laura, 166, 276
Gramsci, Antonio, 24, 29, 193, 213
Greene, Graham, 159
Gruber, Lili, 253
Gruppo '63, 43, 275
Guattari, Felix, 58, 114
Gumpert, Carlos, 176, 195, 208, 212, 215, 216, 281
Gumpert Melgosa, Carlos, 176, 186, 197, 201, 202, 203, 204, 206, 208, 212, 215, 280–83

Harvey, David, 23, 26, 29, 34, 49, 216–17, 254, 255
Heffernan, James A. W., 194, 195, 244
Hemingway, Ernest, 159
Hernández, Domingo-Luis, 192, 209
Horney, Karen, 103, 278
Hurvich, Marvin S., 226, 284–85
Hutcheon, Linda, 52

Jacobson, Edith, 269
Jankélévitch, Vladimir, 186
Jameson, Fredric, 16, 50, 56, 97, 194, 245, 246
Jeffreys, M. D. W., 286
Jennings, J. L., 65
Jensen, Viggo W., 106, 107
Joyce, James, 196, 212

INDEX

Kant, Immanuel, 261
Kaplan, Harvey, 87
Kaplan, Linda Joan, 76, 78, 87, 264, 270
Karon, Bertram P., 223, 270, 271, 284, 287, 288
Kellner, Douglas, 22, 23-24, 26, 114, 177, 254-55, 255
Kerry, John, 23
Kilborne, Benjamin, 41, 89, 139, 194, 199, 249, 271, 272, 290
Klein, Melanie, 151, 152, 263, 271
Klopp, Charles, 18, 19, 284, 288
Kramer, Jane, 276, 277
Kristeva, Julia, 186
Kuhn, Thomas S., 57

Lacan, Jacques, 33, 50, 81, 182, 269
Latrive, Florent, 54
Le Goff, Jacques, 55
Leone, Giuseppe, 166, 275
Leopardi, Giacomo, 222, 284
Lepschy, Anna Laura, 288
Lepschy, Giulio, 287, 288
Lopes, Fernando, 183, 184, 278, 280
López, Adelaida, 53, 214
Luperini, Romano, 57
Lustiger, Jean-Marie, 265
Lynn, Steven Jay, 140
Lyotard, Jean François, 19, 57, 175, 213-14

Maddocks, Ian, 231
Maiello, Francesco, 255
Manacorda, Giuliano, 162
Marcuse, Herbert, 25, 27-29, 46, 160, 162, 163, 168, 255-56, 273
Mari, Giovanni, 255, 261
Mandralisca, Enrico Pirajno di, 165
Manzoni, Alessandro, 281
Marramao, Giacomo, 25
Martini, Carlo Maria, 18, 62, 105, 106, 108, 260-61, 267
Masciandaro, Franco, 264
Mattei, Paolo, 282
Mauri, Paolo, 188, 193
Mazzini, Giuseppe, 286
McHale, Brian, 43, 97, 260
Mitchell, W. J. T., 192, 194, 195, 282

Mitgang, Herbert, 95
Mitterand, François, 265
Mohacsy, Ildiko, 82, 152, 264, 265, 272
Montefeltro, Guido da, 289
Moore, Michael, 28
Moro, Aldo, 91
Murphey, C. M., 65
Mussolini, Benito, 228, 233, 289

Neri, Francesca, 276
Nicolao, Mario, 160, 164, 273
Norton, Charles Eliot, 47

Orengo, Nico, 199, 206, 283

Padovani, Marcelle, 60, 258
Pagano, Tullio, 169, 171, 257, 275
Palmer, Allen J., 286
Palmieri, Giovanni, 199
Parazzoli, Ferruccio, 19, 21, 254
Parri, Ferruccio, 229, 286, 289
Pasolini, Pier Paolo, 16-17, 19, 146, 158, 161-64, 284
Pavese, Cesare, 16
Pavone, Claudio, 287
Peirce, Charles Sanders, 261
Pericoli, Tullio, 196, 205-6, 280
Pessoa, Fernando, 36, 176, 183, 186-88, 191, 198, 200-201, 210, 217, 258, 277, 278, 282, 284, 285
Petri, Romana, 176, 207, 218, 283
Petty, Thomas A., 106, 107
Pike, Burton, 48, 49, 50, 180
Pintar, Judith, 140
Pirandello, Luigi, 188, 191, 273, 274, 282
Pires, José Cardoso,
Piromalli, Antonio, 161
Placido, Beniamino, 256, 262
Potash, Herbert M., 272, 284

Ragland-Sullivan, Ellie, 138, 199
Reagan, Ronald, 22, 259
Rhue, Judith W., 140
Rich, Frank, 28
Rice, Condaleeza, 27
Rilke, Rainer Maria, 190
Rimbaud, Arthur, 278

Rivoire, Annick, 54
Rodowick, D. N., 34–35, 52, 217
Roelens, Nathalie, 282
Rosengarten, Frank, 273
Rossi, Andrea, 157, 158
Rosso, Stefano, 54, 57
Rutenberg, Jim, 28

Said, Edward W., 273
Salgot, José Antonio, 280
Samuels, Robert, 263
Sancis Antonio, Emma, 207, 212, 220, 283
Sanna, Salvatore A., 158, 159, 162, 164, 273
Savary, Alain, 91, 265
Savino, Giancarlo, 280, 282
Scafoglio, Domenico, 161
Scaglione, Aldo, 148, 270
Sciascia, Leonardo, 171, 176, 273
Searle, John, 142
Segneri, Giampiero, 276
Segre, Cesare, 165, 275
Shakespeare, William, 36, 200, 252
Shanon, Benny, 188
Shumway, David R., 261
Sobieraj, Sarah, 30, 141
Sontag, Susan, 168
Smith, Jonathan, 20, 175
Spielberg, Warren E., 226
Stalin (Joseph Vissarionovich Djugashvili), 160, 247, 289
Stauder, Thomas, 48, 92, 117, 260, 261, 266
Steiner, George, 198, 199, 213, 283

Sterba, Richard, 63, 85, 107, 121, 215, 264, 266, 270
Stevenson, Robert Louis, 206, 280
Surdich, Luigi, 183
Surdich, Mavi, 183
Svevo, Italo (Ettore Schmitz), 281

Tabucchi, Antonio, 15–38, 52, 174–242, 243–45, 253–54, 257–58, 276–89
Teroni, Sandra, 223
Thatcher, Margaret, 22
Tito (Josip Broz), 289
Togliatti, Palmiro, 262
Tomkins, Silvan, 99, 102
Tranfaglia, Nicola, 227

VandenBos, Gary R., 284, 287, 288
Van Eekhout, Fabienne, 192
Vassalli, Sebastiano, 51, 162
Vattimo, Gianni, 23, 260
Velázquez de Silva, Diego, 281
Verga, Giovanni, 159, 162, 274
Vettori, Giuseppe, 288
Viegnes, Michel, 266
Vittorio Emmanuele III di Savoia, 226, 247
Vittorini, Elio, 57, 175, 214

Weiner, Bernard, 265
White, Hayden, 234
Wolf, Mauro, 28

Zamora, Lois Parkinson, 90, 96, 114